AUSTRALIA

THE BEAUTIFUL
COOKBOOK

AUSTRALIA
THE BEAUTIFUL
COOKBOOK

RECIPES BY
ELISE PASCOE

REGIONAL AND FOOD TEXT BY
CHERRY RIPE

FOOD PHOTOGRAPHY BY
PETER JOHNSON

FOOD AND PROP STYLING BY
JANICE BAKER

SCENIC PHOTOGRAPHY BY
RAY JOYCE

CollinsPublishersSanFrancisco
A Division of HarperCollinsPublishers

First published in USA 1995
by Collins Publishers San Francisco

Produced by Weldon Owen Inc.
814 Montgomery Street
San Francisco, CA 94133 USA
Phone (415) 291-0100   Fax (415) 291-8841

Weldon Owen Inc.:
Chairman: Kevin Weldon
President: John Owen
General Manager: Stuart Laurence
Co-Editions Director: Derek Barton
Co-Editions Production Manager (US): Tarji Mickelson
Publisher: Jane Fraser
Associate Publisher: Anne Dickerson
Project Editor: Judith Dunham
Editorial Assistant: Jan Hughes
Copy Editor: Sharon Silva
Proofreaders: Sharilyn Hovind, Julia Cain
Production: Stephanie Sherman
Design: John Bull
Design Layout: Ruth Jacobson
Photography Editor: Sandra Eisert
Map: Kenn Backhaus
Illustrations: Diana Reiss-Koncar
Index: Ken Dellapenta
Assistant Food Stylists: Liz Nolan, Marianne Rudd, Amanda Biffin
Assistant to Food Photographer: Simon Edie

Library of Congress Cataloging-in-Publication Data:

Pascoe, Elise.
Australia the beautiful cookbook / Elise Pascoe ; regional and food
text by Cherry Ripe ; food photography by Peter Johnson ; food and
prop styling by Janice Baker ; scenic photography by Ray Joyce.
    p.   cm.
    Includes index.
    ISBN 0–00–255372–4 (hardcover)
    1. Cookery, Australian. 2. Food crops -- Australia. 3. Food
habits -- Australia. I. Ripe, Cherry. II. Title

TX725.A9A96   1995
641.5994--dc20   94–23523
                                              CIP

Manufactured by Mandarin Offset, Hong Kong
Printed in China

A Weldon Owen  Production

Endpapers: Hundreds of species of the genus Acacia, *commonly known as
wattle, thrive in Australia, from the arid interior to the temperate coastlands.*
*Pages 2–3: Years of erosion have softened The Olgas, or Kata Tjuta, the
place of 'many heads', in the Northern Territory.*
*Page 4: Sydney Rock Oysters with Six Garnishes (recipe page 36)—
photographed at Cremorne Point, Sydney Harbour.*
*Right: The restaurants, pizzerias and gelaterias along Lygon Street in
Carlton, Melbourne, are a mecca for people seeking an upbeat ambience
and delicious food.*
*Pages 8–9, left to right: Semolina Gnocchi with Italian Tomato Sauce and
Pesto (recipe page 175), Eggplant Lasagne with Sun-Dried Tomatoes
(recipe page 161)—photographed at Woodbyne Park Gallery, Jasper's
Brush, on the south coast, NSW*
*Page 10, clockwise from top: Tropical Fruit Soup with Asian Spices (recipe
page 235), Stuffed Quinces in Their Own Jelly (recipe page 247),
Tamarillo and Kakadu Plum Tartlets with Cumquat Cream (recipe page
231)—photographed at Goomoolahra Falls, Queensland*
*Pages 12–13: Many of South Australia's acclaimed wines originate in the
area around McLaren Vale on the Fleurieu Peninsula.*

CONTENTS

A grower proudly displays the products of his orchards in the Barossa Valley of South Australia.

INTRODUCTION

A FOOD PARADISE

'If it's this hot in January, what must it be like in July!' was the incredulous reaction of one of the First Fleeters, arriving to establish a British settlement on 26 January 1788. Forgotten, of course, was the fact that Australia's seasons are the reverse of those of the Northern Hemisphere: they had arrived in the middle of summer.

Although more than one-third of its landmass is in the tropics, Australia is the world's second driest continent. It stretches from forty-four degrees latitude in the south (the same distance between Toronto, Canada, and the equator) to well north of the Tropic of Capricorn. If you were to turn Australia upside down and set it in the Atlantic Ocean, it would stretch from Nova Scotia down past Panama to Caracas in Venezuela, one of the greatest latitudinal reaches of any single country, except perhaps Chile or China. This not only offers an enormous diversity of climates, but also permits the growing of a vast array of produce.

From the tropical fruits of Far North Queensland to the salmon and rock lobster off the coast of Tasmania, Australia is blessed with an abundance of food. In between, everything is possible, from the cool-climate berry farms of northern Tasmania, the farmhouse cheeses of Gippsland in Victoria, the rice fields of the Riverina and the oranges of the Riverland, to the bananas and mangoes of the Gascoygne in Western Australia and the dates—and even wine—in the Red Centre. Beef thrives in every state and territory, and wheat abounds in all but the far north.

Except for seafood and the macadamia nut, however, nearly all the foodstuffs Australians cultivate and eat today have been introduced since European settlement. Australia was settled as a result of the American War of Independence, when England was forced to look elsewhere to offload the inmates of its overcrowded prisons. European settlement in the form of a penal colony was established in Port Jackson (now Sydney Harbour) on that January day in 1788. A small fleet, comprising eleven sailing ships (six transports, three store ships, a flagship and a tender), brought 1473 people aboard, including 778 convicts, 192 women and 32 children. They were expected to become self-sufficient in food in a short time, despite there being only one farmer amongst them.

Australian agriculture had a literally riotous beginning. In a wild thunderstorm on the day the women were landed—the men and women having been separated during the eight-month voyage—the convicts broke loose and much debauchery ensued. In the melee, all but one of the cattle (five cows and two bulls) brought from the Cape of Good Hope escaped, not to be found again until seven years later, some sixty-five kilometres (forty miles) away, in what became known as the Cow Pastures. (By then their numbers had grown to sixty, and they had gone wild.)

Paradoxically, given today's abundance of fresh produce year-round, early attempts at cultivation were a series of disasters. The first crop failed so disastrously that

The village of Richmond in Tasmania preserves many old structures, such as this historic stone church and bridge.

within two years the colony was on the brink of starvation and strict rationing was imposed. These were the Hungry Years, when the situation was so bad that if you were invited to dine at Government House, you were expected to take if not your own food, certainly your own bread. Perhaps thus began the great Aussie BYO ('bring your own', as in a bottle of wine) tradition, still common today when dining in friends' homes, and even practised in some restaurants.

It took a decade or more to establish any real agricultural base, and for some considerable time after settlement, the early Australian diet consisted almost entirely of imported foods. Convict rations for a week, based on the maritime diet of the time, were two-thirds of a seaman's ration: three-and-a-half kilograms (seven pounds) bread (dried biscuit) or flour, three-and-a-half kilograms (seven pounds) beef or two kilograms (four pounds) pork, plus peas, oatmeal, butter, cheese and vinegar. Women got less.

Because of the time it took to develop self-sufficiency in agriculture—and because people were moving inland and clearing the land for farming—the early regimen continued to be largely portable, consisting mainly of dried preserved goods: tea, flour, sugar and salted meat. (A comprehensive history of Australian food is illustrative of that portability. It's appropriately entitled *One Continuous Picnic,* as indeed Australia's early food history was, for people carried their food with them.)

But even in the early 1800s, when the colony began to feed itself, the interior was being opened up and a significant wool industry had developed, the staple diet continued to be tea, damper (a bread initially unleavened,

One young resident rides the shoulders of another in the country north of Adelaide.

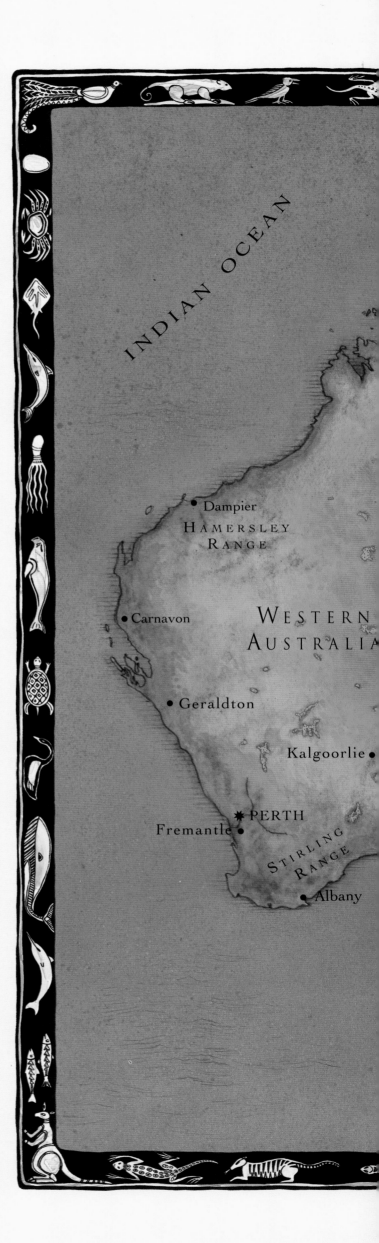

DARWIN ✴ Kakadu
National
Park

ARNHEM
LAND

Gulf of
Carpentaria

CAPE
YORK
PENINSULA

GREAT

PACIFIC

OCEAN

KIMBERLEY
PLATEAU

BARKLY
TABLELAND

BARRIER

Cairns

NORTHERN
TERRITORY

Mount Isa

Townsville
Charters Towers

GREAT

REEF

IBSON DESERT

Alice Springs

QUEENSLAND

DIVIDING

Rockhampton

Uluru

SIMPSON

Birdsville

Bundaberg

DESERT

RANGE

Charleville

BRISBANE ✴

Oodnadatta

SOUTH
AUSTRALIA

Lake
Eyre

Lamington
National Park

NEW
SOUTH
WALES

Armidale

NULLARBOR PLAIN

Lake
Torrens

Lake
Gairdner

FLINDERS

RANGE

Darling R

Broken Hill

Great Australian
Bight

Murray R

Orange

BLUE MTS

Port Lincoln

✴ ADELAIDE

Murrumbidgee R

SYDNEY ✴

CANBERRA

KANGAROO
ISLAND

VICTORIA

Mt Kosciusko

Bendigo

Wangaratta

TASMAN SEA

Geelong

✴ MELBOURNE

Launceston

TASMANIA

✴
HOBART

The magnificent view of Sydney from Vaucluse takes in the city skyline and the succession of bays leading to the Sydney Harbour Bridge.

but later leavened with beer or bicarbonate of soda, and baked in the embers of a camp fire) and mutton, three times a day.

Surprisingly little attention was paid by the early colonists to the diet of the Aborigines, from whom they could have learned much about alternative food sources. Although the Aborigines did employ some agricultural practices, such as burning tracts of land (understanding that many Australian native plants germinate only after fire) and harvesting a type of grass seed, they did not practise cultivation in the conventional sense. They were largely foragers and, to a lesser extent, hunters. Some of their harvesting methods, however, were extremely sophisticated. For example, in certain areas pools of freshwater fish were treated with poisonous alkaloids from particular trees, allowing the Aborigines to wade in and gather the stunned fish floating on the surface.

Although indigenous foods sustained the Aboriginal population for at least forty thousand—some say as long as one hundred thousand—years before the colonising British arrived, when agriculture was established it was based entirely on European crops. Even today, surprisingly few native plants are cultivated; the quandong, or South Australian native peach, is one of the few. The macadamia nut is the only Australian native farmed on any scale, and that was first cultivated commercially in Hawaii! Australia's native spinach, tetragonia, is more widespread in France (as *tetragone)* than in Australia.

Australians eat relatively little of their native fauna. For many years, in most states it was illegal to eat kangaroo on health grounds, despite the fact that up to four million are killed a year, often as many as one million in the state of New South Wales alone. (Kangaroos are not an endangered species as some suggest. Indeed, there are more kangaroos than people in Australia. Their large numbers are made possible by the increased availability of drinking water for farmed animals.) Kangaroo does appear on the menus of many restaurants. Other species of native animals, such as farmed crocodile and emu and wallaby, turn up on menus, though their use in the home remains limited. Yet these major protein sources sustained the Aboriginal population as part of a diet that nutritionists today see as having been close to ideal: low in fat and high in protein, vitamins and fibre.

'Bush tucker', although popular with visitors looking for uniquely Australian flavours, is still largely unfamiliar to most Australians. While there are cottage industries producing jams, jellies and sauces using these bush fruits, the average Australian is unlikely to harvest these wild foods because they are largely scattered throughout the remote, uncultivated parts of the continent.

Australia's bountiful harvest, of every imaginable introduced fruit and vegetable, has grown up mainly in the two centuries since settlement, with the most significant and rapid changes having taken place in the last forty years. The country was progressively colonised from Sydney, first by sea to Van Diemen's Land, later called Tasmania, which became a separate colony in 1825, and then slowly across the rest of the continent. Victoria (named after the English queen) was established in 1851, followed by South Australia in 1855, Queensland in 1859 and Western Australia in 1890. Australia became a nation, rather than remaining this collection of British colonies, only at the time of Federation in 1901.

For much of its history, Australia was a country of migrants principally from the British Isles. Although Irish were brought in on the early fleets of convict ships—one-third of the convicts were Irish—they began to arrive in greater numbers following the Potato Famine of the late 1840s, and many more came during the gold rushes of the subsequent decades. Indeed, gold precipitated Australia into nationhood. In the 1850s, the population trebled, and many who had come to seek fortunes stayed on after the gold was exhausted, providing labour for the new rural industries that were developing in the interior.

As the world's first postindustrial society, Australia never had the chance to develop regional cuisines. Regional differences are—and were—slight. No place in Australia was sufficiently isolated for long enough to develop uniquely local dishes. A regional cuisine develops in isolation, when cooks in a specific area treat the produce of that region in a particular way for a considerable period of time, without much interference or influence from outside. But people were continually moving from one place to another, and the same (largely portable) ingredients travelled with them.

While there are ingredients that are identified with particular places, such as Queensland mud crabs, Streaky Bay scallops, Port Parham blue swimmer crabs and West Australian marrons, these are regional products, not descriptions of the way they are cooked. Certain areas, too, have become known for particular ingredients that were not native to those regions. Tasmanian Atlantic salmon and Pacific oysters, Milawa cheese and even Illabo milk-fed lamb fall into this category, but the way they are treated is not exclusive to those particular areas. So it is even with Australia's culinary icons: lamingtons were not exclusive to Queensland, nor were puftaloons; jaffles don't 'belong' to either New South Wales or South Australia, but to both and beyond; pavlova is not confined to Western Australia. Historically, there is no geographical

Every Saturday, Salamanca Place in Hobart, Tasmania, becomes a lively market filled with flowers and food, crafts and music.

Vast and varied, Kakadu National Park in the Northern Territory is home to a distinctive array of plant and animal life.

exclusivity to billy-boiled yabbies, crumbed lamb chops, drop scones or damper. And without regional dishes, there are no regional cuisines.

Even after Federation, Australia's migration was relatively homogeneous, with 90 percent of the nation's population Anglo-Celtic at the end of World War II. Today, by contrast, it is 73 percent Anglo-Celtic and rapidly declining. By the early 1990s, one in five Australians had been born overseas and a quarter of all Australians had a parent who was a migrant. At least one in five Australians has Irish forebears.

Of Australia's current population of some seventeen million, only a couple hundred thousand are Aborigines. Australia's early settlers did a fairly comprehensive job— often deliberate—of wiping them out, helped by diseases like measles to which the Aborigines had no resistance.

Australia's greatest migration has occurred largely since World War II, when it was perceived that the country needed to 'populate or perish'. Four million migrants have been welcomed since then. By the early 1990s, nearly half of all arrivals were coming from Asia, and about one-third from Europe. Ten years prior to that, it was almost the reverse, with more than half from Europe and one-quarter from Asia.

Until the 1950s, Australians ate pretty much the same food as the British, however inappropriate it might have been in the warmer Australian climate. The culinary changes that have taken place in Australia since then are therefore all the more astonishing for their rapidity. Soon after the war, the government began actively encouraging migrants from Europe, first from the Baltic, and subsequently from countries around the Mediterranean, principally Italy and Greece and to a lesser extent Lebanon. The third largest urban concentration of Greeks after Athens and Thessalonika is said to be in Melbourne.

These new migrants dramatically changed the Australian dinner table, introducing Anglo-Celtic Australians to a wide range of new tastes, cuisines and foodstuffs. They increased the variety of foods available, first in greengrocers, then in delicatessens (salamis, southern European cheeses like fetta, olives, cured meats like prosciutto and *pancetta*) and subsequently in supermarkets. They also created an explosion in the types of restaurants—Italian, Greek and Lebanese—and introduced Australians to good espresso coffee.

In the 1950s and early 1960s, the Australian diet was exceptionally unadventurous. In those days, a typical Australian evening meal at home, consumed around six o'clock, almost always comprised meat and two or even three overcooked vegetables. The centrepiece of the meal was a large portion of meat—quite often mutton—in the form of chops or roasts, or even sometimes rissoles and gravy, always served with potatoes, perhaps pumpkin and one type of green vegetable, such as stringy green beans. Stodgy flour-based puddings in the English style, like jam roly-poly, and cakes were eaten to fill one up.

In small-town cafés (rather than the more formal restaurants, found only in cities), if you ordered a steak, it would come with a salad of a couple of slices of tomato, some lettuce, onion rings, the ubiquitous canned pickled beetroot (beet) garnished with a twisted slice of orange and probably mashed potatoes. This was the standard dinner out for much of the country.

Thirty years ago, one faced the same limitations when making a salad at home. The typical greengrocer carried only minimal ingredients: one variety of lettuce (iceberg), one variety of cucumber (dry, short, fat ones, which

The mound-building termites near Moreston Station in Queensland construct villages of towering nests interconnected by chambers and tunnels.

consisted mostly of indigestible seeds) and one type of tomato. Along with rings of raw onion, that was the sum total of *the* Australian salad. How things have changed!

In the late 1960s, 'new' foods started appearing in neighbourhood greengrocers largely run by Italian, Greek or Lebanese migrants. There were long telegraph and short Lebanese cucumbers, snake and borlotti (cranberry) beans, Italian flat-leaf parsley, endive, okra and fennel. These migrants wanted to eat these vegetables themselves, so they encouraged market gardeners to grow them.

The impact of migration on the availability of foodstuffs accelerated wildly in the 1980s. For example, greens that Australians now take for granted were beginning to fill the shops: cos (romaine) and butter lettuces, frisée, endive, scarola (escarole) and rocket (arugula).

More recent waves of migration have brought about the appearance of a wide variety of Asian vegetables and ingredients. In the mid-1970s, a large number of Asians— particularly Vietnamese—began coming to Australia to live. This further increased the food choices, and introduced a whole new range of Asian flavours, foods and cuisines, many ingredients of which—ginger, fresh coriander (cilantro), lemongrass—have been embraced with such fervour and to such an extent that they have become part of Australia's culinary mainstream.

Today, an evening meal in the home commonly consists of pasta, a stir-fry or even a prepared meat mix such as honey-sesame chicken, Thai lamb curry or skewered kebabs picked up at a butcher shop or other retail outlet. A 1993 survey found that people ate pasta twice as often as Australia's supposed national dish, the

The sandstone peaks of the Three Sisters, a familiar landmark, survey Jamison Valley in the Blue Mountains of New South Wales.

Vineyards and wineries, and plenty of opportunities for wine-tasting, abound in the Barossa Valley of South Australia.

Breathtakingly steep cliffs along the Western Australia coast plunge into the Great Australian Bight.

meat pie. Many people in the home turn to stir-frying, the Asian technique of wok cooking that has been locally adapted as a quick and nutritious way to feed a family.

What we drink has also changed. Where once Australians were a nation of tea drinkers—at the time of Federation, we were the largest consumers of tea per head in the world—increasingly people are drinking other beverages. Coffee has become highly popular, and wine is regularly drunk with meals.

Not only has Australia become a significant wine exporter, but the types of wines Australians make have also changed. Whereas after World War II, 90 percent of Australian wine was fortified (port, sherry and so on), the proportions are now reversed: 90 percent of Australian wine is table wine and only 10 percent is fortified. Evidence of the centrality of wine production is apparent

in the fact that more than one-third of Australia's fruit-growing area is devoted to grapes.

Australians are some of the world's most enthusiastic travellers. Initially the focus was on Europe, but more recently attention has turned to Australia's closer Asian neighbours. These experiences abroad have made once-foreign tastes familiar to the Australian palate.

Today, Australians are among the world's most eclectic eaters, with their enthusiasm for new tastes and different cuisines showing no signs of abating. The dazzling array of available produce combined with a wide variety of cooking methods and ingredients is a reflection of the dynamic multicultural society Australia has become. Australia is now home to some of the most exciting food in the world, and its citizens can rightfully claim they live in a food lover's paradise.

New South Wales

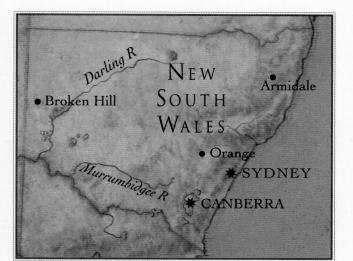

NEW SOUTH WALES

E U R O P E A N
B E G I N N I N G S

'I AM THE FIRST WHITE MAN to see it and I think I will undoubtedly be the last', wrote John Oxley, the surveyor-general, in 1817. 'There is a uniformity of barren desolation in this country which wearies one more than I am able to express'. Admittedly, it was a drought year, and he had stopped forty kilometres (twenty-four miles) short of the Murrumbidgee River, but thankfully, history has proved him wrong. From this region, 'which for bareness and desolation has no equal', now comes nearly one-third of Australia's citrus crop, one-fifth of its wine and almost all (98 percent) of its rice. It symbolises the nation's triumph over climate and the odds.

In a mammoth feat of engineering, ten thousand kilometres (six thousand miles) of canals and channels were dug in the three years between 1910 and 1913. The Murrumbidgee Irrigation Area—or MIA, as it's known—the largest public works irrigation programme in the world, was dug without bulldozers or the petrol engine, by backbreaking manual work, with the help of horses. Today, there are some 160 000 hectares (395 200 acres) under gravity-fed irrigation in this appropriately named operation: *murrumbidgee* is the local Wiradjuri tribe's word for 'never-failing water supply'. From here in the Riverina come tomatoes—sun-dried, in cans and as tomato paste— both honeydew and rockmelons (musk melons), figs, carrots and many other vegetables.

In view of such fecundity, it is paradoxical that European agriculture in Australia should have had such inauspicious beginnings. Captain Arthur Phillip, commander of the First Fleet, was a naval man, not a farmer. It is claimed that he chose the worst possible place on which to try and establish agriculture: the soils of

Previous pages: The south coast town of Central Tilba is surrounded by small farms and big expanses of grazing land. Left: A team of surf lifesavers takes a wave at Narrabeen in Sydney.

Sydney Cove were shallow and sandy and of very poor quality. Had he been a farmer, he might have looked farther afield for better soils, such as those settled in November that year at The Crescent, upriver at Parramatta.

From the first days of settlement, when the cattle escaped in a thunderstorm, it was obvious that agriculture was going to be hard work. Lacking beasts of burden to pull ploughs and with agricultural implements breaking or going missing, convicts without tools could not be forced to clear the land or saw down scrub or dig never-tilled earth. Cultivation was further frustrated by drought and by the presence of only one farmer on the First Fleet. On top of already poor fortune, much of the wheat and barley that hadn't been eaten by weevils rotted in the ground. Fortunately, many of the fruits brought from the Cape of Good Hope—oranges, lemons, limes, figs and grapes— did thrive, thanks to the similarity of the two climates.

The colony suffered other setbacks. The *Guardian,* which had set sail in 1789 with a cargo of cast-iron pots, wheelbarrows and ploughs, plus plants in a glasshouse on deck, hit an iceberg after Capetown (two nights before Christmas), and the plant material destined for the new colony was turfed overboard. Nevertheless, by 1791, about three-quarters of a hectare (two acres) of potatoes was under cultivation at Parramatta, and when Captain Phillip left in 1792, the hardest years were over. There were three producing government farms, and ships were coming in from the American west coast and Calcutta carrying supplies to help the settlement.

It was 1793 before free settlers started arriving in response to the then governor's request to come and farm the land. (Even then, of the fourteen free settlers that arrived on the *Bellona* in January that year, only four could seriously have been considered farmers.) By 1798, botanist Joseph Banks, who by then presided over the Royal Society in London, was sending sage, mint, tarragon, sorrel, capers, olives, ginger, lemongrass and tea to New South Wales on board the *Porpoise,* all destined for cultivation. The *Porpoise* also carried hops for brewing, raisin grapes, apples for cider, pears, raspberries, walnuts, quinces, nectarines, peaches, small hazelnuts (filberts), chestnuts, greengages (a particularly sweet green plum), strawberries and several varieties of grapes, including Tokay and Frontignac.

The First Fleet had brought vine cuttings from both Rio de Janeiro and the Cape, and the first grape plantings were in Phillip's garden on the eastern side of Sydney Cove. They were too near the water, however, and suffered from excess moisture. The first viable vineyard was planted at Parramatta in November 1788, near where New Government House would be built. By December 1791, there were eight thousand vines growing there. But the colony's alcohol was still being imported—and how.

In the early 1800s, alcohol became the main form of currency. Convicts were paid in rum or arrack, with a gallon worth ten shillings. Until the silver coins of 1813, the only form of currency was the cumbersome Georgian penny, a small-denomination, large English coin.

On the Second Fleet, which docked 28 June 1790, John and Elizabeth Macarthur arrived. In 1793, they were granted forty hectares (one hundred acres) at Parramatta, which became Elizabeth Farm, and by the following year John Macarthur had 100 'hogs' (his word) and 130 goats.

The first merino sheep were brought to the colony in 1797, by a Captain Waterhouse (not Macarthur, as is sometimes thought), and Macarthur was one of a number of people who obtained breeding stock. During involuntary exile in England from 1809 to 1817 (thanks to

Snow dusts a dense forest of gum trees in the aptly named Snowy Mountains, part of the Kosciusko National Park.

Sand, sun, surf and sports, as well as people watching, draw crowds to Bondi Beach in Sydney.

an altercation with William Bligh that saw Bligh deposed as governor of New South Wales), Macarthur became an expert in which wools were best suited to the London market and in the procedures necessary to assure sales of colonial wool overseas. In so doing, he, more than anyone else, was responsible for the development of wool as an export industry and, more significantly in food terms, its by-product: sheep meat. Lamb, hoggett (a young sheep from the age of ten months up to the cutting of the first two adult teeth) and mutton formed a great proportion— a staple, almost—of the Australian diet for the next century and a half.

Exploration pushed ahead—by water—up the Hawkesbury and Hunter rivers, but it took twenty-five years (until 1813) before explorers scaled the escarpments and gorges of the Blue Mountains and discovered the fertile grazing lands beyond. These mountains are part of the Great Dividing Range, the watershed that runs like a spine down the east coast from Queensland to the Snowy Mountains—on average some 150 kilometres (90 miles) from, and parallel to, the coast. As late as 1836, New South Wales comprised two-thirds of the continent. It reached across to what ultimately became the Western Australian border, and until then incorporated what was to become three other states and the Northern Territory.

Gold was discovered in 1823 not far from Bathurst, northwest of Sydney. This and other early gold discoveries were kept quiet, however, in what was still a penal settlement, fearing that the news might aggravate the labour shortage. (How are you going to keep convicts

under control when they catch gold fever?) In 1840, transportation of convicts ceased. Then, when the California gold rush of 1848 began draining off the Australian population, in 1849 it was decided to exploit the mineral resources of New South Wales. Returning from California, Edward Hargraves washed the first pan of gold-bearing gravel at the junction of Summer Hill and Lewis Pond creeks on 12 February 1851. In April the same year, the first gold of payable quantity was discovered at Ophir. Finds were made in other places and tent cities sprang up. The main track was lined with improvised 'coffee tents', 'sly grog shops' and butchers' shops constructed out of calico and canvas.

This gold rush, and subsequent ones, brought an influx of Chinese, many of whom stayed on after the gold era as storekeepers and market gardeners. These expert farmers were to demonstrate what could be grown in bush conditions. Some descendants of these first arrivals started Chinese restaurants in country towns, thereby introducing Australians to Asian food, albeit modified to Australian tastes. Even in the 1960s, Chinese menus offered steaks alongside chop sueys and chow meins.

It's much easier to list what doesn't grow in New South Wales than what does. From the wealth of peaches harvested in the Riverina and the apples from cooler Batlow in the foothills of the Snowy Mountains to the bananas of the north coast, almost everything will grow here. Durum wheat for pasta is grown on the slopes around Tamworth, an area that is hot and dry, conditions that keep the wheat's protein content high. Aside from

*Sydney Harbour Bridge rises above Lower Fort Street,
near the city's first settlement at Sydney Cove.*

being a major producer of wool and wheat, New South Wales is the country's second biggest beef producer (after Queensland) and second ranked lamb producer (after Victoria). In addition to grass-fed and grain-fed beef, organic beef is being produced at Elmswood in the Upper Hunter. Specialty-lamb producers can be found, too, like those who raise the wonderful Illabo milk-fed lamb.

From the state's coastal waters comes an immense variety of fish. The coast can be divided into three regions. The main fishing areas of the south coast—Eden, Bermagui and Ulladulla—yield flathead and morwong, redfish (or nannygai), warehou, blue-eye (sometimes called cod, but actually trevalla), large octopus (a different species than the smaller ones up north), mirror dory, John Dory, abalone, swordfish and yellowfin tuna. There are wild mussels from Tuross Lakes south of Ulladulla and farmed mussels from Eden.

The central area, from Wollongong up to Port Stephens, offers royal red prawns, cuttlefish, kingfish, yellowfin tuna, black flathead (estuarine) and sand flathead. From the Hawkesbury estuary come calamari (squid), said to be the best in Australia.

The north coast above Forster is home to blue-eye, baby snapper, large quantities of small octopus (a by-catch of the prawn trawl) and kingfish, plus a lot of travelling fish like silver bream and mullet. King prawns and school prawns come out of the Clarence River, where black tiger prawns are now farmed. Balmain bugs are found this far up the coast, too (although a different species from Moreton Bay bugs, found over the border in Brisbane's waters), and there are the wonderful eastern green crayfish, unique to the New South Wales coast.

Up and down the coast, from the Richmond and Clarence rivers in the north to the Hawkesbury and Shoalhaven farther south, river mouths offer prawn grounds and oyster beds. The major shellfish of the whole coastline is the native Sydney rock oyster—exclusive to the New South Wales coast. The introduced Pacific oysters are allowed to be grown only in Port Stephens; an eradication programme has been established to rid all other estuaries of them because they have been competing too vigorously with the Sydney rock oysters.

Given this wealth of fish and shellfish, it's hardly surprising that the people of New South Wales consume significantly (25 percent) more seafood per head than those of Western Australia, the next rated state. Nearly one-third of Australia's population lives in New South Wales, clustered mainly on the coastal strip in cities like Wollongong, Sydney and Newcastle. The last stands at the mouth of the Hunter River, whose upper reaches offer two of the state's most prestigious wine-producing regions. Although there are more than a dozen others, the Hunter Valley boasts two wine regions with distinctively different climates, the Lower Hunter, northwest of Cessnock, and the Upper Hunter, around Denman. Overall, New South Wales produces one-third of the country's wine.

Nestled under the scarp of the Broken Back Range, part of the Great Dividing Range, the Lower Hunter around Pokolbin also features a variety of wonderful restaurants, and there is much local produce for them to draw on. Quail, venison and yabbies come from Port Stephens, and the asparagus from near Maitland is said to be the best in Australia. To the south of the Hunter, near Galston, is the Game Farm, which produces pheasant, squab, pigeon, spatchcock (poussin), guinea fowl and quail.

Although the Hunter may be the best known of the state's wine regions, wine is produced as far north as Port Macquarie, and as far south as Cooma and Bombala, and even Tumbarumba. There have been more recent plantings around Canberra and Yass, although not in as significant quantities as around Cowra and in the Riverina. The wines of Mudgee are receiving increasing acclaim, and there are more plantings every year on the Central Tablelands, around Orange.

Orange is arguably the most interesting food region in New South Wales. Once known largely for its apples, the area is becoming known for its produce, and thereby developing a sense of regionalism. The Orange region's lack of humidity means quinces, cherries and many other cool-climate fruits can flourish. Producers have also branched out into venison, golden trout—an albino rainbow trout—river trout, brook trout, black Genoa figs, chestnuts, goat's milk ice cream, goat's milk cheese and pickled walnuts. Wild mushrooms—*matsutake* (pine) mushrooms, cèpes, wood blewitts—are harvested by dedicated forager Rob Robinson in a national park. Several different breeds of cattle are raised in the area—Angus, Simmental and Maine Anjou—as well as lamb, and a number of wineries have been established.

Before World War II, Australians drank nearly twenty times more beer than wine. By 1989, although beer consumption had doubled, we were drinking ten times more wine than we had been drinking before the war. Wine has become one of Australia's biggest exports and deserving of its description 'bottled sunshine'.

First Fleet officer Watkin Tench showed extraordinary prescience when he wrote of those earliest grapes grown at Parramatta in the 1790s: 'I am convinced that . . . their juice will probably hereafter furnish an indispensable article of luxury of European tables'. How right he was.

Rugby players head down the field during a spirited game at Cranbrook College in Sydney.

SNACKS AND APPETISERS

At Ballarat, Victoria, a greengrocer prepares for a busy marketing day.

SNACKS AND APPETISERS

COFFIN BAY SCALLOPS grilled in the shell, spicy Thai fish balls with a dipping sauce, tartlets made from Western Australian goat cheese, bluefin tuna sashimi and *bruschetta* are all taste delights barely dreamt of a decade ago that have become nearly commonplace. The most delicious morsels imaginable are today served regularly both in restaurants and at home.

With the wide range of ingredients now available, the number of dishes for serving with drinks or before a meal is constantly growing. Australians' familiarity with cuisines and cooking styles around the world, in particular Italian and Thai food, has exponentially increased the types of foods served. These days eclecticism rules. It is not unusual to be served a mixture of Mediterranean and Asian dishes, sometimes in sequence and at other times even on the same plate.

Whether it is exploring the sharpness of pineapple set off against the sweetness of caramelised pork mince in the Thai delight *ma hor* (literally, 'galloping horses', possibly because it transports one?) or the luscious explosions of flavour hidden in golden salmon 'caviar' served on baby pikelets (pancakes), the Australian palate has become one of the most adventurous in the world.

How different it was even twenty years ago. Throughout the 1950s, the Australian diet was relatively homogeneous. Most people ate essentially the same thing, whether they lived in a town or in the country. Not only had the Australian diet remained relatively static for

Freshly picked tomatoes lay out in the sun to dry in Griffith, NSW.

Previous pages, clockwise from top: Cornmeal Muffins with Tomato, Borlotti and Basil Salad (recipe page 45), Lamb Prosciutto with Rocket and Citrus Fruits (recipe page 43), Pacific Oysters with Pickled Ginger, Daikon and Lime (recipe page 36)—photographed at Balmoral, Sydney

decades, but what we then ate was not that far removed from the English fare of the time. Certainly the cooking methods, the cooking times (the overcooked vegetables) and the omnipresent brown gravy were similar, although there were minor variations. Australians, for instance, ate a great deal more meat than the British, and the Sunday roast was more likely to be mutton than beef.

Even as late as 1973, in an introduction to the new edition of Mrs Forster Rutledge's 1899 *Goulburn Cookery Book,* Helen Rutledge wrote: 'Our taste in food has not altered, only our ability to buy it or our diets to indulge in it'. But things were changing even as the ink was drying.

Not only has the Australian mealtime shifted since Helen Rutledge made that observation—whereas thirty years ago the evening meal (called tea) was served around 6.30 p.m., now it's more likely to be called dinner and eaten at 7.30 or even 8.00 p.m.—but what is served has also undergone a revolution. And perhaps no other area of Australian food has changed so much as the choice of things eaten before or between meals. The afternoon tea, with its filling cakes, scones and sandwiches, has all but disappeared, replaced by an explosion of the savoury foods handed around at parties or before meals when friends are gathered. Even the guests at a children's party are more likely to be reaching for the salami and olives put out for the parents than for buttered bread sprinkled with multicoloured hundreds and thousands.

One uniquely Australian snack is the jaffle. A kind of toasted sandwich, the jaffle is an example of a portable snack that was traditionally cooked outdoors in an open fire. It is remembered nostalgically as a feature of many a childhood camping trip; so, too, is burning your fingers as you tried to break off the charred corners of crusts protruding from inside the iron. The jaffle iron consists of two hinged pieces of concave moulded metal with long handles. Two slices of bread, buttered on the outside, are put into the iron's indentations, filled and closed tight. The iron is then latched and shoved into the hot coals. Fillings range from baked beans to tomato and bacon to a whole raw egg. Today's electric-toasted sandwich makers simply cannot produce the same taste.

Casual entertaining has also come a long way. If you were invited to a party in the 1960s, you were lucky to be offered anything more than cubes of cheddar cheese skewered on cellophane-frilled cocktail sticks, tiny white cocktail onions and wine out of a flagon. Perhaps the host might have run to cocktail frankfurters with tomato ketchup to dip them in, but in those days Jatz crackers were the one thing no party was without. The *Women's Weekly* of the time recommended garnishing these bite-sized savoury crackers with sliced eggs, capers, pickled onions and sprigs of parsley and serving them along with cubes of cheddar cheese. By the 1970s, dips were commonplace—made from a packet of powder mixed with sour cream—again served with the ubiquitous Jatz crackers.

These days even Jatz have veered upmarket. Their packets now abound with depictions of the crackers adorned with much more exotic ingredients: a sun-dried tomato with a triangle of mozzarella and a couple of basil leaves, half a quail egg, smoked salmon on a sprig of curly endive, a wedge of camembert or two gleaming olives on a slice of fetta dusted with chopped chives. Gone are the curried stuffed eggs of yesteryear.

Today, to take advantage of the country's mild climate, entertaining is as likely to be done outdoors as in. Reflecting Australians' increasing informality, the gathering is more commonly a barbecue or a stand-up affair with drinks

Melbourne's Victoria Markets overflow with the bounty of 'The Garden State'.

(usually wine) and finger food rather than a sit-down dinner. Smoked Tasmanian salmon on rye bread, chicken satays or skewered prawns with a zesty sauce, sushi or a simple platter of freshly steamed asparagus might be handed around at just such a party.

The biggest change has been the switch to fresh ingredients. Even twenty years ago, today's crudités were a rarity. Packet-based dips have been replaced by freshly made guacamole, and by such Lebanese dishes as hommos and *baba ghannouj* served with unleavened pitta bread for scooping. Other breads, like the Italian *ciabatta* or the Turkish *pide,* rare a decade ago, have also been welcomed with gusto.

These days instead of 'the shrimp'—actually it would have been a king prawn—from the barbecue, there might appear a platter of grilled baby octopuses. At an outdoor twilight drinks party, a plate of Asian steamed crab rolls or cherry tomatoes stuffed with pesto might be passed among guests.

Migrants have provided the opportunity to taste flavours not just from around the Mediterranean—from Kalamata olives to Sicilian *caponata*—but from around the world. Recent Asian arrivals are introducing us to a bounty of new tastes, and we seem to be embracing these exotic flavours even more rapidly than we took to those from the Mediterranean.

SKEWERED TIGER PRAWNS WITH HONEY-LIME BUTTER

Tiger prawns grow up to 20 centimeters (8 inches) in length and have distinct brown, yellow or orange stripes on their bodies, legs and whiskers. They are caught in the Gulf of Carpentaria, into Torres Strait and farther south to Princess Charlotte Bay in north Queensland. Other large species can be substituted in this dish.

FOR THE HONEY-LIME BUTTER:

200 g (6½ oz/¾ cup plus 2 tablespoons) unsalted butter, at room temperature
60 ml (2 fl oz/¼ cup) dry white wine
80 ml (3 fl oz/⅓ cup) fresh lime juice
1½ tablespoons mild-flavoured honey
1 piece gingerroot, about 2.5 cm (1 in) long, peeled and grated
1 tablespoon finely chopped brown onion
paprika

24 green (raw) tiger prawns (shrimp), peeled and deveined
6 fresh coriander (cilantro) sprigs
3 limes, halved lengthwise

❧ Soak 12 wooden skewers in water to cover for 20 minutes. Preheat a griller (broiler) on high.
❧ To make the butter, in a small food processor fitted with the metal blade or in a blender, combine all the ingredients, including paprika to taste. Process until smooth. Scrape into a small, heavy pan and place over low heat. Cook gently for 5 minutes to blend the flavours. Set aside.
❧ Line a heatproof grilling plate or barbecue plate with heavy-duty aluminium foil. Drain the skewers and thread 2 prawns onto each of the skewers. Arrange the skewers on the foil-covered plate. Brush the prawns with some of the butter.
❧ Grill (broil), turning once and brushing with the butter to keep the prawns moist and well flavoured, until cooked through, about 2 minutes on each side.
❧ Transfer to warmed individual plates and garnish with the coriander sprigs and lime halves. Serve at once.

SERVES 6

STEAMED CHILLI CRAB PARCELS WITH THAI DIPPING SAUCE

Cooks all over Australia prepare these little mouthfuls in various shapes. Any type of crabmeat can be used in the recipe, but the meat of Australia's blue swimmer crabs is particularly delicious.

100 g (3½ oz) green (raw) crabmeat
2 teaspoons fresh lime juice
leaves from ¼ bunch fresh coriander (cilantro), finely chopped
½ fresh red chilli, finely chopped, optional
10 sheets rice paper, each 16 cm (6½ in) in diameter (see glossary)

FOR THE DIPPING SAUCE:

2 fresh red chillies, finely sliced
1 clove garlic, finely chopped
100 ml (3½ fl oz/6½ tablespoons) fresh lemon juice
80 ml (3 fl oz/⅓ cup) fish sauce (see glossary)

❧ In a bowl, stir together the crabmeat, lime juice, coriander leaves and chilli. Working with 1 round at a time, dip the rice paper in cold water briefly to soften. Drain. Lay the rice paper on a work surface. Place a heaped spoonful of the crab mixture on the lower one-quarter of the rice paper round. Fold the end

over the filling, fold in the sides and then roll up into a tidy elongated parcel.
❧ Arrange the crab parcels seam side down on a steamer rack over boiling water, cover the steamer and steam until the crab filling is cooked and the parcels are just firm, 8–10 minutes.
❧ Meanwhile, to make the sauce, in a small bowl, stir together all the ingredients. Set aside. Serve the parcels hot on a platter with the bowl of dipping sauce.

MAKES 10

PACIFIC OYSTERS WITH PICKLED GINGER, DAIKON AND LIME

Pacific oysters, first introduced in the 1940s from Japan, are currently being farmed in three states. They grow where Sydney rock oysters, their much smaller cousins, do not.

18 Pacific oysters, freshly opened in the shell
30 g (1 oz) pickled ginger slices, cut into fine julienne (see glossary)
75 g (2½ oz) daikon, cut into fine julienne (see glossary)
18 fresh coriander (cilantro) leaves
2 limes, halved lengthwise, for garnish

❧ Arrange the oysters on a platter. Scatter the ginger and daikon evenly over the top. Place a coriander leaf on each oyster. Garnish the platter with lime halves.
❧ Refrigerate until well chilled, then serve.

MAKES 18   *Photograph pages 32–33*

SYDNEY ROCK OYSTERS WITH SIX GARNISHES

The rock oyster is the most commonly farmed oyster in Australia, although natural oyster beds are also found along the coast. It is widely believed that to cook these delicious molluscs is a crime.

6 dozen Sydney rock oysters, freshly opened in the shell
2 shallots, finely diced
1½ tablespoons balsamic vinegar
1½ tablespoons white wine vinegar
coarsely ground pepper
3 tablespoons salmon roe
juice of 1 lemon
3 tablespoons black lumpfish roe
1 hard-boiled egg, yolk and white sieved separately
3 tablespoons onion juice (see glossary)
¼ teaspoon wasabi paste (see glossary)
3 tablespoons light soy sauce
12 pieces pickled ginger (see glossary)

❧ Arrange 1 dozen oysters on each of 6 large flat dinner plates. In a small bowl, stir together the shallots, vinegars and pepper to taste and spoon the mixture over 2 of the oysters on each plate. Garnish 2 more of the oysters with the salmon roe and a few drops of the lemon juice, and then another 2 oysters with the lumpfish roe and lemon juice. Garnish 2 more oysters on each plate with the egg yolk and white and a drizzle of the onion juice. Top the next 2 oysters with the wasabi and a drizzle of the soy sauce. Garnish the final 2 oysters with pieces of the pickled ginger. Serve immediately.

SERVES 6   *Photograph page 4*

Top to bottom: Skewered Tiger Prawns with Honey-Lime Butter, Steamed Chilli Crab Parcels with Thai Dipping Sauce— photographed on Moreton Island, Queensland

Grilled Figs with Prosciutto and Milawa Roquefort-Style Cheese

NEW SOUTH WALES

PINK-SKINNED POTATO CHIPS WITH CHILLI AIOLI

This is bistro food that is easy to do at home. Its success depends on the quality of the ingredients. Yandilla brand mustard seed oil, produced at Wallendbeen in central New South Wales, is low (5.5 percent) in saturated fats. It has a nutty flavour and can be used to replace other fats in all types of cooking, including cakes. Its distribution has increased in recent years, but if you cannot find it, use any high-quality vegetable oil. Desirée potatoes, with their pink shiny skins and cream-coloured flesh, make fabulous chips.

1 kg (2 lb) desirée potatoes or other frying potatoes
1 teaspoon regular table salt, or to taste
Yandilla brand mustard seed oil, for deep-frying

FOR THE CHILLI AIOLI:

4 cloves garlic
1 fresh red chilli, or to taste
2 egg yolks
½ teaspoon regular table salt, or to taste
250 ml (8 fl oz/1 cup) virgin olive oil
sea salt, optional

❧ Scrub the potatoes but do not peel. Place in a saucepan with water to cover barely. Add the table salt and bring to a boil. Reduce the heat to medium and simmer, uncovered, until just tender, 8 minutes or longer, depending on their size. Drain and let cool completely.
❧ In a heavy, straight-sided pan, pour in mustard seed oil to a depth of 5 cm (2 in). Heat the oil slowly, keeping an eye on it while you make the aioli.
❧ To make the aioli, in a small food processor fitted with the metal blade or in a blender, place the garlic and chilli and process to chop. Add the egg yolks and salt and process until

thick. With the motor running, slowly add half of the olive oil, drop by drop, until incorporated. Then add the remaining oil in a thin, steady stream and process until thickened. Spoon into a bowl and set aside.
❧ Cut the potatoes lengthwise into eighths. Test the oil to see if it is at the correct temperature for frying the chips by dropping a small piece of bread into it. If it rises to the surface immediately, the oil is ready. Working in batches, slip the potatoes into the oil and fry until golden, about 8 minutes. Using a slotted spoon, lift out and place on crumpled paper towels. Cook the remaining potatoes in the same manner.
❧ Reheat the oil and recook the chips, again in batches, until crisp, about 3 minutes. Using the slotted spoon, lift out and drain on crumpled paper towels. Scatter with sea salt, if using.
❧ Serve piping hot on warmed individual plates or on a platter. Pass the aioli.

SERVES 6

MELBOURNE

GRILLED FIGS WITH PROSCIUTTO AND MILAWA ROQUEFORT-STYLE CHEESE

An Italian-inspired starter or appetiser to enjoy with a chilled Victorian or South Australian sparkling Burgundy or smooth, bottle-aged Shiraz. The contrasting flavours of the sweet figs, the pleasantly salty prosciutto and the distinctive Australian blue mould cheese are fabulous.

100 g (3½ oz) Milawa roquefort-style blue cheese or other blue cheese, rind removed and cut into 18 equal pieces

9 firm ripe black figs, cut in half lengthwise
9 thin slices lean prosciutto, cut in half

❧ Preheat an oven to 190°C (375°F). Line a baking tray (sheet) with aluminium foil.
❧ Place a piece of cheese on top of each fig half. Wrap each fig in a piece of prosciutto. Secure with a wooden toothpick and place, cheese side up, on the prepared baking tray.
❧ Bake until the cheese begins to melt and the prosciutto is sizzling, 8–12 minutes. Transfer to a platter and serve hot.

MAKES 18

ADELAIDE

GRILLED EGGPLANT TOPPED WITH CAPONATA

This recipe is for eggplant lovers. It includes a double dose, with the vegetable turning up in the base and in the topping. The latter, called caponata, *is a specialty of Sicilian cooks. Use Australian black olives for the best flavour.*

FOR THE *CAPONATA*:

1 kg (2 lb) eggplants (aubergines), peeled and cut into 2-cm (¾-in) dice
salt
200 ml (6½ fl oz/¾ cup plus 1½ tablespoons) olive oil
1 large brown onion, cut into slices 1 cm (⅜ in) thick
12 fresh celery leaves
pinch of sugar, or to taste
100 ml (3½ fl oz/6½ tablespoons) tomato purée (paste)
100 ml (3½ fl oz/6½ tablespoons) white wine vinegar
1 tablespoon pine nuts
2 tablespoons chopped fresh oregano
3 tablespoons well-drained capers
100 g (3½ oz/⅔ cup) pitted black olives, chopped
4 anchovy fillets in olive oil, drained and roughly chopped
salt and freshly ground pepper

FOR THE EGGPLANT BASES:

750 g (1½ lb) eggplants, cut crosswise into slices 1 cm (⅜ in) thick
4–5 tablespoons olive oil

❧ To make the *caponata,* place the eggplant in a colander and salt liberally. Let stand for 30 minutes to drain off the bitter juices. Rinse off the salt under running cold water, squeeze by hand to remove excess water and pat dry with paper towels.
❧ In a large, heavy frying pan over medium heat, warm the oil. Add the eggplant and cook, stirring, until softened, about 15 minutes. Using a slotted spoon, transfer to a plate.
❧ Add the onion to the oil remaining in the pan and cook, stirring, until softened, about 5 minutes. Add the celery leaves, sugar and tomato purée and cook, stirring occasionally, for 5 minutes. Add the vinegar and cook over medium heat, stirring occasionally, until the mixture forms a good thick consistency, about 10 minutes.
❧ Return the cooked eggplant to the pan and add the pine nuts, oregano, capers, olives and anchovies. Season to taste with salt and pepper, mix well and remove from the heat. Let cool.
❧ To prepare the eggplant bases, preheat a griller (broiler) on high. Arrange the eggplant slices on a baking tray (sheet). Brush the slices with about half of the olive oil. Slip under the griller and grill (broil) until just beginning to colour, 2–3 minutes. Turn and brush the second side with the remaining olive oil and grill until tender, about 2 minutes longer; do not overcook. Transfer to a plate and let cool.
❧ Arrange the eggplant slices on a large platter, top evenly with the *caponata* and serve.

MAKES ABOUT 30

SYDNEY

CAPSICUMS PUTTANESCA ON GRILLED PIDE

Turkish pide, *a long, flat bread topped with sesame seeds, is increasingly popular in Australia. It could eventually even rival Italian focaccia. Pide is ideal for splitting and filling for sandwiches or for simply topping as is done here. This bread can also be toasted over a charcoal fire. If you cannot find* pide, *Italian ciabatta can be substituted.*

2 red capsicums (bell peppers), roasted, peeled, seeded and cut into long strips 6 mm (¼ in) wide (see glossary)
6 anchovy fillets, packed in olive oil, drained and chopped into large pieces
1½ tablespoons well-drained small capers
12 black olives, pitted and halved
2 teaspoons fresh oregano leaves
1½ tablespoons virgin olive oil
freshly ground pepper
8 *pide* slices, each 1 cm (⅜ in) thick (about ½ loaf)
3 fresh Italian (flat-leaf) parsley sprigs, stems removed and leaves chopped

❧ Preheat a griller (broiler) on high.
❧ In a bowl, combine the capsicums, anchovies, capers, olives, oregano, olive oil and pepper to taste. Mix well, taste and adjust the seasonings.
❧ Arrange the *pide* slices on a griller rack and grill (broil) on both sides, turning once, until just beginning to colour. Arrange the slices on a platter. Spoon the capsicum mixture on top of the slices and strew with the parsley. Serve at once.

MAKES 8

Top to bottom: Capsicums Puttanesca on Grilled Pide, Pink-Skinned Potato Chips with Chilli Aioli, Grilled Eggplant Topped with Caponata

ROASTED TOMATO HEARTS

These always win a few hearts in my house. I have them assembled, waiting for the guests to arrive, then they're popped into a hot oven until they are puffed and golden.

3 sheets frozen puff pastry, each 25 cm (10 in) square,
    thawed (see glossary)
3 tablespoons Dijon mustard
6 Roma (plum) tomatoes, thinly sliced
125 g (¼ lb) cherry tomatoes, sliced
¼ bunch fresh thyme, preferably flowering
sea salt and freshly ground pepper

☙ Position a rack in the upper part of an oven and preheat the oven to 220°C (425°F). Spray 2 heavy baking trays (sheets) with nonstick cooking spray.

☙ Lay the pastry sheets out on a floured work surface. Using large and small heart-shaped cutters, stamp out hearts and arrange well spaced on the prepared trays.

☙ Spread each heart with some mustard and then top with a tomato slice; use larger slices on large hearts and smaller ones on small hearts.

☙ Bake in the upper part of the oven until the pastry is puffed and the tomatoes are beginning to colour around the edges, 12–15 minutes.

☙ Arrange the hearts on a platter. Scatter with sprigs of thyme and season with salt and pepper. Serve at once.

MAKES ABOUT 25

COCKTAIL PASTIES WITH HOMEMADE TOMATO SAUCE

Here is a little piece of our English heritage. The tomato sauce is about as Australian as you can get. Beware, however: it's so good, you'll find it turning up on everything!

FOR THE TOMATO SAUCE:

10 whole cloves
1 piece gingerroot, about 10 g (⅓ oz)
1 tablespoon whole allspice
2 kg (4 lb) ripe tomatoes, chopped
150 g (5 oz/⅔ cup) sugar
2 tablespoons salt, or to taste
300 ml (9½ fl oz/1¼ cups) malt vinegar
2 spring (green) onions, including tender green tops, chopped
1 small clove garlic, chopped
pinch of cayenne pepper

FOR THE FILLING:

100 g (3½ oz) lean minced (ground) beef
½ brown onion, coarsely grated
1 small carrot, peeled and coarsely grated
1 piece peeled butternut pumpkin or other firm pumpkin
    variety, 50 g (1½–2 oz), coarsely grated
1 small zucchini (courgette), coarsely grated
½ celery stalk, coarsely grated
1 small potato, peeled and coarsely grated
2 tablespoons frozen peas, thawed
salt and freshly ground pepper

6 sheets frozen puff pastry, each 25 cm (10 in) square,
    thawed (see glossary)
1 egg yolk, beaten with 2 teaspoons water

☙ To make the sauce, place the cloves, gingerroot and allspice in a small square of muslin (cheesecloth), bring together the corners and tie securely with kitchen twine.

☙ Place all the sauce ingredients, including the cloth bag, in a heavy pot and bring slowly to a boil. Cover the pot and simmer over low heat until the mixture has thickened to a sauce consistency, 1½ hours.

☙ Let the sauce cool, then discard the cloth bag. Strain the sauce through a sieve to remove the skins and seeds. You should have about 300 ml (10 fl oz/1¼ cups).

☙ While the sauce cooks, preheat an oven to 210°C (400°F). Butter 2 baking trays (sheets).

☙ To make the filling, in a large bowl, mix together the beef, onion, carrot, pumpkin, zucchini, celery, potato and peas. Season to taste with salt and pepper and mix well.

☙ Separate the pastry sheets and, working in batches if necessary, arrange on a work surface. Using a sharp knife, cut out 4 rounds, each 10 cm (4 in) in diameter, from each sheet.

☙ Spoon an equal portion of the filling into the centre of each pastry round, leaving a 2-cm (¾-in) uncovered border around the edges. Dampen the uncovered edges with cold water and fold each round in half. Crimp the pastry edges together to seal well.

☙ Arrange the pasties well spaced on the prepared trays. Brush the tops with the egg yolk mixture. Bake until puffed and golden, about 18 minutes.

☙ Let rest for 5 minutes, then transfer to a platter and serve. Pass the sauce.

MAKES 24

PARMESAN CHEESE BISCUITS

These light, flavoursome biscuits are perfect for serving with a glass of fine Australian sparkling wine. They can be made up to 3 days in advance and stored at room temperature, but the container must be absolutely airtight. Since there is no good parmesan-style cheese currently produced in Australia, it is best to use imported Italian parmigiano.

60 g (2 oz) parmesan cheese, preferably imported, finely
    grated
130 g (4 oz/¾ cup) plain (all-purpose) flour
½ teaspoon salt, or to taste
½ teaspoon baking powder
⅛ teaspoon cayenne pepper, or to taste
120 g (4 oz/½ cup) unsalted butter, at room temperature,
    cut into small bits

☙ Position a rack in the centre of an oven and preheat the oven to 180°C (350°F). Butter and flour 2 baking trays (sheets).

☙ In a large bowl, stir together the cheese, flour, salt, baking powder and cayenne. Add the butter and, using a knife, work it into the dry ingredients until the mixture comes together in a rough mass. Shape the dough into a ball, wrap in plastic wrap and refrigerate for 30 minutes.

☙ On a lightly floured surface, roll out the dough 8 mm (⅓ in) thick. Dip a biscuit cutter 5 cm (2 in) in diameter in flour and cut out rounds, dipping the cutter as needed to prevent sticking. Place the rounds 2.5 cm (1 in) apart on the prepared baking trays. Prick each biscuit twice with a fork.

☙ Bake on the centre rack until golden, 8–10 minutes. Transfer to wire racks to cool.

☙ Serve warm or at room temperature.

MAKES ABOUT 40

Top to bottom: Roasted Tomato Hearts, Parmesan Cheese Biscuits, Cocktail Pasties with Homemade Tomato Sauce— photographed at Pittwater, Sydney

Outside to center: Spinach Pancakes with Sour Cream and Salmon Roe,
Smoked Tasmanian Salmon Lavash Rolls (recipe page 45)

SPINACH PANCAKES WITH SOUR CREAM AND SALMON ROE

The roe from Tasmanian salmon is pure bliss. It is slightly salty and slightly oily, and the eggs are large and the colour of salmon. Combined here with spinach and cream, they make for a particularly attractive appetiser.

FOR THE PANCAKES:

250 g (½ lb) frozen chopped spinach, thawed
2 tablespoons finely chopped fresh parsley
2 spring (green) onions, including tender green tops, finely chopped
2 eggs
3 tablespoons milk, or more as needed
3 tablespoons sour cream
1 tablespoon unsalted butter, melted
120 g (4 oz/¾ cup) plain (all-purpose) flour
pinch of freshly grated nutmeg
salt and freshly ground pepper

about 80 ml (3 fl oz/⅓ cup) olive oil
250 g (8 oz/1 cup) sour cream
200 g (6½ oz) Tasmanian salmon roe or other high-quality salmon roe

❊ To make the pancakes, wrap the spinach in a clean kitchen towel and wring out any excess water. Place in a medium bowl, add the parsley and spring onions and stir to mix.
❊ In a large mixing bowl, beat the eggs. Add the 3 tablespoons milk, sour cream and melted butter and mix well. Stir in the flour, nutmeg and salt and pepper to taste. Fold in the spinach mixture. Let stand for 30 minutes.
❊ In a large frying pan (preferably nonstick) over medium heat, warm 1 tablespoon of the olive oil. Working in batches, spoon in 1 tablespoon of the spinach mixture to form each pancake; do not crowd the pan. Add more milk to the mixture if it seems too thick. Cook until the edges are golden, about 2 minutes. Flip the pancakes and cook until the second side is golden, about 2 minutes longer. Transfer to a serving plate and let cool. Repeat with the remaining oil and batter.
❊ Top each cooled pancake with a spoonful of sour cream and then a spoonful of salmon roe. Serve at room temperature.

MAKES ABOUT 20 PANCAKES

LAMB PROSCIUTTO WITH ROCKET AND CITRUS FRUITS

John Wilson of Mohr Foods at Botany flavours lamb legs with tarragon, garlic and native pepperleaf, then smokes them lightly and, finally, air-dries them. He calls his product lamb prosciutto, even though the pork prosciutto of Italy is never smoked. If you cannot find this all-Australian specialty, regular prosciutto can be used in its place.

500 g (1 lb) Mohr Foods lamb prosciutto, thinly sliced
2 oranges, segmented and membranes removed
2 grapefruits, segmented and membranes removed
1 bunch rocket (arugula), carefully washed and crisped
extra-virgin olive oil
freshly ground pepper

❊ Arrange the lamb slices in a single layer on 8 large flat dinner plates. Top with the citrus fruits and rocket. Anoint lightly with olive oil. Grind pepper over the top and serve.

SERVES 8   *Photograph pages 32–33*

South Pacific Ceviche—photographed at Blue Lagoon, Moreton Island, Queensland

SOUTH PACIFIC CEVICHE

Ceviche (also spelled seviche) originated in Latin America, but has become popular wherever there is a plentiful supply of fresh fish. The lime juice cures the fish and firms the flesh—essentially 'cooking' it without means of heat. Each region in Australia has its own version of this dish using the local fish. This one was given to me by food writer and caterer Consuelo Guinness. She says

making ceviche with whiting fillets turns it into a particularly special dish. Snapper or bream fillets can be substituted.

6–8 whiting fillets, about 1.25 kg (2½ lb) total weight skinned
juice of 6–8 limes, plus 2 limes, sliced
90 g (1 cup) baby spring (green) onions, very finely sliced
2 or 3 small fresh red, preferably birdseye chillies, chopped
salt and white pepper
1 bunch fresh coriander (cilantro) sprigs

❧ Cut each fillet into 4–6 pieces. Place in a single layer in a shallow glass or ceramic dish. Pour the lime juice evenly over the fish, then turn the fish to coat it evenly. Scatter the onion and chillies over the fish. Cover and refrigerate for 2 hours.

❧ Season the fish to taste with salt and pepper, re-cover and refrigerate for 2 hours longer, or as long as overnight. The fish is ready when it is opaque and appears cooked.

❧ Chop half of the coriander, including some of the stems. Add to the fish and toss. Transfer to a glass serving dish and decorate with the lime slices and the remaining coriander sprigs. Serve at once.

SERVES 8

SYDNEY

CORNMEAL MUFFINS WITH TOMATO, BORLOTTI AND BASIL SALAD

Cornmeal has become a popular food with many Australians. Yellow cornmeal (also sometimes called by its Italian name, polenta) is available in three grinds, fine, medium and coarse. Use coarse grind unless the recipe specifies differently. This recipe calls for fresh borlotti beans, but other fresh shell beans, such as broad (fava) beans, can be substituted. Adjust the cooking time as needed.

FOR THE SALAD:

250 g (½ lb) fresh borlotti (cranberry) beans, shelled (150 g/ 5 oz shelled)
4–6 tomatoes, peeled, seeded and coarsely diced
1 teaspoon balsamic vinegar
1 teaspoon red wine vinegar
100 ml (3½ fl oz/6½ tablespoons) extra-virgin olive oil
sea salt and freshly ground pepper
12 fresh basil leaves, finely shredded

FOR THE MUFFINS:

200 ml (6½ fl oz/¾ cup plus 1½ tablespoons) milk
2 tablespoons unsalted butter
80 g (2½ oz/½ cup) yellow cornmeal
3 egg yolks
4 egg whites
pinch of regular table salt
1 teaspoon sea salt

❧ To make the salad, fill a saucepan with water and bring to a boil. Add the shelled beans and cook until tender, about 15 minutes. Drain and place in a bowl. Add the tomatoes, vinegars and oil and toss to coat well. Season to taste with salt and pepper and toss again. Top with the basil and set aside.

❧ To make the muffins, position a rack in the centre of an oven and preheat the oven to 200°C (400°F). Butter 6 standard muffin-tin cups.

❧ In a large, heavy pot, bring the milk and butter to a boil. Add the cornmeal in a thin, steady stream, whisking constantly. Remove from the heat at once and let cool a little. Whisk in the egg yolks, one at a time.

❧ In a bowl, beat the egg whites and the table salt until the whites form soft, shiny peaks. Using a rubber spatula, fold the whites into the cornmeal mixture. Divide the mixture evenly among the muffin cups. Scatter the sea salt over the top.

❧ Bake in the centre of the oven until puffed and golden, about 15 minutes. Remove from the oven and let stand for 2 minutes, then turn out of the muffin tin onto a wire rack and let cool completely.

❧ Split the muffins and place in individual bowls. Top with the salad and serve.

SERVES 6   *Photograph pages 32–33*

SYDNEY

GALLOPING HORSES

One of the best small offerings from Thailand, galloping horses, called ma hor *in Thai, are perfect for serving at stand-up parties or as an opener to a Thai meal. The sweetness and acidity of the fresh pineapple are a wonderful contrast to the taste of the pork. Assemble the* ma hor *while the pork mixture is warm, as it will bind together better. This is Cherry Ripe's recipe.*

1½ teaspoons peanut or vegetable oil
1 clove garlic, crushed
1 fresh red chilli, seeded and chopped
3 fresh coriander (cilantro) roots with sprigs attached, stems and roots chopped and leaves left whole (see glossary)
175 g (6 oz) finely minced (ground) pork with some fat
3 tablespoons salted peanuts, coarsely crushed in a mortar with a pestle
1 tablespoon fish sauce (see glossary)
2 teaspoons palm sugar (see glossary) or brown sugar, or to taste
freshly ground pepper
3 fresh pineapple slices, each 6 mm (¼ in) thick

❧ In a wok or large frying pan over medium heat, warm the oil. Add the garlic and chilli and stir-fry until softened, 20–30 seconds; do not allow to brown. Add the coriander stems and roots and the pork and cook until the colour changes, about 2 minutes. Add the peanuts, fish sauce, sugar and pepper to taste and continue cooking, stirring occasionally, until the mixture is cooked but not too dry, about 10 minutes.

❧ To serve, cut each pineapple slice into 6 equal pieces. Arrange the pieces on a serving dish and top each piece with a spoonful of the pork mixture. Lightly press with your fingertips to bind the mixture together. Garnish with the coriander leaves. Serve at room temperature.

MAKES 18   *Photograph page 47*

HOBART

SMOKED TASMANIAN SALMON LAVASH ROLLS

Lavash, also spelled lavoche *and* lovash, *is the oldest form of bread found in the Middle East. It is very thin and crisp when made in the traditional way. A commercial version that is soft and pliable, allowing you to roll it, is the one you need for this recipe. In this soft form,* lavash *is also called mountain bread.*

160 ml (5 fl oz/⅔ cup) mayonnaise
2 teaspoons snipped fresh dill or pinch of dried dill
coarsely cracked pepper
finely grated zest of 1 lemon
2 soft *lavash* slices, each about 20 by 30 cm (8 by 12 in), halved lengthwise
250 g (8 oz) smoked salmon slices

❧ In a small bowl, stir together the mayonnaise, dill, pepper to taste and lemon zest until well mixed. Lay the halved *lavash* slices on a flat work surface and spread the mayonnaise mixture evenly over them. Cover with the salmon slices in a single layer. Starting from a short end, roll up each sheet firmly but not tightly. Wrap each roll in plastic wrap and refrigerate for 1 hour before slicing.

❧ To serve, remove the plastic wrap and, using a serrated knife, cut crosswise on the diagonal into slices about 2.5 cm (1 in) thick. Arrange on a serving tray and serve at once.

MAKES 16   *Photograph page 42–43*

SPICY THAI FISH BALLS WITH DIPPING SAUCE

Judging from the number of suburban Thai restaurants and the many exotic ingredients appearing on supermarket shelves, Thai food is the fastest-growing ethnic cuisine in Australia.

FOR THE FISH BALLS:

500 g (1 lb) redfish fillets, cut into pieces
1 tablespoon red curry paste (see glossary)
1 egg, lightly beaten
2 spring (green) onions, including tender green tops, finely sliced
4 fresh kaffir lime leaves, finely chopped (see glossary)
1 tablespoon finely chopped fresh coriander (cilantro) root and leaves (see glossary)
1 teaspoon sugar
½ teaspoon salt, or to taste

400 ml (13 fl oz/1⅔ cups) vegetable oil, for deep-frying
fresh coriander (cilantro) sprigs and cucumber slices for garnish
dipping sauce for steamed chilli crab parcels (recipe on page 36)

☙ To make the fish balls, in a food processor fitted with the metal blade, place the fish. Process until minced (ground). Add the curry paste and pulse to mix. Add the egg and process until the mixture just comes together. Transfer to a bowl and add the onions, lime leaves, coriander, sugar and salt. Alternatively, mince the fish with a sharp knife and stir in the remaining ingredients. Stir until the mixture is well mixed and comes together. Roll the mixture into small balls about 2 cm (¾ in) in diameter and refrigerate until firm, about 30 minutes.
☙ In a small, deep saucepan over high heat, pour in oil to a depth of 5 cm (2 in). Heat to 190°C (375°F) on a deep-fat thermometer, or until a small piece of bread dropped into the oil immediately rises to the surface. Carefully slip about 10 fish balls into the hot oil and deep-fry until evenly golden, about 3 minutes. Using a slotted spoon, remove to crumpled paper towels to drain. Cook the remaining balls in the same manner.
☙ Arrange the fish balls in a serving bowl and garnish with the coriander sprigs and cucumber slices. Place the dipping sauce in a smaller bowl. Serve at room temperature.

MAKES ABOUT 48

VEGETABLE BRUSCHETTA

Bruschetta makes an ideal finger food or snack. An Italian (saltless) baguette or loaf that has been baked in a wood-fired oven is good for this recipe. The best Italian breads are found in certain suburbs and other areas with large Italian populations, such as Carlton in Melbourne and Leichhardt in Sydney.

3 tablespoons unsalted butter
2 tablespoons olive oil
1 yellow capsicum (bell pepper), about 100 g (3½ oz), seeded and cut into 2-cm (¾-in) dice
2 Roma (plum) tomatoes, diced
80 g (2½ oz) yellow teardrop tomatoes, halved lengthwise
120 g (¼ lb) asparagus, tips removed and stalks cut into 1-cm (⅜-in) pieces
2 teaspoons chopped fresh parsley
2 teaspoons balsamic vinegar
sea salt and freshly ground pepper
12 baguette slices, each 2 cm (¾ in) thick
2 cloves garlic, halved

☙ Preheat a griller (broiler) on high.
☙ In a heavy frying pan over medium heat, melt the butter with the oil until sizzling. Add the capsicum, Roma and teardrop tomatoes and asparagus tips and stalks and sauté until just tender, about 10 minutes. Stir in the parsley and vinegar and season to taste with salt and pepper. Remove from the heat and cover to keep warm.
☙ Arrange the baguette slices on a griller rack and grill (broil) on both sides, turning once, until lightly golden. Rub one side with the cut garlic and arrange, garlic side up, on 1 or 2 platters. Spoon the hot vegetable mixture on top of the bread slices and serve at once.

MAKES 12

GOAT CHEESE FILO TARTLETS

The cheese in this recipe comes from Gidgegannup, east of Perth, where Gabrielle Kervella creates her remarkable goat cheeses. The filo pastry cases can be used for various soft fillings, but the fillings must not be too moist. These cases go together much more quickly than those made from short pastry.

FOR THE FILLING:

60 g (2 oz/¼ cup) unsalted butter, plus 2 tablespoons unsalted butter, softened
½ bunch spring (green) onions, white part only, sliced
200 g (6½ oz) Gabrielle Kervella Frais goat cheese or other fresh goat cheese
125 ml (4 fl oz/½ cup) thickened (double/heavy) cream
salt and freshly ground pepper

8 filo sheets, each 20 cm (8 in) square (see glossary)
60 g (2 oz/¼ cup) unsalted butter, melted

☙ Position a rack in the centre of an oven and preheat the oven to 180°C (350°F). Butter 16 tartlet moulds, each 7 cm (2¾ in) in diameter and 1.5 cm (⅗ in) deep or, preferably, use nonstick moulds.
☙ To make the filling, in a frying pan over medium heat, melt the 60 g (2 oz/¼ cup) butter. Add the onions and sauté until softened, about 8 minutes. Let cool.
☙ Place the goat cheese, 2 tablespoons softened butter and cream into a food processor fitted with the metal blade, in a blender or in a bowl. Process or beat with a wooden spoon until well mixed. Fold in the onions until thoroughly combined. Season to taste with salt and pepper. Set aside.
☙ To make the tartlet moulds, cut the filo sheets into quarters. Keep any filo sheets you are not working with covered with plastic wrap to prevent them from drying out. Place 1 filo quarter in a tartlet mould and cover with a second piece, positioning it on the diagonal to the first so you have 8 evenly spaced points of filo around the rim of the mould. Paint lightly with the melted butter. Repeat with the remaining filo and moulds.
☙ Divide the filling among the prepared tartlet moulds. Bake in the centre of the oven until the filo is golden and the filling is just set, about 18 minutes. Let cool for 5 minutes in the moulds, then, using a small eggslice (metal spatula), ease the tartlets out of the moulds, being careful not to break the filo 'petals'.
☙ Serve warm or at room temperature.

MAKES 16

Clockwise from top right: Goat Cheese Filo Tartlets, Galloping Horses (recipe page 45), Vegetable Bruschetta, Spicy Thai Fish Balls with Dipping Sauce—photographed at Gwinganna estate, Queensland

TASMANIA

TASMANIA

ISLAND OF PLENTY

Paradise and Plenty could be descriptions of this island state, but they're actually names of two of its hamlets. Such names must have expressed the feelings of their original settlers upon finding themselves somewhere so temperate and so fertile.

Tasmania might have been left off the national map so often that it's become a cliché to say it is Australia's 'best-kept secret'. The island's food producers have used this geographical isolation—which has protected it from many of the pests, such as the fruit fly, and diseases that beset the mainland—to promote a clean, 'green' image. From its wilderness honey to its crisp apples, Tasmania produces some of the best food, in terms of both quality and flavour, in Australia, thanks to both its latitude and its unique maritime climate.

Australia's second oldest colony, Tasmania was discovered by Dutch explorer Abel Tasman in 1642, who named it Van Dieman's Land, after the then governor of the Dutch East Indies. It was circumnavigated by George Bass and Matthew Flinders in 1798, proving it was not part of the mainland. A British settlement was established some six years later, largely to forestall the French, who had been snooping about. The French explorers nevertheless left their mark on the landscape in names that still mark many parts of the island: Bruni (Bruny Island), d'Entrecasteaux (Channel), Huon (River) and Freycinet (Peninsula).

The impenetrability of the Australian bush also contributed to the settlement of Tasmania. It was easier to travel south by sea than to penetrate the thickly vegetated escarpment of the Great Dividing Range. The initial settlement was established in 1803 at Risdon Cove

Previous pages: The penal colony at Port Arthur, abandoned in 1877, stands as an evocative ruin on the Tasman Peninsula. Left: Striking examples of Georgian architecture fill the meandering streets of Battery Point in Hobart.

Roving musicians serenade both shoppers and vendors at the weekly open-air market in Hobart.

(later Hobart Town) on the east side of the Derwent, ten years before the explorers Blaxland, Lawson and Wentworth had even managed to cross the Blue Mountains, a distance of fewer than one hundred kilometres (sixty miles). The first cattle (139 cows, 1 bull and 60 oxen imported from India) reached Hobart Town in August 1804. In November that same year, a settlement was established in the north, then moved two years later to what is now Launceston. When, in 1811, Governor Macquarie visited from New South Wales—still two years before the Blue Mountains were crossed—he travelled overland between the two settlements. Convict labour sped development—by 1846 there were just under thirty thousand convicts on the island, which had been settled as a penal colony—and soon Tasmania was sending wheat to New South Wales.

Despite its latitude (Hobart at forty-three degrees south of the equator is equivalent to Boston), Tasmania's maritime climate modifies its temperatures; no place is more than 115 kilometres (66 miles) from the sea. Climatically more similar to the British Isles than to the rest of Australia, the island has retained much of its charming early architecture, which recalls British buildings of that period.

Not for nothing did Tasmania become known as the Apple Isle. Its first apples were planted by no less than Captain Bligh on his way to Tahiti in 1788. (The infamous mutiny occurred the following April.) The *Bounty* anchored in Adventure Bay on Bruny Island on 20 August, a mere eight months after the arrival of the First Fleet in Port Jackson. Bligh could be said to have started

Hops for brewing beer, a crop with a long history in Tasmania, can still be seen growing in fields north of Hobart.

A grazier herds his sheep through the Derwent Valley, one of Tasmania's wine-producing regions.

European horticulture in Tasmania. In addition to apples, he planted vines, oranges, lemons, cherries and various vegetables, probably to ensure himself fresh supplies on subsequent voyages. By the time of his next visit in February 1792, again on his way to Tahiti, only one of the apple trees had survived.

The seeds were sown, however. The *Van Diemen's Land Almanac* of 1833 reported that the success of growing certain fruits—apples and plums—'was so astonishing that it needs to be seen to be credited'. Commercial apple plantings began in the Huon Valley in the 1840s. A flourishing dried-apple industry developed in the late 1890s; one early drying shed now houses the Apple Museum.

Until the 1970s, literally millions of cartons of apples were exported to Europe—particularly Britain—each year. When Britain joined the European Economic Community, this lucrative market largely dried up, and Tasmania had to take up planting different varieties to suit new markets. This has literally changed the landscape. The orchards of full-sized trees of three decades ago have been replaced by comparatively miniature trees, with both old and new varieties grafted onto dwarfing root stock. (This enables the fruit to be picked largely from the ground rather than pickers having to scale ladders.)

Old varieties that were grown to suit British tastes, such as Cox's Orange Pippins, Sturmers and Cleopatras, have given way to plantings of newer varieties to

accommodate contemporary tastes, both on the mainland and in the developing markets in Asia, particularly Singapore and Taiwan. In Asia the taste is for a sweeter apple, and so these days new plantings are more likely to be Red Fuji (a variety bred in Japan by crossing an old variety, Rall's Jennet, with a Red Delicious strain), Pink Lady from Western Australia or the locally developed Tassie Snow Apple, so-called because of its contrasting crispy white flesh and red skin. The latter is a descendant of Geeveston Fanny, named after Fanny Tyson, a local grower's wife. Still grown in large numbers are varieties like Democrat, Hi Early Delicious and, to a lesser extent, that traditionally popular Australian variety, Granny Smith. Thanks to its official fruit fly–free status, which also means less use of pesticides, Tasmania can export such fruits as these more easily to Japan and the United States.

Following harvest, the Apple Museum, just outside Huonville, displays some three hundred varieties—many of them no longer grown commercially.

The cool climate offers further advantages. The longer fruits and vegetables take to grow, the more flavour they develop, so such berry fruits as raspberries develop fuller flavour and fragrance than those grown on the mainland because they ripen more slowly. Tasmania's longer days and cooler growing conditions also cause the same grape varieties cultivated on the mainland to behave very differently in Tasmanian conditions. This was recognised

The well-preserved colonial architecture along Hobart harbour is the setting for the popular market held every Saturday.

by Claudio Alcorso, an Italian and a former textile manufacturer, in the late 1950s, when he successfully planted vines at Moorilla Estate on the banks of the Derwent, now within the confines of suburban Hobart. While he was not the first to realise its potential as a grape-growing region—Tasmania's first vineyard had been planted in 1823—he is considered the father of the present-day Tasmanian wine industry. These days there are six grape-growing regions, including the Tamar Valley northeast of Launceston, Piper's River, the East Coast, the Coal River Valley, the Derwent Valley (which includes Hobart) and the Huon Valley.

From around Nubeena near Port Arthur on the Tasman Peninsula come wonderful pear varieties like Beurre Bosc, Winter Cole and Doyenne de Comice, the last considered by its many growers to be the ultimate in pears.

Tasmania also grows large quantities of potatoes. Some of them are exceptional, such as the wonderfully waxy, yellow-fleshed pink-eye. Sometimes called Pink Lady and also sold in Victoria as Southern Gold, the pink-eye is not to be confused with the more common red-skinned pontiac.

Up in the north of the island, a Dutch potato variety called Bintjes (pronounced binjies) is grown. Here, too, in the dark-chocolate basalt soil around Forth, are grown tens of thousands of tonnes of onions for export each year to the Northern Hemisphere. Also cultivated are the deliciously nutty Japanese kabocha pumpkins, with flesh the colour of an avocado's.

Aquaculture industries flourish in Tasmania's unpolluted waters, with the farming of Atlantic salmon being the most successful. Since the mid-1980s, salmon farms have sprung up along the lower east coast. In 1986, the first year of marine production, the harvest was a mere fifty-three tonnes; by 1993, it had grown to well over three thousand tonnes, and the season had been extended from three months a year to year-round.

The eggs are hatched in fresh water at Wayatinah, high in the mountainous centre of Tasmania. After fifteen months, when the smolts reach eighty to eighty-five grams (about two and one-half ounces), they are transferred to the sea to large pens. In the next fifteen months in sea water, their growth rates are explosive: they go from that eighty-five grams to an average of three to three and a half kilos (six to seven pounds) at harvest. This rate is double the average in the Northern Hemisphere.

Although Atlantic salmon is farmed in Canada, Norway and Scotland, Tasmania's farms are 'greener' than their counterparts elsewhere. There are fewer fish to each pen, and, being free of the diseases and parasites (like sea lice) found in the Northern Hemisphere, Tasmanian salmon don't need to be fed antibiotics or treated with parasite-killing chemicals.

Aside from abalone—wild and farmed—one of the most innovative of all the state's aquaculture ventures is the farming technique used for raising Pacific oysters (*Crassostrea gigas*) employed at Eagle Hawk Neck, on the way to Port Arthur. The novel method, which was adapted from a Japanese system, was introduced by the Commonwealth Scientific Industrial Research Organisation (CSIRO) back in 1947 for states that didn't have an oyster industry. It calls for suspending the oysters in 'modules'—a stack of eight trays—about three metres (three yards) under the surface, on long lines attached to buoys. Because the oysters are constantly submerged, they have access to food twenty-four hours a day, whereas in a tidal environment on fixed poles or trays, they can feed only when the tide is in. Thus these oysters grow faster and more uniformly.

Once a month the oysters are hauled aboard a boat, taken ashore and graded. In the process, the frill on the end of the shell is deliberately knocked off. Pacific oysters, if left alone, have a tendency to grow long, narrow and deep, cigar-shaped shells. Knocking off the frill causes them to grow fatter and rounder—more like the Sydney Rock oyster. Thanks to these growing methods, the oysters grow more than twice as quickly as the Sydney Rock, achieving maturity in eighteen months.

Also from Tasmania's waters come wonderful crustaceans and molluscs, such as crabs, rock lobsters, scallops, mussels, baby clams (vongole) and sea urchins prized for their roe. There are all manner of fish, too, including the superb stripey trumpeter, deep-sea trevalla, blue warehou and the most recently discovered—because they live at such depths—orange roughy (sometimes called ocean perch) and deep-sea dories.

The king crabs found in Tasmanian waters are said to be the biggest in the world. They must be handled carefully out of the water, because the weight of their claws is so great, they can easily snap off.

Freshwater trout were introduced to Tasmania in 1864. The Ranicars at the Tasmanian Smokehouse effectively began the island's smoking industry, first handling river trout and eels in the 1970s, and then Atlantic salmon. Now many people smoke salmon, and there are other cottage smoking industries as well, such as the Wursthaus, which produces smoked sausages and venison.

Deer were brought by early Scottish settlers, but some escaped and adapted well to conditions in the wild. The current deer farms captured animals in the hills to start their operations and are now farming them free-range.

From Tasmania's wilderness comes leatherwood honey. Stephens' Golden Nectar (real leatherwood) honey is gathered by transporting the beehives from Mole Creek in the north of the island over to the rainforest wilderness area on the west around the Franklin River. This trip is made in late December, when only the leatherwood is in flower. The result is one of the most distinctively perfumed honeys in the world.

With nothing lying between it and South Africa, except the Roaring Forties, Tasmania prides itself on being so free of pollution that it bottles and sells its rainwater, as well as a range of mineral waters. Although Tasmania had long been wonderful dairy country—supplying milk to Cadbury's chocolate factory—the first of the new wave of artisan cheeses, which began an explosion of boutique and farmhouse cheeses around the country—had its beginnings on King Island, in Bass Strait, off Tasmania's north coast, in the early 1980s. King Island's wonderfully lush pastures are due to its unique grasses, the seeds of which are said to have been washed ashore in mattresses from shipwrecks on its treacherous coastline. King Island Dairy makes a range of some one dozen artisan cheeses (the milk coming from more than one farm), including its famous brie, camembert and cheddar. In 1992, the dairy also started producing blue-mould cheeses, for which a separate dairy was built so the moulds don't get mixed up. The first of these was the Bass Strait Blue, which was followed by others like Endeavour Blue. Next door to the cheese factory is a small operation that produces smoked beef, pastrami and salamis.

Driving around King Island, you may see huge dark swathes hanging on giant clotheslinelike frames. This is kelp for export to Scotland, which uses its alginates in ice-cream making.

Some of the best farmhouse (that is, the milk coming only from a single farm) cheese in Australia is from Tasmania, particularly those from Frank and Elisabeth Marchand at Heidi, a family operation near Deloraine. They make their own starter cultures and a range of matured cheeses, from wonderful gruyère wheels to the Heidi cheddar 'barrels'. In addition to a number of large cheese producers such as Lactos, also in the north of the island, there are many small farmhouse businesses springing up.

Although now disappearing, hops for beer making traditionally were grown on the island. In the Derwent Valley, where you see rows of poplars acting as windbreaks between fields, there once were hop fields.

Other newer crops being grown are fennel (exported for the aniseed flavour in Pernod), dill (for use in pickles) and buckwheat (for Japanese soba noodle manufacturers). In development are Japanese green tea and ginger. The wine industry, although still small in comparison to that of other states, is growing, and increasingly its wines are achieving wider acclaim.

Tasmania is a significant food exporter—with Asia an increasingly important market. More than half of all its fruit and vegetable exports, two-thirds of its dairy exports and two-thirds of its seafood—rock lobster, Atlantic salmon, abalone and oysters—now go to Asia. Such a wealth and diversity of foods show it to be truly the island of plenty.

The town of Franklin greets the Huon River as it tumbles down the forested mountains towards the sea.

SOUPS AND STARTERS

A variety of shops occupy the well-preserved nineteenth-century buildings in Beechworth, Victoria, a town that prospered in the gold-rush era.

SOUPS AND STARTERS

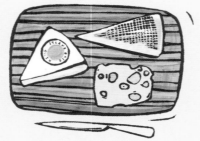

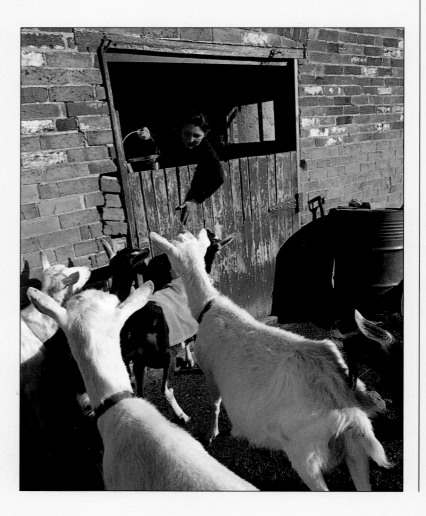

FEW DISHES ARE MORE QUINTESSENTIALLY—and uniquely— Australian than kangaroo tail soup. Although it was unobtainable for nearly three decades almost everywhere but in South Australia, these days it is again turning up on restaurant menus, sometimes even flavoured with lemon-grass, or the native lemon myrtle, and a touch of chilli.

Certainly stews—rather than soups—loomed large in the early Australian culinary repertoire. When faced with only a camp fire to cook on, one can fairly easily suspend a large pot over the flames. The early colonists' disdain for local game, however, is summed up in a facetious recipe for the native cockatoo from Australian folklore: 'Take a cockatoo, a large stone, and a pot of boiling water', run the instructions for preparing this large, raucous parrot. 'Put the cockatoo and the stone in the pot. When the stone is soft, throw away the cockatoo and eat the stone'. In the early days in the bush, serving starters would have been a luxury. Even during the transition from convict rations to such bush staples as damper and grilled or fried meat three times a day, people were working too hard to think of appetisers: food was fuel to help get the country settled.

Previous pages, clockwise from right: Rustic Cheese Pie (recipe page 64), Kumara Soup with Green Pea and Lettuce Soup (recipe page 67), Farmhouse Barley-Vegetable Soup with Herb Damper (recipe page 67), Kangaroo Tail Soup (recipe page 62)—photographed at Mount Canobolas in NSW. Right: Orange, NSW, where this grazier has his herd, is known for cheese and other products made from goat's milk.

The aroma of freshly baked bread and German pastries permeates a bakery at Tanunda, a South Australia town with a strong European heritage.

Once station life was established, and homesteads acquired vegetable gardens, things began to look up. Australia's first cookbook—*The English and Australian Cookery Book* by Tasmanian Edward Abbott—was published in 1864. By the end of the century, the squattocracy were eating better than they had before. In 1899, country cook Mrs Forster Rutledge offered recipes for some thirty-eight soups, including such stand-bys as mutton broth, sheep's head and oxtail, as well as chowders, mulligatawnys and even lettuce and asparagus soups. Certainly, in less affluent homes, when the backyard chook—the laying hen—had finished her usefulness, she ended up in the pot, first as boiled chicken, and then as chicken broth.

Soup was an integral part of all formal banquets, modelled as they were along French lines. It would frequently be described as a 'potage' on the menu, and appeared along with many courses now abandoned. Today's diner would find the amount of food served quite daunting. Even in the 1930s, a 'simple dinner' in winter for six people or fewer, decreed Amy Schauer (the doyenne of Queensland cooks of the period) in the *Schauer Australian Cookery Book,* should begin with a cocktail, say of orange and mint. This should be followed by an hors d'oeuvre—perhaps oysters in the shell—and then a soup (she suggested a tomato purée). Next came a fish course of steamed whiting fillet with shrimp sauce, followed by an entrée of chicken cutlets. All this, and the main course—the 'joint'—was still to come, as were a further four courses!

A 'simple menu for summer' along the same lines recommended a cocktail of iced fruit, an hors d'oeuvre of asparagus boats, a julienne soup, fried whiting fillets for the fish course, sheep's tongue in aspic as the entrée, and (no doubt with some relief in the Queensland heat) cold chicken and boiled ham. This summer menu for an informal dinner—even in the tropical heat—also ran to eight courses. One wonders how the diners ever got up from the table after such a repast.

Thankfully, these days not only is our food lighter, but there is a good deal less of it, and it incorporates a much greater proportion of vegetables. A warming winter meal might comprise only a hearty farmhouse soup, a crusty bread like damper and a salad. Or it might start with duck livers on polenta, or even an Italian-inspired sausage-and-lentil soup. Tomato soup might be given a new twist with the addition of avocado and shallots, or a lettuce soup might be enlivened with the addition of sweet potato and fresh peas.

Gone are the grapefruit cocktails of the past. In their place is perhaps a seafood salad, such as squid tossed with roasted capsicums (bell peppers) and olives and a dressing made with the wonderful Western Australian anchovies, or one concocted from lime juice, shallots and chilli.

Whereas Australians used to go out to eat Asian food—particularly Chinese—with its increasing popularity and people's familiarity with it, there is more enthusiasm for cooking Asian dishes at home. Nowadays, a soup is quite likely to be Asian—perhaps a Malaysian *laksa,* or a hot-and-sour prawn soup, like the Thai *tom yum goong.* An Asian-inspired salad, such as mussels marinated in lemongrass and other Asian spices, or a more old-fashioned but equally delicious Chinese dish like *san choy bow* rolled up in lettuce leaves, is also a popular choice.

A spring meal might commence with linguine tossed with sweet young broad (fava) beans and *pancetta.* On a balmy summer evening outdoors, a wonderful citrus-laced Tasmanian salmon tartare or a roulade of capsicum (bell pepper) and eggplant (aubergine) might be served. A summer lunch might feature a terrine of goat cheese, or a lobster and mango salad.

In contemporary Australian homes, inspiration for dishes might originate anywhere in the world, but at their root they are a celebration of our plethora of fresh ingredients.

This robust cauliflower crop in South Werribee, Victoria, reflects the state's abundant harvests of a wide array of vegetables and fruits.

Top to bottom: Squid Salad with Roasted Capsicums, Black Olives and Anchovy Dressing, Capsicum and Eggplant Roulade, Sautéed Duck Livers on Polenta with Tomato Vinaigrette

CAPSICUM AND EGGPLANT ROULADE

Gay Bilson and Janni Kyritsis, two well-known Australian chefs, gave me this recipe, which has been copied by other chefs, surely the greatest accolade. Gay describes the dish as a salad of capsicum and eggplant served as 'a neat round package'.

6 large red capsicums (bell peppers)
350 ml (11 fl oz/1⅓ cups) olive oil
3 or 4 eggplants (aubergines)
sea salt

2 tablespoons finely snipped fresh chives
2 tablespoons finely chopped fresh parsley
freshly ground pepper
about 80 ml (3 fl oz/⅓ cup) virgin olive oil

❧ Preheat an oven to 210°C (400°F).
❧ Remove the stem and the seeds from each capsicum. Oil a baking tray (sheet) with 2 tablespoons of the olive oil. Place the whole capsicums on the tray. Roast in the oven, turning as needed, until evenly blackened and blistered on all sides, about 15 minutes. Remove from the oven and place in a paper bag. Close the top and let sweat and cool for almost 10 minutes. When cool enough to handle, peel off the skins with your fingertips. Cut lengthwise along one side of each pepper and open out flat. Remove and discard the stems, seeds and ribs.

✁ Cut the eggplants lengthwise into slices 6 mm (¼ in) thick. Sprinkle the slices with salt and place in a single layer on wire racks. Let stand for at least 30 minutes, or for up to 1 hour, to draw off the bitter juices. Wipe the slices dry with paper towels.

✁ In a frying pan over medium-high heat, warm the remaining olive oil. When the oil is hot, deep-fry the eggplant slices, a few at a time, until golden and tender, 5–8 minutes. Using a slotted spoon, remove to crumpled paper towels to drain.

✁ Lay a sheet of plastic wrap on a work surface. The sheet should be larger than the capsicums laid out side by side in a rectangle. Arrange the flattened capsicum pieces on the sheet of plastic wrap, forming a rectangle. Do not leave any gaps. Lay the fried eggplant slices on top of the capsicums, again leaving no gaps.

✁ Sprinkle the top with the chives and parsley and then season to taste with salt and pepper. Splash with about 2 tablespoons of the virgin olive oil.

✁ Using the plastic wrap as a guide, roll up the rectangle into a tight roll (roulade). Carefully bring this roll back towards you, still on the plastic wrap, and roll it again, this time wrapping it up in the plastic wrap. Now the shape can be adjusted by twisting the ends of the plastic wrap as if the roll were a bonbon. Wrap the roulade again in another generous layer of plastic wrap and tie the ends with kitchen twine. The cylinder should be about 5 cm (2 in) in diameter. Refrigerate for about 1 hour.

✁ Remove the roulade from the refrigerator and place on a serving plate. Using a very sharp knife, carefully cut the plastic wrap, remove and discard. Splash the roulade with the remaining virgin olive oil, grind pepper over the top and sprinkle with a pinch of sea salt. Cut into portions to reveal the twist of capsicum and eggplant. Serve at once.

SERVES 8

QUEENSLAND

SAUTÉED DUCK LIVERS ON POLENTA WITH TOMATO VINAIGRETTE

Polenta has become extremely popular in Australia. Italians who migrated here after World War II introduced it, and though it took years for Australians to take to it, now there's no stopping us. Australia produces cornmeal at Bundaberg in Queensland.

FOR THE POLENTA:

500 ml (16 fl oz/2 cups) chicken stock
175 g (6 oz/1⅛ cups) polenta (cornmeal)
1½ tablespoons unsalted butter
salt and freshly ground pepper

vinaigrette for healthy salad (recipe on page 164), plus 1 ripe tomato, peeled and finely diced
olive oil

FOR THE LIVERS:

2 tablespoons unsalted butter
2 tablespoons olive oil
1 clove garlic, finely chopped
500 g (1 lb) duck livers, trimmed and cut into bite-sized pieces
1½ tablespoons red wine vinegar
2 tablespoons chopped mixed fresh herbs

✁ To make the polenta, lightly oil a 20-cm (8-in) square cake pan. In a heavy pot over high heat, bring the stock to a boil. Whisking constantly, add the cornmeal in a thin, steady stream. Continue stirring until the cornmeal forms a thick dropping consistency, 4–5 minutes. Reduce the heat to low and cook, stirring often, until the polenta is no longer granular, about 30 minutes. Stir in the butter and salt and pepper to taste.

Immediately pour the polenta into the prepared pan and let stand until cold and firm.

✁ While the polenta cools, prepare the vinaigrette and stir the tomato into it. Set aside.

✁ Preheat a griddle pan until hot. Unmould the cooled polenta onto a work surface and cut into 4 equal squares. Brush the squares with oil and grill on both sides in the griddle pan, turning once, until marked with the griddle ridges. Keep warm.

✁ To cook the livers, in a frying pan over medium heat, melt the butter with the oil. Add the garlic and stir-fry until softened, about 2 minutes; do not allow to colour. Add the livers and sauté until lightly browned on the outsides, about 4 minutes. The insides should be pink and juicy; do not overcook. Remove to a plate and keep warm.

✁ Add the vinegar to the pan over medium-high heat and scrape up the caramelised juices on the pan bottom. Add the herbs and stir briefly until bright green. Remove from the heat. Arrange a polenta square on each of 4 warmed plates. Top with the livers and pour on the pan juices. Spoon the vinaigrette over the tops and serve at once.

SERVES 4

WESTERN AUSTRALIA

SQUID SALAD WITH ROASTED CAPSICUMS, BLACK OLIVES AND ANCHOVY DRESSING

Jim Mendolia's Western Australian Bella del Tindari anchovies are the best in the country. Here, they are used to make a delicious dressing to complement squid. The squid are seasoned with oregano, the only herb I believe has a better flavour dried than fresh. The best dried oregano comes not from Australia but from Greece, where it is picked in full flower. The flower heads give it a wonderful aromatic quality.

FOR THE DRESSING:

4–6 Bella del Tindari anchovy fillets, drained
1 tablespoon red wine vinegar
120 ml (4 fl oz/½ cup) virgin olive oil
freshly ground pepper
1 tablespoon finely chopped fresh parsley

1 kg (2 lb) small to medium squid
80 ml (3 fl oz/⅓ cup) olive oil
4 cloves garlic, finely chopped
1 teaspoon dried oregano
salt and freshly ground pepper
100 g (3½ oz) small black olives
2 red capsicums (bell peppers), roasted, peeled, seeded and cut into long strips 1 cm (⅜ in) wide (see glossary)

✁ To make the dressing, using a fork, mash the anchovies in a bowl. Add the vinegar and whisk until blended. Slowly add the oil, whisking constantly to make an emulsion. Season to taste with pepper and stir in the parsley. Set aside.

✁ To clean each squid, twist the head and then pull out the head, guts and quill. Remove the 'wings' and cut off the purply skin. Rinse the tubes well and cut crosswise into rings 1 cm (⅜ in) wide.

✁ In a heavy frying pan over medium-high heat, warm the olive oil. Add the garlic and squid and stir-fry until the squid is tender, 2–3 minutes. Stir in the oregano, salt and pepper to taste, olives and capsicum strips.

✁ Divide the squid salad evenly among 6 individual salad plates. Stir the dressing and drizzle it over the salads. Serve at once.

SERVES 6

Spiced Squid Salad

SPICED SQUID SALAD

The best squid to use for this spicy cold Thai salad, called nam pla muk, *is the calamari, or arrow squid, caught in Bass Strait (between Tasmania and Victoria) and in New South Wales. Many Thai restaurants in Australia's capital cities serve a version of this salad. For a particularly attractive presentation, cut the chillies for garnish into flower shapes.*

3 tablespoons fresh lime juice
2 tablespoons fish sauce (see glossary)
2 or 3 fresh birdseye chillies, thinly sliced
about 2 garlic cloves, thinly sliced crosswise to measure
    1 tablespoon
1 tablespoon thinly sliced, peeled fresh galangal (see glossary)
    or gingerroot
500 g (1 lb) fresh squid, each about 10 cm (4 in) long
salt
½ lemon

FOR THE GARNISH:

18 fresh coriander (cilantro) leaves
3 spring (green) onions, very thinly sliced
1–3 fresh red serrano or other red chillies, thinly sliced

In a glass or ceramic bowl, mix together the lime juice, fish sauce and chillies. Add the garlic and galangal or gingerroot, stir well and set aside.

To clean each squid, twist the head and then pull out the head, guts and quill. Remove the 'wings' and rub off the purply skin. Slit the tubes open lengthwise, then rinse them. Using a sharp knife, score the insides of the now-flattened tubes in a fine diamond pattern.

Bring a saucepan three-quarters full of water to a boil. Salt lightly and add the lemon. Add the squid and reduce the heat so the water simmers gently. Poach until the squid pieces curl and are opaque, then simmer for 1 minute longer. Lift out with a slotted spoon and drain briefly on paper towels. Add the warm squid to the lime juice mixture and toss to mix well. Cover and refrigerate for 30 minutes to cool completely.

Spoon into a serving dish. Garnish with the coriander, spring onions and chillies. Serve at room temperature.

SERVES 4–6

KANGAROO TAIL SOUP

The tail and the fillet are the prize of this native Australian mammal. Now that kangaroo meat is so readily available in New South Wales, Queensland and South Australia (where kangaroo has been on the table for more than a decade), it is worth seeking out the tail to make this very Australian soup. Ask your butcher for the larger, upper portion of the tail, which contains the most meat. Soups such as this taste best if allowed to sit for a couple of days before serving, so make the soup at least 2 days ahead of time to ensure the fullest flavour. There's a madeira-style wine made in northeastern Victoria that is excellent used in this recipe.

3 kg (6 lb) kangaroo tail, sawed into joints
2 tablespoons unsalted butter
2 tablespoons vegetable oil
1 veal shank, sawed into 3-cm (1¼-in) pieces
3 brown onions, quartered
3 carrots, peeled and quartered
2 celery stalks
1 fresh parsley sprig
2 or 3 fresh thyme sprigs
1 bay leaf

125 ml (4 fl oz/½ cup) madeira
125 ml (4 fl oz/½ cup) cognac
3 l (3 qt) water
salt and freshly ground pepper

FOR SERVING:

1 carrot, peeled and thinly sliced

❧ Rinse the kangaroo tail pieces well and pat dry with paper towels. In a large, heavy pot over medium heat, melt the butter with the oil. Add the kangaroo, veal shank, onions and quartered carrots and sauté, stirring frequently, until evenly brown, 7–8 minutes. Meanwhile, to make a bouquet garni, cut 1 celery stalk in half. Sandwich the parsley and thyme sprigs and bay leaf between the celery pieces and tie in place with kitchen twine.

❧ Add the madeira, cognac, bouquet garni and remaining celery stalk to the pot. Cover and simmer over low heat for 15 minutes, stirring occasionally. Add the water and salt and pepper to taste and bring slowly to a boil. Simmer, uncovered, over low heat until the meat is tender, about 4 hours. If too much liquid cooks away and the kangaroo joints are no longer immersed, add enough water to cover them.

❧ Strain the soup through a fine sieve into a clean pot. Set the kangaroo meat aside to cool and discard the remaining solids. Boil the strained soup, uncovered, until reduced to 1.5 l (48 fl oz/ 6 cups). Remove from the heat and cool the soup by resting the bottom of the pot in ice water. Cover and refrigerate the cooled soup until the fat rises to the surface.

❧ While the soup is chilling, remove the meat from the bones and discard the bones. Set aside.

❧ Remove and discard the congealed fat from the top of the soup. Stir in the kangaroo meat. Cover and refrigerate for at least 2 days or for up to 5 days to gather flavour.

❧ To serve, reheat the soup in a saucepan. At the same time, bring a small saucepan three-quarters full of water to a boil and add the carrot slices. Boil just until tender, a few minutes, and then drain and add to the soup. Taste and adjust the seasonings. Ladle the soup into warmed bowls and serve piping hot.

SERVES 6–8   *Photograph pages 56–57*

SYDNEY

SEAFOOD LAKSA

Kit Chan a talented young chef, shares her recipe for laksa, *a seafood noodle soup from Malaysia. Thai mint, also called* laksa herb, *or* ra ran, *is becoming more readily available and could be used instead of English mint. Shrimp paste has several names, depending on which Asian country it is made in, but* blachan *from Malaysia is one of the most common. Look for it and other exotic ingredients in Asian markets.*

FOR THE SOUP BASE:

2 fresh red chillies, seeded
40 g (1½ oz) dried shrimp paste (see glossary)
1 brown onion, roughly chopped
2 fresh gingerroot slices
1 lemongrass stalk, roughly chopped (see glossary)
1 teaspoon coriander seeds
1½ tablespoons macadamia nuts
60 ml (2 fl oz/¼ cup) safflower oil
1 teaspoon paprika
1 teaspoon ground turmeric
1 bunch fresh coriander (cilantro), coarsely chopped
500 ml (16 fl oz/2 cups) fish stock (see glossary)
500 ml (16 fl oz/2 cups) coconut milk (see glossary)

FOR THE *LAKSA*:

300 g (9½ oz) rice vermicelli, soaked in hot water to cover for 10 minutes and drained (see glossary)
100 g (3½ oz) bean sprouts
4 cubes deep-fried bean curd (tofu) or regular firm bean curd

8 large prawns (shrimp)
12 scallops
4 pieces salmon fillet, each about 50 g (2 oz)
4 pieces white fish fillet, each about 50 g (2 oz)
4 small red mullet fillets or other firm white-fleshed fish fillets
salt and freshly ground pepper
1 tablespoon vegetable oil
1 bunch spinach, carefully washed, blanched in boiling water until wilted and drained
45–60 g (1½–2 oz/about ¼ cup) cucumber strips
1 tablespoon fresh mint leaves, cut into fine shreds
1 tablespoon dried onion, deep-fried or sautéed in safflower oil until golden
4 lime halves
chilli sambal (see glossary)

❧ To make the soup base, in a blender, combine the chillies, shrimp paste, onion, gingerroot, lemongrass, coriander seeds and macadamia nuts. Blend to a fine paste.

❧ In a heavy saucepan over medium heat, warm the oil. Add the paste and fry until fragrant, about 5 minutes. Add the paprika, turmeric and fresh coriander and fry for a few more minutes. Add the stock and bring to a boil. Reduce the heat to medium and simmer for 20–30 minutes, to reduce the stock by one-third. Add the coconut milk and bring back to a boil. Then pass the mixture through a sieve into a large pot and taste for seasoning.

❧ To make the *laksa,* bring the soup base to a boil. Add the rice vermicelli, bean sprouts and bean curd. Return to a boil and remove from the heat; keep warm. Do not cook the rice vermicelli too long or it will be mushy.

❧ Season all the shellfish and fish with salt and pepper. In a frying pan over high heat, warm the oil. Add the shellfish and fish and fry, turning once, until cooked through; the timing will depend on the thickness of the pieces.

❧ To assemble the soup, divide the vermicelli among 4 deep bowls. Fill each bowl three-quarters full with the soup. Place some spinach on one side of the bowl and then arrange the fish and shellfish on top of the noodles. Top with the cucumber, mint and fried onion. Serve immediately with the lime halves and sambal.

SERVES 4

Seafood Laksa—photographed at Pittwater, Sydney

VICTORIA

RUSTIC CHEESE PIE

Belinda Jeffery is a food editor and a great cook. We have shared many happy hours cooking together. This pie of hers will have you making two at a time because there will never be enough to go around! Milawa blue cheese is the nearest Australian cheese to gorgonzola. It is made by David and Anne Brown at Milawa in northeastern Victoria.

FOR THE PASTRY:

235 grams (7½ oz/1½ cups) plain (all-purpose) flour
¼ teaspoon freshly grated nutmeg
¼ teaspoon salt
125 g (4 oz/½ cup) unsalted butter, chilled, cut into small cubes
60 ml (2 fl oz/¼ cup) ice water

FOR THE FILLING:

125 g (¼ lb) *pancetta,* chopped (see glossary)
1 large red capsicum (bell pepper), roasted, peeled, seeded and finely diced (see glossary)
1 tablespoon olive oil
1 large brown onion, thinly sliced
1 clove garlic, finely chopped
300 g (10 oz/1¼ cups) ricotta cheese
80 g (3 oz) firm mozzarella cheese, grated
60 g (2 oz/½ cup) freshly grated parmesan cheese
40 g (1½ oz) fontina cheese, finely chopped
80 g (3 oz) Milawa blue cheese or other creamy blue cheese, crumbled
75 ml (2½ fl oz/¼ cup plus 1½ tablespoons) thickened (double/heavy) cream
3 eggs, lightly beaten
4 fresh parsley sprigs, chopped
salt and freshly ground pepper
freshly grated nutmeg
5 small fresh thyme sprigs, optional

1 egg yolk beaten with 2 teaspoons water

To make the pastry in a food processor fitted with the metal blade, combine the flour, nutmeg and salt. Process to mix. Add the butter and process until the mixture resembles fine breadcrumbs, about 15 seconds. Pour in the water and process only until the mixture forms a ball around the blade.
To make the pastry by hand, in a bowl, combine the flour, nutmeg, salt and butter. Using a pastry blender, 2 knives or your fingertips, cut in the butter until the mixture is the consistency of fine breadcrumbs. Add the water and, using a fork, work the ingredients together until the mixture comes together in a rough ball.
Remove the dough from the processor or bowl and, on a floured work surface, flatten into a disc 3 cm (1¼ in) thick. Wrap in plastic wrap and refrigerate for 30 minutes. (The pastry can be made the day before and brought almost to room temperature before rolling.)
Preheat an oven to 220°C (425°F) and place a rack in the centre of the oven. Butter a shallow 23-cm (9-in) pie pan.
To make the filling, in a frying pan over medium heat, sauté the *pancetta* for 2 minutes. Transfer to a bowl, add the capsicum and mix well. In the same frying pan over medium heat, warm the olive oil. Add the onion and garlic and sauté just until soft. Add to the capsicum mixture and mix well.
Place the ricotta in a large bowl and mash with a fork to break it up. Add all the remaining cheeses and mix well. Then add the cream, eggs and parsley and stir to mix thoroughly. Season lightly with salt, pepper and nutmeg. Stir in three-quarters of the capsicum mixture; reserve the remainder for the topping.
On a lightly floured work surface, roll out the dough into a round 34 cm (13½ in) in diameter. Carefully transfer the pastry round to the prepared pan and gently ease into place. Do not trim the overhang. Spoon the filling into the pan and level. Fold the overhanging pastry over the filling (it will not cover the top

entirely). Press down gently on the pastry. Sprinkle the remaining capsicum mixture evenly over the uncovered portion of the filling and then scatter on the thyme sprigs, if using. Brush the pastry with the egg mixture.
Place the pan on a baking tray (sheet). Bake for 15 minutes in the centre of the oven. Reduce the temperature to 180°C (350°F) and bake until the centre is wobbly but set, 45–50 minutes longer. Check that the pie is done by inserting a thin knife blade; it should come out clean, free of filling. Transfer to a wire rack to cool for at least 10 minutes.
Serve warm, at room temperature or cold.

SERVES 4–6   *Photograph pages 56–57*

SYDNEY

LOBSTER AND MANGO SALAD WITH BASIL VINAIGRETTE

Chef Jean Luc Lundy was a restaurateur in the Sydney area for some years before moving to France. This is his signature dish. I see it in other guises now and again, but I believe its original simplicity cannot be improved upon. The major components must all be in season for this dish to be the way Jean Luc meant it to be. The best mangoes in the world are arguably from Bowen in Queensland. They should be married with South Australian or Tasmanian lobsters and peak-of-summer basil.

FOR THE COURT BOUILLON:

250 ml (8 fl oz/1 cup) water
250 ml (8 fl oz/1 cup) dry white wine
1 bay leaf
2 fresh parsley sprigs
4 peppercorns
1 small brown onion, quartered
1 small carrot, peeled and sliced
1 small celery stalk, chopped
¼ teaspoon salt

500 g (1 lb) green (raw) lobster tails

FOR THE SAUCE:

2 tablespoons white wine vinegar
120 ml (4 fl oz/½ cup) olive oil
1 small clove garlic
40 fresh basil leaves
salt and freshly ground pepper

2 large ripe mangoes, peeled and thinly sliced

In a large pot, combine all the court bouillon ingredients and bring to a boil. Add the lobster tails and simmer until the shells turn red, 6–8 minutes. Remove the tails from the pot and let cool.
Remove the meat from the lobster tails and cut into slices 1 cm (⅜ in) thick.
To make the sauce, in a blender or in a food processor fitted with the metal blade, combine the vinegar, oil, garlic and basil leaves. Process until smooth. Season to taste with salt and pepper.
To assemble the salads, set out 4 large flat plates. Arrange one-quarter of the mango slices on each plate in a circle, leaving a space in the centre. Heap medallions of lobster in the centre and spoon the sauce in a ribbon around the outside of the mango slices.

SERVES 4

Lobster and Mango Salad with Basil Vinaigrette— photographed at Cremorne Point, Sydney Harbour

Left to right: Celeriac Soup with Parsley Purée, Lentil and Sausage Soup

NEW SOUTH WALES

CELERIAC SOUP WITH PARSLEY PURÉE

Celeriac has a fairly short season beginning in autumn and lasting into winter. This recipe is from Robin Howard, the chef and owner of a restaurant in Goulburn.

FOR THE SOUP:

2 tablespoons unsalted butter
4 celeriac (celery roots), about 800 g (26 oz) total weight, peeled and diced
1 cooking apple, peeled, cored and diced
1.5 l (48 fl oz/6 cups) full-flavoured chicken stock
salt and freshly ground pepper

FOR THE PARSLEY PURÉE:

1 bunch Italian (flat-leaf) parsley, stems removed
100 g (3½ oz/⅔ cups) pine nuts, lightly toasted
salt and freshly ground pepper
250 ml (8 fl oz/1 cup) light olive oil

To make the soup, in a heavy pot over medium-low heat, melt the butter. Add the celeriac and cook, stirring occasionally, until golden, about 20 minutes. Add the apple and cook, stirring, until the apple is tender, another 10 minutes. Stir in the stock. Pass the soup through a fine-mesh sieve or a food mill fitted with the coarse blade. Return the soup to the pot, season to taste with salt and pepper, and reheat.

To make the parsley purée, in a food processor fitted with the metal blade, place the parsley, pine nuts and salt and pepper to taste. Process until smooth. With the processor running slowly, gradually pour in the olive oil; the mixture should be thick.

To serve, spoon 1 tablespoon of the parsley purée into each warmed soup bowl. Ladle the soup into the bowls and serve immediately.

SERVES 8–10

VICTORIA

LENTIL AND SAUSAGE SOUP

This soup recalls middle Europe and is ideal during our cooler months. It can be made up to 2 days ahead of serving, cooked, covered and refrigerated. The flavour improves upon reheating.

90 ml (3 fl oz/6 tablespoons) olive oil
375 g (¾ lb) mild pepperoni, cut into 1-cm (⅜-in) dice
½ teaspoon ground coriander
1 large brown onion, finely chopped
1 large carrot, peeled and finely chopped
2 celery stalks, finely sliced
3 fresh Italian (flat-leaf) parsley sprigs, roughly chopped
50 ml (2 fl oz/¼ cup) dry white wine
1¼ l (40 fl oz/5 cups) veal or beef stock
300 g (9½ oz/1⅓ cups) brown lentils, picked over and rinsed
salt and freshly ground pepper

In a large, heavy pot over medium heat, warm 1 tablespoon of the oil. Add the pepperoni and sauté until the fat is fully rendered. Drain off and discard the fat; set the pepperoni aside.

In the same pot over medium heat, warm the remaining oil. Add the coriander and stir until fragrant, about 2 minutes. Add the onion and sauté until softened, about 5 minutes. Add the carrot, celery and parsley and sauté until soft and just beginning to colour, about 10 minutes.

Add the wine and cook over medium heat until reduced by half. Add the stock and lentils and cook gently, uncovered, until the lentils are tender, 30–35 minutes.

Return the pepperoni to the pot and heat through. Season to taste with salt and pepper, if necessary. (The sausage can be both salty and peppery, so the soup may not need additional seasoning.) Serve in warmed individual bowls.

SERVES 6

N E W   S O U T H   W A L E S

FARMHOUSE BARLEY-VEGETABLE SOUP WITH HERB DAMPER

My paternal grandmother, Matilda Julia Swaffer Garrett, whose ancestors came to Australia with explorer Charles Sturt, used to make vegetable soups like this for Sunday night supper. Although she didn't make herb damper to go with it, the damper complements the soup beautifully.

FOR THE DAMPER:

530 g (17 oz/3⅓ cups) self-raising flour
pinch of salt
1 large ripe avocado, halved, pitted and peeled
⅓ bunch fresh parsley, finely chopped
⅓ bunch fresh chives, finely chopped
⅓ bunch fresh dill, finely chopped
285–300 ml (9–9½ fl oz/1⅛–1¼ cups) freshly opened beer
    (use smaller amount in warm weather)
1 tablespoon milk
2 tablespoons finely grated cheddar cheese

FOR THE SOUP:

2 carrots, peeled and finely chopped
1 turnip, peeled and finely chopped
1 parsnip, peeled and finely chopped
2 celery stalks, finely chopped
1 potato, peeled and finely chopped
1 l (32 fl oz/4 cups) chicken or beef stock
3 fresh parsley sprigs, chopped
80 g (2½ oz/⅓ cup) pearl barley
salt and freshly ground pepper

To make the damper, position a rack in the upper part of an oven and preheat the oven to 200°C (400°F). Butter a baking tray (sheet).

In a large bowl, sift together the flour and salt. Mash the avocado in a separate bowl. Add the avocado to the flour and rub in with your fingertips until the mixture resembles rolled oats.

Make a well in the centre of the flour mixture. Add the chopped herbs and beer to the well. Using a fork, gradually stir the dry ingredients into the wet ingredients until a soft dough forms. Turn out onto a floured board and knead until smooth and shiny, 5–6 minutes.

Shape the dough into a tall round and place on the prepared baking tray. Paint all over with the milk. Using a floured knife, score the top. Scatter with the cheese.

Bake in the hottest part of the oven until golden all over and the bottom sounds hollow when tapped, about 1 hour.

While the damper is baking, make the soup. Place the carrots, turnip, parsnip, celery, potato and stock in a large pot. Bring slowly to a boil. Reduce the heat to medium-low and simmer, uncovered, for 30 minutes.

Add the parsley and barley and simmer until the barley is tender, about 20 minutes.

Season to taste with salt and pepper and serve with the hot damper.

SERVES 6   *Photograph pages 56–57*

V I C T O R I A

KUMARA SOUP WITH GREEN PEA AND LETTUCE SOUP

Here are two soups in one bowl. The trick to making this dish successfully is to have both soups exactly the same consistency, so that when they are poured into the soup bowls simultaneously they meet perfectly in the centre. The apricot colour of the flesh of the kumara contrasts beautifully with the green of the peas. Cos is the ideal lettuce to use with the peas. Do not use iceberg lettuce as it gives off too much water. The soups will taste best if they are made one day in advance and reheated.

FOR THE KUMARA SOUP:

2 tablespoons vegetable oil
1 small brown onion, chopped
1 l (32 fl oz/4 cups) chicken stock
1 kg (2 lb) kumaras, peeled and coarsely chopped
    (see glossary)
1 potato, peeled and sliced
salt and freshly ground pepper
freshly grated nutmeg

FOR THE GREEN PEA AND LETTUCE SOUP:

2 tablespoons butter
1 small brown onion, chopped
800 ml (26 fl oz/3¼ cups) chicken stock
1 potato, peeled and sliced
250 g (½ lb) cos (romaine) lettuce, shredded
500 g (1 lb) frozen peas
salt and freshly ground pepper

To make the kumara soup, in a large pot over medium heat, warm the vegetable oil. Add the onion and cook, stirring, until it begins to caramelise, about 12 minutes. Add the stock, kumaras, regular potato and salt, pepper and nutmeg to taste. Bring slowly to a boil. Reduce the heat to low and simmer, uncovered, until the potatoes are tender, about 30 minutes. Let cool a little. Working in batches, transfer the potatoes to a food processor fitted with the metal blade or to a blender and purée until smooth. Return to the pan.

Meanwhile, to make the pea soup, in a large saucepan over medium heat, melt the butter. Add the onion and cook, stirring, until it begins to caramelise, about 12 minutes. Add the stock and potato and bring to a boil. Add the lettuce, peas and salt and pepper to taste. Reduce the heat to low and simmer, uncovered, until the potato is tender, about 25 minutes. Let cool a little. Working in batches, transfer to a food processor fitted with the metal blade or to a blender and purée until smooth. Return to the pan.

To serve, reheat both soups to serving temperature and pour each into a jug with a spout. Holding 1 jug in each hand and positioning them on opposite sides of each warmed soup plate, pour the soups into the plates at the same time so they meet in the centre. Serve at once.

SERVES 8–10   *Photograph pages 56–57*

FRESH TOMATO SOUP WITH AVOCADO AND SHALLOTS

I adore this soup. It's so easy and colourful and the balance of the acid in the soup with the buttery texture of the avocado is wonderful. It should only be made during the autumn when tomatoes have had the benefit of the long ripening hours of the summer sun and avocados have just come into season.

2 tablespoons olive oil
4 shallots, finely chopped
1 small clove garlic, finely chopped
1 teaspoon sugar, or to taste
½ teaspoon finely chopped fresh red chilli
850 g (1¾ lb) ripe tomatoes, roughly chopped
375 ml (12 fl oz/1½ cups) water
salt and freshly ground pepper
1 firm but ripe avocado

In a saucepan over medium heat, warm the olive oil. Add half of the shallots and all of the garlic and sauté until softened, about 10 minutes. Do not allow to colour. Add the sugar and chilli and sauté for 1 minute. Add the tomatoes and water, cover and cook gently over medium heat for 20 minutes. The vegetables should be soft. Remove from the heat and let cool.

Pass the soup through a food mill or sieve placed over a bowl. Season to taste with salt and pepper. If the weather is very hot, cover and chill the soup well.

To serve, halve and pit the avocado. Peel and cut into slices 1 cm (⅜ in) thick. Arrange one-quarter of the avocado in the bottom of each of 4 shallow soup plates. Ladle the soup around the avocado. Scatter the remaining shallots over the top and serve.

SERVES 4

TOP PADDOCK BLUE CHEESE TART

Fred Leppin makes this cheese at Bena, in Victoria's Gippsland. This is chef and restaurateur Barry Mieklejohn's recipe, which he makes for his restaurant in Newcastle, two hours' drive north of Sydney.

FOR THE PASTRY:

250 g (8 oz/1⅔ cups) plain (all-purpose) flour
2 teaspoons plus a pinch of salt
125 g (4 oz/½ cup) butter, chilled, cut into small cubes
125 ml (4 fl oz/½ cup) ice water
1 egg yolk plus 1 whole egg

FOR THE FILLING:

300 g (9½ oz) Jumbanna Top Paddock blue cheese or any creamy blue cheese
9 egg yolks
salt and freshly ground pepper
freshly grated nutmeg
600 ml (18 fl oz/2¼ cups) thickened (double/heavy) cream

To make the pastry in a food processor fitted with the metal blade, combine the flour, 2 teaspoons salt and butter. Process until the mixture resembles coarse rolled oats, about 40 seconds. Add the ice water and egg yolk and process only until the dough forms a ball around the blade.

To make the pastry by hand, in a bowl, combine the flour, 2 teaspoons salt and butter. Using a pastry blender, 2 knives or your fingertips, cut in the butter until the mixture is the consistency of coarse rolled oats. Add the ice water and egg yolk and, using a fork, work the ingredients together until the mixture comes together in a rough ball.

Remove the dough from the food processor or bowl and, on a floured work surface, flatten into a disc 3 cm (1¼ in) thick. Wrap in plastic wrap and refrigerate for 30 minutes.

On a lightly floured work surface, roll out the dough into a round large enough to fit a deep 26-cm (10½-in) tart tin with a removable base. Carefully transfer the pastry round to the tart tin and gently ease into place. Trim off the overhang. Cover with plastic wrap and refrigerate for 30 minutes.

Position a rack in the centre of an oven and preheat the oven to 170°C (325°F). Line the pastry-lined tin with aluminium foil and then fill with pie weights. Bake in the centre of the oven for 20 minutes. Remove the weights and foil and return to the oven. Bake until the pastry is pale gold and dry, about 5 minutes.

In a bowl stir together the whole egg and the pinch of salt. Brush the egg over the inside bottom and sides of the pastry. Return to the oven and bake until a deep gold, about 5 minutes. Remove from the oven and reduce the oven temperature to 150°C (300°F).

To make the filling, in a food processor fitted with the metal blade, combine the cheese, egg yolks and salt, pepper and nutmeg to taste. Process until thoroughly mixed. Add the cream and blend for only a moment. Alternatively, mix the ingredients together in a bowl with a wooden spoon.

Pour the cheese mixture into the baked pastry. Bake in the centre of the oven until set, about 1¼ hours. Watch the top of the tart for signs of burning and cover with aluminium foil if it begins to brown too much. Let cool completely on a wire rack. Remove the pan sides and slide onto a serving plate.

Serve at room temperature.

SERVES 8–10

RISOTTO PATTIES WITH BROAD BEANS AND SPRING ONIONS

I imagine that risotto patties were originally made to use up leftover risotto. Now that they have been discovered, risotto is cooked especially to make these delicious morsels. This is well-known food editor Joan Campbell's version of risotto patties. Use a good homemade chicken stock if you can.

FOR THE RISOTTO:

750 ml (24 fl oz/3 cups) chicken stock
2 tablespoons unsalted butter
1½ tablespoons olive oil
½ brown onion, finely chopped
1 clove garlic, crushed
200 g (6½ oz/1 cup) arborio rice (see glossary)
60 ml (2 fl oz/¼ cup) dry white wine
15 g (½ oz/½ cup) dried porcini mushrooms, soaked in 60 ml (2 fl oz/¼ cup) water
salt and freshly ground pepper
75 g (2½ oz) parmesan cheese, freshly grated

FOR THE PATTIES:

30 g (1 oz/½ cup) fresh white breadcrumbs
2 eggs, beaten
salt and freshly ground pepper
olive oil

400 g (13 oz) shelled young, tender broad (fava) beans, cooked in boiling water 5–10 minutes, drained and cooled
4 cloves garlic, thinly sliced and fried until crisp in olive oil
1 bunch spring (green) onions, cut into 8-cm (3¼-in) lengths and fried until crisp in olive oil
salt and freshly ground pepper

To make the risotto, pour the stock into a saucepan and bring to a boil. Reduce the heat so the stock barely simmers. In

Clockwise from top: Fresh Tomato Soup with Avocado and Shallots, Top Paddock Blue Cheese Tart, Risotto Patties with Broad Beans and Shallots

a large, heavy saucepan over low heat, melt the butter with the oil. Add the onion and sauté until soft, about 5 minutes. Add the garlic and cook for a few minutes longer. Add the rice and stir until well coated with the butter and oil. Sauté for a few minutes until the rice is opaque.

❧ Add the wine and cook, stirring occasionally, until it is absorbed. Drain the mushrooms, chop them and then stir into the rice. Add 1 or 2 ladlefuls of the simmering stock and continue to cook, stirring, until the stock is absorbed.

❧ Add 1 or 2 more ladlefuls of stock and again cook, stirring, until the stock is absorbed. Continue to cook in this manner until all the stock is used and the rice is creamy but the grains are still slightly firm in the centre. Season to taste with salt and pepper and stir in the cheese. Set aside to cool completely.

❧ To make the patties, in a bowl, combine the breadcrumbs, eggs, cold risotto and salt and pepper to taste. Mix well. Form the mixture into 6 patties about 2.5 cm (1 in) thick and 12 cm (4½ in) in diameter. To cook the patties, in a frying pan over medium heat, warm the olive oil. Add the patties and fry, turning once, until crisp, brown and heated through, about 2–3 minutes on each side. Using an eggslice (metal spatula), transfer to paper towels to drain briefly.

❧ To serve, in a bowl, quickly toss together the broad beans, garlic, onions and salt and pepper to taste. Place the patties on 6 warmed individual plates and spoon some of the bean mixture over each patty. Serve at once.

SERVES 6

SYDNEY

HOT AND SOUR PRAWN SOUP

Here is a Thai classic, tom yum goong, *which is available in every Thai restaurant. The quality of the fresh produce will determine the success of the soup.*

400 g (13 oz) medium-sized green (raw) prawns (shrimp)
3 tablespoons vegetable oil
1.5 l (48 fl oz/6 cups) water
2 cloves garlic, finely chopped
1 fresh coriander (cilantro) root, finely chopped (see glossary)
4 peppercorns, crushed
3 lemongrass stalks, cut into 3-cm (1¼-in) lengths
    (see glossary)
1 piece galangal, 1.5 cm (⅔ in) long, peeled and sliced
    (see glossary)
4 spring (green) onions, tender green tops only, sliced
4 fresh kaffir lime leaves, finely shredded (see glossary)
1½ tablespoons fish sauce (see glossary)
1½ tablespoons fresh lime juice
2 fresh red chillies, thinly sliced
2 tablespoons finely shredded fresh coriander (cilantro) leaves

❧Remove the heads and shells from the prawns and reserve. Devein the prawns and set aside. In a large, heavy pot over high heat, warm the oil. Add the prawn heads and shells and stir-fry until well coloured. Add the water and bring to a boil. Reduce the heat to medium, cover and simmer for 15 minutes.
❧Meanwhile, in a mortar with a pestle, pound together the garlic, coriander root and peppercorns to form a smooth paste. Strain the simmering liquid into a clean pot and discard the heads and shells. Add the garlic paste, lemongrass, galangal, spring onions, lime leaves and prawns. Bring to a simmer and simmer gently until cooked, 2–3 minutes; the timing will depend on the size of the prawns. Add the fish sauce, lime juice and chillies and stir for a few seconds. Add the coriander leaves and immediately ladle into warmed individual bowls. Serve at once.

SERVES 4–6

MELBOURNE

DUCK AND GRAPE SOUP

This is a simplified version of a duck soup, gaeng phed ped yang, *that I first tasted in southern Thailand. You will need access to a Chinese duck shop or friendly Chinese restaurant to take advantage of using a ready-cooked duck.*

420 ml (14 fl oz/1¾ cups) coconut cream (see glossary)
2–3 tablespoons red curry paste (see glossary)
½ roast duck (about 600 g/1¼ lb), skinned, boned and flesh
    cut into chunky pieces
250 ml (8 fl oz/1 cup) coconut milk (see glossary)
100 g (3½ oz) cherry tomatoes, halved
100 g (3½ oz) seedless black or green grapes
100 g (3½ oz) finely diced pineapple
1 tablespoon fish sauce (see glossary)
8 kaffir lime leaves, torn (see glossary)
8 fresh basil leaves
sugar

❧In a wok or saucepan, bring the coconut cream to a boil. Stir in the curry paste, reduce the heat to low and simmer gently until aromatic, about 5 minutes. Add the duck and simmer for 1 minute. Add the coconut milk, tomatoes, grapes and pineapple and simmer for 2 minutes. Add the fish sauce, lime and basil leaves and sugar to taste and simmer for 3 minutes.
❧Ladle into warmed individual bowls and serve piping hot.

SERVES 4

MELBOURNE

CHICKEN SAN CHOY BOW

Often called Chinese hamburgers, these lettuce-wrapped parcels of minced chicken are on most Chinese restaurant menus. They should be eaten grasped in the fingers. Traditionally iceberg lettuce is used, but you can substitute butter lettuce, which is softer, if you wish.

8–12 perfect iceberg lettuce leaves
1 teaspoon cornflour (cornstarch)
1 tablespoon dry sherry or water
2–3 tablespoons vegetable oil
½ brown onion, finely chopped

Clockwise from top: Duck and Grape Soup, Chicken San Choy Bow, Hot and Sour Prawn Soup

½ teaspoon grated, peeled gingerroot
½ celery stalk, finely chopped
100 g (3½ oz) fresh white button mushrooms, finely diced
250 g (½ lb) minced (ground) chicken
1 tablespoon light soy sauce
100 g (3½ oz) bamboo shoots, finely chopped

Stack a few of the lettuce leaves on top of one another, invert a saucer on top of them and cut around the saucer with a sharp knife to make perfectly round leaves. Repeat with the remaining lettuce leaves. Refrigerate to keep crisp until needed.

In a small bowl, stir the cornflour into the sherry or water until dissolved; set aside. In a wok or a frying pan over medium-high heat, warm 2 tablespoons of the oil. Add the onion and stir-fry until softened, about 2 minutes. Add the gingerroot and cook until fragrant, about 45 seconds. Add the celery and mushrooms and stir-fry until the mushrooms release their juices. Add the chicken and stir-fry until cooked through, 2–3 minutes; the meat should be opaque. If the chicken begins to stick before it is cooked, add the remaining 1 tablespoon oil.

Reduce the heat to low, stir the cornflour mixture and add it to the pan. Cook, stirring, until the mixture thickens slightly, about 10 seconds. Add the soy sauce and bamboo shoots and stir-fry until heated through.

Transfer to a warmed serving dish. Serve at once with the lettuce leaves stacked on a plate alongside.

SERVES 4

Clockwise from top right: Goat Cheese Terrine,
Cappuccino of Cauliflower and Parsley, Barbecued Chicken Wings

MELBOURNE

CAPPUCCINO OF CAULIFLOWER AND PARSLEY

The charm of this easy and inexpensive soup from Fabrice Boone is its lightness. The trick is to blend and aerate it as close to service as possible. As with all soups, it will have a more pronounced flavour if made 1 or 2 days ahead. Reheat the soup and spoon on the parsley purée at the very last moment.

3 tablespoons olive oil
50 g (1⅔ oz/⅓ cup) finely chopped celery
50 g (1⅔ oz/⅓ cup) finely chopped onion
50 g (1⅔ oz/⅓ cup) finely chopped leeks
800 ml (26 fl oz/3¼ cups) chicken stock
300 g (9½ oz/2½ cups) finely chopped cauliflower
200 ml (6½ fl oz/¾ cup plus 2 tablespoons) thickened (double/heavy) cream
1 bunch curly-leaf parsley, coarsely chopped

In a heavy pot over medium heat, warm the oil. Add the celery, onion and leeks and sauté until softened, about 5 minutes. Add the chicken stock and cauliflower and bring to a boil. Reduce the heat to medium and simmer until the cauliflower is tender, 5–10 minutes.

Working in batches, transfer to a blender and purée until smooth. Return the soup to a clean pot and add half of the cream. Reheat to serving temperature; keep warm.

Rinse out the blender container and add the parsley to it. Blend to chop finely. Add the remaining cream and blend until well mixed and frothy. If the mixture needs more liquid, add a tablespoonful of the cauliflower soup and blend until smooth. Transfer the purée to a small pan and bring to a boil. Remove from the heat.

Ladle the cauliflower soup into warmed individual bowls. Spoon the parsley mixture onto the hot soup. Serve at once.

SERVES 4

AUSTRALIA

BARBECUED CHICKEN WINGS

Every Australian cook prepares a version of these chicken wings. However bad for you they may be (much of the fat of the chicken is in the wings), they are irresistible when sizzling on a backyard barbecue. Buy plump wings for the best results. You will need to allow 4 hours for marinating the wings.

FOR THE BARBECUE SAUCE:

2 tablespoons peanut or safflower oil
1 small brown onion, finely chopped
½ teaspoon dry hot mustard, or to taste
1 tablespoon Worcestershire sauce
2 tablespoons red wine vinegar
1 tablespoon brown sugar
300 ml (10 fl oz/1¼ cups) commercial tomato sauce (ketchup)
pinch of chilli flakes, optional
1 lemon, sliced
salt and freshly ground pepper

16 chicken wings (about 1 kg/2 lb)

To make the sauce, in a heavy pot over medium heat, warm the oil. Add the onion and sauté gently until it caramelises, 12–15 minutes.

Add all the remaining ingredients, including salt and pepper to taste, and bring to a simmer, stirring frequently. Simmer, uncovered, for 20 minutes to blend the flavours, but do not allow to boil. Remove from the heat and let cool.

Place the chicken wings in a nonreactive dish and pour the cooled barbecue sauce over the top. Turn the chicken wings to coat well, then cover and refrigerate 3–4 hours.

Prepare a fire in a barbecue. Using tongs, arrange the chicken wings on the barbecue rack and cook, turning to brown all sides, until crisp and golden, 12–15 minutes.

Arrange on a serving platter and serve at once.

SERVES 4

SYDNEY

GOAT CHEESE TERRINE

We are fortunate in Australia to have a number of brilliant cheese makers who do us proud with their world-class products. David and Anne Brown are cheese makers at Milawa in northeastern Victoria, where they make cheeses not only from cow's milk but also from goat's and sheep's milks. This is chef Paul Merrony's recipe, which is on the menu at his restaurant in Sydney. You will need to begin making this recipe 1 day before serving.

FOR THE TERRINE:

500 g (1 lb) Milawa fresh goat cheese or other fresh goat cheese, room temperature
150 g (5 oz/⅔ cup) plain yoghurt
150 g (5 oz/⅔ cup) sour cream
1 tablespoon olive oil
freshly grated nutmeg
salt and freshly ground pepper

FOR THE DRESSING:

1 red capsicum (bell pepper), roasted, peeled, seeded and cut up (see glossary)
2 ripe tomatoes, peeled, seeded and cut up
about 180 ml (6 fl oz/¾ cup) vinaigrette for healthy salad (recipe on page 164)
2 tablespoons snipped fresh chives
salt and freshly ground pepper

To make the terrine, line a terrine 24 cm (9½ in) long with plastic wrap. Pass the goat cheese through a sieve or a food mill into a large bowl. Add the yoghurt, sour cream, olive oil and nutmeg, salt and pepper to taste and mix thoroughly. Spread the mixture in the terrine and tap the terrine on a firm surface to settle the ingredients. Cover with plastic wrap and refrigerate overnight.

To make the dressing, in a blender or in a food processor fitted with the metal blade, combine the capsicum and tomatoes. Purée until smooth. Add enough of the vinaigrette to make a good coating consistency. Add the chives and season to taste with salt and pepper. Mix well.

To serve the terrine, grasp the plastic wrap, gently lift and place on a serving dish. Accompany with the dressing.

SERVES 12

SOUTH AUSTRALIA

WARM SHERRIED LAMB KIDNEYS ON SALAD GREENS

Try to include some curly endive with the mesclun, as it contrasts beautifully with the richness of the kidneys. Use a fine dry sherry such as the Barossa Valley's Seppelts DP117 Show Fino. It's so dry and elegant that even the Spanish admire it.

125 g (¼ lb) mesclun, picked over (see glossary)
3 tablespoons olive oil
3 cloves garlic, finely chopped
600 g (1¼ lb) lamb kidneys, halved, trimmed and roughly chopped
80 ml (3 fl oz/⅓ cup) dry sherry
4–5 teaspoons redcurrant jelly
salt and freshly ground pepper

Pile the mesclun in the centres of 4 large dinner plates.

In a large, heavy frying pan over low heat, warm the oil. Add the garlic and sauté gently for 2 minutes; do not allow it to colour. Raise the heat to high, add the kidneys and sauté, constantly shaking the pan, until just sealed on all sides, 2–3 minutes. Using a slotted spoon, remove to a warmed serving dish; cover to keep warm.

Add the sherry to the pan over high heat and scrape up any browned bits on the pan bottom. Add the jelly, reduce the heat to medium-low and crush with the back of the spoon until it melts. Taste the juices and season to taste with salt and pepper. Spoon the kidneys around the mesclun and spoon the pan juices over the greens and kidneys. Serve at once.

SERVES 4   *Photograph page 74*

ROASTED CAPSICUM, GOAT CHEESE AND BASIL PIE

Karen Carnie makes this recipe for her customers at her seafood and gourmet outlet in North Adelaide, where it is very popular. She attributes its success to its summery colours and flavours. Karen uses South Australian Caprino goat cheese and says to serve the pie at room temperature.

FOR THE PASTRY:

385 g (12 oz/2¼ cups) plain (all-purpose) flour
155 g (5 oz/⅔ cup) butter
1 whole egg plus 1 egg yolk
4 tablespoons cold water, or as needed

FOR THE FILLING:

3 eggs
250 ml (8 fl oz/1 cup) thickened (double/heavy) cream
125 ml (4 fl oz/½ cup) milk
salt and freshly ground pepper
olive oil
1 large brown onion, chopped
2 cloves garlic, finely chopped
4 large red capsicums (bell peppers), roasted, peeled, seeded
    and cut into long, narrow strips (see glossary)
200 g (6½ oz) Caprino goat cheese, sliced
30 fresh basil leaves, torn

1 egg, lightly beaten

❧ To make the pastry in a food processor fitted with the metal blade, combine the flour and butter. Process until the mixture resembles fine breadcrumbs. Add the whole egg and egg yolk and then the water, 1 tablespoon at a time, and process only until the mixture forms a ball around the blade.

❧ To make the pastry by hand, in a bowl, combine the flour and butter. Using a pastry blender, 2 knives or your fingertips, cut in the butter until the mixture is the consistency of fine breadcrumbs. Add the whole egg and egg yolk and then add the water, 1 tablespoon at a time, and, using a fork, work the ingredients together until the mixture comes together in a rough ball. Knead the dough briefly until it is smooth, up to 1 minute.

❧ Remove the dough from the processor or bowl and divide into 2 portions, one somewhat larger than the other. On a floured work surface, form each portion into a disc about 3 cm (1¼ in) thick. Wrap the disks separately in plastic wrap and refrigerate for 30 minutes.

❧ Preheat an oven to 160°C (325°F) and place a rack in the centre of the oven. Butter a 23-cm (9-in) pie tin.

❧ To make the filling, in a bowl, whisk together the 3 eggs, cream, milk and salt and pepper to taste. In a frying pan over medium heat, warm the oil. Add the onion and garlic and sauté until soft and golden, about 10 minutes. Remove from the heat.

❧ On a lightly floured work surface, roll out the larger disk of dough into a round 3 mm (⅛ in) thick. Carefully transfer the round to the prepared pie tin and gently ease it into place. Arrange the capsicum strips, cheese slices, basil and sautéed onion and garlic in the pastry shell. Pour in the egg mixture. Roll out the remaining pastry disk in the same manner. Brush the edges of the bottom crust with the beaten egg. Carefully lay the pastry round over the filling and trim off the overhang. Press the edges together and flute if desired. Brush the top of the pie with the remaining beaten egg.

❧ Bake until cooked through and the pastry is golden and crisp, about 25 minutes. Serve at room temperature.

SERVES 8–10

Top to bottom: Roasted Capsicum, Goat Cheese and Basil Pie, Warm Sherried Lamb Kidneys on Salad Greens (recipe page 73)

LINGUINE WITH PANCETTA AND BROAD BEANS

South Australia's Joseph brand extra-virgin olive oil is produced at Primo Estate Winery, located at Virginia, north of Adelaide, where the Mediterranean climate is ideal for making premium olive oil. It is one of Australia's best and I am never without a bottle beside my stove for both cooking and dressing salads. Always ask to taste the pancetta *before you buy, as it is often overly salty. Blanch it in boiling water for a minute or so if it is.*

salt
300 g (10 oz) fresh linguine
200 g (6½ oz) *pancetta,* cut into julienne (see glossary)
200 g (6½ oz) shelled young, tender fresh or frozen broad
    (fava) beans
80 ml (3 fl oz/⅓ cup) Joseph olive oil
freshly ground pepper

❧ Bring a large pot of water to a boil. Salt the water lightly and add the linguine. Cook until al dente, about 5 minutes. Drain and refresh in cold water.

❧ In a heavy frying pan over medium heat, fry the *pancetta,* shaking the pan from time to time to prevent sticking, until well rendered, about 10 minutes. Add the beans and cook, stirring occasionally, until tender, 5–10 minutes; the timing will depend on their age.

❧ Drain the linguine and add to the pan. Toss with the *pancetta* and beans until heated through.

❧ Divide the linguine among 4 warmed pasta bowls. Drizzle with the oil and grind pepper over the top. Serve immediately.

SERVES 4

Left to right: Linguine with Pancetta and Broad Beans, Penne with Béchamel, Pepperoni and Spinach with Toasted Breadcrumbs—photographed at Bondi, Sydney

MELBOURNE

PENNE WITH BÉCHAMEL, PEPPERONI AND SPINACH WITH TOASTED BREADCRUMBS

As the pepperoni is the most prominent flavour in this dish, it is important that you buy a sausage that is peppery hot and at the same time has a good balance of salt and sweetness.

FOR THE BÉCHAMEL SAUCE:

80 g (2½ oz/5 tablespoons) unsalted butter
40 g (1¼ oz/3½ tablespoons) plain (all-purpose) flour
1 l (32 fl oz/4 cups) milk
salt and freshly ground white pepper
freshly grated nutmeg

160 g (5 oz) pepperoni, cut into julienne
1 bunch spinach, carefully washed, stems removed and
   leaves coarsely shredded
250 g (½ lb) penne
3 tablespoons unsalted butter
2 tablespoons olive oil
80 g (2½ oz/1⅓ cups) fresh breadcrumbs

To make the sauce, in a large pan over medium heat, melt the butter. Add the flour and whisk for 2 minutes. Slowly add the milk, whisking constantly, and cook, continuing to whisk, until the sauce thickens. Reduce the heat and cook gently, stirring occasionally, for 10 minutes. Season to taste with salt, pepper and nutmeg.

Position a rack in the centre of an oven and preheat the oven to 180°C (350°F). Butter a 2-l (2-qt) baking dish.

In a heavy frying pan over medium heat, sauté the pepperoni until well rendered, about 7 minutes. Using a slotted spoon, remove to paper towels to drain. Raise the heat to high, add the spinach and sauté in the pepperoni drippings until wilted, 4–5 minutes. Set aside.

Bring a large pot of water to a boil. Salt the water lightly and add the penne. Cook until al dente, 8–10 minutes. Drain and refresh in cold water. Drain again, shaking well, and transfer to a bowl.

Fold three-quarters of the béchamel into the penne. Layer half of the penne in the prepared baking dish and top with the spinach mixture. Scatter the remaining penne evenly over the top, then evenly spoon on the remaining béchamel.

In a heavy frying pan over high heat, melt the butter with the oil until it sizzles. Add the breadcrumbs and sauté until toasted and golden, 2–3 minutes. Spoon the breadcrumbs evenly over the penne.

Bake in the centre of the oven until hot and bubbling, 20–25 minutes. Serve immediately.

SERVES 4

SPANNER CRAB NAPOLEONS

Chef Megan Brown creates menus that are deliciously innovative, as you will discover with this recipe. It is her adaptation of napoleons, the popular jam-and-cream-filled pastry stacks or sandwiches. This dish may take a little time to execute perfectly, but it is worth the extra effort. Spanner crabs are caught in northern New South Wales and Queensland and are available year-round.

200 ml (6½ fl oz/¾ cup plus 1½ tablespoons) vegetable oil,
    for deep-frying
12 wonton wrappers (see glossary)
10 fresh basil leaves, finely shredded, plus 1 bunch fresh
    basil, stemmed
3 red capsicums (bell peppers), roasted, peeled, seeded and
    diced (see glossary)
3 ears sweet corn, steamed or boiled and kernels removed
salt and freshly ground pepper
½ bunch fresh chives, finely snipped
125 ml (4 fl oz/½ cup) mayonnaise for egg salad with
    kalamata olives (recipe on page 172)
125 ml (4 fl oz/½ cup) olive oil or light vegetable oil
300 g (9½ oz) cooked spanner crabmeat or other crabmeat
1 bunch watercress, carefully washed and crisped

☙ In a deep, heavy saucepan over high heat, pour in the vegetable oil to a depth of 4 cm (1½ in). Heat to 190°C (375°F) on a deep-fat thermometer or until a dry crust of bread dropped into the oil immediately rises to the surface and bubbles at the edges. Add the wonton wrappers, 4 at a time, and deep-fry, flattening them with tongs, until golden and crisp, about 2 minutes. Using tongs, remove to crumpled paper towels to drain.
☙ In a large bowl, mix the shredded basil leaves, capsicums and corn. Season to taste with salt and pepper. Set aside. In another bowl, stir the chives into the mayonnaise. Set aside.
☙ In a blender, combine the whole basil leaves with the olive oil or light vegetable oil. Blend until smooth. Strain through a very fine sieve; there will be only tiny particles of basil remaining in the oil. Set aside.
☙ To assemble, place a spoonful of the chive mayonnaise on each of 4 serving plates and place a wonton wrapper on top. Place a spoonful of capsicum mixture, a spoonful of crab and 2 sprigs watercress on each. Repeat the layers, beginning again with the mayonnaise. Top with the remaining wonton wrappers. Be sure to stack the layers very lightly. Drizzle the basil oil around each stack. Serve immediately.

SERVES 4

GRILLED FRESH SARDINES WITH ROAST TOMATO DRESSING

When sardines are in season, they should be snapped up for grilling. Don't be put off by the fact that they must be gutted: it is a straightforward task that takes only a matter of seconds for each one. Sardines are caught along the southern stretches of Australia and are available year-round.

FOR THE DRESSING:

250 g (½ lb) cherry tomatoes
2 teaspoons balsamic vinegar
1 teaspoon white wine vinegar
120 ml (4 fl oz/½ cup) virgin olive oil
sea salt and freshly ground pepper

24 fresh sardines
olive oil, for brushing on griller tray

☙ Preheat an oven to 150°C (300°F). Oil a baking dish large enough to accommodate the tomatoes.
☙ To make the dressing, place the tomatoes in the prepared dish and roast until very soft, about 45 minutes. Transfer the tomatoes to a bowl and, when cool enough to handle, remove some of the loose skins. Stir in the vinegars and leave to cool to room temperature. Stir in the oil and season to taste with salt and pepper. Divide the sauce evenly among the centres of 4 flat plates.
☙ To clean the sardines, twist off the heads. Working with 1 sardine at a time, hold it under running cold water, slip your thumb under the backbone and pull the bone out. Dry the sardines thoroughly with plenty of paper towels.
☙ Preheat a griller (broiler) on high. Brush a griller tray with oil. Arrange the sardines side by side on the tray. Slip under the griller and grill (broil) until beginning to brown, about 2 minutes. Very carefully turn the sardines over and grill the other side until browned, about 2 minutes longer.
☙ Serve the sardines at once on top of the sauce.

SERVES 4

TASMANIAN ATLANTIC SALMON TARTARE

Cheryl Mohr is a cofounder of Mohr Foods, well-known salmon smokers at Botany in New South Wales. Her delightful version of salmon tartare doesn't mask the fresh flavour of this fine Australian fish. The crispness of the toast is a necessary contrast to the softness of the tartare.

200–250 g (6½–8 oz) salmon fillet, finely diced
1 small purple onion, finely diced
2 teaspoons well-drained small capers, roughly chopped
2 teaspoons fresh chervil leaves, chopped
1 lemon, peeled and diced
1 teaspoon sea salt
freshly ground pepper
16 very thin slices sandwich bread
1 tablespoon olive oil
1 cucumber, thinly sliced

☙ In a large bowl, mix together the salmon, onion, capers, chervil, lemon, salt and pepper to taste. Cover and refrigerate until ready to serve.
☙ Preheat a griller (broiler) on high. Arrange the bread slices on a baking tray (sheet) and slip under the griller. Grill (broil) lightly, turning once, until evenly golden and crisp. Let cool on a wire rack.
☙ Just prior to serving, stir the olive oil into the salmon mixture. Arrange the cucumber slices on individual plates and spoon the salmon tartare on top. Serve with the toast.

SERVES 4

Clockwise from top: Tasmanian Atlantic Salmon Tartare, Grilled Fresh Sardines with Roast Tomato Dressing, Spanner Crab Napoleons

VICTORIA

T H E G A R D E N

B LUE LEEKS, white carrots, yellow beetroots (beets), tiny tomatoes the size of redcurrants—all centuries-old heirloom varieties—are found growing in an extraordinary garden on Victoria's Mornington Peninsula. Flanked by the peninsula's apple orchards and, more recently, vineyards, this heritage garden, Heronswood at Dromana, is possibly the most significant in Australia. Standing on its lawn, looking out across Port Phillip Bay, you can believe the cliché of this state's vehicle number plates that proclaims it 'The Garden State'. Victoria grows such an enormous variety of produce that an annual event, the Harvest Picnic, is held every autumn in celebration. On most days of the week further evidence is found at Melbourne's Victoria Markets. Both are manifestations of the state's horticultural abundance.

Heronswood's importance is that it keeps alive old domestic varieties of fruits and vegetables, the sorts of plants our grandparents and their parents grew in their gardens. Here, the biodiversity of vegetable varieties is preserved as an alternative to the commercial hybrids. It is the showplace of Digger's Seeds, whose catalogue offers more than fifty varieties of tomato alone. This garden, the passion of seed-saver Clive Blazey, grows over one hundred tomato varieties, each with different features that make it better for eating, for drying, for making tomato paste and so on. There are the original tiny currant tomatoes, a quarter the size of a cherry tomato, from which many others are descended. In late summer there are apricot-sized yellow tomatoes, a white tomato—White Beauty—with purple tinges, and Green Zebra, which has yellow stripes through its green skin and is greeny-yellow when ripe. Nearly forty types of

Previous pages: Constellations of lights illuminate Bourke Street in Melbourne. Left: Actors reach a dramatic moment during a performance of street theatre in Melbourne.

capsicums (peppers) are grown as well. Among them are a variety called evergreen, which doesn't change colour like the others and is thus ripe when it's green; purple ones; dark chocolate brown ones; and many different shapes, including miniature capsicums the size of cherry tomatoes. Aside from the conventional deep purple eggplants (aubergines), there are pale cream ones with lavender flecks.

Although Victoria's climate is cooler than that of much of the rest of Australia, this small haven of Heronswood demonstrates, in microcosm, what can be cultivated in this fertile state. Despite its relatively small size, Victoria boasts a quarter of Australia's total area devoted to growing vegetables. It produces nearly three times as many apples as Tasmania; grows nearly as many potatoes as the next two states, Tasmania and South Australia, combined, and more lettuce—and significantly more tomatoes—than even Queensland; and is also Australia's largest pear grower, producing nearly the country's entire crop. The nashi, an Asian pear first brought here by the Chinese in the mid-1800s, is also

A fisherman at Mallacoota repairs his nets as he looks forward to the next day's catch.

being grown commercially, mostly in the Goulburn Valley. There are three main varieties, the green Nijisseiki and the newer russet Kosui and Hosui.

The settlement in Port Jackson was nearly half a century old before any attempt was made to settle what is now Victoria. Fears that the French might establish settlements in Port Phillip Bay—along with a search for more grazing lands—drove explorer Hamilton Hume in his overland expedition south. (Later his name was given to the main highway between Sydney and Melbourne.) Settlements were established at Portland (1834) and Melbourne (1835). Almost immediately the first fruit plantings—apples—took place. Although agricultural expansion was slow at first, this was to change dramatically within fifteen years.

The rush to the New South Wales goldfields caused such a serious decline in the Victorian population that a Gold Discovery Committee was formed in the hope that gold would be discovered locally. Gold was found in 1851, and fields at Ballarat and Bendigo were in full production by the end of that year.

As with most other colonies (it was separated from New South Wales in 1851), Victoria was largely opened up—and populated—thanks to the gold routes. Melbourne, it is said, was built on gold-rush money. The first gold seekers from overseas arrived in Melbourne in December 1851. Shipload after shipload followed, and Victoria's population of 77 345 in 1851 more than doubled in 1852, with 94 644 people arriving in 1852 alone. Within three years, the numbers had quadrupled.

Like many itinerant Australians of the time, a gold-digger had a meal that usually comprised, wrote an observer of the time, 'a chop or a steak out of the frying pan, placed on a piece of damper [bread] with a pannikin of tea'. (The steak sandwich was to live on as the Australian equivalent of the hamburger for at least another century.)

Although the majority of gold-diggers were European, of the other fortune seekers the most numerous were the Chinese. By 1859, there were forty-two thousand in Victoria alone, one-third of Victoria's mining population and the largest non-British community in any Australian colony in the nineteenth century. Largely only the men came, intending to make their fortunes and return home. They made a significant contribution to goldfield life by growing fruits and vegetables. The Chinese market gardeners essentially kept the goldfields free of scurvy.

It is suggested that the uniquely Australian expression *dinkum*—as in 'fair dinkum', meaning 'real, honest or genuine'—is derived from the Cantonese *ding* for 'topmost' and *gam* for 'gold'. Certainly these Chinese gold seekers came largely from Canton.

Gold also brought French immigrants, many of whom later settled on land in grape-bearing districts. Two such settlers, Truette and Blompied, planted vines in northwestern Victoria in 1863 and established the Great Western vineyards.

The Spanish community of Bendigo demonstrated how tomatoes could be grown using gravity irrigation, long before the establishment of the irrigation systems of the Goulburn and Murray valleys.

The Canadian Chaffey brothers, well-known irrigation pioneers encouraged by the offer of a grant of land, arrived in Melbourne in 1886, to set up an irrigation scheme on the Murray River at Mildura. (Later, when the scheme fell into financial difficulties, they went on to Renmark to set up the Riverland.) By 1890, there were three thousand settlers at Mildura.

The first rice (in temperate southeastern Australia) was planted at Swan Hill, by Japanese-born Jo Takasuka, a member of a samurai family and the son of a chef to the Japanese emperor. He had observed irrigation in California and, in 1906, having seen the amount of rice Australia was importing, persuaded the Victorian government of the day to lease him eighty hectares (two hundred acres) by the Murray. He employed dryland sowing techniques used in wheat cultivation, and then irrigated the land, thereby demonstrating a novel method of growing rice and establishing a precedent for methods used in the Riverina today.

Unfortunately, Takasuka's land was flood-prone, and his crop was washed away year after year. Then it was hit by drought, but he persevered. In 1914, he harvested a successful crop. Some he sold to a miller in Melbourne, and the rest he sold to the Victorian Department of Agriculture. Later, in 1917, he sold seed to the New South Wales Department of Agriculture that was successfully used in trials at the Yanko Agricultural College in the Riverina. By establishing a rice crop in

This intricate crest graces Tanswell's Commercial Hotel in Beechworth, built in the 1870s.

Cows graze in the hills along the Genoa River near the heart of the state's dairy industry in Gippsland.

A field of wattle in Rushworth, the brilliant blooms at their peak, is set off by a backdrop of eucalypts.

the southeast, Takasuka made a significant contribution to the development of rice growing in Australia.

Victoria has a substantial dairy industry, particularly in the northeast. Although it produces butter, yoghurt and cheeses such as cheddar on a large commercial scale, much more exciting has been the explosion in production of farmhouse and artisan cheeses since the mid-1980s, most of which were helped along by the skills of cheese maker Richard Thomas. The greatest proliferation in farmhouse cheeses in Australia has come from Victoria. A farmhouse cheese is, by definition, one made with milk from a single farm, whereas an artisan or specialty cheese is made from the milk of a number of different farms. They are as varied as soft-curd cheeses, white mould cheeses in the style of brie or camembert, or blue cheeses—or even a combination of blue and white mould.

Following the example of King Island, small cheese-making operations were first set up in Gippsland, rich farmland that lies about one hundred kilometres (sixty miles) east of Melbourne. This was the first region to break with the tradition of naming cheeses after the European styles they were emulating; instead, an Australian identity was stamped on each product. For instance, there is nothing in the name Gippsland Blue to suggest it is a gorgonzola-style cheese. Nor do names such as Benadale, Jumbunna, Jeetho, Bass River Red and Moyarra give any indication of what type of cheese they are. Royal Victorian Blue, Mungabareena, Mount Buffalo Blue and King River Gold likewise offer little insight into their style.

These last two cheeses come from Milawa, in the north of the state, in the foothills of the high country known as the Victorian Alps, at the southern end of the Snowy Mountains. The Milawa Cheese Company's range includes not only cow's and goat's milk cheeses, but also sheep's milk cheeses, both blue and white mould, and hard cheeses.

As a region, Milawa has become known for a whole range of foods, including—and probably thanks to—its wine. The area's oldest family vignerons, Brown Brothers, set up their company here in gold-rush times, originally growing grapes to feed the miners. They began making wine in 1889, and these days spend much thought and effort on matching food and wine, in addition to promoting the region's produce.

From the Milawa area come olives from the Hourigans, yabbies (small freshwater crayfish), walnuts from Gapsted, quince paste from Old Emu Inn, Conroy Brothers' beef and many potato varieties from the famed Dobson's Farm. The last show up each year at the Harvest Picnic with at least ten varieties, including the wonderfully waxy kipfler, a short, cigar-shaped potato. There is local cottage mustard and honeys such as red gum, yellow box, blue gum and stringy bark. The stringy bark should come as no surprise, for this is Kelly country: Ned Kelly, Australia's most famous bushranger, was shot against a stringy bark.

Besides the rare (wild) Murray crayfish, the second biggest freshwater crustacean in the world (mottled grey-green, with sweet flesh), there are trout from the Hume Weir and from near Beechworth, both smoked locally. There is farmed Chinook—Pacific rather than Atlantic salmon—from Harrietville in the Snow Country. The area around Beechworth also yields quantities of pears and apples and wonderful apple juice.

Victoria is Australia's third biggest beef producer. Its pastures produce arguably the finest grass-fed beef in the country from breeds like Hereford and Angus.

The state now has nearly a dozen wine-growing areas, its cooler climate range producing a different flavour spectrum in its wines than is found in wines from the warmer regions to its north and west. Areas becoming noted for their wine are the relatively recently developed Mornington Peninsula and, more particularly, the Yarra Valley, where author, wine writer and vigneron James Halliday produces his Coldstream Hills label. The Yarra Valley turns out sparkling wines as well, such as those from Domaine Chandon, and is noted for its berry fruits, especially its strawberries, and cherries.

Victoria's cooler waters offer small sweet mussels, blue-eye, morwong, redfish (nannygai), arrow squid, silver and blue warehou and abalone, as well as orange roughy from its deeper waters. According to anglers, the best flathead in Australia comes from Lakes Entrance.

Wild mushrooms like morels are found in the old gold areas near Kyneton and Castlemaine. Olives are grown in the Grampians near Horsham, as well as around Dimboola, Robinvale and Mildura, and are eagerly snapped up every summer by members of Melbourne's Italian and Greek communities for curing at home.

The contribution to Victorian life made by Italian, Greek and other non-British migrants, most of whom have arrived since the 1950s, has been enormous. The evidence is everywhere: the coffee shops of Carlton, the aged parmesan available at the Lygon Food Store, the range of sausages—*saucisson sec, zampone* and *cotechino*—sold by Jonathan Gianfreda of Jonathan's Meats, the array

The harvest now over, two growers carry the last of their walnut crop through their orchard in Gapsted.

of locally made breads and cheeses like mascarpone and mozzarella, and the whole new range of salad greens and other vegetables previously unavailable. These days migrants from Asia are introducing us to other whole new ranges of ingredients and flavours. Asian vegetables grown by these more recently arrived communities, particularly the Vietnamese, are stocked in shops clustered in Victoria Street, Richmond.

Melbourne restaurants are considered to be amongst Australia's finest, and certainly the city has arguably the best Italian and Chinese establishments in the country. Its restaurants tend to be more formal and more French-oriented—French food is more popular in Melbourne than in decidedly more casual Sydney, perhaps because of its cooler climate. And no visit to the state is complete without a visit to Melbourne's Victoria Markets. The markets, like the Harvest Picnic at Heronswood, are amongst the horticultural and culinary achievements of which Victoria can be proud.

FISH AND SHELLFISH

More than a hundred species of crayfish, including these yabbies from South Australia, are found in the fresh waters throughout Australia.

FISH AND SHELLFISH

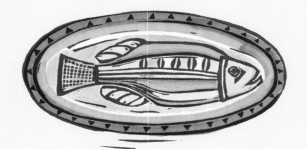

Butterfish, kingfish and jewfish are all names of one and the same fish—depending on which state you happen to be in. Officially known as mulloway, they are found from south Queensland, down right around the Bight into Western Australian waters. This confusion of nomenclature, which is the case with a number of fish, arose when early settlers gave fish the names that they were familiar with at home.

The converse is also true: some species that are actually different go by the same names. Butterfish is the recommended name for a fish called old maid in New South Wales, but known as John Dory in Queensland—although they are not even the same shape. The old maid, a member of the Scatophagidae family, has scales and vertical bands which the latter does not have, and it doesn't even have the distinctive thumb-print marking of the John Dory.

'Bugs', or shovel-nosed lobsters, a type of small crayfish, are known as Balmain bugs (*Ibacus peronii*) in Sydney waters, but are different from—although related to—the (warm-water) Moreton Bay bugs (*Thenus orientalis*) found from Brisbane right up around Cape York into the Gulf of Carpentaria and down into Western Australia.

It's confusing enough if you live here and travel between states, but it is even worse if you're a visitor. What is called snapper in Australia is a different species from the Northern Hemisphere snapper, and Australian whiting bears no resemblance to what is called whiting in

Europe. But no matter what names the fish go by their quality is superb, thanks to Australia's unpolluted waters.

Australian fish is much in demand, particularly in Asian markets, where quality is paramount. Tasmanian Atlantic salmon fetches the highest price of any salmon in the Tokyo fish markets because it is perceived to be the best quality. Live abalone, crayfish and Tasmanian rock lobster (actually a marine crayfish) and chilled southern bluefin tuna are also prized.

Australia's coastline of nearly thirty thousand kilometres (eighteen thousand miles) make it one of—if not *the*—longest of any island or country in the world. This remarkable expanse offers an enormous diversity of fish and shellfish, both temperate and tropical, although not in the quantities that might be expected. There are two reasons for this. One factor is the country's relatively low rainfall, which means there is less nutrient run-off for inshore species, and the other is that Australia's continental shelf is relatively narrow and drops off into very deep water not far offshore.

Australia has a number of native species of freshwater fish, including the estuarine catfish, or cobbler, the Murray perch and the relatively rare Murray cod. The flesh of the latter is marbled like Kobe beef, and much treasured by the Chinese community, making it among the dearest fish on sale in Australia, particularly in Sydney. It is also the biggest of Australia's freshwater fish, and can grow to up to 100 kilograms (220 pounds). Stories about this giant

Previous pages, left to right: Grilled Rock Lobster with Sun-Dried Tomato Butter (recipe page 96), Spicy Prawns with Black Wood Fungus and Snow Peas (recipe page 95)— photographed at Milson's Point on Sydney Harbour

88

abound, including many tall tales: a fisherman trying to land one ties his lines to a tree, only to watch the cod rip the tree out by its roots!

The country also claims almost a hundred species of freshwater crayfish, all of which belong to one family (Parastacidae). This family embraces everything from the relatively rare spiny-tailed Murray River crayfish to the common smooth-tailed yabby. Unique to Western Australia is the black marron, a particularly large freshwater crayfish.

The first records of fish in Australian waters date back to Torres's voyage of 1606, and to engravings from Dampier's second voyage of 1669, published in *A Voyage to New Holland* in 1703. La Perouse's men, on their visit to Botany Bay in 1788, recorded catching 'nearly 2 000 light horsemen [snapper]' in one day.

Like fruits and vegetables, many fish are seasonal. The seasons are also defined by where you are, whether in the tropics or in the Bight. There are even differences on the east coast: Queensland prawns (shrimp) are in season mainly in winter, from March to July, whereas Sydney's season runs from November to April.

Australia boasts three types of oysters. The best and most famous are the native Sydney rock oysters (*Saccostrea commercialis*), found up and down the east coast roughly as far as the Queensland border in the north and the Victorian border in the south. There are the less common native Australian belons (*Ostrea angasi*)—a cousin of the French belon (*O. edulis*)—harvested mainly in Tasmania, and in Jervis Bay in New South Wales. The third is the Pacific oyster (*Crassostrea gigas*), introduced from Japan in the 1940s, and now raised in Tasmania, South Australia and to a lesser extent Victoria.

An increasing number of fish and crustacean species are now being farmed. Prawns (shrimp), freshwater and saltwater rainbow trout, Atlantic and Pacific salmon, abalone, oysters, mussels, tuna and barramundi are all being raised in controlled environments that are not subject to the vagaries of the weather, which can restrict fishing boats to port. Barramundi are even being grown in the saline bore water of inland Griffith!

The Sydney Fish Market offers one of the largest

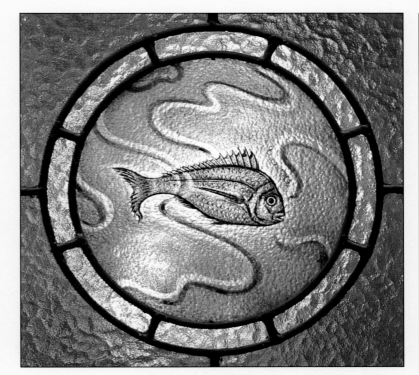

A leadlight window in a Queenscliff hotel highlights Victoria's maritime riches.

arrays of fish species in the world. Only the larger Japanese markets like Tokyo's Tsukiji handle more. Wholesale auctions at the Sydney Fish Market are conducted on weekday mornings, but the retail outlets are open to the public seven days a week. Here you can wander among the mountains of prawns and past tanks of live mud crabs or brilliantly coloured reef fish from Queensland. You can see live rock lobsters from Tasmania, find the strange-looking Balmain bugs, have sashimi sliced from sides of tuna, pick out the smallest of baby octopuses, observe the difference between a spanner crab and a blue swimmer (which are blue when they're raw), and, at a certain time of the year, find *nannata,* the tiny whitebait so popular with the Italian community.

Every visitor to the city should take the opportunity to see this abundance at first-hand. It is irrefutable proof of Australia's bountiful marine harvest.

Devoted to his pursuit—in all weather—an angler casts his fly across the waters at the mouth of the Farmhouse River in Tasmania.

TASMANIA

SMOKED TASMANIAN SALMON AND AVOCADO PARCELS WITH NAAN

There are several excellent commercial salmon smokers in Australia, including Mohr Foods at Botany in New South Wales, Springs Smoked Salmon at Mt Barker in the Adelaide Hills and Tasmanian Smokehouse Deloraine in Tasmania. Smoked salmon from any of these suppliers would be wonderful used for making this delicious first course. If you don't have time to make the naan, *purchase the breads from a well-stocked supermarket or one of the many local Indian restaurants. Indeed, there are so many Indian eateries in suburban Australia now, they will soon rival Thai restaurants.*

FOR THE *NAAN*:

520 g (16½ oz/3¼ cups) plain (all-purpose) flour
1 tablespoon sugar
1 tablespoon baking powder
1 teaspoon bicarbonate of soda (baking soda)
2 teaspoons salt
2 eggs
60 g (2 oz/¼ cup) yoghurt
185 ml (6 fl oz/¾ cup) milk
1½ tablespoons vegetable oil

FOR THE SALMON PARCELS:

6 large smoked salmon slices
2 avocados
juice of 1 lemon
1 tablespoon snipped fresh dill
freshly ground pepper

FOR SERVING:

6 fresh dill sprigs

✄ To make the *naan,* sift together the flour, sugar, baking powder, bicarbonate of soda and salt into a large bowl. Make a well in the centre and add the eggs, yoghurt, milk and oil to the well. Using a fork, mix the ingredients together briskly until the dough comes together. If the mixture is too dry, add a little warm water.

✄ Turn the dough out onto a lightly floured work surface and knead until elastic and smooth, about 5 minutes. Form into a ball and wrap in plastic wrap. Refrigerate for 30 minutes.

✄ Divide the dough into 12 equal portions. Roll each portion into a ball between your palms, then, on a floured work surface, pat out each ball into a thin round about 10 cm (4 in) in diameter.

✄ Heat a large, heavy frying pan or griddle over medium-high heat. Place as many *naan* in the pan as will fit without crowding and cook until the first side has lightly coloured patches, about 3 minutes. Turn the breads over and again cook until coloured patches appear, about 2 minutes longer. Transfer to a plate and cover to keep warm. Cook the remaining rounds in the same way.

✄ To make the salmon parcels, spread the salmon slices out on the work surface. Halve, pit and peel the avocados. Dice the flesh and place it in a bowl. Add the lemon juice and toss to prevent discolouration. Drain off the excess juice and add the snipped dill and pepper to taste. Toss gently. Spoon an equal amount of the avocado on top of each salmon slice and fold in the edges of the salmon to form tidy parcels.

✄ Arrange the salmon parcels, seam side down, on individual plates. Garnish with the dill sprigs. Serve with the warm bread.

SERVES 4–6

Smoked Tasmanian Salmon and Avocado Parcels with Naan—photographed at the blowhole in Kiama , NSW

BRISBANE

KING GEORGE WHITING FILLETS WITH VEGETABLE CONFETTI

Whitings are relatively small, elongated fish that live in shallow coastal waters. The sweetish, delicate white-fleshed fish have fine bones and are considered to be among the tastiest of Australia's fish. King George whiting is one of the six whiting species in our waters and I believe it to be the best. It is found principally in South Australia and Victoria. Judith Henderson operates a Brisbane-based cooking school. She is a natural cook who loves nothing better than talking food and sharing her table with friends and colleagues. This recipe illustrates her rule never to overshadow the mild flavour of whiting with strong ingredients.

FOR THE VEGETABLE CONFETTI:

1 red capsicum (bell pepper), seeded and cut into tiny dice
1 choko (chayote), peeled, seeded and cut into tiny dice
300 g (9½ oz) fresh mushrooms, cut into tiny dice
1 tablespoon finely shredded fresh basil

FOR THE SAUCE:

400 g (13 oz) ripe tomatoes, seeded
1 clove garlic
fresh basil leaves
2 tablespoons olive oil
salt and freshly ground pepper

FOR THE FISH:

800 g (1¾ lb) King George whiting fillets, with skin intact, at room temperature
olive oil
salt
1–2 tablespoons fresh lemon juice
freshly ground pepper

FOR SERVING:

1 tablespoon olive oil

✄ To make the confetti, place the capsicum in a sieve over boiling water for 20–30 seconds. Repeat with the choko. Let the vegetables cool, then pat dry with paper towels. Place the cooled vegetables in a bowl and add the mushrooms and basil. Mix well and set aside.

✄ To make the sauce, place the tomatoes, garlic and basil in a food processor fitted with the metal blade or in a blender. Purée until smooth. Pass the purée through a sieve into a small saucepan and heat to serving temperature but do not boil. Whisk in the olive oil and season to taste with salt and pepper. Keep warm.

✄ To prepare the fish, toss the fillets lightly in a little olive oil so they glisten on all sides. Lightly oil a large, heavy frying pan and place over medium heat. Add the fish, skin side up, and cook for 1–2 minutes; the timing will depend upon the size of the fillets. Sprinkle with a little salt, lemon juice and pepper. Turn the fillets over and cook until just cooked through, 30–60 seconds longer. Lift out onto a plate and keep warm.

✄ To serve, in a heavy frying pan over medium heat, warm the oil. Add the vegetable confetti and toss until heated through. Place the fillets on a warmed serving plate, spoon the vegetables over the top and ladle the sauce around the fish. Serve immediately.

SERVES 4   *Photograph page 93*

Steamed Coral Trout with Chinese Sauce—photographed at Gwinganna estate, Queensland

STEAMED CORAL TROUT WITH CHINESE SAUCE

I first tasted this dish at Hayman Island Resort, a beautiful place in the Whitsunday Islands, off the Great Barrier Reef in Queensland. It is superb made with one of Queensland's favourite fish, coral trout, and, once assembled, resembles a bunch of grapes. Pearl perch or another delicate, small saltwater fish can be used in place of the trout. Haw flakes are reddish waferlike rounds made from haw fruits. They can be found in Asian stores.

1 coral trout, 500 g (1 lb), filleted

FOR THE SAUCE:

1 teaspoon sugar
juice of ½ lemon
2 teaspoons tamarind pulp (see glossary)
10 haw flakes
1 teaspoon commercial tomato sauce (ketchup)

fresh grape leaves for decorating

❧ Using a very sharp knife, cut crosswise slashes in each fish fillet; be careful not to cut all the way through. Place in a shallow dish on a steamer rack over gently boiling water, cover and steam until just cooked through, about 12 minutes; the timing will depend on the thickness of the fillets. Transfer to a warmed platter and keep warm.
❧ To make the sauce, combine the sugar, lemon juice, tamarind pulp and haw flakes in a small saucepan. Bring to a boil, whisking constantly. Add the tomato sauce and cook, uncovered, stirring until the sauce reduces and thickens to a light coating consistency, about 5 minutes.
❧ Pour the sauce over the fish, decorate with the grape leaves and serve at once.

SERVES 4

BAKED COD WITH GINGER AND SOY ON ASPARAGUS

Maori cod, which is found around the top half of Australia, or bar cod, which is fairly plentiful around the east coast of Australia, is good in this dish. Buy Asian sesame oil, which is made from roasted seeds, and add it judiciously, as it has a very strong taste and a little goes a long way.

1 Maori or bar cod fillet or other firm-fleshed white fish
    fillet, about 1 kg (2 lb), with skin intact
2 tablespoons peanut oil
2 tablespoons light soy sauce
1 piece gingerroot, 40 g (1½ oz), peeled and thinly sliced
salt
4 bunches pencil-slim asparagus, about 750 g (1½ lb) total
    weight, tough stem ends removed
1 tablespoon Asian sesame oil (see glossary)
1½ tablespoons well-drained pickled ginger (see glossary)

❧ Position a rack in the centre of an oven and preheat the oven to 200°C (400°F).
❧ Place the fillet, skin side down, in a nonstick or lightly oiled heavy baking pan. Brush with the peanut oil, drizzle with the soy sauce and scatter the gingerroot slices over the top. Cover the pan with aluminium foil and bake in the centre of the oven until the fish is just cooked, 25–30 minutes.
❧ Meanwhile, fill a saucepan three-quarters full of water and bring to a boil. Salt lightly and add the asparagus. Cook until barely tender, 4–5 minutes. Drain well.
❧ Arrange the asparagus in a lattice pattern in the centre of 4 warmed plates. Divide the fish into 4 portions and place a portion on top of each asparagus arrangement. Drizzle with the sesame oil and top with the pickled ginger. Serve at once.

SERVES 4

YABBIES WITH TAMARIND, CHILLI AND COCONUT MILK

When I was growing up, I caught yabbies with my friends in the Onkaparinga River at Port Noarlunga, just south of Adelaide. We would hang a piece of meat in a tree for a week and, when it was really ripe, tie it to a length of string and throw it in the river. The yabbies loved it, and we'd haul them out of the water with a colander. We'd cook them on the beach over an open fire and eat them right out of the shell with just a squeeze of lemon. Today we pay dearly for farmed yabbies to be flown across the continent, as the best come from Western Australia, Victoria and South Australia. They are similar to the Louisiana crawfish native to the southeastern United States. The Asian treatment of yabbies in this dish is wonderful. Do take care when measuring out the tamarind pulp, as it can be overpowering.

1 l (32 fl oz/4 cups) coconut milk (see glossary)
4–6 fresh red chillies, seeded and chopped
2 teaspoons tamarind pulp (see glossary)
salt
10 fresh kaffir lime leaves, finely shredded (see glossary)
2 kg (4 lb) live yabbies (crayfish)

❧ In a large, heavy pot, combine the coconut milk, chillies, tamarind pulp, salt to taste and lime leaves. Bring slowly to just below the boiling point. Add the yabbies, stir, reduce the heat to low, cover and cook as slowly as possible for 15 minutes.
❧ Using tongs, remove the yabbies to a bowl and keep warm. Bring the coconut milk mixture to a rapid boil and boil until reduced a little, about 5 minutes.
❧ To serve, divide the yabbies among individual shallow dishes and ladle some of the reduced coconut milk over each serving. Serve at once.

SERVES 4

Clockwise from top right: Yabbies with Tamarind, Chilli and Coconut Milk, Baked Cod with Ginger and Soy on Asparagus, King George Whiting Fillets with Vegetable Confetti (recipe page 91)—photographed at Kiama Harbour, NSW

Steamed Stuffed Crab Shells

STEAMED STUFFED CRAB SHELLS

Blue swimmer crabs come from many areas around Australia's vast coastline. Here, they are stuffed with a fragrant mixture rich with coconut cream. Offer them as a first course.

8 green (raw) blue swimmer crabs or other small crabs

FOR THE STUFFING:

200 g (6½ oz) minced (ground) pork and veal, in equal
   amounts
1 small brown onion, chopped
1 tablespoon chopped coriander (cilantro) root (see glossary)
2 tablespoons finely chopped fresh coriander (cilantro)
1 tablespoon cornflour (cornstarch)
2 eggs
80 ml (3 fl oz/⅓ cup) coconut cream (see glossary)
salt and freshly ground pepper

❧ Bring a large saucepan three-quarters full of water to a boil. Add the crabs and cook in the simmering water until they turn reddish and are cooked, 7–8 minutes. Using a slotted utensil or tongs, remove the crabs from the water. When cool enough to handle, carefully remove the top shells and set aside. Extract all the flesh from the body and claws and shred finely. Set aside.
❧ To make the stuffing, in a food processor fitted with the metal blade or in a blender, combine all the ingredients, including salt and pepper to taste. Process briefly until all the ingredients are chopped medium-fine and evenly distributed. Fold in the crab flesh.
❧ Spoon the stuffing into the reserved crab shells without packing it down too firmly. Place, stuffed side up, on a steamer rack over simmering water. Cover and steam until cooked, about 15 minutes. Serve hot in the shells.

SERVES 8

SPICY PRAWNS WITH BLACK WOOD FUNGUS AND SNOW PEAS

Ian and Jenny Morphy own an inn in the upper Hunter Valley, where they welcome not only customers, but also friends (as long as they have the capacity for great food and wine—and lots of it!). Here is one of their celebrated recipes. Every Australian surely has a bottle of tomato sauce in the kitchen cupboard, so it's not surprising to see it being used here as the basis for a chilli sauce.

2 tablespoons peanut oil
10 spring (green) onions, trimmed to 8-cm (3¼-in) lengths
20 g (¾ oz) dried black wood fungus, soaked in 1 l (32 fl oz/
   4 cups) hot water for 1 hour and drained (see glossary)
20 snow peas (mangetouts), trimmed
12 medium-sized green (raw) king prawns (shrimp), peeled
   and deveined
125 ml (4 fl oz/½ cup) sweet chilli sauce (see glossary)

❧ In a large frying pan over high heat, warm the oil. Add the spring onions and sauté for 2 minutes. Add the fungus and snow peas. Toss and stir the ingredients constantly for 1 minute. Add the prawns and continue to toss and stir until the prawns have coloured and are cooked, 3–4 minutes.
❧ Add the chilli sauce and toss constantly until all the ingredients are coated with the sauce and heated through. Serve at once.

SERVES 2   *Photograph pages 86–87*

CHILLI FISH STIR-FRY

Choose the freshest, firmest white-fleshed fish available. My choice is blue-eye cod, which is caught off the coast of New South Wales. Flake (shark) is also good; so too is ling (cod). Serve this spicy stir-fry with steamed long-grain white rice.

80–100 ml (3–3½ fl oz/6–6½ tablespoons) safflower oil
2 cloves garlic, finely chopped
½ brown onion, finely chopped
1 or 2 fresh red chillies, seeded and chopped
1 piece gingerroot, about 10 g (⅓ oz), peeled and finely
  chopped
100 g (3½ oz) carrots, peeled and cut into 2-cm (¾-in) dice
100 g (3½ oz) zucchini (courgettes), cut into 2-cm (¾-in) dice
600 g (1¼ lb) firm-fleshed fish fillets, cut into 3-cm (1¼-in)
  dice (see note)
2–3 tablespoons soy sauce, or to taste
100 g (3½ oz) bean sprouts, tails removed
80 ml (3 fl oz/⅓ cup) fish stock (see glossary) or chicken stock
1 tablespoon cornflour (cornstarch)
2 tablespoons water

❧ In a wok or large frying pan over medium-high heat, warm the oil. When it is hot, add the garlic and onion and stir-fry for 2 minutes. Add the chillies, gingerroot, carrots and zucchini and stir-fry until half-cooked, 4–5 minutes.

❧ Add the fish and stir-fry for 1–2 minutes. Add the soy sauce, bean sprouts and stock and stir-fry until the fish is cooked and the bean sprouts are tender, about 2 minutes. In a small bowl, quickly stir together the cornflour and the water and add to the pan. Stir over high heat until the sauce mixture thickens slightly.

❧ Transfer to a warmed platter and serve at once.

SERVES 4   *Photograph pages 98–99*

GRILLED ROCK LOBSTER WITH SUN-DRIED TOMATO BUTTER

Australia has an abundance of lobsters. In the north they are known as northern tropical lobsters. Those native to New South Wales are called eastern lobsters, while in Victoria, South Australia and Tasmania they are referred to as southern crayfish. Then there are also the native western lobsters from Western Australia. All Australian lobsters have firm white flesh and a fabulous flavour and any type can be used for making this simple first course. You will need dry-packed rather than oil-packed sun-dried tomatoes for making the butter. Riverina sun-dried tomatoes are a particularly good choice because of their full flavour. The tomatoes must be rehydrated in very hot water for a few minutes before using.

FOR THE BUTTER:

125 g (4 oz/½ cup) unsalted butter, cut into 8 pieces
10 Riverina dry-packed sun-dried tomato halves or other
  high-quality sun-dried tomatoes, soaked in hot water to
  cover for 5 minutes and drained
½ teaspoon red chilli flakes, optional

4 small green (raw) lobster tails, 150–200 g (5–6 oz) each
2 tablespoons virgin olive oil
2 tablespoons fresh lemon juice
freshly ground pepper

❧ To make the butter, in a food processor fitted with the metal blade, combine all the ingredients. Pulse until the mixture is smooth. Alternatively, in a small bowl, mix the ingredients with a fork. Scrape the butter out of the bowl onto a flat plate and form it into a long block. Wrap well and refrigerate.

❧ Split open lengthwise the shells of the lobster tails and remove the skin covering the flesh. Carefully remove the flesh in a single piece from each tail section and cut into 4 or 5 pieces. Place the pieces back in the same shell in the same order.

❧ In a bowl, whisk together the oil, lemon juice and pepper to taste. Brush evenly over the lobster flesh, then cover and refrigerate until ready to cook.

❧ Preheat a griller (broiler) on high. Arrange the lobster tails, flesh side up, on a heavy griller tray and slip under the griller about 10 cm (4 in) from the heat source. Reduce the heat to medium-high and grill (broil) until beginning to brown. Turn over and grill for 3–4 minutes on the shell side; the timing will depend on the size of the tails. Turn over the tails again and cook until the flesh is just cooked. Again, the timing will depend on the size of the tails. (It is essential that the delicate flesh not overcook and dry out, as it will toughen. It is better to undercook it slightly, and then cover the pan with aluminium foil and finish cooking in a warm oven.)

❧ To serve, transfer the lobster tails to plates. Cut the chilled butter into 8 squares and place 1 piece on top of each tail section. Send to the table as the butter begins to melt.

SERVES 4   *Photograph pages 86–87*

GRAVLAX OF OCEAN TROUT

Gravlax is a Scandinavian method of curing fish that flavours it deliciously. Atlantic salmon as well as ocean trout can be used. If the fish is not cured long enough, it will be soft and difficult to slice; if it is overcured, it will be dry. Simply put, keep an eye on it.

15 g (½ oz/½ cup) snipped fresh dill
200 g (6½ oz/¾ cup plus 1 tablespoon) sugar
100 g (3½ oz/⅓ cup plus 1 tablespoon) coarse salt
1 tablespoon freshly ground pepper
1 ocean trout fillet, about 500 g (1 lb), with skin intact

FOR THE MUSTARD SAUCE:

60 g (2 oz/¼ cup) whole-grain mustard
sea salt and freshly ground pepper
2 tablespoons snipped fresh dill
1½ teaspoons white wine vinegar
100 ml (3½ fl oz/6½ tablespoons) safflower oil

grilled unsalted or low-salt crusty bread for serving

❧ In a small bowl, stir together the dill, sugar, salt and pepper. Place half of the mixture on the bottom of a shallow nonreactive dish just large enough to hold the fillet. Place the fillet, skin side down, on the salt mixture. Scatter the remaining salt mixture evenly over the top of the fillet. Cover with plastic wrap and weight down with canned foods or bricks. Refrigerate for 3 days, pouring off any accumulated juices every 12 hours or so.

❧ Just before serving, make the mustard sauce. In a small bowl, combine the mustard, salt and pepper to taste, dill and vinegar. Whisk until smooth. Add the oil slowly, whisking constantly until the mixture comes together in an emulsion.

❧ To serve, pour off the juices from the fish and scrape off any undissolved pieces of salt. Slice very thinly on an angle and serve with the mustard sauce and grilled bread.

SERVES 6

Top to bottom: Marrons in Tomato-Chive Mayonnaise on Toasted Bread, Gravlax of Ocean Trout—photographed at Bloodwood Estate, Orange, NSW

MARRONS IN TOMATO-CHIVE MAYONNAISE ON TOASTED BREAD

The marron, a native of Western Australia, is one of the largest freshwater crayfish in the country. Ash grey when raw, marrons turn dark red when cooked. Western Australians contend they are the best-tasting crayfish in Australia. Kate Lamont is the chef in her family's restaurant in the Swan Valley east of Perth, not far from where these native marrons are farmed in the Darling Ranges.

4 marrons (large crayfish), cooked

FOR THE MAYONNAISE:

1 egg
½ teaspoon salt, or to taste
½ teaspoon cracked pepper, or to taste

juice of 1 lemon
4 tablespoons snipped fresh chives
250 ml (8 fl oz/1 cup) safflower oil
2 large, firm ripe tomatoes, peeled, seeded and cut into 1-cm (⅜-in) dice

toasted brioche or crusty bread

Remove all the meat, including that from the claws, from the marrons. Cut the meat into 1-cm (⅜-in) dice.

To make the mayonnaise, in a blender or in a small food processor fitted with the metal blade, combine the egg, salt, pepper, lemon juice and chives. Process until thick. With the motor running, add the oil, drop by drop, until half of it has been used. Then, while continuing to process, add the remaining oil in a thin, steady stream until a thick mayonnaiselike consistency forms.

Transfer the mayonnaise to a bowl and fold the marron meat and tomato into it. Serve with toasted brioche or crusty bread.

SERVES 4

NEWCASTLE

Stuffed Squid

Barry Mieklejohn and his partner, Paul Garvan, are restaurateurs on the edge of Newcastle, north of Sydney. Barry is a creative chef who uses only the freshest of ingredients. This is his way of making stuffed squid, which he buys locally. He recommends serving them on a bed of steamed Chinese vegetables.

12 squid, about 600 g (1¼ lb) total weight, each about 10 cm (4 in) long

FOR THE STUFFING:

60 ml (2 fl oz/¼ cup) olive oil
1 small brown onion, finely chopped
2 cloves garlic, finely chopped
200 g (6½ oz) minced (ground) pork and veal, in equal amounts
¼ teaspoon salt, or to taste
¼ teaspoon freshly ground pepper, or to taste
1 or 2 fresh red chillies, seeded and chopped
4 tablespoons finely chopped fresh coriander (cilantro)
2 teaspoons tomato paste

60 ml (2 fl oz/¼ cup) olive oil
500 ml (16 fl oz/2 cups) fish stock (see glossary) or chicken stock
3 lemons, halved
6 fresh coriander (cilantro) sprigs for garnish

To clean the squid, cut off the heads. Trim off the tentacles and set aside. Pull off the 'wings' from each body and set aside. Remove and discard the guts and quill from each body and rinse well inside and out. Set the bodies aside. Finely chop the tentacles and wings and set aside as well.

To make the stuffing, in a heavy frying pan over medium-low heat, warm the olive oil. Add the onion and sauté until it begins to caramelise, about 12 minutes. Add the garlic and sauté for 1 minute. Add the meat and sauté, breaking it up, until it changes colour, just a few minutes. Add the salt, pepper, chillies, coriander, tomato paste and reserved chopped squid and sauté for 2 minutes. Remove from the heat and set aside to cool.

Spoon the cooled mixture into the squid bodies; do not pack too tightly or the squid will be too heavy. Secure the tops closed with toothpicks. Pat dry with paper towels.

In a wide, heavy saucepan over medium heat, warm the olive oil. Working in batches, add the squid in a single layer and sauté, turning, until golden all over. When all the squid have been sautéed, add the stock, cover and simmer until the squid are just cooked, about 5 minutes.

Using a slotted spoon, remove the squid from the stock and place in a serving dish. Remove the toothpicks and garnish with the lemon halves and coriander sprigs.

SERVES 6

VICTORIA

Steamed Chilli Mussels

Black mussels are farmed in Victoria, Tasmania and Western Australia. They are the most flavoursome of all the mussels and should be used in this dish, although other flavoursome mussels can also be used.

1 kg (2 lb) black mussels, scrubbed and debearded
2 tablespoons safflower oil
4 spring (green) onions, white part only, sliced
1 clove garlic, finely chopped
4 fresh red chillies, seeded and sliced
2 teaspoons finely chopped coriander (cilantro) root (see glossary)

2 teaspoons grated galangal (see glossary)
1 piece lemongrass, 4 cm (1½ in) long, thinly sliced (see glossary)
finely grated zest of 1 small lime
2 teaspoons shrimp paste (see glossary)
180 ml (6 fl oz/¾ cup) coconut cream (see glossary)
1 large egg, lightly beaten
2 tablespoons rice flour (see glossary)
salt and freshly ground pepper
fresh basil leaves, as needed

Clockwise from top right: Chilli Fish Stir-Fry (recipe page 96), Steamed Chilli Mussels, Stuffed Squid—photographed at Cremorne Point, Sydney Harbour

❧ Rinse the mussels in salted cold water. Arrange on a steamer rack over boiling water, cover and steam until they open, 5–10 minutes. Discard any mussels that do not open. Remove the mussels from their shells and place in a bowl. Reserve half of the shells, selecting the largest ones.

❧ In a wok or large frying pan over medium heat, warm the oil. Add the spring onions and garlic and stir-fry until soft, 3–4 minutes. Add the chillies, coriander root, galangal, lemongrass, lime zest and shrimp paste and stir-fry until the mixture is aromatic, about 3 minutes. Transfer to a bowl.

❧ Add the coconut cream, egg, rice flour and salt and pepper to taste to the onion mixture and stir until thoroughly mixed.

❧ Bring a small saucepan three-quarters full of water to a boil. Immerse the basil leaves for 30 seconds; drain well. Place 1 or 2 leaves in the bottom of each retained half shell. Place 2 mussels in each shell and spoon a little of the onion mixture on top of each. Arrange on a shallow dish and place on a steamer rack over gently boiling water. Cover and steam until heated through, 4–5 minutes. Serve immediately.

SERVES 6

99

Top to bottom: Lobster Tagliolini with Purple Basil, Barramundi in Fresh Green Herb Sauce, Scallop Mousse—photographed at Gwinganna estate, Queensland

TASMANIA

SCALLOP MOUSSE

The population of the classic Tassie scallop is a fluctuating one. Found in the waters of Victoria and Tasmania, the scallops were almost fished out in the 1980s, but now stocks are building up and we are reaping the benefits. Sea scallops are also available in good quantities. Beware of scallops that have been frozen, as they hold a lot of water even after thawing and will ruin this delicate mousse. Use an Australian white wine vinegar, if possible.

FOR THE MOUSSE:

375 g (¾ lb) scallops
salt and freshly ground pepper
1 whole egg plus 1 egg white
500 ml (16 fl oz/2 cups) thickened (double/heavy) cream

FOR THE SAUCE:

2 shallots, finely chopped
1 tablespoon peppercorns
200 ml (6½ fl oz/¾ cup plus 1½ tablespoons) dry white wine
2 teaspoons white wine vinegar
1 tablespoon thickened (double/heavy) cream
200 g (7 oz/¾ cup plus 2 tablespoons) unsalted butter, cut
    into 8 pieces
cayenne pepper
salt

❧ To make the mousse, place the scallops in a food processor fitted with the metal blade or in a blender and process to a smooth purée. Add salt and pepper to taste, the whole egg and the egg white and process for 1 minute. The mixture should be smooth. Transfer to a bowl, cover and refrigerate until firm, about 30 minutes.

❧ Preheat an oven to 180°C (350°F). Spray ten 100-ml (3½-fl oz) moulds (*oeuf en gelée* moulds work well) with nonstick cooking spray.

❧ Return the firmed-up scallop mixture to the food processor or blender and add the cream. Process for 5 seconds. Transfer to the moulds, filling each three-quarters full. Cover the moulds with aluminium foil and place in a large baking pan. Pour hot water into the pan to reach halfway up the sides of the moulds. Bake until just set, about 25 minutes.

❧ Meanwhile, make the sauce. Place the shallots, peppercorns, white wine and vinegar in a saucepan and cook over medium heat until reduced to 2 tablespoons, about 5 minutes. Strain through a fine-mesh sieve into a clean pan. Add the cream and cook over medium heat for 1 minute. Reduce the heat to low and add the butter, 1 piece at a time, whisking until it melts before adding the next piece. Do not allow the sauce to boil. Season to taste with cayenne and salt.

❧ To serve, ladle the sauce onto warmed individual plates. Run a thin-bladed knife around the edge of each mousse, invert onto a plate and shake gently to ease the mousse out. Serve at once.

SERVES 10

HAYMAN ISLAND

LOBSTER TAGLIOLINI WITH PURPLE BASIL

Small quantities of tropical lobster are caught in the warm waters off Hayman Island in Queensland. Chefs at Hayman Island Resort prepare the tail flesh with fresh pasta with delicious results.

salt
400 g (13 oz) fresh tagliolini or other thin fresh pasta
100 ml (3½ fl oz/6½ tablespoons) olive oil
2 small cloves garlic, finely chopped
1 or 2 fresh red chillies, seeded and finely chopped
4 fresh purple basil leaves, torn

3 canned tomatoes, roughly chopped
1 kg (2 lb) green (raw) lobster tails, shelled and flesh cut into
    bite-sized pieces
3 tablespoons dry white wine
freshly ground pepper
leaves from 2 fresh purple basil sprigs, finely chopped

❧ Bring a large pan three-quarters full of water to a boil. Salt it lightly and add the pasta. Cook, stirring to prevent sticking, until al dente, 1–2 minutes. Drain and refresh in a bowl of cold water.
❧ In a heavy pan over medium-low heat, heat 1 tablespoon of the oil. Add the garlic, chillies and torn basil leaves and sauté gently until softened, about 2 minutes. Add the tomatoes and simmer until a good sauce consistency forms, about 15 minutes. Set aside.
❧ In another large, heavy pan over medium heat, warm the remaining oil. When the oil is hot, add the lobster and sauté for 3 minutes. Add the wine and the reserved tomato mixture and cook until a good consistency forms, about 3 minutes. Season to taste with salt and pepper.
❧ Drain the pasta and shake well to remove any excess water. Add to the pan holding the lobster and cook over medium-high heat until heated through. Transfer to a warmed serving dish and add the chopped basil. Toss well and serve at once.

SERVES 6

WESTERN AUSTRALIA

BARRAMUNDI IN FRESH GREEN HERB SAUCE

Barramundi, or barra as it is known in Far North Queensland, is farmed in warm brackish bore water all over Australia, except in Tasmania. The plate-sized barramundi, which the Far North Queensland restaurateurs love, lacks the flavour of its large wild relative because it is young and has no fat. A steak or fillet off a large fish is full of flavour and has a marvellous texture. Barramundi is a soft-fleshed fish, so treat it carefully.

FOR THE HERB SAUCE:

1 shallot, finely chopped
80 ml (3 fl oz/⅓ cup) dry white wine
salt
leaves from ½ bunch fresh curly-leaf parsley
leaves from ½ bunch watercress
½ bunch fresh chives
125 g (4 oz/½ cup) sour cream
2 tablespoons unsalted butter, cut into 4 pieces
freshly ground pepper

1.25 kg (2½ lb) barramundi
salt and freshly ground pepper
2 tablespoons olive oil

❧ To make the sauce, combine the shallot and wine in a small saucepan and boil over high heat until reduced to 1 tablespoon. Strain into a blender. Finish the sauce after cooking the fish.
❧ Cut the barramundi into 4 fillets each about 10 by 15 cm (4 by 6 in) and 2.5 cm (1 in) thick. Season the fillets lightly with salt and pepper. Brush a nonstick pan with the olive oil and place over medium heat. When the pan is hot, pan-fry the fillets, turning once, until they are beginning to brown and the centres are just cooked, about 4 minutes on the first side and 3–4 minutes on the second. Remove from the heat and keep warm.
❧ Return to the sauce. Bring a large pot three-quarters full of water to a boil and salt lightly. Immerse the parsley, watercress and chives in the water for 1 minute. Drain well and refresh in ice water. Drain again and wring out any remaining water by hand. Drop the herbs into the blender holding the reduced wine mixture and chop finely. In a small saucepan, heat the sour cream to just below the boiling point and pour it over the herbs. Blend until smooth. With the motor running, add the

butter pieces, one at a time, and blend until smooth. Stir in salt and pepper to taste.
❧ Ladle the sauce onto 4 large flat plates. Place the barramundi fillets on top and serve at once.

SERVES 4

NORTHERN TERRITORY

STIR-FRIED CHILLI MUD CRAB

Mud crabs are essentially from Queensland, the Northern Territory and northern New South Wales. They are sold live, with their claws bound so they cannot cause any harm. I believe it is kinder to put them quietly to sleep in the freezer before chopping and cooking. This recipe can also be offered as a starter, in which case it will serve four.

1 kg (2 lb) live mud crab or other large crab
1 tablespoon safflower oil
3 or 4 small fresh red chillies
2 cloves garlic, finely chopped
1 gingerroot slice, about ½ cm (¼ in) thick
250 ml (8 fl oz/1 cup) fish stock (see glossary)
6 spring (green) onions, white part only, chopped
4 fresh coriander (cilantro) sprigs

❧ Place the mud crab in a freezer for 30–40 minutes, to kill it. Pull off the top shell of the crab and discard. Remove and discard the tail portion, gills and spongy organs. Twist off the legs and claws and crack them. Cut the body into serving-sized pieces.
❧ In a wok or large frying pan over medium-high heat, warm the oil. When the oil is hot, add the crab pieces, chillies, garlic and gingerroot and stir-fry until the crab pieces turn bright red, 4–5 minutes. Add the stock and bring to a boil. Add the onions and stir-fry until wilted, about 2 minutes.
❧ Transfer to a warmed platter. Garnish with the coriander sprigs and serve at once.

SERVES 2

Stir-Fried Chilli Mud Crab—photographed at Pittwater, Sydney

Billy-Boiled Yabbies with Tomato Mayonnaise—photographed at Berry, on the south coast, NSW

BILLY-BOILED YABBIES WITH TOMATO MAYONNAISE

Restaurateur-turned-potter Anders Ousback and restaurateur Michael McMahon had fresh farmed Western Australian yabbies flown into famed vintner Len Evans's birthday gathering at his estate in the lower Hunter Valley a couple of years ago. The yabbies were cooked this way in the vineyard by Anders and Michael. Everyone sat on hay bales beside the dam, pulling yabby tails from the shells and dipping them in this excellent mayonnaise. Anders insists that the triple-refined Australian peanut oil made by Chefol is the only one to use for this dish.

FOR THE TOMATO MAYONNAISE:

4 egg yolks
½ teaspoon salt, plus salt to taste
500 ml (16 fl oz/2 cups) peanut oil
2–3 teaspoons fresh lemon juice
2 teaspoons Dijon mustard
75 ml (2½ fl oz/5 tablespoons) fresh tomato purée (paste)
freshly ground pepper

3 kg (6 lb) live yabbies (crayfish)

◊ To make the court bouillon, place all the ingredients in a large billy can. Add cold water to cover by 25 cm (10 in) and bring slowly to a boil. Reduce the heat and simmer for 30 minutes.
◊ Meanwhile, to make the mayonnaise, in a food processor fitted with the metal blade or in a blender, combine the egg yolks and the ½ teaspoon salt. Process until thick. With the motor running, add the oil, drop by drop, until half of it has been used. Then, while continuing to process, add the remaining oil in a thin, steady stream until a thick mayonnaiselike consistency forms. Add the lemon juice, mustard and tomato purée and season to taste with salt and pepper.
◊ Add the yabbies to the simmering bouillon, stir and cook until they change colour, 4–5 minutes. Using a large slotted spoon, scoop out the yabbies and pile them on a large platter. Serve the yabbies warm or cold with the tomato mayonnaise.

SERVES 6

ADELAIDE

TOMMY RUFFS WRAPPED IN VINE LEAVES WITH TAPENADE

Tommy ruffs are plentiful in South Australia and Western Australia. Gordon Parkes, an Adelaide chef, loves using this South Australian fish. He gets the vine leaves for this recipe from the Adelaide Hills vineyard of his friend, Michael Hill Smith.

FOR THE *TAPENADE:*

3 cloves garlic
60 ml (2 fl oz/¼ cup) virgin olive oil, or more as needed
100 g (3½ oz/¾ cup) pitted black olives
2 anchovy fillets, drained
salt and freshly ground pepper

12 grape leaves, preferably fresh and young
12 tommy ruffs or tailor (bluefish), filleted

◊ Prepare a fire in a barbecue or preheat a griller (broiler) on high.
◊ To make the *tapenade,* combine all the ingredients, including salt and pepper to taste, in a blender or in a food processor fitted with the metal blade. Process until smooth. Add more oil, if necessary, to achieve a spreadable consistency.
◊ Bring a saucepan three-quarters full of water to a boil. Add the grape leaves, boil for 30 seconds and drain. Refresh the leaves in cold water and drain again. Pat dry with paper towels. (If using brined grape leaves, simply rinse and pat dry.)
◊ Spread the grape leaves, shiny side down, on a work surface. Season the fillets with salt and pepper and place 1 fillet from each fish on each leaf. Spread the fillet with *tapenade* and top with the other fillet of the fish. Wrap each fish in the grape leaf and secure the leaf in place with a toothpick.
◊ Place the fish packets on a barbecue rack or on a griller tray and barbecue or grill (broil) very quickly, 4–5 minutes; the timing will depend on the size of the fish.
◊ Place the fish packets on plates and serve.

SERVES 6   *Photograph page 105*

FOR THE COURT BOUILLON:

1 carrot, peeled and finely chopped
½ brown onion, finely chopped
1 celery stalk, finely chopped
3 fresh parsley sprigs, bruised
3 eucalypt leaves
9 peppercorns

SYDNEY

Scallops with Witlof and Roquefort

Damien Pignolet is one of the most highly regarded chefs and successful restaurateurs in Australia. Here is one of his especially interesting and easy bistro dishes. It has a fine balance of flavours among the richness of the scallops, the bitterness of the endive and the intensity of the roquefort.

20 hazelnuts (filberts)

FOR THE VINAIGRETTE:

80 ml (3 fl oz/⅓ cup) hazelnut oil
2½ tablespoons olive oil
½ clove garlic crushed with a little salt
1–1½ tablespoons cider vinegar
salt and freshly ground pepper

olive oil
3–4 heads witlof (chicory/Belgian endive)
750 g (1½ lb) sea scallops
salt and freshly ground pepper
180–200 g (6–6½ oz) roquefort cheese, crumbled

❧ Preheat an oven to 200°C (400°F). Spread the hazelnuts in a shallow pan and place in the oven. Toast until the skins begin to flake, about 12 minutes. Remove from the oven and place the still-warm nuts in a kitchen towel. Rub vigorously to remove the skins. Then return the nuts to the pan and place in the oven once again. Toast until lightly browned, about 3–4 minutes. Remove from the oven and chop coarsely; set aside.
❧ To make the vinaigrette, combine all the ingredients, including salt and pepper to taste, in a good-sized glass bowl and whisk to blend well.
❧ Heat a heavy frying pan over high heat and drizzle it with oil. Reduce the heat to low. (This step seasons the pan and prevents the scallops from sticking.)
❧ While the pan is heating, remove the bitter core from each witlof and carefully remove the leaves. Divide the leaves evenly among 6 flat plates, arranging them in a single layer.
❧ Increase the heat to high and place the scallops in the pan. Sear on the first side for about 1 minute. Turn and sear on the second side for 1 minute longer, or until cooked through.
❧ Season the scallops with salt and pepper and transfer to the vinaigrette. Toss well. Using a slotted spoon, remove the scallops from the vinaigrette, reserving the vinaigrette, and arrange them on the witlof leaves.
❧ Top each serving with a heaped spoonful of the roquefort and some of the hazelnuts. Drizzle the vinaigrette over the witlof. Serve at once.

SERVES 6

SYDNEY

Fish in Coconut Milk

Charmaine Solomon, Australia's best-known Asian food writer and a highly successful cookbook author, says that it is now easy to cook authentic Asian food in Western kitchens in Australia. The influx of Asian refugees to Australia in the mid-1980s brought a dramatic change in our markets, so that now we can buy, in the capital cities at least, practically any ingredient needed to cook good Asian food. This recipe, she says, is an everyday dish that children and adults alike enjoy. Ling (cod) is the ideal fish to use, as it has firm flesh and is available year-round. Red snapper can also be used. Serve the dish with steamed rice.

4 firm white fish fillets or steaks, about 125 g (4 oz) each (see note)
½ teaspoon ground turmeric
1 teaspoon salt, plus salt to taste
1 tablespoon *ghee* (see glossary) or vegetable oil
1 brown onion, thinly sliced
2 cloves garlic, finely chopped
1 teaspoon finely chopped, peeled gingerroot
2 fresh curry leaf sprigs or 12 dried curry leaves (see glossary)
3 fresh green chillies, seeded but left whole
400 ml (13 fl oz/1⅔ cups) coconut milk (see glossary)
fresh lime or lemon juice

❧ Pat the fish dry with paper towels, then rub with the turmeric and the 1 teaspoon salt.

Left to right: Salmon with Citrus Sauce, Scallops with Witlof and Roquefort—photographed at Huskisson Harbour, NSW

Clockwise from top: Thai Marinated Fish (recipe page 108), Tommy Ruffs Wrapped in Vine Leaves with Tapenade (recipe page 103), Fish in Coconut Milk

In a saucepan over medium heat, warm the ghee or oil. Add the onion, garlic, gingerroot, curry leaves and chillies and sauté until the onions are soft and golden, about 10 minutes.

Divide the coconut milk in half. Dilute half of it with an equal amount of water and add to the pan holding the onions. Stir as it comes to a simmer.

Add the fish, bring back to a simmer and cook, uncovered, over medium heat until the fish is cooked through, about 10 minutes. Add the remaining undiluted coconut milk, heat through and remove from the heat.

Add the lime or lemon juice and salt to taste. Serve at once.

SERVES 4

T A S M A N I A

SALMON WITH CITRUS SAUCE

Belinda Jeffery gave me this recipe. She particularly likes it because the acidity of the sauce is a good counterpoint to the richness of the salmon. She uses Tasmanian salmon, which is farmed off the southeastern coast in cold unpolluted waters. A lemonade fruit is a cross between a lime and a tangelo.

FOR THE CITRUS SAUCE:

125 ml (4 fl oz/½ cup) fresh orange juice, plus 2–3 tablespoons fresh orange juice, if needed
1 teaspoon finely chopped, peeled gingerroot
1 spring (green) onion, white part only, finely chopped
1 teaspoon light soy sauce
2 tablespoons fresh lemon juice
½–1 teaspoon Asian sesame oil (see glossary)
125 ml (4 fl oz/½ cup) light olive oil
1 teaspoon honey

1 teaspoon white wine vinegar
1 teaspoon drained pink or green peppercorns
salt and freshly ground black pepper

FOR THE GARNISH:

2 oranges
1 or 2 limes or lemonade fruits
1 grapefruit

FOR THE SALMON:

4 salmon fillets with skin intact or salmon steaks, 200 g (6½ oz) each
1 tablespoon fresh lemon juice

To make the sauce, place the 125 ml (4 fl oz/½ cup) orange juice in a small saucepan and bring to a boil. Boil until reduced to 2 tablespoons; set aside. In a bowl, whisk together the gingerroot, onion, soy sauce, lemon juice, sesame oil, olive oil, honey, vinegar and peppercorns. Add the reduced orange juice and season to taste with salt and pepper. The sauce should be acidic. Taste and add more orange juice, if needed. Set aside. Preheat an oven to 200°C (400°F).

To make the garnish, cut the zest from 1 orange into fine slivers. Bring a small saucepan filled with water to a boil, add the slivered zest and boil for 1 minute. Drain and set aside. Peel both oranges, the limes or lemonade fruits and the grapefruit; make sure no white pith remains. Working with 1 piece of fruit at a time, hold it over a bowl and cut between the membranes to release the segments into the bowl.

To cook the salmon, place it, skin side down if using fillets, in a lightly oiled, heavy baking dish. Drizzle with the lemon juice and cover tightly with aluminium foil. Bake until just tender, 8–10 minutes. Remember, the fish will continue to cook a little once it is removed from the oven. Transfer the salmon to warmed flat plates. Drizzle with the sauce and scatter the citrus fruits and zest over the top. Serve at once.

SERVES 4

BARBECUED OCTOPUS

I can remember when octopus and almost every other creature from the deep was used only for bait. But now Australians, thanks to our Mediterranean immigrants, cannot get enough of them. Octopuses are by-products of trawling and are available year-round. The best coriander roots are sold in shops in Asian neighbourhoods, where the Asian market gardeners are supplying a species that has a large, plump root. This Asian-inspired recipe makes an excellent starter to an Asian or a Western meal.

1 kg (2 lb) baby octopuses

FOR THE SAUCE:

4 large cloves garlic, finely chopped
4 large coriander (cilantro) roots, finely chopped (see glossary)
1 tablespoon fish sauce (see glossary)
3–4 tablespoons fresh lime juice
sugar

3–4 tablespoons soy sauce

❧ Prepare a fire in a barbecue. Meanwhile, cut off the head of each octopus and remove and discard the beak and guts. Rub off the purplish skin, if desired, then rinse well.
❧ To make the sauce, place the garlic and coriander roots in a mortar and pound with a pestle until a paste forms. Add the fish sauce and stir in the lime juice and sugar to taste. Set aside.
❧ Brush the octopus with the soy sauce. Arrange the octopuses in a single layer on the barbecue rack and cook, turning often, until they are beginning to brown on all sides, 4–6 minutes; the time will depend upon the size of the octopuses.
❧ Transfer to a large bowl and spoon the sauce over the top. Serve hot or at room temperature.

SERVES 6

BAKED RED SNAPPER WITH TOMATOES, CAPSICUMS AND PURPLE ONIONS

Captain Cook named red snapper in his logbook upon catching it off Cape Capricorn in Queensland. He had seen a similar species in America, where there is a family of snappers resembling those found in Australia. The same fish is called pink snapper in Western Australia.

1 kg (2 lb) red snapper fillets, with skin intact
salt and freshly ground pepper
100 ml (3½ fl oz/6½ tablespoons) olive oil
2 purple onions, cut into slices 1 cm (⅜ in) thick
1 red capsicum (bell pepper), seeded and sliced lengthwise
1 yellow capsicum (bell pepper), seeded and sliced lengthwise
1 clove garlic, finely chopped
6 firm tomatoes, peeled, seeded and cut into long strips 1 cm (⅜ in) wide
3 tablespoons chopped fresh parsley
leaves from 4 fresh basil sprigs, finely shredded
juice of 1 lemon

❧ Position a rack in the centre of an oven and preheat the oven to 200°C (400°F).
❧ Season the snapper fillets generously with salt and pepper. Set aside. In a large, heavy frying pan over medium heat, heat half of the olive oil. Add the onions and sauté until softened, about 10 minutes.
❧ Add the capsicums to the pan and sauté over medium heat for 5 minutes. Reduce the heat to low and add the garlic and tomatoes. Cover and cook for 5 minutes. Stir in the parsley and basil. Taste and adjust the seasonings. Keep warm over low heat.
❧ Brush the fish fillets with the remaining olive oil and place in a single layer in a baking dish. Place in the centre of the oven and bake until just cooked through but still firm, 10–12 minutes. The cooking time will depend upon the thickness of the fillets.
❧ To serve, arrange the fillets on a warmed oval serving dish. Spoon the warm vegetable mixture over the top, sprinkle with the lemon juice and serve immediately.

SERVES 6

RAGOUT OF SHELLFISH

Diane Holuigue is a food writer and owns one of Australia's best-known and oldest cooking schools. This is her Australian version of a French shellfish ragout, and it makes a lovely first course. School prawns are caught in New South Wales and as far north as Noosa Heads on the Sunshine Coast in Queensland. They are almost always trawled and are occasionally caught in pocket nets. For the larger prawns in this dish, be sure to use medium-sized prawns and not large ones. When preparing the julienned vegetables, put together a colourful combination.

12 black mussels, well scrubbed and debearded
500–600 ml (16–18 fl oz/2–2¼ cups) medium-strength fish stock (see glossary)
4 tablespoons julienned mixed vegetables such as carrots, leeks, turnips, green beans and/or snow peas (mangetouts) and celery
18 scallops
6 medium-sized green (raw) prawns (shrimp), peeled and deveined
12 live yabbies or 6 Moreton Bay or Balmain bugs (crayfish)
18 green (raw) tiny school prawns (shrimp)
12 oysters, well scrubbed
1½–2 tablespoons unsalted butter
salt and freshly ground pepper
2 tablespoons finely chopped fresh parsley

❧ Put the mussels in a pot, cover and place over medium-high heat, shaking the pan periodically, until they open, 5–10 minutes. Discard any mussels that do not open.
❧ Pour the fish stock into a large saucepan and bring to a boil. Add the julienned vegetables and boil them until they soften. If you are using leek, add it last, as it softens quickly. Add the seafood, starting with the scallops and followed by the medium-sized prawns, yabbies or bugs and school prawns. (If you have bought the yabbies, bugs, prawns and so on precooked rather than raw, they need to go in only long enough to reheat.) Add the oysters, which need only to be heated so that they open, and the precooked mussels last.
❧ When all the seafood is cooked and piping hot, lift it out with a slotted spoon and distribute it among 6 wide soup bowls. Reduce the fish stock over high heat until you have about 310–375 ml (10–12 fl oz/1¼–1½ cups). If you fear this will take so long that the seafood will cool, keep the seafood together in a single covered bowl while you reduce the stock. You can also discard a little of the stock before starting to reduce it, to hasten the process.
❧ Stir the butter into the reduced stock to enrich it. Season to taste with salt and pepper and spoon over the seafood. It will be fairly soupy, but taste strongly of fish. Garnish with the parsley and serve.

SERVES 6

Clockwise from top: Barbecued Octopus, Baked Red Snapper with Tomatoes, Capsicums and Purple Onions, Ragout of Shellfish—photographed at Pittwater, Sydney

GRILLED TUNA ON LENTILS WITH SPICY TOMATO VINAIGRETTE

The best tuna can be categorised in this order: big eye, bluefin and yellowfin running third. It is available year-round, coming mainly from New South Wales. If you buy sashimi-quality tuna, you pay a little more, but it is worth the cost as there is no waste.

FOR THE LENTILS:

2 tablespoons olive oil
2 tablespoons finely chopped brown onion
2 tablespoons finely chopped carrot
2 tablespoons finely chopped celery
250 g (8 oz/1 cup) green lentils, picked over and rinsed

FOR THE VINAIGRETTE:

sea salt and freshly ground pepper
1 tablespoon red wine vinegar
½ teaspoon red chilli flakes
100 ml (3½ fl oz/6½ tablespoons) extra-virgin olive oil
2 ripe tomatoes, peeled, seeded and cut into small dice

2 tablespoons olive oil
4 tuna steaks, about 200 g (6½ oz) each
sea salt and freshly ground pepper

❧ To prepare the lentils, in a heavy saucepan over medium heat, warm the oil. Add the onion, carrot and celery and sauté until softened, about 5 minutes. Add the lentils and water to cover by about 7.5 cm (3 in). Bring to a boil, reduce the heat to medium and simmer, uncovered, until tender, about 25 minutes. Drain and keep warm. Preheat a griller (broiler) on high.
❧ To make the vinaigrette, in a small bowl, whisk together salt and pepper to taste and the vinegar, red chilli flakes and oil. Fold in the tomato and set aside.
❧ To cook the tuna, brush the griller rack with some of the oil and then place the tuna on the rack. Brush the remaining oil on

Top to bottom: Grilled Tuna on Lentils with Spicy Tomato Vinaigrette, Steamed Red Emperor with Ginger, Onions and Kaffir Lime Leaves

the tuna. Grill the tuna, turning once, 2–4 minutes on each side or until done the way you like it. I like it well sealed on both sides but still rare in the centre. Season to taste with salt and pepper.
❧ To serve, spoon the lentils onto 4 warmed flat plates. Place the tuna on top, spoon on the sauce and serve at once.

SERVES 4

STEAMED RED EMPEROR WITH GINGER, ONIONS AND KAFFIR LIME LEAVES

Red emperor, from the Barrier Reef in Queensland, is a joy to cook. The subtle flavours of ginger, spring onions and kaffir lime leaves complement its delicate flavour. Other firm-fleshed saltwater fish can be substituted. Here is a fabulous dish for people watching their weight and cholesterol level.

2 teaspoons vegetable oil
1 red emperor, about 2.5 kg (5 lb), cleaned
10 spring (green) onions, including tender green tops, cut into 4-cm (1½-in) lengths
1 piece gingerroot, 25 g (¾ oz), peeled and cut into fine julienne
6 fresh kaffir lime leaves, torn (see glossary)

❧ Brush a steamer rack with the oil. Place the fish on the rack. (If you do not have a steamer large enough for the whole fish, cut off the head and tail.) Place over the steamer pan filled with water to a depth of 3–4 cm (1¼–1½ in). Scatter the spring onions, gingerroot and lime leaves over the fish. Cover and bring to a boil. Reduce the heat to medium and steam until the fish is just cooked, about 30 minutes. Test that the fish is done by inserting a knife into the flesh behind the head, the thickest part.
❧ Lift the fish onto a warmed platter and serve at once.

SERVES 8

THAI MARINATED FISH

Ocean trout is rainbow trout raised in salt water. It is farmed in the cold waters of Bruny Island off southern Tasmania. In this dish, called yam pla *in Thai, the trout is complemented by a bouquet of Asian ingredients.*

750 g (1½ lb) ocean trout fillets
125 ml (4 fl oz/½ cup) fresh lime juice
2 tablespoons green peppercorns in brine, rinsed, drained and crushed
1 teaspoon finely chopped fresh green chilli
1 large clove garlic, finely chopped
½ teaspoon grated, peeled gingerroot
3 lemongrass stalks, tender part only, thinly sliced (see glossary)
2 tablespoons fish sauce (see glossary)
250 ml (8 fl oz/1 cup) coconut milk (see glossary)
leaves from ½ bunch fresh mint, finely shredded
leaves from ¼ bunch coriander (cilantro), finely chopped

❧ Cut the fish into thin slices on the diagonal and against the grain. Place in a shallow nonreactive dish. Pour the lime juice evenly over the top. In a mixing bowl, combine the peppercorns, chilli, garlic, gingerroot and lemongrass. Add to the fish and toss gently to mix. Cover with plastic wrap and refrigerate for at least 4 hours or as long as overnight.
❧ Just before serving, add the fish sauce, coconut milk, mint and coriander. Stir gently and serve.

SERVES 4–6   *Photograph page 105*

Top to bottom: Ling and Mango Curry, Yabbies with Garlic and Ginger Butter—photographed at Bondi, Sydney

QUEENSLAND

LING AND MANGO CURRY

I make this with ling, which keeps its shape beautifully. Other firm-fleshed fish, such as blue-eye cod or jewfish, can be substituted. Wait for when mangoes are in full season and choose those that are highly perfumed yet still firm. Thai pickled green peppercorns are available in cans in Asian markets. This recipe should be made 2–3 days in advance of serving to allow the flavours to intensify. Serve with steamed long-grain white rice.

2 tablespoons vegetable oil
1 tablespoon red curry paste (see glossary)
1 red capsicum (bell pepper), seeded and cut into long, narrow strips
1 tablespoon fish sauce (see glossary)
500 ml (16 fl oz/2 cups) coconut cream (see glossary)
500 g (1 lb) ling (cod) or other firm-fleshed fish fillets, cut into 3-cm (1¼-in) dice
750 g (1½ lb) mangoes, peeled, pitted and sliced
1 teaspoon Thai pickled green peppercorns
2 limes, halved

❧ In a heavy saucepan over medium heat, warm the oil. Add the curry paste and sauté until aromatic, about 3 minutes. Add the capsicum and sauté until softened, 3–4 minutes.
❧ Add the fish sauce and coconut cream and simmer over medium heat until reduced and thickened a little, about 5 minutes.
❧ Add the fish and simmer over medium heat for 4 minutes. Add the mango slices and peppercorns and simmer until the fish is just cooked, 1–2 minutes.
❧ Remove from the heat, let cool, cover and refrigerate for 2–3 days to gather flavour.
❧ To serve, reheat gently. Serve with the lime halves.

SERVES 4–6

WESTERN AUSTRALIA

YABBIES WITH GARLIC AND GINGER BUTTER

Stir-frying is becoming one of the most popular ways to prepare good fresh ingredients, especially when you are short of time.

60 g (2 oz/¼ cup) unsalted butter
about 5 tablespoons olive oil
4 cloves garlic, finely chopped
1 tablespoon grated, peeled gingerroot
2 kg (4 lb) green (raw) yabbies (crayfish), heads discarded
salt and freshly ground pepper
3 celery stalks, julienned
2 carrots, peeled and julienned
4 Roma (plum) tomatoes, diced
3 zucchini (courgettes), julienned

❧ In a large nonstick frying pan over medium-high heat, melt half of the butter with 1–1½ tablespoons of the oil. Add the garlic and gingerroot and stir-fry for 1 minute. Add half of the yabbies and stir-fry until the colour changes and the flesh is opaque, 4–5 minutes. Season to taste with salt and pepper. Using tongs, lift out the yabbies and keep warm in a bowl. Add the remaining butter and 1–1½ tablespoons of the oil to the pan. When sizzling hot, add the remaining yabbies and cook in the same way. Transfer to the bowl holding the yabbies.
❧ Reheat the pan juices over medium-high heat. Add the remaining 2 tablespoons olive oil (if not using a nonstick pan, you will probably require more oil). When the oil is sizzling, add the celery, carrots, tomatoes and zucchini and stir-fry until just tender, about 4 minutes. Season to taste with salt and pepper.
❧ To serve, pile the vegetables on 4 warmed individual plates. Top with the yabbies and serve at once.

SERVES 4

109

SOUTH AUSTRALIA

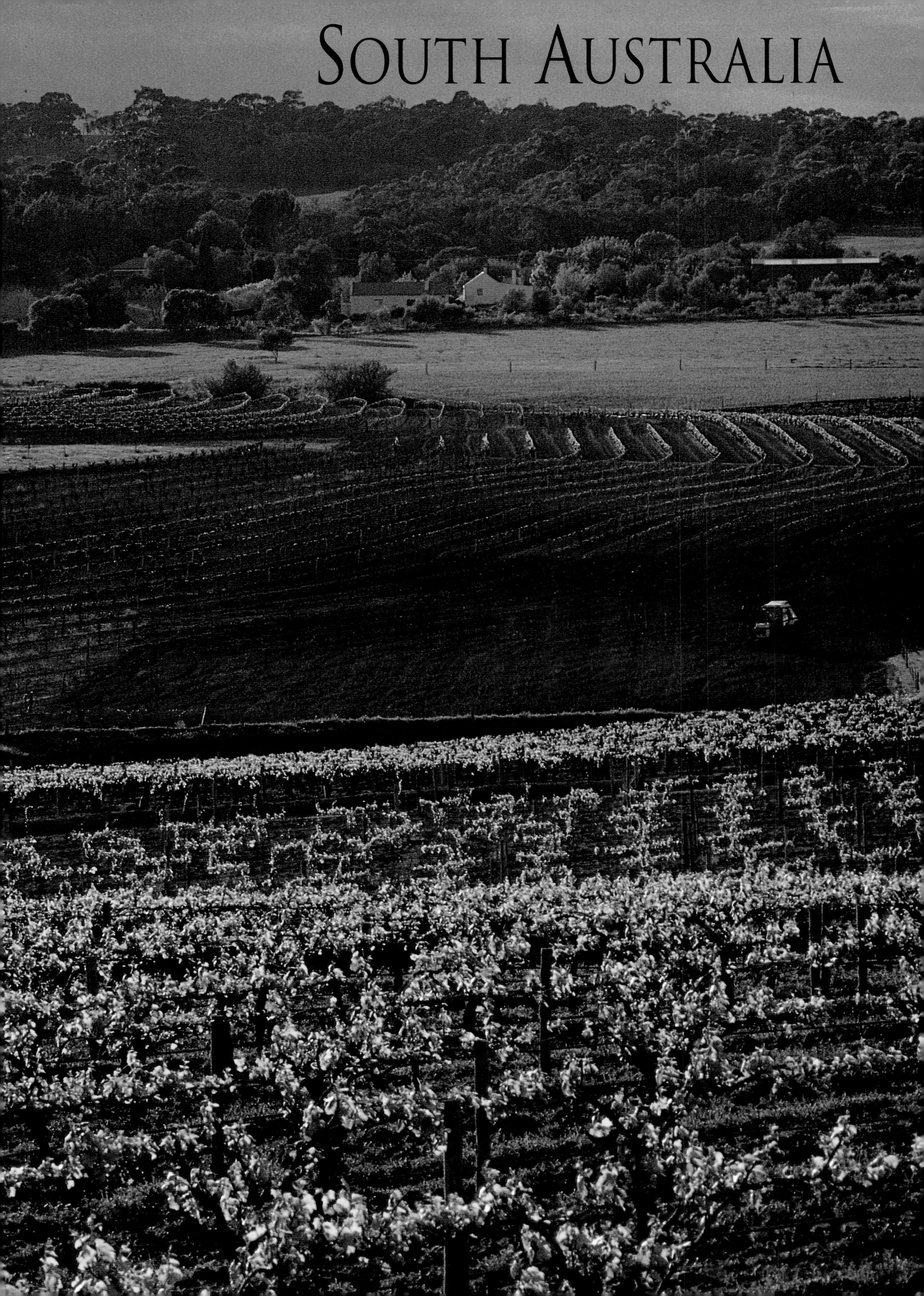

SOUTH AUSTRALIA

M E D I T E R R A N E A N
A B U N D A N C E

Wild olive trees are dotted here and there along the roadside, looking at first like eucalypts with their shimmering, silvery leaves. Behind them stand vineyards, and then small towns, spaced at walking distance from one another. Both offer a clue to the area's European heritage.

The distinctive church spires give it away: this is the Barossa, a valley thirty-two kilometres (nineteen miles) long and eight kilometres (five miles) wide that lies to the north of Adelaide. Of any area in Australia, the Barossa Valley has the strongest regional identity, and this is particularly reflected in its food.

Settled 150 years ago by a German-speaking Lutheran community from Silesia in Prussia that was escaping religious persecution, the valley has a sense of regionalism that is due to this 'German' heritage. Aided financially by early pioneer George Fife Angas (for whom the local town Angaston is named), these Lutherans began arriving in 1838 and brought with them northern European food traditions. Such early settlements as Hanhdorf supplied Adelaide with vegetables and dairy products, making it self-sufficient for the first time. By 1861, there were nearly nine thousand German settlers in the colony.

Australia as a whole has much to thank them for. They were responsible for some of the earliest vine plantings, and thus the development of the wine industry in the Barossa (and later the establishment of the vineyards in the Clare Valley as well). Families like Seppelt, Gramp and, later, Henschke and Lehmann gave their names to the famous wines of the region. Even the small, but sweet and juicy Corella pears originate from seedlings brought by these Silesian settlers to the Barossa in the last century.

Previous pages: The vineyards of South Australia account for nearly half of the country's entire wine production. Left: A picturesque stone building serves as the tasting room of the Rockford Winery in the Barossa Valley.

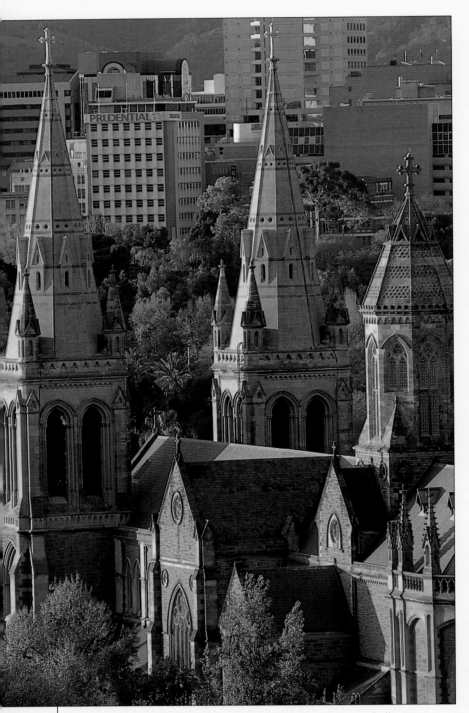

St Peter's Cathedral, with its twin spires and its sonorous bells, is a well-known Adelaide landmark.

By the 1950s, there were more than twenty thousand descendants of these Lutherans in the Barossa.

The original settlers were farmers who mixed livestock and horticulture, and that blend continues to permeate the local culture. Today, as in the past, some people kill their own pigs to make sausages, and almost every farm has its own small orchard. Because they have maintained the culinary traditions of their forebears, within the homes there is a regional cuisine based on northern European dishes adapted to local products.

Simply put, the Barossa exemplifies the best of everything that is local and regional. Its culinary reputation is helped by the efforts of local chefs like former restaurateur Maggie Beer, whose dedication to regional ingredients at her restaurant, The Pheasant Farm, saw the valley receive a well-deserved broader recognition.

The rich variety of produce grown locally is exceptional. Besides grapes and other fruits like figs, olives and quinces, there's a wide variety of game, including wild rabbit and hare from the vineyards, wonderful plump pheasant and partridge from The Pheasant Farm, venison, spatchcock (poussin) from Springton, emu and guinea fowl. There are

pigeons and quail, too, crossbred merino-Suffolk lambs, and, of course, kangaroo, which was to be found on menus in South Australia a decade before it was permitted in the eastern states.

The German tradition of smoking food is alive throughout the Barossa. Traditionally, every farmhouse had its own smokehouse, and these days each Barossan butcher has a different way of smoking, with different butchers vying to be acknowledged as the best. Each has recipes handed down from generation to generation, and they all follow the seasons, so for smoking at times one might use ground almond husks and yet another mallee, South Australia's dwarf eucalypt. Besides smoked meats like *kassler, lach schinken* and *mettwurst,* these butchers also make a whole variety of other sausages and smallgoods, from black (blood) and white puddings to wursts and *speck.* Their customers also have preferences—some people go to one butcher for *lach schinken* and another for wurst. The smoked kangaroo from Schulz, a small butcher in Angaston, is widely regarded as the best in the country.

German baking traditions are still carried on, too, especially by the Lyndoch Bakery and Linke's in Nuriootpa. The Fechner family's Apex Bakery in Tanunda, a town of around three thousand, still uses a wood-fired oven to produce their locally famed savoury pastries. There are also German-style egg noodles from Wiech's, a small family concern that is almost a cottage industry and, although going for years, is hardly known outside the valley.

Good hard-wheat flour with the qualities of durum semolina is available from Laucke's mill just down the road from Wiech's. Nearby, you can even find locally smoked salmon, from Springs at Mount Barker in the Adelaide Hills, and a local goat's milk cheese.

South Australia, with its Mediterranean climate, is also the country's major olive producer. The first seedlings were imported from Brazil in the 1830s; in the 1840s, the South Australian Company brought five of the best oil-producing varieties from Marseilles—Bouquetier, Silouen, Blanquet, Redonaou and Verdale. Its first batch of olive oil—produced in 1851—received an honourable mention at the Great Exhibition in London! Many more varieties were introduced, and by 1914 thirty-five olive varieties were being grown. Production of olive oil declined in the 1950s due to high labour costs, but renewed interest in its health benefits has led to more people pressing olive oil commercially. The most highly regarded oils come from Joe Grilli at Primo Estate, Joseph, and Coriole extra-virgin olive oil from Mark Lloyd in the McLaren Vale, although they are relatively small producers. Mark Lloyd also produces wood-fermented red wine vinegar under the Coriole label and is currently ageing balsamic vinegar in old port barrels. From here, too, come the juicy McLaren Vale Kalamata olives, which are more fruity and less salty than the imported Greek ones. For people who grow their own olives, or harvest wild ones along the roadside, there are presses to which they can take the fruits for turning into their own oil.

Olives are grown around Angle Vale, a market gardening area between Adelaide and the Barossa that also produces tomatoes, almonds, artichokes and more olive oil. These days there are many Asian vegetables, too, although not necessarily grown by Asian immigrants: Italians in the Adelaide Hills are growing bok choy.

As it is the driest state, South Australia offers the perfect climate for drying food. During the hot, dry days of summer, fruits like tomatoes and apricots are put out on wire mesh to dry in the sun. The best tomato variety

From Victor Harbour on the Fleurieu Peninsula—at the mouth of Inman River—a causeway leads across Encounter Bay to small Granite Island just offshore.

for sun-drying is the Roma (plum or egg). Because of its low liquid content, the Roma dries quickly and retains its bright red colour.

In addition to its dried fruits from Angas Park, South Australia is also renowned for its glacé fruits, such as quinces, figs, pears, peaches and nectarines, and for Moore Park apricots, a particularly loved local variety from Gawler Park. Adelaide institutions like Ditters are noted for dried fruits and nuts, and Haigh's for chocolates.

If this weren't enough, the Piccadilly Valley, a market gardening area near Uraidla, produces some of the finest vegetables in the state, as well as chestnuts. Milk-fed veal comes from Tilbaroo near Currency Creek in the Adelaide Hills.

Kangaroo Island off South Australia's southern coast offers exciting prospects. With its maritime climate, rich soil and closeness to the Adelaide market, its sheep's milk cheese and vineyards, and the aquaculture carried out in its clean waters, it is set to become South Australia's King Island. Yabby farming and other expanding aquaculture enterprises are adding to South Australia's multiplicity of food choices.

Over to the east of the state, where the Murray River crosses the border into South Australia, is the Riverland. This sizeable irrigation scheme round Renmark produces vines, all manner of citrus fruits—oranges, lemons, grapefruit, tangelos (a cross between a tangerine and a grapefruit)—and stone fruits. The irrigation system was initially set up as a private operation in the 1880s by the Chaffey brothers, George and William, two Canadians, who prior to their work at Renmark had set up the irrigation system at what is now Sunraysia at Mildura, farther up the Murray. Sunraysia is also famous for its abundant citrus harvest, some of which is used for juice (by the likes of Berri-Renmano); for its apricots and peaches, which are sold fresh and in the form of nectar; and for its grapevines, from which come not only raisins, currants and sultanas, but also wine.

Despite its relatively small size, South Australia produces nearly half of all of Australia's wine. Of its many grape-growing regions, the three best known are the Barossa and Clare valleys and the McLaren Vale, although Coonawarra and Langhorne Creek are equally respected.

Waterbirds find sanctuary amidst the marshes and saltpans of the Coorong, a long, narrow national park along the coast southwest of Adelaide.

Fine wine, farm-raised game and German smallgoods are among the regional specialties listed on the menus of Barossa Valley cafés.

The first vines were planted in South Australia by a Dr Hamilton around 1838. In 1844, Dr Penfold, a friend of Louis Pasteur, obtained vine cuttings from Pasteur and brought them to Australia for propagation. These he planted for medicinal purposes—wine was served to patients in surgery—at Magill in the foothills just above Adelaide, once some distance from the city, but now surrounded by suburbs.

South Australia had been founded in 1836, but unlike the eastern colonies, it was settled by 'private initiative', that is, by free settlers. This fact gave it a sense of moral superiority, for it was the only state never to have had convicts. Although regarded as much more conservative than the rest of Australia, it was ahead of much of the world in granting women the vote as early as 1894. Its capital, Adelaide, is frequently referred to as the City of Churches.

There was never a gold rush in South Australia, so it opened up more slowly than other states. Its population growth wasn't helped by numbers of people rushing off to the gold-diggings in Victoria in the early 1850s, although the Bullion Act of 1852 set a higher price for gold in Adelaide than elsewhere, which encouraged people to send their gold home to sell—and return home themselves. Various schemes to encourage migration (such as assisted passages) increased the population to 110 000 by 1857. It was given 'responsible government' in 1855, at the same time as its eastern neighbours, and until 1911 also included the Northern Territory.

Surrounded on three sides by deserts and separated from Western Australia by the Nullarbor Plain, South Australia is rich in sheep and wheat. The state is the nation's third biggest lamb producer. It is a major grower of bread wheat, and durum wheat for pasta making is now being grown.

Much of the wheat comes from the Eyre Peninsula, which is so big you could fit Tasmania into it. On the peninsula's east coast, quandongs, Australia's native peach—described as tasting like a cross between a quince and an apricot—are farmed. They are used mainly for jams and chutneys, but are also dried and made into fruit chews. From the peninsula's west coast come oysters and the unique Coffin Bay scallops, whose males carry a treasured purply roe. In the cooler waters farther up the coast, Streaky Bay scallops can be found. Port Lincoln, on the tip of the peninsula, is renowned for its crayfish, many of which are exported as far afield as the United States. Robe is also known for its crayfish, although to a much lesser extent.

Also from Port Lincoln's waters come abalone and the famous bluefin tuna. With the introduction of tuna harvest quotas, some fishers have turned to tuna farming. Large fish are netted, brought inshore and put into huge marine cages where they are fed a gourmet diet; they double their size in twelve months, at which stage they are highly prized by the Japanese.

The tuna farms are clustered in the bays of Boston

Island in the middle of Boston Bay, near Port Lincoln, a vast expanse of water variously described as being either three or five times the size of Sydney Harbour. (It was nearly the site for Adelaide, but it was found to have insufficient fresh water.) The bay is also home to unique pale-coloured, almost white prawns, and on its shores grow the grapes for the trophy-winning Boston Bay wines.

South Australia's coastline—disproportionate to its landmass because it is extended by the indentations of two gulfs, St. Vincent and Spencer—abounds with all manner of fish and shellfish, such as King George whiting (the best in the country), garfish and blue swimmer crabs. From the waters off the Eyre Peninsula come tommy ruffs, the usual diet of wild tuna.

All these fish are to be found on the menus of restaurants in Adelaide, which, despite its relatively small population in comparison to other state capitals, has been at the forefront of Australia's culinary endeavours since the mid-1970s. Its position in the front ranks is probably thanks to the enlightened political and artistic climate of that time, and to its culinary-minded then-premier, Don Dunstan. Like the city's unique bluestone architecture, this culinary distinction has lasted.

The state's restaurants continue to serve up some of the most adventurous and exciting food in the country. (They were doing their own fusion of Asian and European—more natural and authentically Asian—some years before the dreadful soubriquet 'East meets West' was even dreamt up for that culinary shotgun marriage in California.) South Australia's rich and varied produce comes as no surprise, however. In the state's Mediterranean climate, everything to do with good food thrives.

The southern tip of the Mount Lofty Ranges is softened by the lush Fleurieu Peninsula landscape.

Adelaide's colonial architects chose a regional sandstone with a distinctive hue for buildings that range from majestic churches to elegant residences.

MEAT, POULTRY AND GAME

Classic Aussie snacks entice shoppers at the Salamanca Markets in Hobart.

MEAT, POULTRY AND GAME

'THE FLESH OF THE KANGAROO IS EXCELLENT', wrote French novelist Alexandre Dumas in his 1870 *Grand Dictionnaire de Cuisine* (which he found time to write between novels), describing it as 'greatly preferable to that of cow or sheep in that it is much more tender than the first, and much more abundant and nutritious than the second'. He advocated farming kangaroo in Europe, although he didn't go so far as to describe how high the fences might need to be!

Kangaroo is a particularly lean meat, flavoursome, very low in cholesterol and, after decades of being out of fashion on Australian tables, increasingly popular. It is suggested that the Chinese knew of the existence of the kangaroo long before Europeans sighted our coastline: Chinese literature of the eleventh century reportedly mentions a 'leaping hare'.

Australia has been blessed with a variety of native game, from kangaroo, emu and possum (a dish of the early settlers was 'possum in a pumpkin') to wallaby, all of which Australia's original inhabitants lived on for perhaps a hundred thousand years before European settlement. The early settlers were quick to turn up their noses at the native game as soon as domestic animals became more plentiful, however; no doubt their preference was in part due to the fact that farm-raised animals were far easier to catch!

Native game was undoubtedly on the menu of the First Fleet settlers. With their cattle having run away in the first few days, fresh beef was not available. It is recorded that when two animals were killed in January 1793, it was only the third time the colonists had tasted fresh beef since their arrival five years earlier.

The first emu killed by the European newcomers was shot by a convict for the table of Governor Phillip in February 1788. Its flesh was found to taste like beef, and hunting parties were promptly organised. (Some of the Aborigines' hunting methods were much more intelligent. Rather than expending energy tracking and spearing them, they would 'dope' the emus' drinking water.)

In the early days, the dietary staples were salt beef or salt pork and carbohydrates, and the quantity of fresh meat consumed was determined by social class. Although fresh meat would have been a luxury beyond the means of the petty thieves—pickpockets, horse stealers and poachers—who were transported, it was embraced as soon as it could be afforded. Once the wool industry got going, mutton became plentiful—so plentiful in fact that it was sometimes given facetious names. For example, 'colonial goose' was actually stuffed shoulder of mutton.

Australians were—and still are—some of the world's greatest carnivores. Not so long ago, it was not uncommon for Australians to consume meat three times a day, something that seems almost unbelievable today. As late as the 1960s, even in the cities, a typical breakfast would have been a cooked one, possibly consisting of both chops and sausages. In the country, a steak with fried eggs

Previous pages, clockwise from top: Swaggie's Lamb Shanks (recipe page 126), Lamb Fillets with Braised Capsicums on a Crispy Potato Cake (recipe page 124), Irish Stew (recipe page 134)

was commonly set out on the morning table. The more refined might have had bacon and eggs, along with porridge in winter.

The main meal of the day was invariably built around some sort of meat, even rissoles (meatballs) or a stew. Shepherd's pie was a standard on Mondays, to use up the leftover Sunday roast leg of lamb. Much more of the animal was used: tongue, tripe in white sauce, lamb's fry (sheep's liver) with onions and bacon, pig's trotters, meat loaf and curried sausages were common fare. Corned beef has also faded from its former popularity. As strange as it may seem today, chicken was a luxury reserved for Sundays or Christmas Day.

'Underground mutton'—as rabbit was humorously known—was a staple source of protein during the Depression, when many out-of-work men made a living by trapping (wild, although introduced) rabbits and selling them door-to-door, with the cry 'rabbitoh'. For many years afterwards, the rabbit's image remained poor because of a certain amount of snobbery. Now, however, rabbit is being reappraised by adventurous cooks and is again turning up on restaurant menus.

The changes in meat consumption are further evidence of how Australian eating habits have shifted. These days we are eating less meat in general. Beef and veal consumption has dropped by half, and lamb and mutton consumption is down to a quarter of what it once was. We are, however, eating more chicken and more meat of better quality. People are turning to leaner cuts such as boned lamb loins and trimmed pork cuts, which have been introduced to meet with the demand for less animal fat in the diet.

Butchers now frequently make the distinction between grain- and grass-fed beef. Milk-fed lamb and veal are available, as well as farmed rabbit, venison, crocodile and all manner of feathered game, from pheasant and quail to emu.

Kangaroo, a particularly tasty game meat, has recently begun to achieve deserved gastronomic recognition. People are realising that we should make more use of this

An Aboriginal stockman musters cattle in the Kimberleys, Western Australia's cattle country.

Sheep stations and farms are scattered throughout the rolling country in southwest NSW.

uniquely Australian food resource, which is also less damaging to Australia's fragile topsoils than such introduced cloven-hooved animals as sheep and cattle. Kangaroo is a lean, sinewy meat, and its taste is often compared with that of venison.

As with other areas of food, meat and game can be cooked in many ways, with a nod in the direction of any number of cuisines. They can be roasted, braised, pan-fried, grilled or barbecued, and might then be served with flavours or accompaniments derived from a variety of cuisines, such as kangaroo paired with Italian polenta.

Meat, poultry and game dishes are being flavoured in new ways, too. We are seeing the incorporation of the singularly Australian flavours of indigenous bush berries, leaves and seeds, such as lilly pillies; riberries, which have a clove flavour; or lemon myrtle leaves, which taste similar to lemongrass. A sauce might be made from muntharies, a small South Australian berry described as a native cranberry with an apple flavour. Also increasingly popular are the wonderful pepperberries from the highlands of Tasmania. They are quite hot—certainly hotter than black pepper—but with a zing rather than chilli heat and a subtle flavour as well as a spiciness. Both the leaves and the berries are used. Flavours such as these make the perfect accompaniment to meats such as beef—or kangaroo. And you can't get much more Australian than that.

MELBOURNE

THAI LAMB SALAD WITH MINT AND LEMONGRASS

Australians' love affair with Thai food is one of the delights of the modern Australian table. In the mid-1970s, I first went to Thailand and I adored the food but couldn't buy enough of the ingredients back home to cook any of the dishes successfully. Today, most Thai ingredients are sold in suburban supermarkets and the more obscure ones can be found in Asian markets or your local Chinatown.

200 g (6½ oz) minced (ground) lean lamb
1 tablespoon fish sauce (see glossary)
2 tablespoons finely chopped lemongrass (see glossary)
3 tablespoons water
1½ tablespoons fresh lemon juice
½ purple onion, thinly sliced
1 tablespoon chopped spring (green) onion
1 tablespoon finely chopped fresh coriander (cilantro) root
   (see glossary)
4 tablespoons fresh mint leaves
1 teaspoon sliced fresh red chilli

FOR SERVING:

6 lettuce leaves
10 fresh mint leaves
10 fresh coriander (cilantro) leaves
2 long fresh red chillies
½ lemon, cut in half lengthwise
½ lime, cut in half lengthwise

In a saucepan over medium heat, combine the lamb, fish sauce, lemongrass and water, and cook gently, stirring to break up the lamb. If necessary, add a little more water to keep about 3 tablespoons of liquid in the pan at all times. Simmer until the lamb is cooked through, but still moist, about 3 minutes. Add the lemon juice, purple onion, spring onions, coriander root, mint leaves and sliced chilli and cook for 5 minutes. Remove from the heat and let cool to room temperature.

To serve, arrange the lettuce leaves on a small platter. Heap the cooled lamb salad on top and then scatter the mint and coriander leaves over the top. Cut the 2 long chillies to form flowers and place on top. Place the lemon and lime halves at the ends of the platter. Serve at room temperature.

SERVES 4

SYDNEY

RED CURRY OF LAMB NECK CHOPS

Lamb neck chops (also called rosette chops because of their shape) are the sweetest chops of all. They are ideal used in slow-cooked dishes such as curries, casseroles, braises and stews. Aficionados will frown at the use of a commercial red curry paste in this recipe. I offer no excuse except time and the fact that very good Asian curry pastes are available. Serve this dish with steamed rice.

1 kg (2 lb) lamb neck chops
2 lemongrass stalks
4 cans (400 ml/13 fl oz each) coconut cream (see glossary)
3 tablespoons red curry paste (see glossary)
1¼ tablespoons sugar
3 tablespoons fish sauce (see glossary)
leaves from 3 fresh basil sprigs
6 fresh kaffir lime leaves, finely shredded (see glossary)

Place the chops in a large, heavy pot. Remove and discard the tough, outer leaves of the lemongrass; bruise the tender, inner portions and cut into 2 or 3 pieces. Place in the pot. Spoon the thick coconut cream off the tops of the cans into a measuring jug to measure 600 ml (19 fl oz/2⅓ cups); set aside. Pour the remaining coconut cream (the thin part) over the chops. Bring to a boil and simmer until the chops are tender, 30–40 minutes.

Meanwhile, in another heavy pot over medium heat, warm the reserved coconut cream. Add the curry paste and cook, stirring constantly, until fragrant and oil rises to the surface, about 10 minutes. Then reduce the mixture over medium heat until thick, about 30 minutes. Add the curry paste mixture to the chops along with the sugar and fish sauce. Bring to a boil and simmer for 10 minutes. Stir in the basil and lime leaves and serve.

SERVES 4

NEW SOUTH WALES

LAMB FILLETS WITH MELTED EGGPLANT AND CAPSICUM

The backstrap of lamb is the eye of the fillet from the loin. This colourful dish is one of my favourite stand-bys for entertaining overseas guests.

FOR THE VEGETABLES:

1 large eggplant (aubergine), cut crosswise into slices 1 cm
   (⅜ in) thick
75 ml (2½ fl oz/5 tablespoons) olive oil
2 large red capsicums (bell peppers), halved lengthwise
2 teaspoons finely chopped fresh oregano
2 teaspoons finely chopped fresh marjoram
1 fresh red or green chilli, seeded and chopped
salt and freshly ground pepper

FOR THE LAMB AND SAUCE:

2 tablespoons olive oil
4 lamb backstraps, about 180 g (6 oz) each
salt and freshly ground pepper
80 ml (3 fl oz/⅓ cup) dry red wine
2 teaspoons redcurrant jelly
125 ml (4 fl oz/½ cup) chicken stock

To cook the vegetables, preheat a griller (broiler) on high. Paint the eggplant slices with a little of the oil and place on a griller pan. Grill (broil), turning once, until just tender, a few minutes. Let cool and cut into long strips 1 cm (⅜ in) wide.

While the eggplant slices are cooling, paint the capsicums with a little of the oil, place them on the griller pan and grill, turning if needed, until the skin is blistered evenly. Remove from the griller, place in a paper bag and seal airtight. Let cool, then, using your fingertips, peel off the skins. Remove the stems, seeds and ribs and discard. Cut the capsicums into long strips 1 cm (⅜ in) wide.

In a large, heavy frying pan over medium heat, warm the remaining oil. Add the eggplant, capsicums, oregano, marjoram and chilli and stir until the vegetables are well mixed and almost falling apart. Season to taste with salt and pepper; keep warm.

To cook the lamb, in a heavy frying pan over medium-high heat, warm the oil. Add the lamb and sear to seal on all sides. Season to taste with salt and pepper and cook, turning once, until done to your liking, 4–6 minutes for medium-rare. Remove to a plate, cover and keep warm. Reserve the juices in the pan.

To make the sauce, whisk pan juices over medium heat until caramelised. Add the wine and whisk to deglaze the pan, scraping up any browned-on bits. Add the jelly and mash with a whisk. Heat until melted. Add the stock and reduce the mixture until it forms a good sauce consistency. Add any juices that accumulated under the lamb. Taste and adjust the seasoning with salt and pepper.

To serve, cut each lamb backstrap in half at a sharp angle and arrange the halves resting on each other on a warmed serving plate. Spoon the eggplant mixture around the lamb. Moisten with the sauce and serve at once.

SERVES 4

Clockwise from top: Red Curry of Lamb Neck Chops, Lamb Fillets with Melted Eggplant and Capsicum, Thai Lamb Salad with Mint and Lemongrass—photographed at Woodbyne Park Gallery, Jasper's Brush, NSW

Left to right: Barbecued Racks of Lamb with Mustard and Lemon Thyme, Chargrilled Lamb Steaks with Garlic and Rosemary

CHARGRILLED LAMB STEAKS WITH GARLIC AND ROSEMARY

Just about everyone who enjoys a steak will love this alternative to beef steak. Ask your butcher to saw a leg of lamb (bone in) into steaks. Because the steaks have been marinated, they will cook very quickly. Begin to prepare this dish 1 day in advance of serving.

6 lamb steaks cut from the top of the leg, each about 1.5 cm (⅔ in) thick

FOR THE MARINADE:

3 cloves garlic, bruised and cut into small pieces
1 tablespoon fresh rosemary
125 ml (4 fl oz/½ cup) olive oil
salt and freshly ground pepper

❧ Remove the small, round bone from the centre of each lamb steak. To make the marinade, place the garlic in a large, shallow nonreactive dish and place the steaks on top. Sprinkle with the rosemary and pour the olive oil over the top. Cover and refrigerate for 24 hours, turning once.

❧ Preheat a griller (broiler) on high or prepare a fire in a barbecue. When very hot, lift the steaks from the marinade, reserving the marinade, and place on the griller tray or barbecue rack. Sear quickly on both sides to seal in the juices. Then sprinkle on some salt and grind some black pepper over each steak and leave to cook to individual taste, painting with the marinade during cooking.

❧ The steaks are best when cooked until they are still a little pink inside, about 5 minutes on the first side and 3 minutes on the second side. Serve at once.

SERVES 6

LAMB FILLETS WITH BRAISED CAPSICUMS ON A CRISPY POTATO CAKE

These lamb fillets are from the 'eye' of the middle loin. They are small, only about 14 cm (5½ in) long and 1.5–2 cm (⅔–¾ in) wide, so you need to allow 3 or 4 fillets per person. These are the most tender portions of the loin, so be careful not to overcook them. This dish is from Glenn Barber and Kim Walker, chefs at a restaurant in the Lower Hunter Valley.

FOR THE POTATO CAKE:

300 g (10 oz) pontiac potatoes or other baking potatoes, peeled and thinly sliced
300 g (10 oz) kumaras, peeled and thinly sliced (see glossary)
80 g (2½ oz/5 tablespoons) unsalted butter, melted
salt and freshly ground pepper

FOR THE BRAISED CAPSICUMS:

80 ml (3 fl oz/5 tablespoons) plus 1 tablespoon olive oil
2 brown onions, cut into 3-cm (1¼-in) dice
2 yellow capsicums (bell peppers), seeded and cut into 3-cm (1¼-in) dice
2 red capsicums (bell peppers), seeded and cut into 3-cm (1¼-in) dice
2 green capsicums (bell peppers), seeded and cut into 3-cm (1¼-in) dice
1 small clove garlic, finely chopped
60 g (2 oz/4 tablespoons) well-drained tiny capers

FOR THE LAMB:

1 tablespoon olive oil
salt
24 lamb fillets (see note)

freshly ground pepper
watercress sprigs

To cook the potatoes, preheat an oven to 150°C (300°F). Place all the potato slices in a large bowl and add the melted butter. Stir well so each slice is coated with butter. Arrange the slices of both potatoes together in slightly overlapping concentric rings to form 6 dinner plate–sized circles on 2 baking trays (sheets). Season to taste with salt and pepper. Place in the oven and cook until crisp and golden, 20–25 minutes.

To cook the capsicums, in a large, heavy frying pan over medium-low heat, warm the 80 ml (3 fl oz/5 tablespoons) of the oil. Add the onions, capsicums and garlic and cook gently, turning occasionally, until softened, about 30 minutes. If the pan begins to dry out, top it with a cover slightly ajar.

Meanwhile, in a small frying pan over medium-high heat, warm the remaining 1 tablespoon oil. Add the capers and sauté until crisp, about 2 minutes. Add the capers to the capsicum mixture.

To cook the lamb, heat a heavy frying pan or griddle pan over medium heat and brush with the oil. Rub salt into the lamb fillets and add to the pan. Sauté quickly for 1 minute. Turn and cook for 30–60 seconds longer, for medium-rare, or until cooked to your preference. Remove from the heat and let rest for 3 minutes in a warm oven.

To serve, place each potato cake in the centre of a warmed dinner plate. Arrange the lamb fillets on top of the cakes and spoon the braised pepper mixture over the lamb. Grind black pepper over the top. Garnish with watercress and serve.

SERVES 6 *Photograph pages 118–119*

SYDNEY

Barbecued Racks of Lamb with Mustard and Lemon Thyme

Australian lambs feed on natural pastures of clover and rye and are finished on lucerne to bring them to their peak for market. During the drier summer months, their diet is supplemented with crops of turnips and lucerne. The two major breeds for lamb meat are Dorset and Border Leicester. Rea Francis, a publicist and great home cook, barbecues this lamb on her trusty backyard Weber overlooking Sydney Harbour at Balmain, just west of the city. She serves it with barbecued new potatoes in their skins. If young lamb under 8 months is used, select 6-cutlet racks. If more mature lamb is used, choose meatier 4-cutlet racks.

6 lamb racks (see note)
2 cloves garlic, cut in half
1½ tablespoons Dijon mustard or 1 tablespoon English (hot yellow) mustard
½ bunch fresh lemon thyme or regular thyme
freshly ground pepper
1 lemon, thinly sliced

Prepare a fire in a barbecue and allow the coals to burn down until they are white.

Meanwhile, trim the excess fat off the lamb and trim the meat from the ends of the ribs, to form French chops. Rub both sides of each rack with the cut garlic cloves. Spread some mustard on the flesh side of each rack and arrange flesh side up on the barbecue rack. Place generous handfuls of thyme sprigs under and on top of the lamb. Grind pepper over the top and then top with the lemon slices.

Barbecue until the lamb is done to your satisfaction, turning once, about 8 minutes on each side for medium-rare. Replace the lemon slices when the racks are turned.

Remove from the barbecue and let rest near the barbecue for 10 minutes before serving.

SERVES 6

SYDNEY

Green Curry of Duck

Purchase fresh ducks from specialist game suppliers. Many outlets sell frozen ducks, which makes it difficult to tell the condition of the bird. Ask for plump ducks with good breast meat, such as the Muscovy. You can make your own green curry paste, but a good commercial one is infinitely quicker. Serve with steamed white rice.

300 ml (10 fl oz/1¼ cups) coconut cream (see glossary)
3 tablespoons green curry paste (see glossary)
1 duck, 2 kg (4 lb), cut into bite-sized pieces on the bone (see note)
400 ml (13 fl oz/1⅔ cups) thin coconut milk (see glossary)
400 ml (13 fl oz/1⅔ cups) thick coconut milk (see glossary)
2 teaspoons sugar
8 fresh kaffir lime leaves, shredded (see glossary)
1 teaspoon salt
1 tablespoon fish sauce (see glossary)
3 fresh long green chillies, slivered
16 fresh basil leaves, plus 8 small fresh basil leaves
2 fresh red chillies, slivered

Spoon the coconut cream into a wok or deep frying pan. Stir over medium-high heat until the coconut oil begins to separate. Add the curry paste and cook over medium-high heat, stirring constantly, until aromatic, about 2 minutes. Add the duck pieces and stir to coat with the coconut cream. Reduce the heat, cover and cook slowly for 10 minutes.

Scoop off any fat that has risen to the top and discard. Add the thin and thick coconut milks, sugar, lime leaves, salt and fish sauce. Bring slowly to a boil, reduce the heat and simmer gently, uncovered, until the duck is fork tender, about 45 minutes.

Again scoop off any fat that has risen to the top and discard. Add the green chillies and the 16 basil leaves and simmer for 3–4 minutes.

Serve the duck garnished with the red chillies and the small basil leaves.

SERVES 4–6

Green Curry of Duck

PERTH

EMU STEAKS ON A BED OF CARAMELISED PEAR AND ROCKET

Emu is being farmed for the table primarily in Western Australia, but other states are gearing up to get into this affluent market. The best cuts come from the hind and fore saddles. This is a lean meat, so be sure not to overcook it or it will dry out.

FOR THE MARINADE:

100 ml (3½ fl oz/6½ tablespoons) olive oil
1½ tablespoons balsamic vinegar
1½ tablespoons sherry vinegar
1 clove garlic, finely chopped
freshly ground pepper

2 emu fore or hind saddle fillets, about 250 g (½ lb) each,
    cut into thin strips 6 cm (2½ in) long and 1 cm (⅜ in) wide
4 firm Packman pears or other firm, ripe pears, unpeeled,
    halved and cored
juice of 1 lemon

FOR THE DRESSING:

1½ tablespoons balsamic vinegar
100 ml (3½ fl oz/6½ tablespoons) extra-virgin olive oil
salt and freshly ground pepper

2 tablespoons olive oil
60 g (2 oz/¼ cup) unsalted butter
90 g (3 oz/⅓ cup) sugar
400 g (13 oz) rocket (arugula) leaves
125 g (4 oz/1 cup) walnut pieces

To make the marinade, in a shallow nonreactive dish, combine all the marinade ingredients, including pepper to taste, and whisk together to mix well. Add the emu strips and turn to coat evenly. Cover and refrigerate for 24 hours.

To assemble the dish, slice the pear halves lengthwise, place in a bowl and sprinkle with the lemon juice. Toss to coat evenly.

To make the dressing, in a small bowl, whisk together all of the dressing ingredients, including salt and pepper to taste. Set aside.

Remove the emu strips from the marinade. In a heavy frying pan over high heat, warm the oil. When hot, add the emu strips and stir-fry just until well seared, about 2 minutes. Remove to a plate and keep warm.

Add the butter to the same pan and place over medium-high heat. When it sizzles, add the pear slices and sugar and sauté until caramelised. Remove from the heat and keep warm.

Divide the rocket leaves evenly among 6 large dinner plates, stacking them in the centre of each. Arrange the emu strips around the rocket. Scatter the pears and walnuts over the emu and drizzle with the dressing.

Serve immediately.

SERVES 6

SOUTH AUSTRALIA

SWAGGIE'S LAMB SHANKS

A swaggie (swagman) is someone who carries a swag on his back and roams around the country on foot, living off his earnings doing odd jobs here and there and from gifts of money and food. This inexpensive cut of lamb is one a swaggie might be given and is a real treat when cooked this way and served sitting around a camp fire under the stars in the Australian bush. It is more likely, though, that a swaggie would use beer rather than wine. This dish can be made at home in a heavy pot and finished on a barbecue or under a hot griller, but I know it tastes better when cooked in a camp oven

over an open fire and then finished, clamped in a grill rack, over the coals until the outsides are crisp and golden. You will need to begin making this dish 2 days ahead of serving.

6 lamb shanks
1 carrot, peeled and diced
1 onion, diced
1 celery stalk, diced
3 fresh parsley sprigs
3 fresh thyme sprigs
1 head garlic, cut in half across the cloves
1 piece gingerroot, 5 cm (2 in) long, peeled and sliced
6 peppercorns

Emu Steaks on a Bed of Caramelised Pear and Rocket—photographed at Blackheath, in the Blue Mountains, NSW

125 ml (4 fl oz/½ cup) peanut oil
1 bottle (750 ml/24 fl oz/3 cups) red wine

Arrange the shanks in a large, shallow baking dish. Scatter the vegetables, herbs, garlic, gingerroot and peppercorns over the top. Pour in the oil and the wine. Turn the shanks over in the marinade to coat evenly. Cover and refrigerate overnight.

Position a rack in the centre of an oven and preheat the oven to 180°C (350°F).

Transfer the shanks to a heavy pot with a lid and pour the marinade evenly over the top. Cover and cook in the centre of the oven until fork tender, about 2 hours. During cooking, turn the shanks over from time to time. Remove from the oven and let cool, then refrigerate overnight in the marinade.

To serve, preheat a griller (broiler) on high.

Drain the shanks over a pot, catching the marinade. Place the marinade over medium-high heat and cook until reduced to a good coating consistency.

Arrange the shanks on a griller tray and slip under the griller. Grill (broil) until glazed and crisp, about 5 minutes, then turn and grill until glazed and crisp on the second side and heated through, 2–3 minutes longer.

Serve the shanks at once with the reduced sauce spooned around them.

SERVES 6   *Photograph pages 118–119*

SYDNEY

ROAST GAME DUCK WITH SHALLOTS AND WILD MUSHROOMS

Serge Dansereau is executive chef at one of Sydney's top hotels. He is a friend to everyone in the food industry, loyal to his beliefs and an excellent and innovative chef. This is his way of cooking game ducks in the autumn when wild mushrooms are plentiful. Rob Robinson is a forager with a state licence for collecting wild fungi in the state forests. He calls his business The Market Cat, which epitomises what Rob does best. He can rustle up wild berries, game, river trout and rare produce of stunning quality in a matter of hours.

2 game ducks
½ small brown onion, plus 4 small brown onions
1 small leek, carefully washed
1 carrot
½ bunch fresh thyme
2 tablespoons madeira
100 ml (3½ fl oz/6½ tablespoons) dry red wine
sea salt and cracked pepper
4 large cloves garlic
olive oil
24 tiny new potatoes
8 shallots
500 g (1 lb) wild mushrooms such as field, cèpes, *matsutake* (pine) or morels
4½ tablespoons unsalted butter
4 bunches young spinach, blanched in boiling water for 1–2 minutes and drained

❧ Preheat an oven to 150°C (300°F). Remove the necks and legs from the ducks and place them in a small roasting pan with the ½ onion, leek, carrot and thyme. Roast until browned, about 30 minutes. Remove from the oven and transfer the contents to a saucepan. Place the roasting pan over high heat, add the madeira and red wine and deglaze the pan by scraping up any browned bits. Add the juices to the saucepan along with enough water to cover the bones. Bring to a simmer and simmer, uncovered, while the duck and vegetables cook.

❧ To roast the ducks, rub the breasts with sea salt and cracked pepper. Cut 1 garlic clove in half and rub half over each breast.

Roast Game Duck with Shallots and Wild Mushrooms

❧ Lightly oil a heavy roasting pan and add the 4 onions, potatoes, shallots and remaining garlic. Roast in the oven for 30 minutes. Add the mushrooms and season to taste with salt and pepper. Increase the oven temperature to 200°C (400°F). Place the ducks on top of the vegetables and roast until medium-rare, 20–25 minutes. Turn off the oven and let the duck and vegetables rest in the warm oven for 20 minutes before serving.

❧ Meanwhile, in a frying pan over medium heat, melt 1 tablespoon of the butter. Add the spinach and sauté just until wilted. Keep warm.

❧ To finish the sauce, strain the stock and then discard any fat from the surface. Return the strained stock to the saucepan and reduce it over high heat until it forms a good sauce consistency. Season to taste with salt and pepper. Reduce the heat to medium and add the remaining 3½ tablespoons butter to the sauce, whisking constantly. Do not let it boil. Keep the sauce warm in the top pan of a double boiler or in a flameproof bowl placed over hot water until serving.

❧ To serve, arrange the mushroom mixture and the spinach on warmed plates. Remove the breasts from the ducks and place on top of the vegetables. Serve the sauce on the side.

SERVES 4

SYDNEY

CHICKEN WITH WALNUTS

Jane Tennant is a long-time food writer who lives in Sydney. She loves entertaining her family and friends and says this dish is very easy to cook. You can find already diced chicken meat labeled stir-fry chicken in the market.

FOR THE MARINADE:

1 egg white, lightly beaten
1 tablespoon soy sauce
1 tablespoon cornflour (cornstarch)
1 tablespoon dry sherry

1 kg (2 lb) chicken meat, cut into thin strips 5 cm (2 in) long and 12 mm (½ in) wide
vegetable oil for deep-frying
300 g (10 oz/2½ cups) walnut halves
1 small red capsicum (bell pepper), seeded and thinly sliced
1 small green capsicum (bell pepper), seeded and thinly sliced
1 tablespoon minced, peeled gingerroot
2 cloves garlic, crushed
4 shallots, chopped
1 teaspoon sugar
1 teaspoon white wine vinegar
1 tablespoon soy sauce
1 tablespoon dry sherry
3 tablespoons chicken stock, optional

❧ To make the marinade, combine all the ingredients in a nonreactive bowl and stir well. Add the chicken pieces and stir to coat. Cover and refrigerate for 1 hour.

❧ Drain the chicken pieces and pat dry with paper towels. In a wok or deep frying pan, pour in the oil to a depth of 5 cm (2 in) and heat to 190°C (375°F). Add the walnuts and deep-fry for 1 minute. Using a slotted spoon, remove to crumpled paper towels to drain. Then, add half of the chicken and deep-fry until just tender, about 1 minute. Using a slotted spoon, remove to crumpled paper towels to drain. Repeat with the remaining chicken.

❧ Pour off all of the oil except for 2 tablespoons. Heat the pan over medium heat. Add the capsicums, gingerroot, garlic and shallots and stir-fry for 1 minute. Return the chicken to the pan and immediately add the sugar, vinegar, soy sauce and sherry. Add a little chicken stock if the mixture seems too dry. Stir-fry for a few seconds, then remove the wok from the heat. Mix in the walnuts. Transfer to a serving dish and serve immediately.

SERVES 4

Left to right: Grilled Chicken Steaks with Indonesian Peanut Sauce, Chicken with Walnuts

GRILLED CHICKEN STEAKS WITH INDONESIAN PEANUT SAUCE

Even though Indonesia is one of our closest northern neighbours, Indonesian food is not well known in Australia. Make this peanut sauce, which commonly accompanies satay, with Australian peanuts and serve it with grilled or barbecued chicken steak. It also goes well with grilled vegetables.

FOR THE MARINADE:

1 teaspoon grated, peeled gingerroot
1 clove garlic, finely chopped
1 spring (green) onion, including tender green tops, finely
    chopped
1 piece lemongrass, 5 cm (2 in) long, thinly sliced (see glossary)
1 fresh coriander (cilantro) root, finely chopped (see glossary)
1 tablespoon finely chopped fresh coriander (cilantro)
1 or more fresh red chillies, chopped
80 ml (3 fl oz/⅓ cup) dry white wine
3 tablespoons peanut oil

4 large whole chicken breasts, boned and skinned

FOR THE PASTE:

1 small brown onion, coarsely chopped
1 piece lemongrass, 6 cm (2½ in) long, chopped
¾ teaspoon shrimp paste (see glossary)
3 dried red chillies, or to taste
2 cloves garlic

1 teaspoon ground cumin
1 teaspoon ground coriander
2 fresh coriander (cilantro) roots, coarsely chopped

FOR THE SAUCE:

1 teaspoon peanut oil
200–250 ml (6½–8 fl oz/¾–1 cup) water
150 ml (5 fl oz/⅔ cup) coconut milk (see glossary)
150 g (5 oz/scant 1 cup) roasted peanuts, finely chopped
2 teaspoons tamarind juice (see glossary)
1½ tablespoons sugar

peanut oil for grilling

To make the marinade, in a large, shallow nonreactive dish, combine all the ingredients and stir to mix well. Add the chicken and turn to coat well with the marinade. Cover and refrigerate for 2–4 hours.

To make the paste, combine all the ingredients in a blender. Blend until finely chopped.

To make the sauce, in a heavy saucepan over medium heat, warm the oil. Add the paste and sauté, stirring, until aromatic, 2–3 minutes. Add the water and coconut milk and whisk until well mixed. Add the peanuts and cook over low heat for 2 minutes. Add the tamarind juice and sugar and cook until heated through. Remove from the heat and let cool.

Place a griddle pan over high heat or prepare a fire in a barbecue.

Lift the chicken from the marinade. Brush the hot griddle pan or barbecue rack with oil. Place the chicken on the hot surface and cook, turning once, until well seared and just cooked through, about 4 minutes on each side.

Serve the chicken with the sauce.

SERVES 4

Clockwise from top: Braised Duck with Vegetables (recipe page 133), Rabbit with Creamy Garlic Potatoes, Kangaroo and Emu Steaks with Two Fruit Sauces, Seared Kangaroo Fillet with Kumara Purée—photographed at Orange, NSW

PORT DOUGLAS

SEARED KANGAROO FILLET WITH KUMARA PURÉE

The credit for this magnificent way to cook kangaroo goes to Anthony Hendre in Port Douglas. It is among the most successful ways for the home cook to prepare this uniquely Australian meat. The trick is to cook the 'roo quickly without allowing the heat to reach the centre of the meat, which, because it is a very lean meat, would dry it out. Always undercook rather than overcook the meat; you can always cook it longer, although it is better to time it properly the first time. Bottled demiglace can be found in gourmet delicatessens. Begin making this dish the day before you plan to serve it.

FOR THE KANGAROO:

1 kangaroo fillet, 900 g (2 lb), trimmed of sinews
125 ml (4 fl oz/½ cup) olive oil
2 teaspoons cracked pepper

FOR THE SWEET POTATO PURÉE:

60 g (2 oz/¼ cup) unsalted butter
1 brown onion, chopped
800 g (1⅔ lb) kumaras, peeled and cut into small dice (see glossary)
salt and freshly ground pepper

FOR THE SAUCE:

150 ml (5 fl oz/⅔ cup) bottled demiglace (see glossary)
1 tablespoon julienned sun-dried tomato
2 teaspoons well-drained capers, chopped
½ fresh red chilli, or to taste
1 teaspoon finely chopped fresh parsley

FOR SERVING:

1 bunch young silverbeet (Swiss chard)

❄ Cut the kangaroo fillet into 4 steaks. Place in a shallow dish in a single layer. Pour the oil evenly over the steaks and grind pepper over the top. Turn the steaks over in the marinade, cover

MEAT, POULTRY AND GAME

and refrigerate 24 hours, turning the steaks over from time to time.

To cook the sweet potato purée, in a heavy pot over medium heat, melt the butter. Add the onion and cook until softened, about 5 minutes. Add the kumaras, cover partially and cook gently over low heat until tender, about 20 minutes. Mash and season to taste with salt and pepper.

To make the sauce, combine the demiglace, sun-dried tomato, capers and chilli in a small pan and bring to a boil. Remove from the heat, add the parsley and keep warm.

To cook the kangaroo steaks, place a heavy pan large enough to hold the 4 steaks without crowding over medium-high heat. Lift the kangaroo steaks from the marinade and slip them into the hot pan. Sear on both sides, turning once, until medium-rare, about 6–10 minutes' total cooking time. Transfer to a platter and keep warm. To the same pan over high heat, add the silverbeet and cook until just wilted, just a few minutes.

Place the kangaroo steaks on warmed dinner plates. Arrange the silverbeet next to the kangaroo and then a spoonful of sweet potato purée next to the silverbeet. Spoon the sauce over the kangaroo and vegetables and serve at once.

SERVES 4

RABBIT WITH CREAMY GARLIC POTATOES

During the Great Depression and for a couple of decades after, rabbits were the staple diet of many Australians. Today, hutch-bred rabbits are available at specialist game suppliers, but they are so different from the wild rabbits available from most suburban butchers that they are hardly interchangeable in recipes. For value and flavour, it's hard to beat young wild rabbits. The creamy garlic potatoes can be served with other meats or simply with a platter of grilled (broiled) or barbecued vegetables.

2 young wild rabbits, 750 g–1 kg (1½–2 lb) each, cut into serving pieces
2½ tablespoons unsalted butter
2½ tablespoons safflower oil
50 g (2 oz) *speck,* cubed (see glossary)
8 small white onions, 2–4 cm (¾–1¼ in) in diameter
salt and freshly ground pepper
250 ml (8 fl oz/1 cup) dry white wine

FOR THE POTATOES:

600 g (1¼ lb) pink-eye potatoes or other baking potatoes, peeled and quartered
salt
2 rounded tablespoons unsalted butter
1 small clove garlic, very finely chopped
about 60 ml (2 fl oz/¼ cup) milk or cream
white pepper

juice of 1½ lemons
2 tablespoons finely chopped fresh parsley

Use the forequarter and hindquarter pieces of the rabbits to make a stock. Place them in a saucepan with water just to cover. Bring to a boil and simmer, uncovered, for 30 minutes. Discard the rabbit pieces and measure out 250 ml (8 fl oz/1 cup) of the stock. Use the remaining stock in another dish.

In a heavy pot over medium heat, melt the butter with the oil. Add the *speck* and sauté until well rendered, about 5 minutes. Add the onions and sauté until they begin to colour, 12–15 minutes. Dry the rabbit loin pieces and add to the pot, a few at a time; brown on all sides. Season to taste with salt and pepper and add the wine and the 250 ml (8 fl oz/1 cup) stock. Bring to a boil. Reduce the heat to medium, cover and simmer gently until the rabbit is tender, 50–60 minutes. The timing will depend on the age and size of the rabbits.

Meanwhile, cook the potatoes. Place the potatoes in a saucepan with water to cover. Add salt to taste and bring to a boil. Reduce the heat and simmer until fork tender, about 10 minutes. Drain and pass the potatoes through a potato ricer or a food mill into a warmed bowl. Add the butter and garlic and mix until soft and creamy. Add as much milk or cream as needed to form a smooth, creamy consistency and season to taste with salt and white pepper. Place in a serving dish and keep warm.

Lift the rabbit out of the pot with a slotted spoon and place on a platter; keep warm. Increase the heat under the pot and reduce the cooking juices until almost evaporated. Add the lemon juice and parsley and mix quickly over high heat for 2–3 minutes.

Spoon the sauce over the rabbit and serve with the creamy garlic potatoes.

SERVES 4

KANGAROO AND EMU STEAKS WITH TWO FRUIT SAUCES

Vic Cherikoff is well known for his knowledge and marketing of Australian bush foods. This is his recipe for two of Australia's indigenous meats. Native bush foods are sold through health-food stores and selected delicatessens.

500 g (1 lb) kangaroo rump or fillet, cut into 6 medallions
500 g (1 lb) emu hind saddle, cut into 6 medallions
8 native pepperleaves, ground to a powder (see glossary)
200 ml (3½ fl oz/6½ tablespoons) macadamia nut oil
50 g (2⅓ oz) dried quandongs (see glossary) or other wild fruit
125 ml (4 fl oz/½ cup) dark grape juice
250 ml (8 fl oz/1 cup) beef stock
250 ml (8 fl oz/1 cup) dry red wine
250 ml (8 fl oz/1 cup) thickened (double/heavy) cream
salt and freshly ground pepper
200 g (6½ oz) Kakadu plums (see glossary)
10 g (⅓ oz) ground dried akudjura (see glossary)

Dust the kangaroo and emu medallions with the native pepperleaves. Place each type of meat in a separate shallow nonreactive dish and add half of the oil to each. Turn the meat to coat both sides with the oil. Marinate for 2 hours at room temperature.

In a bowl, combine the quandongs and grape juice and let stand for 15 minutes.

Drain the meats. Heat 2 heavy frying pans over high heat until very hot. Sear the meats separately on both sides for 2 minutes on each side. Remove the meats from the pans, cover and set aside to rest in a warm place for 15 minutes. Add half each of the beef stock and wine to the pan used for cooking the kangaroo and place over medium heat to deglaze. Drain the quandongs and add them and half of the cream to the pan. Cook, stirring occasionally, until the sauce reduces and thickens, about 5–10 minutes. Season to taste with salt and pepper.

Meanwhile, place the pan used for cooking the emu over medium heat. Add the remaining stock and wine. Then add the Kakadu plums, akudjura and remaining cream. Cook, stirring occasionally, until the sauce reduces and thickens and the plums are tender, about 5–10 minutes. If the sauce is slightly bitter from the akudjura, add a little salt.

To serve, arrange 1 kangaroo medallion and 1 emu medallion on each of 6 warmed dinner plates. Spoon the quandong sauce over the kangaroo medallions and the plum sauce over the emu medallions. Serve at once.

SERVES 6

Spatchcocks with Couscous Stuffing and Harissa

SYDNEY

SPATCHCOCKS WITH COUSCOUS STUFFING AND HARISSA

Spatchcocks, also called poussins, are young chickens. Look for birds that weigh 400–600 grams (¾–1¼ pounds) each for this recipe. Order them in advance to be sure to secure fresh rather than frozen ones. Look for new-season dried dates; those that have been on the shelf too long are hard and dry. Harissa, a spicy North African condiment, can be purchased, but it is easy to make and tastes much better when fresh.

FOR THE STUFFING:

2 tablespoons peanut oil
1 brown onion, finely chopped
pinch of ground cinnamon
2 small firm tomatoes, diced
1 small carrot, peeled and finely diced
1 small zucchini (courgette), finely diced
4 dates, pitted and chopped
90 g (3 oz/⅔ cup) couscous (see glossary)
250 ml (8 fl oz/1 cup) chicken stock

FOR THE *HARISSA*:

6 large fresh red chillies, seeded
2 cloves garlic, peeled
2 teaspoons caraway seeds
pinch of salt
2 teaspoons olive oil

4 spatchcocks, about 600 g (1¼ lb) each
salt and freshly ground pepper
2 tablespoons peanut oil

To make the stuffing, in a heavy frying pan over medium heat, warm the peanut oil. Add the onion and sauté until soft, about 5 minutes. Add the cinnamon, tomatoes, carrot and zucchini and sauté for 2 minutes. Stir in the dates and couscous and add the stock. Bring to a simmer and simmer gently until all the stock is absorbed and the couscous is cooked, about 5 minutes. Remove from the heat and let cool.

To make the *harissa,* in a mortar, combine the chillies, garlic, caraway seeds and salt and pound with a pestle to form a

paste. Add the olive oil, drop by drop, and work it into the chilli paste. Set aside.

Preheat an oven to 180°C (350°F). Lightly oil a heavy baking pan.

Rinse the spatchcocks inside and out under running cold water and pat dry with paper towels. Season the cavities with salt and pepper. Spoon the stuffing into the cavities and truss closed with kitchen twine. Place breast sides up in the prepared pan and brush with peanut oil.

Roast in the centre of the oven until crisp and golden and cooked through, about 45 minutes. Shake the pan from time to time to ensure the birds do not stick. Clip and remove the twine from each bird. Serve with the *harissa*.

SERVES 4

SOUTH AUSTRALIA

BARBECUED KANGAROO WITH ANCHOVY VINAIGRETTE AND SOFT POLENTA

This is Maggie Beer's favourite way to cook kangaroo meat and, as she points out, it is the most Australian way of cooking it. Maggie, one of Australia's best authorities on cooking kangaroo, lives in South Australia, the only state where human consumption of the meat has been legal for over a decade.

180 ml (6 fl oz/¾ cup) fruity extra-virgin olive oil
1 clove garlic, finely chopped
finely grated zest of 1 lemon
1 generous tablespoon well-drained top-quality capers
4 anchovy fillets
8 fresh mint sprigs
4 kangaroo fillets (preferably from the double fillet), trimmed of sinews
1.25 l (40 fl oz/5 cups) rich chicken stock
235 g (7½ oz/1½ cups) fine polenta (cornmeal)
sea salt and freshly ground pepper
100 g (3½ oz) imported parmesan cheese, freshly grated
2 tablespoons butter
juice of 1 lemon

In a large, shallow nonreactive dish, stir together the oil, garlic, lemon zest, capers and anchovies. Remove the leaves from the mint sprigs and set aside. Chop the stems and add to the oil mixture. Add the kangaroo fillets, turn to coat and let stand for 30 minutes. Prepare a hot fire in a barbecue.

Meanwhile, to make the polenta, in a saucepan heat half of the stock to a simmer. In another saucepan, mix the other half of the cold stock with the polenta to make a paste. Slowly add the hot stock, stirring constantly to avoid lumping. Season to taste with sea salt and pepper and stir continuously over low heat until the polenta begins to come away from the sides of the saucepan, about 20 minutes. Add the parmesan and butter and spoon into a warmed bowl. Cover and keep warm.

Remove the fillets from the marinade and pat dry. Reserve the marinade. Place the fillets on the barbecue rack and sear, turning once, until well sealed, about 2 minutes on each side. This will be sufficient if the fillets are thin; if they are thick, turn them one more time to sear for 2 minutes. Season to taste with salt and pepper. Remove from the rack to a platter and let rest near the warmth of the barbecue for approximately 10 minutes before carving.

Pour the marinade into a small saucepan. Finely chop the reserved mint leaves and add to the marinade along with the lemon juice to form a vinaigrette. Place over medium-low heat and warm to until just under a boil.

Carve the kangaroo and drizzle generously with the warm vinaigrette. Pass the polenta at the table.

SERVES 4

Braised Duck with Vegetables

Duck is too often tough and dry. This method, which calls for braising the birds, keeps them moist and tender. Because each duck can differ in weight and size, the best way to check that the ducks are done is to poke each bird with a fork. Use only fresh, rather than frozen, ducks for this dish for the finest flavour. This dish is from Adelaide chef Gordon Parkes.

2 carrots, peeled and roughly chopped
2 brown onions, roughly chopped
2 turnips, peeled and roughly chopped
2 parsnips, peeled and roughly chopped
3 cloves garlic
4 bay leaves
10 juniper berries
½ bunch fresh oregano
60 ml (2 fl oz/¼ cup) water
3 ducks, 1.6 kg (3¼ lb) each
1 teaspoon salt
1 teaspoon cracked pepper

❧ Preheat an oven to 200°C (400°F). Place all the vegetables, garlic, bay leaves, juniper berries and oregano in a large, heavy roasting pan. Pour the water evenly over the vegetables. Place the ducks on top and season with the salt and pepper.
❧ Cook the ducks until they brown, about 40 minutes. Reduce the heat to 160°C (325°F) and cover the pan with aluminium foil. Continue to cook until fork tender, about 30 minutes. Check to be sure the water does not evaporate completely and add a few spoonfuls as needed.
❧ Remove the ducks and vegetables to a platter and cover to keep warm. Strain the cooking juices into a tall vessel. Spoon the fat off the top of the juices and discard. Pour the juices into a saucepan and heat to serving temperature. To serve, cut each duck in half. Serve with the vegetables and hot juices.

SERVES 6 *Photograph page 130*

Roast Fillet of Buffalo with Peppercorns and Mustard

Food writer and cooking-school owner Diane Holuigue gave me this recipe and said that the buffalo should be well aged for the best results. The fillet can also be cooked over charcoal, in which case she advises to leave some of the fat on the fillet intact, as its dripping helps to keep the fire going. Spit roasting the fillet in an oven or over a fire simplifies the cooking even further.

1 buffalo fillet, 2 kg (4 lb), partially trimmed of fat
3 large cloves garlic, cut into slivers
90 g (3 oz/6 tablespoons) smooth or whole-grain Dijon mustard
3 tablespoons cracked peppercorns

❧ Preheat an oven to 190°C (375°F). Using the point of a sharp knife, make slits in the fillet. Stick the garlic slivers into the slits and then spread the mustard on all sides of the fillet. Roll in the peppercorns. Place in a roasting dish. Roast, turning from time to time to brown easily, for 20–25 minutes for medium-rare.
❧ Transfer to a warmed platter and let rest for a few minutes, then slice and serve.

SERVES 8–10

Left to right: Roast Fillet of Buffalo with Peppercorns and Mustard, Barbecued Kangaroo with Anchovy Vinaigrette and Soft Polenta

STUFFED ROAST LAMB TOPSIDE

The success of the Trim Lamb program has been phenomenal. These healthful lamb cuts are trimmed of all fat and are ready to cook, allowing the home cook more time for unwinding at the end of a busy working day. Not only are these cuts quick to prepare, but there is also no waste. The leg is broken into primal cuts such as this topside, the boneless top portion of the leg. Now that the family unit is smaller, many families do not want a large piece of meat such as a whole leg of lamb. Sun-dried capsicums packed in canola oil, marketed by Sunhurst, are yet another addition to Australia's growing pantry of sun-dried foods. Serve this dish with layered eggplant, tomatoes and purple onions (recipe on page 192).

FOR THE STUFFING:

125 g (4 oz/¾ cup) drained, canned artichoke hearts, chopped
75 g (2½ oz/⅓ cup) drained sun-dried capsicums (bell peppers) in canola oil, chopped
2 tablespoons chopped pitted black olives
1 tablespoon chopped fresh oregano or 1 teaspoon dried oregano
salt and freshly ground pepper

4 lamb topsides, 185 g (6 oz) each, trimmed of all fat
1 clove garlic, halved
2 tablespoons olive oil
sea salt and freshly ground pepper

❧ Position a rack in the centre of an oven and preheat the oven to 200°C (400°F).
❧ In a bowl, combine all the ingredients for the stuffing, including salt and pepper to taste, and mix well. Cut a horizontal pocket two-thirds of the way through the centre of each topside. Rub the cut surfaces and outside surfaces of each topside with the garlic. Stuff each pocket with one-quarter of the artichoke mixture and secure closed with a toothpick.
❧ Heat a griddle pan or heavy frying pan over medium-high heat. Rub the oil over all surfaces of the topsides. Slip them into the pan and sear on both sides to seal in the juices. Transfer to a roasting pan and roast in the centre of the oven until cooked as desired, about 10 minutes for medium-rare.
❧ Remove from the oven to a warmed plate, cover loosely and let rest for 10 minutes. Remove the toothpicks and serve.

SERVES 4

N O R T H E R N   T E R R I T O R Y

OXTAILS WITH ORANGES AND NOODLES

Offal are not nearly as popular as they used to be. One reason is because they are generally extremely high in cholesterol. Oxtails can be very fatty, so make this dish at least 1 day ahead to allow time for the fat to set on the top so it can be discarded before reheating the dish. Long, slow cooking is necessary to tenderise oxtails. Always cook the meat until it is fork tender, but not falling off the bones.

80 ml (3 fl oz/⅓ cup) olive oil
2 brown onions, finely chopped
2 carrots, peeled and finely chopped
1 celery stalk, finely chopped
3 oxtails, about 1.75 (3½ lb) total weight, jointed
pinch of ground mace
grated zest of 3 oranges
250 ml (8 fl oz/1 cup) fresh orange juice

750 ml (24 fl oz/3 cups) beef stock
250 ml (8 fl oz/1 cup) dry red wine
salt and freshly ground pepper
2 navel oranges, sectioned with all white membrane removed
500 g (1 lb) fresh or dried egg noodles
2 tablespoons unsalted butter

❧ In a large, heavy pot over medium heat, warm the oil. Add the onions, carrots and celery and sauté until beginning to colour. Lift out with a slotted spoon and set aside. Working in batches, add the oxtail pieces in a single layer and sauté until browned on all sides. Lift out and place with the vegetables.
❧ When all the oxtails are browned, return them and the vegetables to the pot. Add the mace, orange zest and juice, stock, wine and salt and pepper to taste. Bring slowly to a boil and simmer until the meat is fork tender, 3–4 hours. Remove from the heat and let cool in the pot.
❧ Pour the contents of the pot into a colander placed over another heavy pot. Cover and chill the meat and liquid separately overnight.
❧ Lift the fat off the liquid and discard. If the liquid is too thin, cook rapidly until reduced to a good sauce consistency. Add the meat to the liquid and heat through. Add the orange sections and warm through in the sauce for 2 minutes.
❧ Meanwhile, bring plenty of salted water to a boil. Add the noodles and boil until al dente; the timing will depend upon the type of noodles used. Drain and transfer to a serving dish. Add the butter and toss well.
❧ To serve, place some noodles on each plate and spoon the oxtails and oranges alongside. Serve at once.

SERVES 6–8   *Photograph page 136*

T H E   G R A M P I A N S

IRISH STEW

This stew is made with mutton, lamb or sometimes beef and potatoes and onions. Australia's early Irish immigrants had already learned to survive on potatoes, so the addition of mutton or beef must have seemed like a great luxury. Although no longer a fashionable dish, Irish stew is one of the best one-pot meals I know. Made from shoulder chops, the sweetest part of the lamb, and served in cold weather, it is a truly marvellous feast.

1.5 kg (3 lb) shoulder chops, boned and the meat cut into large pieces
1 kg (2 lb) potatoes, peeled and cut into slices 1 cm (⅜ in) thick
750 g (1½ lb) brown onions, cut into slices 5 mm (¼ in) thick
1 tablespoon finely chopped fresh parsley leaves
1 tablespoon finely chopped fresh thyme
salt and freshly ground pepper

❧ Preheat an oven to 150°C (300°F).
❧ Arrange the lamb in the bottom along the sides of a large, heavy pot with a tight-fitting lid. Put the vegetables and herbs in the centre and pour in almost enough water to cover the lamb (about 500 ml/16 fl oz/2 cups). Season liberally with salt and pepper. Cover with aluminium foil and then with the lid, to ensure a good seal.
❧ Bake until tender, about 1¾ hours. Check from time to time to make sure there is still water in the pan and add more if needed. Serve piping hot.

SERVES 6   *Photograph pages 118–119*

Stuffed Roast Lamb Topside—photographed at Orange, NSW

Clockwise from top: Oxtails with Oranges and Noodles (recipe page 134), Beef Cheeks Braised in Rough Dry Red,
Roast Fillet of Beef with Tasmanian Alpine Pepperberries (recipe page 139)

SOUTH AUSTRALIA

BEEF CHEEKS BRAISED IN ROUGH DRY RED

Beef cheeks may sound a little obscure, but let me assure you they are a joy to eat with plenty of fresh vegetables, here with green beans, potatoes and carrots. You will have to order them ahead from the butcher, as they generally are not stocked. Use a rough dry red wine (a wine not yet matured) to give this slow-cooked dish the best flavour. Begin this dish 2 days before serving.

6 beef cheeks, about 400 g (13 oz) each, trimmed of excess
    sinew and cut in half
3 cloves garlic, cut into slivers

FOR THE MARINADE:

2 carrots, peeled and finely chopped
2 brown onions, finely chopped
3 pinches of mixed dried herbs
¼ bunch fresh Italian (flat-leaf) parsley, stems twisted
    and bruised
2 bay leaves
3 orange zest strips
2 tablespoons olive oil
1 bottle (750 ml/24 fl oz/3 cups) dry red wine
100 ml (3½ fl oz/6½ tablespoons) brandy

3 tablespoons olive oil
500 ml (16 fl oz/2 cups) beef stock
8 small desirée potatoes or other red-skinned young
    potatoes, unpeeled
salt
4 carrots, cut into batons 4 cm (1¼ in) long and 1 cm (⅜ in) thick
250 g (8 oz) green beans, trimmed

✂ Using the point of a sharp knife, make deep incisions in the beef. Stick a sliver of garlic into each slit.

✂ Choose a large nonreactive dish that will accommodate the beef cheeks in a single layer. Place one-third of the carrots and onions on the bottom of the dish and top with one-third of the mixed herbs, parsley, bay and zest. Drizzle with one-third of the oil and place half of the beef on top. Place half of the remaining vegetables, herbs and zest on top and drizzle with half of the remaining oil. Top with the remaining beef. Scatter the remaining vegetables, herbs and zest over the top and drizzle with the remaining oil. Pour the wine and brandy over the top. Cover and refrigerate, turning the beef over in the marinade several times to ensure even flavouring, for 36 hours.

✂ Position a rack in the lower third of an oven and preheat the oven to 140°C (280°F).

✂ Drain the beef in a colander placed over a large bowl to catch the juices. Remove the parsley and orange zest strips and discard. In a large, heavy pot with a tight-fitting lid, over medium heat, warm the oil. Dry the beef on paper towels. Working in batches, add the beef and brown on all sides. Lift out with tongs and set aside on a large plate. Add the drained vegetables to the same pan and sauté until golden, about 10 minutes. Add to the beef. Now add the strained liquid to the pan and boil, whisking up the caramelised juices on the bottom, until reduced by half. Add the stock and return the beef and sautéed vegetables to the pot.

✂ Bring to a boil and skim off fat as necessary. Cover with aluminium foil and then with the lid to ensure a tight fit. Place in the lower third of the oven and cook until the beef is tender, 2½–3 hours.

✂ Just before the beef is done, place the potatoes in a saucepan with water to cover, add salt to taste, bring to a boil and cook until tender, about 10 minutes. Drain and keep warm. In another saucepan, combine the carrots with water to cover and salt to taste, bring to a boil and cook until tender, about 5 minutes.

Drain and keep warm. Finally, cook the green beans in yet another saucepan in the same way for about 5 minutes. Drain and keep warm.

❧ Remove the beef to a large plate and keep warm. Strain the juices into a clean pot and bring to a boil. Skim the fat off the top and simmer until the juices are reduced to a good sauce consistency.

❧ Serve the beef cheeks in large warmed bowls. Pour the sauce around the cheeks and surround with the boiled potatoes, carrot batons and green beans. Serve immediately.

SERVES 4

AUSTRALIA

STEAK AND MUSHROOM PIE

Aussies love a good meat pie. The individual meat pie we queue for at the local bakery is not usually made at home, for two reasons. Firstly, it never tastes the same as the manufactured pie. Secondly, who has the time to make individual pies? On the other hand, making a large steak and mushroom pie to feed a crowd is hard to beat during the colder months. For the best flavour, use steak with some age and a strong homemade beef stock. To save time, pick up some ready-rolled puff pastry at the supermarket freezer.

FOR THE FILLING:

plain (all-purpose) flour for dusting
salt and freshly ground pepper
freshly grated nutmeg
1.25 kg (2½ lb) chuck steak, cut into 2-cm (¾-in) dice
2 tablespoons finely chopped mixed fresh herbs such as parsley, thyme and chives
225 g (7 oz) fresh white button mushrooms, quartered
1 tablespoon fresh lemon juice

500–600 ml (16–20 fl oz/2–2½ cups) beef stock
1 tablespoon commercial tomato sauce (ketchup)
1 tablespoon Worcestershire sauce

FOR THE PASTRY:

1 sheet frozen puff pastry, 25 cm (10 in) square, thawed (see glossary)
1 egg yolk
pinch of salt

❧ Position a rack in the upper third of an oven and preheat the oven to 200°C (400°F). Butter a 1¼-l (40-fl oz/5-cup) pie dish 23 cm (9 in) in diameter and place a pastry funnel in the centre (or cut vents once the pastry is in place). Butter the top of the funnel so the dough will not stick.

❧ To make the filling, in a shallow bowl, stir together the flour and salt, pepper and nutmeg to taste. Dust the beef with the flour mixture and place it in the prepared dish. Scatter the herbs over the meat and then add the mushrooms. Drizzle the lemon juice over the top. Add just enough of the stock to cover the meat and mushrooms, then stir in the tomato sauce and Worcestershire sauce.

❧ Cover the filling with the pastry, pressing it down well around the rim of the dish and trimming off the overhanging pastry with a sharp knife. In a small bowl, stir together the egg yolk and salt and add a few drops of water. Brush the mixture over the pastry without touching the cut edges (or it will not puff). Cut out small decorative shapes from the pastry trimmings and place on top of the pastry. Then brush the cutouts with the egg yolk glaze, again being careful not to brush the cut edges of the decorations.

❧ Bake the pie in the upper part of the oven until the pastry is puffed and golden, 25–30 minutes. Place a sheet of aluminium foil over the top, reduce the oven temperature to 180°C (350°F) and bake for 2 hours longer. Serve the pie straight from the dish.

SERVES 6

Steak and Mushroom Pie

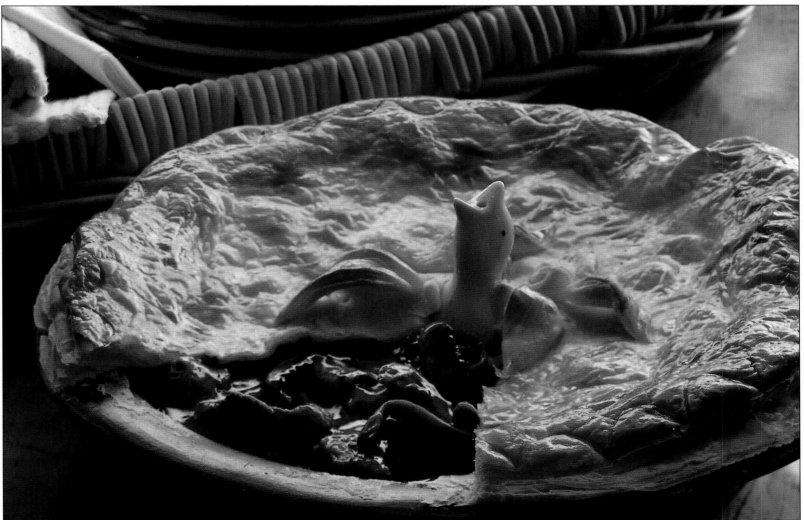

VENISON CHILLI

Venison is increasing in popularity as it becomes more readily available and people realise its nutritional value. It is a lean meat that is low in cholesterol and has the tick of approval from the Australian Heart Foundation. This hearty dish, which comes to us by way of Texas and Mexico, is gaining a following in Australia. It's an excellent dish to cook for a crowd and is worth making several days ahead, to allow the flavours to develop. It can also be made with beef or lamb. If you like, pass sour cream for diners to add as desired.

60 ml (2 fl oz/¼ cup) olive oil
2 brown onions, chopped
2 celery stalks, chopped
4 cloves garlic, crushed
500 g (1 lb) minced (ground) lean venison
1 can (880 g/28 oz) Roma (plum) tomatoes
300 ml (10 fl oz/1¼ cups) venison stock or beef stock
2 tablespoons tomato paste
1 tablespoon ground cumin
1 teaspoon salt, or to taste
1 teaspoon unsweetened cocoa powder
1 teaspoon small dried red chillies
½ teaspoon dried oregano
½ teaspoon ground allspice
1 can (780 g/25 oz) drained red kidney beans

In a large, heavy saucepan over medium heat, warm the oil. Add the onions and sauté until just beginning to brown, about 10 minutes. Add the celery and garlic and cook until golden; sauté about 4 minutes longer. Stir in the venison and cook, stirring, until crumbly. Add the tomatoes and their juice, stock and tomato paste and mix well. Stir in all the spices, herbs and seasonings, bring to a simmer and cook, uncovered, for 1¼ hours.

Add the beans and simmer for another 20–30 minutes, to blend the flavours. Serve the chilli piping hot.

SERVES 6

ROAST FILLET OF BEEF WITH TASMANIAN ALPINE PEPPERBERRIES

Both the leaves and the berries of Australia's native pepper are reasonably easy to find in large food stores in capital cities. Canola oil, which was once commonly known as rapeseed oil, has become popular, in part due to its reasonable price. The MacSmith family, in central-west New South Wales, began developing Australian Country canola oil on their property nine years ago. They make the oil on their property at Cudal. This is Jean-Paul Bruneteau's recipe. He is the owner-chef of Sydney's best-known native-ingredient restaurant.

1 eye of beef fillet, 1.5 kg (3 lb), trimmed of fat
freshly ground pepper or native pepperleaf
   (see glossary)
salt
Australian Country cold-pressed canola oil or other good-
   quality canola oil

FOR THE SAUCE:

canola oil for frying
2 tablespoons chopped pepperberries (see glossary)
2 tablespoons brandy
100 ml (3½ fl oz/6½ tablespoons) dry red wine

1 l (32 fl oz/4 cups) clear beef stock, heated
2 tablespoons madeira
salt and freshly ground pepper

1 carrot, peeled and sliced
1 celery stalk, sliced
1 large brown onion, sliced
2 tablespoons brandy

Preheat an oven to 220°C (425°F).

Tuck the tail of the fillet under to obtain a uniform thickness and tie the fillet with kitchen twine so that it holds its shape, or ask your butcher to do this for you. Rub all over with the pepper or pepperleaf, salt and oil. Let stand for 15 minutes.

To make the sauce, place a nonreactive frying pan over medium heat. Brush the pan with oil, add the pepperberries and sauté for 2 minutes. Add the brandy, ignite it with a long match and, when the flame dies, add the wine. Bring to a boil and add the warm stock. Simmer until reduced by half and the sauce is a good consistency. Add the madeira and season to taste with salt and pepper. Keep warm.

On the stove top, heat a roasting pan over medium-high heat. Add the beef and sear on all sides to seal in the juices. Remove the meat and set aside. Add the carrot, celery and onion and sauté for 2–3 minutes to soften slightly. Drain off any oil from the roasting pan.

Place the beef on top of the vegetables. Roast for 15 minutes. Transfer the beef to a warmed platter and let stand for 10 minutes before carving.

Meanwhile, remove the vegetables from the pan and discard. Remove any visible oil from the pan and place the pan over high heat. Add the brandy and deglaze the pan by scraping up any browned bits. Add the pan juices to the sauce and stir well.

Slice the beef across the grain and serve with the hot sauce.

SERVES 6   *Photograph page 136*

BUFFALO BURGERS

Northern Territory wild buffalo meat can be marvellously tender and flavoursome. But if it is handled incorrectly—cooked too fast or for too long—it will be very tough and dry. Burgers, in particular, must be cooked with these cautions in mind. MacFarms pure macadamia oil, produced in Queensland at Woombye; is a cold-pressed monounsaturated oil made from Australia's indigenous nut. It is a first-class oil for cooking and for dressing salads. This recipe is from Vic Cherikoff.

2 tablespoons MacFarms macadamia oil
1 small brown onion, finely chopped
1 kg (2 lb) buffalo tenderloin, minced (ground)
2–3 tablespoons dried native mint, finely crushed
3 dried native pepperleaves, ground to a powder
   (see glossary)
1½ tablespoons soy sauce
1 egg

In a small frying pan over medium heat, warm 1 tablespoon of the oil. Add the onion and sauté until soft, about 5 minutes. Transfer to a large bowl and let cool completely. Add the buffalo, mint, pepperleaves, soy sauce and egg to the onion and mix well. Form the mixture into 4–6 patties each 3 cm (1¼ in) thick.

Place a large, heavy frying pan over medium-high heat. Brush the pan with the remaining 1 tablespoon oil. Add the patties and fry until well sealed and a good crust has formed, about 3 minutes. Turn over the patties and fry until a good crust forms, about 2 minutes longer. Serve the burgers piping hot.

SERVES 4–6

Clockwise from top right: Venison Chilli, Barbecued Crocodile Steaks with Asian Flavours (recipe page 142), Buffalo Burgers—photographed at Bend of the River estate, Queensland

Left to right: Roast Chicken Stuffed with Granny Smith Apples and Sausages, Saffron Chicken (recipe page 142), Quails Roasted with Speck and Sage Leaves

ROAST CHICKEN STUFFED WITH GRANNY SMITH APPLES AND SAUSAGES

Most Australians dish up roast chicken several times a year. The combination of our much-loved Granny Smith apples with the small, fresh pork sausages known as chipolatas results in a sweet yet subtle chicken that is deliciously moist and flavoursome. Other small fresh sausages can be substituted for the chipolatas.

325 g (10 oz) chipolata sausages (see glossary)
1 roasting chicken, 1.8 kg (4 lb)
salt and freshly ground pepper
1 small brown onion, chopped
1 Granny Smith apple, peeled, cored and chopped
1 teaspoon chopped fresh sage or ½ teaspoon dried sage
1½ tablespoons unsalted butter, melted, or 1 tablespoon
    safflower or peanut oil

✲ Position a rack in the upper third of an oven and preheat the oven to 180°C (350°F).
✲ Bring a saucepan three-quarters full of water to a boil. Add the sausages and boil for 2 minutes. Drain and let cool.
✲ Remove the excess fat from the chicken and wash inside and out under running cold water. Dry with paper towels. Season the cavity with salt and pepper. Place 1 tablespoon of the onion, one-quarter of the apple, a pinch of the sage and 4 or 5 sausages in the cavity. Do not fill the cavity tightly or the sausages will not cook through. Set the remaining onion, apple, sage and sausages aside.
✲ Paint the chicken with the butter or oil and sprinkle with salt and pepper. Place in a heavy nonstick baking pan and roast in the upper third of the oven for 1 hour and 40 minutes. Add the remaining onion, apple, sage and sausages to the pan and continue to roast until the chicken juices run clear when tested with a fork in the thickest part of a leg, about 20 minutes longer.
✲ Let the chicken rest for 10 minutes. Remove the sausages, apple and onion from the pan and the cavity and arrange on a serving platter. Set the chicken on the platter and serve at once.

SERVES 4–6

QUAILS ROASTED WITH SPECK AND SAGE LEAVES

This is one of the simplest yet loveliest quail dishes I know. Best of all for the busy cook, the quail can be readied for cooking 8 hours in advance and refrigerated. Serve with your favourite polenta.

8 quails
180 g (6 oz) *speck,* cut into 24 pieces (see glossary)
16 fresh sage leaves
3 tablespoons olive oil
sea salt and freshly ground pepper

✲ Place 8 bamboo skewers in a shallow dish or pan and add water to cover. Let soak for 20 minutes. Meanwhile, preheat an oven to 180°C (350°F). Lightly oil a heavy roasting pan.
✲ Place a piece of *speck* inside each quail. Drain the skewers and thread the following onto each of them, in the order given: a piece of *speck,* a sage leaf, a quail (under the wings and through the rib cage), another sage leaf and finally another piece of *speck.* Brush the olive oil over the quail and place in the prepared pan.
✲ Roast in the hottest part of the oven until golden and crisp on the outside and pink and juicy within, 15–20 minutes.

SERVES 4

VICTORIA

HAM HOCKS WITH BORLOTTI BEANS

These ham hocks are the hock end of the leg after the ham has been used. They are often used as a base for a thick split-pea soup, but I prefer them this way. Buy the fresh borlotti beans in their pink-flecked pods in the autumn when they are in season. Out of season, use dried borlotti beans, soaked first in cold water, and allow plenty of time for cooking—up to 2 hours. Accompany this dish with boiled potatoes and with spinach cooked in olive oil.

375 g (12 oz/1¾ cups) fresh shelled borlotti (cranberry) beans or 200 g (6½ oz/1 cup) dried borlotti beans
80 ml (3 fl oz/⅓ cup) olive oil
2 brown onions, cut into slices 6 mm (¼ in) thick
4 cloves garlic, bruised
2 or 3 meaty ham hocks, sawn crosswise into pieces 4 cm (1½ in) thick
3 fresh sage sprigs or 1 tablespoon dried sage
2 teaspoons cracked pepper

✿Pick over the beans and discard any discoloured ones. If using dried beans, place in a bowl, add water to cover and let soak overnight. The next day, drain the beans in a colander, rinse well in running cold water and drain. Set aside.
✿Preheat an oven to 190°C (375°F).
✿In a heavy, flameproof terracotta or cast-iron casserole (pot) over medium heat, warm the oil. Add the onions and sauté until softened, about 5 minutes. Add the garlic, drained dried beans, ham hocks, sage, pepper and water just to cover. Bring slowly to a boil, cover with a tight-fitting lid and place in the oven. Bake until the beans and ham are tender, about 2 hours. If using fresh beans, add after the first hour of cooking.
✿Remove from the oven and let cool in the pot. Pour the contents of the pot into a colander placed over a bowl. Pour the captured juices into a tall vessel and place in the freezer until the fat solidifies on top, about 2 hours.
✿Remove the skin, fat and gristle from the ham hocks, then bone them and discard the trimmings and bones. Discard the sage sprigs, if used, as well. Return the meat and the other ingredients still in the colander to the pot.
✿Spoon the fat off the top of the juices and discard. Pour the juices (if they are good they will have jelled) back over the ham and beans and then reheat on the stove top when ready to serve. Spoon into large warmed bowls and serve piping hot.

SERVES 4–6

NEW SOUTH WALES

PORK CHOPS WITH CABBAGE AND ONION MARMALADE

The range of new pork cuts is very tempting. Many of the lean cuts have been approved by the National Heart Foundation. The onion marmalade can be made several days beforehand and refrigerated. Simply heat gently when needed.

FOR THE ONION MARMALADE:

100 ml (3½ fl oz/6½ tablespoons) olive oil
1 kg (2 lb) purple onions, cut into slices 1 cm (⅜ in) thick
1 teaspoon dried oregano
salt and freshly ground pepper
70 g (2½ oz/⅓ cup) firmly packed dark brown sugar
125 ml (4 fl oz/½ cup) chicken stock
80 ml (3 fl oz/⅓ cup) red wine vinegar
2 tablespoons redcurrant jelly
fresh lemon juice, optional

FOR THE PORK:

1 tablespoon olive oil
4 thick pork loin chops, trimmed of fat
coarsely grated zest of 1 orange
juice of 1 orange
80 ml (3 fl oz/⅓ cup) dry white wine
¼ head green cabbage, cut into large chunks
¼ teaspoon cumin seeds
salt and freshly ground pepper

✿To make the marmalade, in a large, heavy pot over medium heat, warm the oil. Add the onions and cook, stirring, until they begin to caramelise, about 15 minutes. Add the oregano, salt and pepper to taste and sugar and cook gently for 10 minutes.
✿Add the stock and vinegar and cook over high heat until most of the liquid evaporates, 4–5 minutes. Add the jelly and stir until melted. Taste and adjust with lemon juice, if needed. Spoon into a heatproof bowl and cover to keep warm.
✿To cook the pork, in a heavy pot over medium heat, warm the oil. Add the chops in a single layer and sauté, turning once, until golden on each side. Add the orange zest and juice and the wine, cover tightly and cook gently until fork tender, 12–15 minutes. Transfer the pork chops to a platter and keep warm.
✿Add the cabbage and cumin seeds to the same pan and cook over high heat, stirring, for 3 minutes. Then partially cover and cook until the cabbage is just tender, 4–5 minutes. Season with the cumin seeds and salt and pepper to taste.
✿To serve, divide the marmalade among 4 warmed dinner plates. Place the cabbage on top and lean the chops against the vegetables. Spoon the pan juices over the top and serve at once.

SERVES 4

*Left to right: Ham Hocks with Borlotti Beans,
Pork Chops with Cabbage and Onion Marmalade*

PORT DOUGLAS

BARBECUED CROCODILE STEAKS WITH ASIAN FLAVOURS

Crocodile tastes similar to chicken but with a mild fish flavour. The tail is definitely the best part. This is how chef Anthony Hendre prepares it in Port Douglas in Far North Queensland.

2 carrots, peeled and cut into julienne
2 leeks, including tender green tops, cut into julienne
1 piece gingerroot, 2.5 cm (1 in) long, peeled and cut into fine julienne
2 lemongrass stalks, tender part only, chopped (see glossary)
6 crocodile tail steaks
6 lime slices
120 ml (4 fl oz/½ cup) oyster sauce (see glossary)
1 tablespoon sesame oil
6 fresh coriander (cilantro) sprigs
1 tablespoon finely chopped fresh mint
1 tablespoon sesame seeds

Prepare a fire in a barbecue and let the coals burn down until they are white.

Meanwhile, cut out six 30-cm (12-in) squares of aluminium foil and spread out on a work surface. Place an equal portion of the carrots, leeks, gingerroot and lemongrass in the centre of each square. Top with a crocodile steak. Add a slice of lime and pour about 1 tablespoon oyster sauce and ½ teaspoon sesame oil over each parcel. Wrap the foil to seal securely. Place the packets on the barbecue rack and cook for 6 minutes; at this point the crocodile should be tender. Open one package to check that the steak is done.

Once cooked, slide the steaks out of the foil onto serving plates. Top with the coriander, mint and sesame seeds and serve.

SERVES 6   *Photograph page 138*

PERTH

CHICKEN AND VEAL TERRINE

A delectable terrine that is easy to make has a place in everyone's recipe repertoire. The blanched leeks wrapped around the terrine keep it moist and impart a delicious flavour. This terrine makes a great starter or luncheon dish and packs well for taking on picnics.

125 g (¼ lb) chicken livers, trimmed
3 tablespoons brandy
freshly ground pepper
1 large leek
salt
1 tablespoon unsalted butter
1 brown onion, finely chopped
3 tablespoons finely chopped fresh parsley
125 g (¼ lb) minced (ground) veal
125 g (¼ lb) minced (ground) chicken
125 g (¼ lb) fresh pork fat, minced (ground)
1 bay leaf, torn into 4 pieces
¼ teaspoon dried oregano
½ teaspoon drained green peppercorns
1 egg, lightly beaten
1 tablespoon plain (all-purpose) flour

Place the livers in a nonreactive dish, add the brandy, stirring to coat, and grind pepper over the top. Cover and marinate in the refrigerator for 2 hours.

Position a rack in the middle of an oven and preheat the oven to 180°C (350°F).

Trim off the root end of the leek. Cut down one side of the leek and remove the first 8 layers. Wash the removed leaves well. Bring a saucepan three-quarters full of water to a boil and add salt to taste. Add the leek leaves and boil for 1 minute. Drain, refresh in cold water and drain well.

Line a terrine 24 cm (10 in) long with the leek leaves, allowing them to overhang the edge so that they can be folded over the mixture when it is added. In a frying pan over medium heat, melt the butter. Add the onion and parsley and sauté until softened, about 5 minutes. Remove from the heat and let cool.

Drain the livers, reserving the brandy. Chop the livers roughly and place in a bowl. Add the cooled onion mixture, veal, chicken, pork fat, bay leaf, oregano, peppercorns, egg and flour. Mix well and then mix in the reserved brandy. Sauté a nugget of the mixture, taste and adjust the seasonings.

Spoon the meat mixture into the leek-lined terrine, level the mixture and fold the leeks over it. Put the lid on the terrine or cover with aluminium foil and place the terrine in a roasting pan. Pour boiling water into the roasting pan to reach halfway up the sides of the terrine.

Bake in the centre of the oven until the terrine is cooked through, about 1½ hours. To check that the terrine is done, insert a metal skewer into the centre of the terrine and leave it there for 30 seconds, then remove it; it should be very hot to the touch.

Uncover the terrine and carefully pour off as much liquid as possible. Let cool for 30 minutes. Cover the terrine with plastic wrap and weight it down with cans of food or bricks. Refrigerate overnight. To serve, carefully invert the terrine onto a serving plate and cut into thick slices.

SERVES 8–10

SYDNEY

SAFFRON CHICKEN

Sri Lankan–born Charmaine Solomon, one of the most prolific cookbook authors in Australia, says this is a good example of how fragrant and spicy an Indian dish can be without being fiery hot. Serve it with steamed white rice or chapattis.

¼ teaspoon saffron strands
1 tablespoon hot water
3 tablespoons *ghee* (see glossary)
1 large brown onion, finely chopped
3 cloves garlic, finely chopped
2 teaspoons finely chopped, peeled gingerroot
3 fresh red chillies, seeded and sliced, optional
1 teaspoon ground cardamom
1 roasting chicken, 1.5 kg (3 lb), cut into serving pieces and breasts halved
salt

Place the saffron in a dry pan over low heat and toast for 1 minute; take care not to scorch it. Turn out into a small shallow dish to cool and become brittle. Crush with the back of a spoon into a powder. Add the hot water and stir to dissolve.

In a heavy saucepan over low heat, warm the *ghee*. Add the onion, garlic, gingerroot and chillies and fry gently, stirring frequently, until the onion is soft and golden, about 10 minutes. Add the dissolved saffron and the cardamom to the pan and then add the chicken. Increase the heat to medium and turn the chicken until each piece is coated with the saffron mixture.

Add the salt, cover and cook over medium heat for 15 minutes. Uncover and continue cooking until almost all the liquid evaporates and the chicken is tender, 20–30 minutes longer. Serve at once.

SERVES 4   *Photograph page 140*

*Chicken and Veal Terrine—
photographed under a jacaranda tree in Sydney*

SOUVLAKI WITH BABA GHANNOUJ

There are many takeaway outlets in Australia selling souvlaki, spit-cooked lamb, wrapped in pitta bread with hommos and tabbouleh. I particularly like this combination of warm crusty pide, a Turkish bread, with moist sliced lamb and creamy eggplant. Lamb backstrap is the eye of the loin.

FOR THE MARINADE:

125 ml (4 fl oz/½ cup) olive oil
100 ml (3½ fl oz/6½ tablespoons) dry white wine
1 tablespoon fresh lemon juice
1 teaspoon dried oregano
3 bay leaves, torn

3 lamb backstraps, cut into slices 2 mm (⅛ in) thick
salt and freshly ground pepper
baba ghannouj (recipe on page 190)
1–2 *pides*

To make the marinade, in a shallow nonreactive dish, whisk together the oil, wine, lemon juice, oregano and bay leaves. Add the lamb, turn to coat and let stand for 30 minutes at room temperature.

Meanwhile, preheat a griller (broiler) on high or prepare a fire in a barbecue. Working in batches, place the lamb on a griller tray or on the barbecue rack. Grill (broil) until it begins to colour, about 1 minute. Turn over and cook on the second side until it begins to colour, about 1 minute longer. Remove to a platter and keep warm while cooking the remaining lamb. Season to taste with salt and pepper.

To serve, split and grill the *pide* until golden and crusty. Spread the *pide* with the *baba ghannouj* and top with the lamb. Place on a platter and serve at once.

SERVES 6

22-MINUTE MONGOLIAN LAMB

This is a simple dish for the family made from lean lamb strips marketed under the Trim Lamb label. Serve with the rice of your choice.

2 teaspoons cornflour (cornstarch)
2 tablespoons light soy sauce
1 tablespoon oyster sauce (see glossary)
125 ml (4 fl oz/½ cup) chicken stock
1 tablespoon vegetable oil
750 g (1½ lb) lean lamb, cut into thin strips about 6 cm
    (2½ in) long and 1 cm (⅜ in) wide
4 brown onions, quartered
2 cloves garlic, crushed
3 spring (green) onions, including tender green tops, chopped
2 fresh red chillies, finely chopped

In a small bowl, stir together the cornflour, soy sauce, oyster sauce and stock. Set aside.

In a wok or a deep frying pan over high heat, warm the oil. Add half of the lamb and stir-fry until the lamb is just tender, 2–3 minutes. Using a slotted spoon, transfer to a dish and set aside. Repeat with the remaining lamb and remove in the same manner. Then add the brown onions, garlic, spring onions and chillies and stir-fry until the onions soften, about 2 minutes.

Return the lamb strips to the pan. Quickly stir the cornflour mixture and add it as well. Cook until slightly thickened, 2–3 minutes. Transfer to a serving dish and serve at once.

SERVES 4–6

SICHUAN PORK WITH SPINACH AND STEAMED BUNS

This Chinese dish from Sichuan Province is easy and delicious. It would be impractical for most cooks to make the dough for the steamed buns at home because it is tricky and time-consuming. Fortunately, the buns are available in Chinese food shops ready to steam. Look for them in the refrigerator cabinets; instructions for steaming are on the packet. The soybean paste is sold in jars in the same shops.

750 g (1½ lb) boned lean leg of pork, in one piece
1 piece gingerroot, 4 cm (1½ in) long, sliced

Clockwise from top right: Souvlaki with Baba Ghannouj, 22-Minute Mongolian Lamb, Sichuan Pork with Spinach and Steamed Buns

½ bunch spring (green) onions, including tender green tops, cut into 4-cm (1½-in) lengths
2 tablespoons rice wine
2 tablespoons meat stock or vegetable stock
pinch of sugar
2 tablespoons fermented soybean paste
2 teaspoons cornflour (cornstarch)
3 tablespoons water
80 ml (3 fl oz/⅓ cup) vegetable oil
2 cloves garlic, finely chopped
2 bunches spinach, stems removed and leaves roughly chopped
2 or 3 fresh red chillies, seeded and sliced
salt
8 Chinese buns, each 8 cm (3¼ in) in diameter, steamed (see note)

ℭ Place the pork, gingerroot and spring onions in a pot that accommodates the pork snugly. Add water to cover and bring

slowly to a boil. Reduce the heat to medium-low, cover and simmer for 25 minutes. Remove from the heat and let cool in the pot.
ℭ Drain the pork and cut it into 3-cm (1¼-in) dice, then slice finely. Place in a nonreactive bowl, add 1 tablespoon of the rice wine and mix well.
ℭ In another small bowl, whisk together the stock, sugar, soybean paste and the remaining 1 tablespoon rice wine. In yet another small bowl, stir together the cornflour and water.
ℭ In a wok or large frying pan over high heat, warm the oil. When the oil is hot, add the garlic, spinach and chillies and stir-fry until the spinach wilts. Add the pork and stir and toss until heated through. Quickly whisk the soybean paste mixture, add it to the wok and stir well. Quickly whisk the cornflour mixture, add it to the wok and stir until the mixture thickens slightly and is glossy. Season to taste with salt.
ℭ Serve immediately with steamed Chinese buns.

SERVES 8

145

ROAST VEAL CUTLETS WITH HERB BREADCRUMBS, ROCKET AND LEMON

Gary Skelton, a chef working near where I live in Sydney, has the same ideas about food that I have. Every dish should be made from the freshest and finest-quality ingredients and cooked with loving care and attention. He is clever with food combinations, flavours and textures. This dish is what he likes to eat when he has the time to sit down to a meal and enjoy it.

Veal in Australia is fairly unreliable. Far too much meat is sold as veal (less than a year old) that is actually beef. Look for pale, almost-white veal and cook it gently without ever letting it dry out. Rocket, also called arugula, is a salad leaf with a peppery taste. A bowl of freshly cut rocket (it's very easy to grow) with a drizzle of fruity South Australian Joseph brand extra-virgin olive oil, a splash of Western Australian Berry Farm pear vinegar and shaved parmigiano-reggiano cheese from Italy is my ultimate lunch.

½ loaf day-old bread, 375 g (12 oz)
1 teaspoon finely chopped fresh parsley
1 teaspoon finely chopped fresh oregano
1 teaspoon finely chopped fresh basil
30 g (1 oz/¼ cup) freshly grated parmesan cheese
100 g (3½ oz/6½ tablespoons) unsalted butter, melted
extra-virgin olive oil for frying veal, plus 150 ml (5 fl oz/⅔ cup) extra-virgin olive oil
8 veal cutlets, 100 g (3½ oz) each
500 g (1 lb) baby rocket (arugula) leaves
2 lemons, halved

❧ Cut the bread into chunks. Place in a food processor fitted with the metal blade and process to form fine crumbs. Transfer to a large bowl and add all the herbs, the parmesan cheese and the butter. Mix well.

Roast Veal Cutlets with Herb Breadcrumbs, Rocket and Lemon

❧ Preheat an oven to 220°C (425°F). Heat a large, flameproof heavy frying pan over high heat until quite hot. Paint the pan with a little oil. Add the cutlets and sear quickly on both sides to seal in the juices. Top evenly with the breadcrumb mixture.
❧ Place in the oven until cooked through and the topping is browned, about 6 minutes. Transfer the veal cutlets to a warmed platter, cover and let rest in a warm oven for a few minutes.
❧ Arrange the rocket leaves on 4 warmed dinner plates. Drizzle evenly with the 150 ml (5 fl oz/⅔ cup) oil. Arrange 2 veal cutlets on top of the rocket and garnish each plate with a lemon half. Serve at once.

SERVES 4

TANDOORI CHICKEN AND PAPPADUM STACK WITH MANGO CHUTNEY AND YOGHURT

This is not a true tandoori chicken dish but an adaptation that is easily grilled or pan-fried. The chicken acquires an excellent flavour from the marinade, which is made from a commercial blend of spices labeled tandoori mix. It is available in well-stocked food stores and Indian shops. The pappadums *are crisp, thin Indian wafers made from split pea, rice or other flour and are commonly flavoured with garlic and pepper. Pile up the various elements— crunchy* pappadums, *chicken and yoghurt—to make an eye-catching and unusual dish. Many of the old country cookbooks have recipes for making mango chutney, or you can buy excellent commercial ones.*

1½ tablespoons tandoori mix
500 g (1 lb/2 cups) plain yoghurt
1 tablespoon fresh lemon juice
1 kg (2 lb) boneless chicken pieces, skinned
vegetable oil for deep-frying
18 *pappadums*
300 g (9½ oz/1 cup) mango chutney
6 fresh coriander (cilantro) sprigs

❧ In a shallow dish that will comfortably accommodate the chicken pieces in a single layer, stir together the tandoori mix, 250 g (8 oz/1 cup) of the yoghurt and the lemon juice.
❧ Cut the chicken into long, slender, serving-sized pieces and immerse in the yoghurt mixture. Cover with plastic wrap and refrigerate for 4–6 hours or as long as overnight.
❧ When ready to assemble the dish, in a heavy frying pan, pour in oil to a depth of 2.5 cm (1 in) and heat to 190°C (375°F). When the oil is ready, fry the *pappadums,* one at a time, until enlarged and crisp, about 1 minute. Using a slotted spoon, transfer to crumpled paper towels to drain.
❧ Heat a large, heavy nonstick frying pan over medium heat or preheat a griller (broiler) on high. Paint the pan or griller tray with vegetable oil. Place the chicken pieces in the pan or on the tray and cook, turning to brown both sides, until cooked through, 15–20 minutes; the timing will depend on the size and thickness of the chicken pieces.
❧ To assemble, warm 6 large dinner plates. Place 1 *pappadum* in the centre of each. Top with some of the chicken pieces. Top with another *pappadum,* more chicken pieces and then another *pappadum.* Finally, divide the remaining chicken among the stacks. Spoon some chutney on one side of each plate. Stir the remaining 250 g (8 oz/1 cup) yoghurt to smooth it slightly and spoon it onto the opposite side of the plates. Finish with a coriander sprig. Serve at once.

SERVES 6

Left to right: Tandoori Chicken and Pappadum Stack with Mango Chutney and Yoghurt, Tandoori Quails with Raita and Puri

TANDOORI QUAILS WITH RAITA AND PURI

Quails are farmed in all the Australian states year-round. Look for the plumper birds for the best value. Redgate Farm at Woodville, between Maitland and Raymond Terrace in New South Wales, markets a 300-gram (10-ounce) quail they call the Excel. They also produce a Super Quail that weighs between 195 and 280 grams (6½ and 9 ounces). The most common breed is Coturnix, also called the Japanese quail.

These tandoori-flavoured quails are quick to prepare, making them ideal for the busy cook. The tandoori mix can be found in well-stocked food stores. The black mustard seeds are sold in Indian shops. The crisp Indian flatbreads known as puri are available commercially in upmarket outlets or may be purchased from the local Indian takeaway or neighbourhood restaurant. If you have the time, however, it is rewarding to make them at home. Be sure to allow time for the dough to rest.

12 quails
500 g (1 lb/2 cups) plain yoghurt
3 tablespoons tandoori mix
1½ tablespoons fresh lemon juice

FOR THE *PURI:*

520 g (16½ oz/3¼ cups) plain (all-purpose) flour
500–550 ml (16–18 fl oz/2–2¼ cups) water
200 g (¾ cup) *ghee* (see glossary)

FOR THE *RAITA:*

2 large carrots, peeled and coarsely grated
2 tablespoons olive oil
1 teaspoon black mustard seeds
½ teaspoon ground dried chilli
2 tablespoons sultanas (golden raisins)
80 ml (3 fl oz/⅓ cup) fresh lemon juice

To prepare the quails, slit each bird down either side of the backbone and remove the backbone. Open the bird out and flatten the small rib bones with the side of your fist. In a dish that will accommodate all the quails, whisk together the yoghurt, tandoori mix and lemon juice until well mixed. Place the quails in the mixture and turn each so it is coated on both sides. Cover with plastic wrap and refrigerate for 2 hours.

To make the *puri* dough, place the flour in a large bowl. Make a well in the centre and add 500 ml (16 fl oz/2 cups) of the water. Using a fork, stir the flour into the water, mixing quickly and adding more water as needed to make a soft, pliable dough. Turn out the dough onto a lightly floured work surface and knead lightly until smooth. Cover with a damp cloth and let rest for 1 hour.

To make the *raita,* place the carrots in a bowl. In a heavy frying pan over medium heat, warm the oil. Add the mustard seeds and fry until aromatic. Add the ground chilli and sultanas and cook, stirring, for 2 minutes. Stir in the lemon juice and pour over the carrots. Mix well and let cool.

To finish the *puris,* divide the dough in half. Knead each portion until silky smooth and no sign of stickiness remains. Divide each half into 12 equal portions and then form each portion into a ball. On a lightly floured work surface, roll out each ball into a round the size of a small plate and about 3 mm (⅛ in) thick.

In a deep pan over medium-high heat, melt the *ghee.* When hot, slip 1 *puri* into the pan and cook until puffed and golden, about 2 minutes. Turn and cook until golden on the second side, about 1 minute. Using tongs or a slotted utensil, transfer to crumpled paper towels to drain. Keep warm while cooking the remaining rounds.

Preheat a griller (broiler) on high or prepare a fire in a barbecue.

Lift the quails from the marinade, draining well, and place skin side up on a griller tray or barbecue rack. Cook on the first side until golden and crisp. Turn carefully and cook on the second side until golden and crisp. Total cooking time will be 9–10 minutes. Serve the quails with warm *puri* and *raita.*

SERVES 6

Western Australia

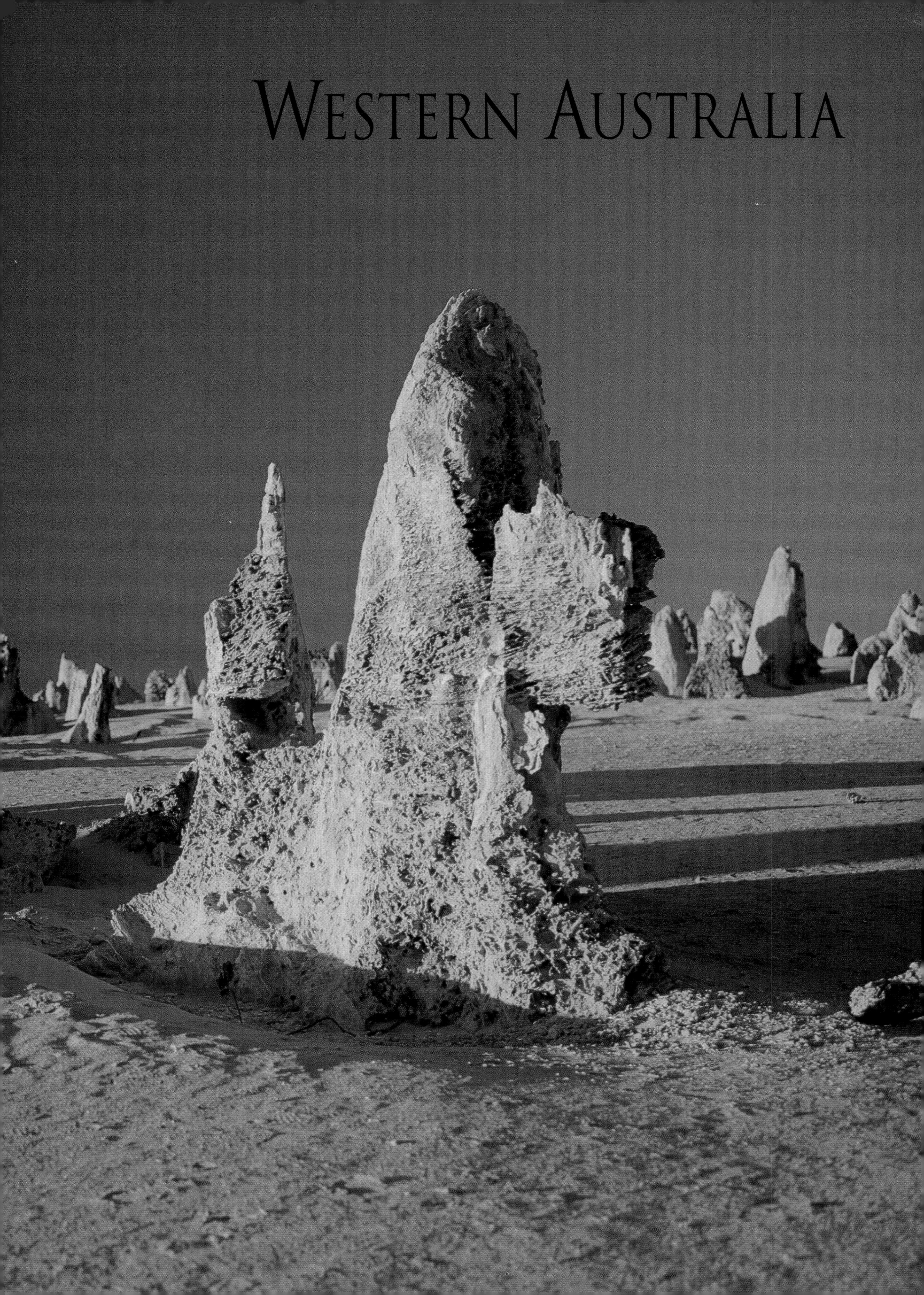

WESTERN AUSTRALIA

W E S T E R N   R I C H E S

KOONACS AND GILGIES (the first g is soft) and marrons are not the only things that set Western Australia apart: it nearly became another country. Were it not for all the t'othersiders—those from 'over east' who flocked to the Western Australia goldfields in the 1890s—voting in favour of joining the federation of states, which became the country of Australia in 1901, Western Australia might not have become part of it.

Koonacs and gilgies are two small, uniquely Western Australian types of yabbies—freshwater crustaceans—bearing their original Aboriginal names. Gilgies are found in the southwest, while the slightly bigger blue and white koonacs are from the north of the state. Marrons—the world's third largest freshwater crustacean (the two biggest are respectively from Tasmania and the Murray River)—are found all along the scarp between Margaret River and Perth.

On the shores of the Indian Ocean, Western Australia, which is nearly twelve times the size of France, comprises one-third of Australia. With a latitudinal stretch of twenty-one degrees, it has the greatest north-south spread of all the Australian states. It also has an enormous coastline of seven thousand kilometres (forty-two hundred miles), which offers a wide variety of fish, both cool water and tropical.

A uniquely Australian fish indigenous to Western Australia waters is the dhufish. Although a first cousin to the pearl perch, which is found in New South Wales waters, dhufish is found only along the five hundred kilometres (three hundred miles) of coastline from Busselton to Kalbarri, and is believed by fishers to have no peer.

Some fish species present elsewhere in Australia are different in Western Australia. For instance, the garfish here have a different flavour from those from South

Previous pages: Limestone towers, many taller than human height, populate the Pinnacles Desert in Nambung National Park. Left: The water of Lake Grace nurtures the rich wetlands in this southwestern part of the state.

Australia. The latter are tastier because they feed in the reedy bottom off the South Australian coast. What South Australians call tommy ruffs are called herrings in Western Australia, where they are larger and much more popular.

Other fish include estuarine catfish—cobbler—gold band snapper, Rankin cod, Spanish mackerel, goatfish (rouget or red mullet), sand whiting, prawns—banana, endeavour and king—scallops, spotted cod, red jewfish and tropical coral trout. Scampi were found by accident off the continental shelf in the mid-1980s—the boats were looking for prawns (shrimp) at the time—and are considered superior to the European scampi.

Since the end of the 1980s, when a new trawl fishery started, increasing numbers of red emperor (red snapper) have been caught. Tuna is available in smaller quantities, because Western Australia sold its tuna harvest quotas to South Australia. There is also a huge crayfish industry; the majority of crayfish are exported live, mainly to Asian destinations such as Tokyo. The annual crayfish season begins at midnight on 15 November. There's a race—the Big Lobster Bash—to land the first crays, and helicopters are even sent out to the boats to bring the first one ashore.

The contribution of migrants, particularly those from Italy and Greece who have arrived since World War II, is arguably more evident in Western Australia than in other states. Their influence has been extensive, particularly in Fremantle and Perth. Migration from around the Mediterranean has also caused changes in the perceptions of what is edible. Squid and octopus, once largely ignored, are now sought after, and whole industries have grown up out of fish that were once considered only good enough for bait.

The Mendolia family came to Australia from Sicily. Obtaining a bait licence, they began to catch anchovies. Jim Mendolia started curing them using traditional Sicilian methods. He now produces the wonderful Auschovies and Bella del Tindari (named for the Madonna in his parents' hometown) anchovies, which are less salty than imported ones.

Sardine fisheries have developed since the 1980s. Where once these fish were only sold as bait, now through the enterprise of southern Italian immigrants, they are sold filleted and even crumbed. Fremantle, where

The Hotel York and other historic buildings in Kalgoorlie are reminders of the town's rich gold-rush past.

most of the fishers are Italian, holds an annual Sardine Festival, and a Blessing of the Fleet each October.

Although the Dutch had mapped the west coast of what they called Terra del Zur—'the South Land'—as far south as Cape Leeuwin by 1628, it wasn't until two centuries later that Europeans attempted to settle here. Separated from the other colonies by great expanses of desert and in the south by the treeless Nullarbor Plain (literally, 'no tree'), it was, as they were, settled by sea.

The presence of French ships had aroused British suspicions, and prompted by fears of their intentions, what was to become Western Australia was annexed on Christmas Day in 1826 where Albany is now. Although Captain Charles Fremantle arrived at the mouth of the Swan on 2 May 1829 to establish the first settlement, by the 1850s only four small pockets were inhabited. Such was the shortage of labour that the colony *requested* the British government to send convicts. Some ninety-seven hundred convicts—all men—were transported between 1850 and 1868, when the policy ceased.

On a visit to Western Australia in 1872, English novelist Anthony Trollope commented on the wishful thinking of many locals that gold might do for the colony what it had done for the eastern states. Within twenty years it had. The first gold finds were in the Kimberleys in 1883. The main rushes came after self-government in 1890. Gold was discovered at Coolgardie in 1892 and at Kalgoorlie in 1893—east of Perth, close to the Great Victoria Desert. The population of Western Australia more than trebled, rising from 39 000 in 1886 to 138 000 in 1896.

Life in the goldfields was harsh. Water, which had to be shipped in, cost an enormous amount per gallon. To supply it, and heavy equipment for the mines (unlike the eastern states this wasn't alluvial gold, so it had to be dug), railways were built, and subsequently great water pipelines to the goldfields were constructed. One alone involved 2900 kilometres (1740 miles) of pipes.

In the 1890s, while the other colonies were undergoing an economic recession, Western Australia boomed. Farmers found markets for their fruit and vegetables in the goldfields, and agriculture flourished to the point that the area under wheat cultivation trebled in the ten years prior to 1900.

The decline of gold mining in the early 1900s coincided with the opening up of the state's vast wheat belt, and with Western Australia's emergence as a major wheat grower and exporter. The wheat belt arcs in a broad sweep halfway between Perth and the deserts.

The state has no fewer than eight wine-growing regions. The best known are probably the Swan Valley and, more recently, Margaret River, south of Perth on the coast, and Mount Barker in the far south.

Thanks to its fertile soils, the Swan Valley was one of the first areas to be settled. Originally it was a market gardening and table-grape growing area. Wine grapes were later planted on the leaner country just beyond that. The region also supports olive trees. There is a marron farm nearby in the Darling Ranges, quail is raised in Wanneroo, and exceptional bread is available from the old monastery at New Norcia.

From Gidgegannup, in the hills of the Avon Valley northeast of the Swan, also in the Darling Ranges, comes Gabrielle Kervella's exceptional goat's milk cheese, widely considered the best cheese in Australia. From her herd of over one hundred goats, Kervella makes around a half-dozen different styles: a fresh cheese, an *affiné* (aged) cheese, a cabecou, what the French might call a *crotin,* and cheese wrapped in a chestnut leaf. These cheeses are in much demand as far away as Sydney and Singapore.

Margaret River sits on the western edge of the food-abundant southwest, which extends from Bunbury down to Albany, its climate modified by its proximity to the Indian Ocean. Originally timber, dairy and sheep country, it is blessed with a Mediterranean climate—long, hot, dry summers and cool, damp winters. The lack of rain in the summer was a handicap to dairying—providing little for the cows to graze on—but not to grape growing, since it means that the vines are free of problems like mildew.

Although grapes were first planted in the Margaret River region in the early 1900s, it wasn't until the 1960s that grape planting began in earnest. They were put in with the help of 'on-shore' labourers—surfers who had drifted there to ride the coast's magnificent waves. They were given this name because as soon as the breeze turned 'on shore' (blowing in the wrong direction), they'd turn up for work!

Now Margaret River is one of the most diverse and food-rich regions in the country. The wines brought tourists, the wineries opened restaurants to cater to them, and then food producers sprang up to supply the restaurants. The area boasts two small cheese makers—Margaret River and Fonti—a marron farm and the Berry Farm, which also produces vinegar, one of only three vinegar producers in the country. There are farmed emu, rabbit and venison, and a trout farm that also has a smokehouse. Just to its north, there's Harvey beef, named for an abattoir rather than a producer, and there is fish offshore. This has led to an ingredient-driven sense of regionalism on local restaurant menus.

There might be Margaret River marron from a local farm, Blackwood Lodge venison or smoked trout from Clover Cottage in Pemberton. There are crayfish, local squid from Bunbury and three types of abalone—of which the best are the green-lip, found in deeper waters—and scallops from Geographe Bay.

An area renowned for its milk, Margaret River boasted a butter factory and a cheddar factory in the 1960s. With the decline in dairying in the region, these closed down, replaced more recently by small operations.

Margaret River Cheese began experimental production in 1986. It now produces eight farmhouse cheeses from its herd of 140 Friesian (Holstein) cows. Although best known for its brie, it also makes camembert, three types of cheddar and two types of fetta, a whole milk and a gourmet in virgin olive oil with herbs and spices. Margaret River brie is one of only three white-mould cheeses in the country that aren't stabilised. (To stabilise a cheese, the curd is 'cooked' to slow down the bacterial action within the cheese; the cheese never ripens properly, remaining a rubbery, almost tasteless curd.)

Farther southeast, in the area around Donnybrook and Manjimup, is fruit country; there, plums, nectarines, pears and, most particularly, apples are grown. From these orchards come some of the most exciting apples grown in Australia, in particular, two new varieties developed locally, the Pink Lady and the Sundowner. They are siblings, sharing Golden Delicious and the Western Australian wild seedling variety, Lady Williams, as parents, although they are quite dissimilar in both flavour and appearance. Pink Lady is a pink, partially blushed apple, while the Sundowner has a bright red stripe against a lime-green background. Their advantage is that they will mature under 'reduced winter chilling', which means they can be grown in warmer conditions

A jackaroo in the Kimberleys takes a welcome break from his work to sip a mug of hot billy tea.

than most other apple varieties, in places such as California, South Africa, northern Italy, southern France and Spain. It is predicted that they will become two of the ten most popular varieties in the world.

Western Australia grows—and exports—vast amounts of vegetables. The Perth Hills produce apples, pears and citrus, while north of Perth, from around Wanneroo, come vegetables and strawberries. Farther north still, around Carnarvon, the Gascoyne (named for the river) produces two-thirds of the state's bananas, as well as such tropical fruits as mangoes, pawpaws (papayas) and ruby grapefruit. Large quantities of tomatoes, beans and capsicums (peppers) are also grown here. Beyond the beef lands of the Kimberleys is Kununurra in the far north, where rockmelons (musk melons), harvested when they are out of season in other parts of Australia, and a variety of tropical fruits are cultivated.

Free from many of the pests and diseases of the eastern states, horticulture has flourished in Western Australia. Large numbers of Italian and Croatian migrants who were the backbone of horticulture forty years ago are now being replaced by the Vietnamese, who have become significant producers.

Two-thirds of the state's population live in Perth, which is one of the most multicultural cities in Australia. Over one-third of the city's population was born overseas, and these migrants have had a significant effect on the quality and types of produce available. Perth now has some of the best smallgoods in the country and even wonderful baby kid—*capretto*—which was originally raised to supply the Italian community and is now enjoyed more widely. The Italian community has also given Perth exceptional butchers. Without its migrants, foodwise t'other side would be a poorer place indeed.

Pastas and Salads

Vegetables and fruits grown in Tasmania gain extraordinary flavour during their slow ripening in the island's cool climate.

PASTAS AND SALADS

AUSTRALIANS HAVE EMBRACED salads and, more particularly pasta with a fervour bordering on passion. We now eat pasta twice as often as that supposed national dish, the meat pie. Indeed, these days pasta has become so familiar that some restaurants even serve Italian rag pasta with Thai-inspired sauces!

In just two decades, pasta has become so popular that it almost could be called a national dish.

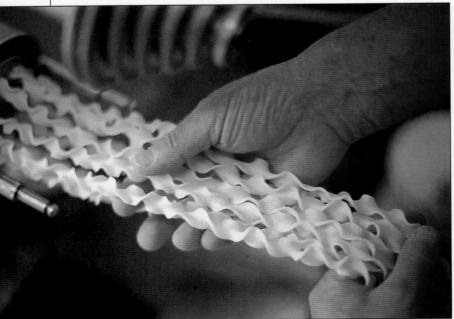

The salad, too, has been redefined. It has been elevated from a mundane garnish on the side of a plate, or a nondescript bowl of undistinguished ingredients, to a dish—a course, even—in its own right that thrills the palate with its combination of textures and flavours. Salads have finally been recognised as ideal fare in the Australian climate. Why it took so long to arrive at this conclusion is a mystery. But for the contribution of migrants, it might have taken even longer.

In the 1960s, what most Australians knew about pasta didn't extend much beyond canned spaghetti or spaghetti bolognese. This has changed dramatically in the intervening decades. First, in the 1960s, students found that some of the cheapest places to eat were cheerful Italian spaghetti joints. Then, with the introduction of fresh pasta in the late 1970s, many more people took to eating it.

Not only has our consumption of pasta changed, but so has its composition. In the past much of Australia's spaghetti was made from bread wheat (*Triticum aestivum*). Although Australia is, and has been, a major wheat producer—and exporter—it is only relatively recently that we have begun to grow hard durum wheat (*T. durum*), which is much better suited to making both fresh and dried pasta.

Pasta is now available in a vast array of shapes—from tagliatelle and rag pasta to delicately flavoured prawn-filled ravioli. What is put with pasta has widened to

Previous pages, clockwise from top right: Warm Balmain Bug and Spinach Salad (recipe page 168), Thai Beef Salad (recipe page 171), Fresh Tuna Salad (recipe page 158), Lobster and Lentil Salad (recipe page 176)—photographed at Balmoral, Sydney

encompass an enormous range and combination of different ingredients. Pasta sauces might include breadcrumbs, baby clams like pipies, the meat from mud crabs or oxtails. Even the pastas themselves are made from new ingredients, such as pumpkin or spinach in place of potato in gnocchi.

Salads, too, have undergone substantial changes. Although they have long been part of the Australian table, in the past they were fairly undistinguished, usually being little more than the mandatory slices of canned pickled beetroot (beet) that accompanied every grilled steak in any country town café.

Back in the 1930s, Amy Schauer (in the *Schauer Australian Cookery Book*) listed salad ingredients as lettuce, tomato, celery, beetroot, apple and cheese, pineapple and cheese, onion, shredded raw carrot, young cabbage, radish parsley and watercress—a fairly unadventurous selection. A simple summer menu from this renowned Queensland (tropical, remember) cook of the 1930s suggests beetroot in jelly and Russian salad to accompany cold chicken and ham.

By the 1960s, the Australian salad had settled into a rut of coleslaw or grated carrot with raisins. The home summer wooden salad bowl, which was as standard as its ingredients, was filled with whole leaves of iceberg lettuce, slices of green-tinged tomatoes and a couple of rounds of tinned beetroot, the whole surmounted by rings of raw onion. In earlier years, the dressing might have been a mix of condensed milk and malt vinegar.

The transformation of the Australian salad has been extreme, with mesclun mixes now available even in supermarkets. The big changes happened in the 1970s, when cos (romaine) lettuce came along, and then, thanks to Italian greengrocers, curly endive, or what the French call frisée. Gradually other salad items began to appear in markets run by Italians and other migrants. By the middle of the 1980s, there was an explosion of salad leaves: witlof (actually witloof, or Belgian endive), butter and oakleaf lettuce, lollo rosso (coral lettuce), radicchio, Japanese mizuna, baby rocket (arugula), mâche (lamb's lettuce) and other wonderful flavours, such as fresh chervil and red witlof. We also have Mediterranean migrants to thank for eggplants (aubergines), fennel, English spinach (as opposed to the previously available silverbeet, also known as Swiss chard) and celeriac (celery root).

Many of these 'new' vegetables were introduced by migrant communities that grew these vegetables for their own use. Then greengrocers from those ethnic communities embraced them and stocked them in their shops, which led to their appearance on a much wider scale. Other ingredients, such as baby salad greens and mesclun mixes, were initially grown at the request of particular chefs, like Serge Dansereau at The Regent of Sydney and Stephanie Alexander of Stephanie's in Melbourne. Their potential having been recognised, and their popularity assured by such exposure, the greens began to be grown commercially for sale in greengrocers.

Migrants from around the Mediterranean have also made us aware of the value—and flavour—of good olive oil. Towards the end of the 1960s, it was possible to buy large tins of olive oil in small supermarkets. Now extra-virgin olive oil is sold in almost every grocery. The subtleties of different vinegars, like those from the Berry Farm near Margaret River in Western Australia, have also become recognised, as people grew aware of their flavour nuances.

Thanks to Australia's enormous range of climates, and with so much of the continent in the tropics, fresh salad

Pasta in every shape and flavour imaginable makes an artistic display at a shop in Carlton, Melbourne's Italian neighbourhood.

ingredients are available all year. These include such tropical foods as green peppercorns, turmeric root and galangal, and such fruits as pineapple, pawpaw (papaya) and mango (used green in Thai salads), as well as avocados.

Salads have embraced all manner of styles and flavours. They can be Asian, tossed with hair-thin slivers of *makrut* (kaffir lime leaves), coriander (cilantro), lime juice and chillies, or a simple mixture of shredded green pawpaw with peanuts. They might include spinach, Lebanese cucumbers, baby beans, rocket, Italian-style cheeses like *bocconcini, pancetta* or pulses (beans) like fresh borlotti (cranberry) beans. They can be based on vegetables such as roasted tomatoes, cooked field mushrooms, or fennel, or they might be an assortment of charcoal-grilled vegetables that forms part of an antipasto platter. They can be cooked or raw, warm or cold, or a combination of all four. One thing is certain, though: salads in Australia today are as far removed as they can possibly be from the old bowl of grated cabbage with condensed-milk-and-malt-vinegar dressing.

BEETROOT, TOMATO AND EGGPLANT SALAD

There's a real art to making a good salad. Top-quality ingredients, time and attention are the major components. Lynette Bignill, who resides in Sydney, makes fabulous salads. This salad of hers is one of my favourites.

salt
500 g (1 lb) Japanese (slender Asian) eggplants (aubergines), halved lengthwise
olive oil for sautéing, plus 3 tablespoons olive oil
250 g (½ lb) carrots, cut into batons 5 cm (2 in) long and 5 mm (¼ in) thick
300 ml (10 fl oz/1¼ cups) chicken stock
1 red capsicum (bell pepper), halved lengthwise
1 green capsicum (bell pepper), halved lengthwise
1 yellow capsicum (bell pepper), halved lengthwise
1 can (800 g/26 oz) baby beetroots (beets), drained and halved
125 g (¼ lb) cherry tomatoes, halved lengthwise
125 g (¼ lb) yellow teardrop tomatoes, halved lengthwise
vinaigrette for healthy salad (recipe on page 166)

Salt the cut sides of the eggplants and leave to drain in a colander for 15 minutes. Rinse under running cold water and squeeze flat between the hands to eliminate juices. In a large, heavy frying pan over medium heat, warm the oil. Add the eggplant and sauté, turning occasionally, until just tender, about 10 minutes. Let cool.

Meanwhile, preheat a griller (broiler) on high.

In a saucepan combine the carrots and stock and bring to a boil. Reduce the heat to simmer and cook until just tender-crisp, 3–4 minutes. Drain and let cool.

Remove the seeds and ribs from the capsicum halves. Place the halves, skin sides up, on a griller (pan) tray. Paint them with the 3 tablespoons olive oil. Grill (broil) until the skins are evenly blackened and blistered, about 10 minutes. Place in a paper bag, close tightly and let stand until cool enough to handle. Using your fingers or a small knife, peel off the skins from the capsicums. Cut into long strips 2 cm (¾ in) wide.

In a serving dish, combine the eggplants, carrots, capsicums, beetroots and tomatoes. Toss to mix well. Drizzle the vinaigrette over the vegetables and toss again. Serve at once.

SERVES 6

FRESH TUNA SALAD

Sashimi-quality bluefin or yellowfin tuna will give the best results.

1 tablespoon light soy sauce
1 tablespoon Chinese rice wine
250 g (½ lb) fresh tuna fillet, thinly sliced against the grain
¼ purple onion, thinly sliced
2 tablespoons Chinese rice vinegar
1 tablespoon chopped fresh coriander (cilantro)
1 large tomato, peeled, seeded and finely diced
1 tablespoon Asian sesame oil (see glossary)
1 large ripe avocado, pitted, peeled and sliced

In a bowl, stir together the soy sauce and rice wine. Add the tuna, toss gently and marinate for 20 minutes.

In another bowl, toss together the onion, rice vinegar and coriander. Marinate for 10 minutes.

In a third bowl, toss together the tomato and sesame oil.

Arrange the tuna, onion, tomato and avocado on 4 large flat plates. Pour the juices collected in the bowls over the salads and serve at once.

SERVES 4   *Photograph pages 154–155*

SHREDDED GREEN BEAN AND TOMATO SALAD

Tomatoes should only be used in salads at the end of the summer, when they have had the full benefit of a long sun ripening and are bright coloured and flavoursome.

700 g (1⅓ lb) young, tender green beans, trimmed
salt
vinaigrette for healthy salad (recipe on page 164)
4 vine-ripened tomatoes, peeled and cut into thin wedges
3 shallots, finely chopped

Push the beans through a bean shredder. Keep the side strips if using stringless beans. Alternatively, shred the beans with a sharp knife. Bring a saucepan three-quarters full of water to a boil. Add salt to taste and the beans and cook until al dente, 4–5 minutes. Drain and toss with half of the vinaigrette while still warm.

Arrange the tomatoes slightly overlapping around the outside edge of a round serving dish. Pile the beans in the centre of the platter. Scatter with the shallots. Drizzle with the remaining vinaigrette 10 minutes before serving.

SERVES 6

RADICCHIO, BORLOTTI BEAN AND GRILLED PROSCIUTTO SALAD

Red radicchio is a round, crisp head of colourful leaves with a bittersweet taste. It makes a delightful salad starter to a menu that is going to be rich or heavy. Grilled prosciutto gives the salad added crispness, which provides a good contrast to the other ingredients.

salt
600 g (1¼ lb) fresh borlotti (cranberry) beans, shelled
1 head radicchio, leaves separated
1 bunch rocket (arugula), stems removed
12 thin slices prosciutto

FOR THE VINAIGRETTE:

1 small clove garlic, finely chopped
1 tablespoon balsamic vinegar
60 ml (2 fl oz/¼ cup) extra-virgin olive oil
salt and freshly cracked pepper

Preheat a griller (broiler) on high.

Bring a small saucepan of water to a boil and salt lightly. Add the beans and simmer until just cooked, about 8 minutes; the timing will depend upon the age and freshness of the beans. Drain and refresh in cold water. Drain and set aside.

Arrange the radicchio and rocket in a serving dish. Place the prosciutto on a griller tray (pan) and slip under the griller. Grill (broil) until crisp, about 1 minute. Spoon the beans over the lettuces.

To make the vinaigrette, in a small bowl, whisk together the garlic, vinegar, oil and salt and pepper to taste.

Drizzle the vinaigrette over the salad, top with the prosciutto and serve at once.

SERVES 4

Top to bottom: Radicchio, Borlotti Bean and Grilled Prosciutto Salad, Beetroot, Tomato and Eggplant Salad, Shredded Green Bean and Tomato Salad

Left to right: Angel Hair Pasta with Smoked Tasmanian Salmon and Salmon Roe, Shiitake and Hazelnut Taglierini—photographed at the Bathers Pavilion, Balmoral, Sydney

SYDNEY

SHIITAKE AND HAZELNUT TAGLIERINI

There is a small commercial hazelnut industry in Australia, but for the most part these wonderful nuts are imported.

FOR THE SAUCE:

2 tablespoons hazelnuts
60 g (2 oz/¼ cup) unsalted butter
2 tablespoons hazelnut oil
200 g (6½ oz) fresh shiitake mushrooms, stems removed
  and caps sliced

400 g (13 oz) fresh taglierini
25 g (1 oz) parmesan cheese, cut into shavings with a
    vegetable peeler

To make the sauce, preheat an oven to 200°C (400°F). Spread the hazelnuts in a small pan and place in the oven until fragrant, lightly toasted and the skins begin to flake, 8–10 minutes.

Remove from the oven and immediately wrap the still-warm nuts in a cloth towel. Rub vigorously between your palms to flake off the skins. Using a heavy chef's knife, cut the skinned hazelnuts into thin shavings and set aside.

Bring a large pot three-quarters full of water to a rapid boil. While the water is reaching a boil, finish making the sauce. In a heavy frying pan over high heat, melt the butter with the oil. Add the mushrooms and sauté until barely tender, about 1 minute. Add the hazelnuts to the pan and stir well. Keep warm.

Add the pasta to the rapidly boiling water and cook until al dente, 1–2 minutes. Drain well and divide among 4 warmed pasta bowls.

Top with the sauce and the cheese and serve at once.

SERVES 4

SYDNEY

EGGPLANT LASAGNE WITH SUN-DRIED TOMATOES

This makes an excellent luncheon or supper dish and is ideal for vegetarians. Choose eggplants that are firm and shiny. Once they soften, they are full of seeds and not worth buying. Macquarie brand sun-dried tomatoes are produced in Narromine from tomatoes grown in Bundaberg in Queensland. If using dry-packed tomatoes, reconstitute first in hot water for a few minutes. If using tomatoes packed in oil, drain and save the oil for brushing over chicken or fish before barbecuing or grilling (broiling).

This is a thin béchamel sauce and unlike the thicker one that accompanies the pasta rolls on page 176. Check to be sure the ricotta cheese is freshly made.

2 large eggplants (aubergines), 1 kg (2 lb) total weight, cut
    crosswise into slices 1 cm (⅜ in) thick
125 ml (4 fl oz/½ cup) olive oil
2 large brown onions, cut into slices 1 cm (⅜ in) thick
salt
300 g (10 oz) fresh lasagne sheets, each about 9 by 15 cm
    (3½ by 6 in)

FOR THE BÉCHAMEL SAUCE:

125 g (4 oz/½ cup) butter
100 g (3½ oz/¾ cup) plain (all-purpose) flour
1.5 l (48 fl oz/6 cups) milk, or as needed
salt and freshly ground pepper

100 g (3½ oz) sun-dried tomatoes, cut into julienne strips
    (see note)
2 teaspoons dried oregano
300 g (10 oz/1¼ cups) very fresh ricotta cheese
100 g (3½ oz/¾ cup) freshly grated parmesan cheese
freshly ground pepper
200 g (6½ oz) mozzarella, sliced

Preheat a griller (broiler) on high. Paint the grill rack with oil. Arrange the eggplant slices on the grill rack and paint with the oil. Grill until golden on the first side, about 3 minutes. Turn the slices over, paint the second side with oil and grill until golden and tender. Total cooking time should be about 5 minutes. Set aside to cool.

In a heavy frying pan over medium heat, warm the remaining oil. Add the onions and cook gently until caramelised, about 15 minutes. Remove from the heat and set aside.

Bring a large pot three-quarters full of water to a boil and add a little salt. Add the lasagne sheets, in batches, and cook until just al dente, 3–4 minutes. Lift them out with a sieve, draining well, and immerse in cold water to refresh. Drain again and set out on kitchen towels until ready to use.

To make the béchamel sauce, in a large, heavy pan over medium heat, melt the butter. Whisk in the flour and cook, whisking constantly, for 2 minutes. Slowly add the milk and cook, whisking, until the sauce thickens. Simmer very gently, stirring occasionally, for 10 minutes. Season to taste with salt and pepper. The sauce must be of a loose coating consistency. Thin with additional milk, if needed.

Position a rack in the centre of an oven and preheat the oven to 180°C (350°F).

To assemble the lasagne, line a baking dish measuring 30 by 26 cm (12 by 10½ in) with a single layer of lasagne sheets, allowing the ends to overhang the two narrow ends of the dish. Ladle one-third of the béchamel sauce evenly over the top and arrange a single layer of half of the eggplant slices over the sauce. Scatter with half of the sautéed onions, sun-dried tomatoes and oregano, and then top with half of the ricotta and one-third of the parmesan. Season lightly with salt and pepper. Top with a single layer of lasagne sheets cut to fit within the dish.

Repeat the layers, finishing with the lasagne sheets. Top with the mozzarella and the remaining béchamel sauce. Then scatter the remaining parmesan over the top.

Cook in the centre of the oven until heated through and golden and bubbling on top, 25–30 minutes. Remove from the oven and let stand for 10 minutes to settle before serving, then cut into squares to serve.

SERVES 6   *Photograph pages 8–9*

TASMANIA

ANGEL HAIR PASTA WITH SMOKED TASMANIAN SALMON AND SALMON ROE

Dried angel hair pasta is available in upmarket delicatessens and well-stocked supermarkets. It can also be found fresh in some specialty outlets. Either type can be used for this recipe.

250 ml (8 fl oz/1 cup) thickened (double/heavy) cream
salt and freshly ground pepper

1 tablespoon virgin olive oil
500 g (1 lb) angel hair pasta
200 g (6½ oz) smoked Tasmanian salmon, cut into long,
    thin strips
125 g (¼ lb) salmon roe
2 tablespoons snipped fresh chives

Bring a large pot three-quarters full of water to a rapid boil. While the water is reaching a boil, pour the cream into a large, heavy frying pan over high heat and bring to a boil. Season to taste with salt and pepper.

Add the oil and pasta to the rapidly boiling water and cook until al dente; this will take a few minutes for dried pasta and only a minute or so for fresh. Drain well, rinse under hot water and drain well again, shaking the pasta to remove excess water. Drop the pasta into the cream and add the smoked salmon. Toss gently over medium heat until warmed through.

Transfer to warmed pasta bowls, top with the salmon roe and chives and serve immediately.

SERVES 6

Top to bottom: Spinach and Goat Cheese Salad, Green Vegetable Pinci with Green Vegetables

SPINACH AND GOAT CHEESE SALAD

Gabrielle Kervella makes premium goat cheese in the country 45 minutes northeast of Perth in Western Australia. I buy her mature goat cheese and age it further in the dairy cabinet of the refrigerator. When it is hard (after 3–4 weeks), I pare off the rind and shave the firm cheese with a chef's knife or swivel-head vegetable peeler. It is the best Australian cheese for topping a salad because it has a mature, although not overly strong, goat taste and a great texture.

FOR THE DRESSING:

60 g (2 oz/⅓ cup) pine nuts, toasted
1 egg, beaten
1 spring (green) onion, including tender green tops, finely sliced
1 teaspoon fresh lemon juice
125 ml (4 fl oz/½ cup) virgin olive oil
1 tablespoon balsamic vinegar

2 tablespoons red wine vinegar
salt and freshly ground pepper

FOR THE SALAD:

1 bunch spinach, carefully washed and stems removed
leaves from 1 small bunch fresh basil
250 g (½ lb) matured Kervella goat cheese or other aged goat cheese, shaved or sliced
60 g (2 oz/⅓ cup) pine nuts, toasted

❀ To make the dressing, place the pine nuts in a food processor fitted with the metal blade. Add the egg, onion and lemon juice and purée until smooth. Gradually add the oil and balsamic and wine vinegars alternately through the feed tube, processing until smooth. Season to taste with salt and pepper. If the dressing is too thick, whisk in a little water and adjust the seasoning.
❀ To assemble the salad, divide the spinach and basil leaves among 6 plates. Spoon the dressing over the spinach. Add the goat cheese and then garnish with the pine nuts.

SERVES 6

GREEN VEGETABLE PINCI WITH GREEN VEGETABLES

Australians love creamy vegetable pastas. This one is for special occasions, as the pinci take some time to make. The greens used for making the pasta dough and the sauce can be varied according to what is available in the market.

FOR THE *PINCI:*

2 spring (green) onions, including tender green tops, chopped
12 spinach leaves, carefully washed and thoroughly dried
8 rocket (arugula) leaves, carefully washed and thoroughly dried
6 fresh parsley sprigs
8 fresh basil leaves
6 snow pea (mangetouts) sprouts (shoots)
about 260 g (8 oz/1⅔ cups) all-purpose (plain) flour
250 g (8 oz/1 cup) ricotta cheese
1 small egg
salt and freshly ground pepper

FOR THE SAUCE:

100 ml (3½ fl oz/6½ tablespoons) extra-virgin olive oil
2 cloves garlic, finely chopped
250 g (½ lb) broccoli, cut into small florets, blanched in boiling water for 30 seconds and drained
3 green zucchini (courgettes), thinly sliced
60 ml (2 fl oz/¼ cup) dry white wine
125 ml (4 fl oz/½ cup) light (single) cream
salt and freshly ground pepper

75 g (2½ oz) parmesan cheese, cut into shavings with a vegetable peeler, plus additional parmesan cheese for serving

✂ To make the *pinci,* in a food processor fitted with the metal blade, combine the onions, spinach, rocket, parsley, basil and pea sprouts. Process to chop finely. Add the flour, ricotta, egg and salt and pepper to taste and process until the mixture comes together in a ball. Remove from the processor and knead on a lightly floured work surface until smooth and no longer sticky, 4–5 minutes. If the dough remains sticky, add a little more flour as needed to reduce the stickiness. Pat into a ball, wrap in plastic wrap and refrigerate for at least 2 hours or for up to 8 hours.
✂ Divide the dough into 6 equal portions. On a lightly floured work surface and, using your palms, roll each portion into a long, narrow log about 1.5 cm (⅔ in) in diameter. Using a sharp knife, thinly slice the roll crosswise. Then, using a floured finger, press out each slice on a floured work surface into a small disc about 2.5 cm (1 in) in diameter. Place the discs in a single layer on a lightly floured tray and cover with a cloth towel. When all of the discs have been formed, refrigerate until ready to cook.
✂ To cook the *pinci,* bring a large pot three-quarters full of water to a rapid boil. While the water is reaching a boil, make the sauce. In a large, heavy frying pan over medium-low heat, warm the oil. Add the garlic and sauté gently for 2 minutes. Increase the heat to medium, add the broccoli and zucchini and sauté for 2 minutes. Add the wine and reduce over high heat by one-quarter. Add the cream and stir over high heat until a good sauce consistency forms, just a few minutes. Season to taste with salt and pepper. Keep warm.
✂ Salt the boiling water lightly and add the *pinci.* Boil until al dente, 2–3 minutes after the pasta has risen to the surface. Drain and immediately divide among 6 warmed bowls. Add the sauce, toss well and scatter on the parmesan. Serve at once. Pass additional parmesan at the table.

SERVES 6

TAGLIERINI WITH PIPIS

Pipis are smooth-shelled bivalve molluscs raised in the coastal waters of New South Wales. They are sold in the shell. Other small molluscs, such as clams, can be substituted. You will need to begin preparing the pipis the day before serving the pasta.

750 g (1½ lb) pipis
salt
2 tablespoons olive oil
2 cloves garlic, finely chopped
1 small fresh red chilli, finely chopped
2 tomatoes, peeled, seeded and diced
freshly ground pepper
400 g (13 oz) fresh taglierini
minced fresh parsley

✂ Rinse the pipis in running cold water. Place in a bowl, add water to cover and refrigerate overnight. Change the water often.
✂ One hour before serving the pasta, add 1 tablespoon salt to the bowl of pipis; this will help them to expel any sand. Drain the pipis and rinse once more.
✂ Bring a large pot three-quarters full of water to a rapid boil. While the water is reaching a boil, prepare the sauce. In a large, heavy frying pan over high heat, warm the oil. Add the garlic and chilli and stir and toss for 2 minutes. Add the pipis, cover and shake the pan over high heat until the pipis open, about 4 minutes. Add the tomatoes and season to taste with salt and pepper. Shake the pan back and forth over the burner to distribute the heat, then cover and keep warm.
✂ Add 1 teaspoon salt and the taglierini to the rapidly boiling water. Cook until al dente, 3–4 minutes. Drain the pasta and place in a large warmed serving bowl.
✂ Pour the pipis over the pasta and toss well. Add the parsley and toss again. Serve at once.

SERVES 4

Taglierini with Pipis

GREEN PAWPAW SALAD

In the southern states, pawpaws are nearly always green. They are picked that way so that they will travel the long distances from the tropics without damaging, and then once they reach their destination, they are ripened with gas. Sadly, pawpaws never taste the same in the south as they do when ripened on the trees in the tropical north. Here is a Thai dish, called som tum, *that is traditionally made from green pawpaw.*

FOR THE SALAD:

salt
100 g (3½ oz) young, tender green beans, cut into 1-cm
   (⅜-in) pieces
1 small green pawpaw (papaya), peeled and seeded
200 g (6½ oz/1–1¼ cups) cooked chicken meat, skinned
   and cut into strips

FOR THE DRESSING:

3 tablespoons fresh lime juice
1 tablespoon fish sauce (see glossary)
2 tablespoons soft brown sugar or palm sugar (see glossary)
1 fresh red chilli, finely chopped
1 fresh green chilli, finely chopped
1 clove garlic, finely chopped
1 piece gingerroot, about 2.5 cm (1 in) long, peeled and grated

FOR THE GARNISH:

10 g (⅓ oz) dried shrimp, finely chopped in a food processor
   (see glossary)
2½ tablespoons roasted peanuts, finely chopped
1 fresh red chilli, finely sliced
1 fresh green chilli, finely sliced

❧ Fill a saucepan three-quarters full of water and bring to a boil. Lightly salt the water, then add the beans. Boil until al dente, about 2 minutes. Drain and refresh in iced water.

❧ Using a grater held over a large bowl, grate the pawpaw into the bowl. Drain the beans well and add to the pawpaw. Add the chicken and toss to mix.

❧ To make the dressing, in a small bowl, combine the lime juice, fish sauce and sugar and stir until the sugar dissolves. Add the chillies, garlic and gingerroot and stir to combine. Pour over the chicken mixture and toss well.

❧ Spoon onto a serving platter. Garnish with the shrimp, peanuts and red and green chillies. Serve at once.

SERVES 6

MOULDED VEGETABLE PASTA

I've seen pasta moulds in Italian kitchens, where they are prepared as a way to use up leftover cooked pasta. A mould such as this is a great asset for a buffet because it can be made—indeed, must be made—some hours before it is needed. Select tubular macaroni about 3 centimetres (1¼ inches) long and 1 centimetre (⅜ inch) in diameter.

salt
200 g (6½ oz) dried macaroni
15 thin lean prosciutto slices
1 tablespoon olive oil
150 g (5 oz) baby Japanese (finger) eggplants (aubergines),
   thinly sliced
250 g (½ lb) zucchini (courgette), diced
250 ml (8 fl oz/1 cup) tomato sauce (see glossary)
60 g (2 oz/⅓ cup) pitted black olives
90 g (3 oz/¾ cup) freshly grated parmesan cheese
1 teaspoon dried oregano
freshly ground pepper

❧ Bring a large pot three-quarters full of water to a boil. Add salt to taste and the macaroni and cook until al dente; the timing will depend upon the type of pasta used. Drain and refresh in iced water.

❧ Position a rack in the centre of an oven and preheat the oven to 180°C (350°F).

❧ Line a 20-cm (8-in) cake pan with overlapping slices of prosciutto. Allow the prosciutto to overhang the edges of the pan so that the slices can be folded back over the mould.

❧ In a large, heavy frying pan over medium heat, warm the oil. Add the eggplant and zucchini and sauté until tender, about 5 minutes. Drain the macaroni, shaking well to remove excess water. Place in a large bowl with the eggplant mixture, tomato sauce, olives, parmesan, oregano and pepper to taste. Mix well. Tip into the prepared pan and fold the prosciutto over the top. Tuck a sheet of aluminium foil down over the top.

❧ Bake until heated through, about 20 minutes. Remove from the oven, then invert onto a serving plate. Serve warm or at room temperature.

SERVES 6–8   *Photograph page 167*

HEALTHY SALAD

Here is my answer to those days when the humidity is trying, the weather is hot and your energy level is low. Needless to say, the ingredients must be super fresh and of good quality. Snow pea sprouts are the tendrils and tiny top leaves of the snow pea plant.

200 g (6½ oz) baby corn
200 g (6½ oz) young, tender green beans
250 g (½ lb) broccoli, cut into bite-sized florets

FOR THE VINAIGRETTE:

sea salt
1 tablespoon balsamic vinegar
2 teaspoons red wine vinegar
100 ml (3½ fl oz/6½ tablespoons) extra-virgin olive oil
freshly ground pepper

⅛ head red cabbage, finely shredded
250 g (½ lb) teardrop tomatoes, halved lengthwise
1 head butter lettuce, separated into halves
50 g (1½ oz) snow pea (mangetouts) sprouts (shoots)

❧ Bring a saucepan three-quarters full of water to a boil and add the corn. Cook until al dente, about 2 minutes. Lift out with a slotted utensil and refresh in cold water.

❧ Add the green beans to the same water and cook until al dente, about 3 minutes. Lift out with a slotted utensil and refresh in cold water.

❧ Add the broccoli to the same water and cook until al dente, about 4 minutes. Lift out with a slotted utensil and refresh in cold water. Drain all the vegetables and pat dry on paper towels.

❧ To make the vinaigrette, in a large salad bowl, whisk together salt to taste, the balsamic and wine vinegars, the oil and pepper to taste. This makes about 125 ml (4 fl oz/½ cup) vinaigrette.

❧ Add the cabbage to the vinaigrette and toss well. Add the tomatoes and the drained vegetables and toss gently.

❧ Arrange the lettuce leaves around the edge of the salad bowl. Top with the sprouts and serve.

SERVES 6   *Photograph page 166*

*Green Pawpaw Salad—photographed at
Bend of the River estate in northern Queensland*

Top to bottom: Healthy Salad (recipe page 164), Spicy Chicken Salad—photographed overlooking Balmoral Bay, Sydney

SPICY CHICKEN SALAD

This is Susan Lowden's recipe. She owns cookware shops in Sydney's eastern suburbs and in Dubbo in New South Wales. Susan and her family are all great cooks, so customers always receive useful information on products and equipment. Palm vinegar, which is the product of the sap from various palm trees, can be found in Asian stores.

1 l (32 fl oz/4 cups) chicken stock
6 chicken breast halves, skinned and boned, about 1.5 kg (3 lb) total weight when boned
1 Spanish (red) onion, finely chopped
1 piece gingerroot, about 4 cm (1½ in) long, peeled and grated
5 fresh coriander (cilantro) roots, finely chopped (see glossary)
3 tablespoons finely chopped fresh coriander (cilantro) leaves
3 tablespoons finely chopped fresh mint
2 tablespoons snipped fresh chives
salt and freshly ground pepper

FOR THE DRESSING:

140 ml (4½ fl oz/½ cup plus 1 tablespoon) light olive oil
2 tablespoons chilli oil (see glossary)
1 clove garlic, finely chopped
3 tablespoons palm vinegar
1 teaspoon sugar
1 or 2 fresh chillies, finely chopped
salt and freshly ground pepper

leaves from 6 fresh coriander (cilantro) sprigs
2 tablespoons sesame seeds, toasted

❧ Pour the chicken stock into a saucepan. Bring to a boil and then reduce the heat until the stock simmers. Add the chicken breasts and poach gently until just cooked, about 15 minutes. Remove from the heat and let cool in the stock.
❧ Remove the chicken from the stock; reserve the stock for

166

another use. Using your fingers, tear the chicken into bite-sized pieces; do not cut with a knife. Place in a bowl. Add the onion, gingerroot, chopped coriander roots and leaves, mint and chives and toss to mix well. Season to taste with salt and pepper and toss again to mix well.

❧ To make the dressing, in a small bowl, whisk together the olive and chilli oils, garlic, vinegar, sugar, chillies and salt and pepper to taste.

❧ Pour the dressing over the chicken and toss well. Arrange a bed of coriander leaves on a platter. Mound the chicken on the leaves. Sprinkle with the sesame seeds and serve at once.

SERVES 6

SYDNEY

NIÇOISE-STYLE SALAD

David Novak Piper, chef at one of Sydney's eastern suburban restaurants, calls this a low-calorie, free-form salad. David uses green beans but I make it with Queensland beanettes when they are in season. They are the closest bean we have to the tiny French green beans.

4 new potatoes
salt
100 ml (3½ fl oz/6½ tablespoons) olive oil
400 g (13 oz) tuna, cut into 4 thick slices
600 g (1¼ lb) beanettes, trimmed (see note)

FOR THE DRESSING:

1 egg, immersed in boiling water for 1 minute and drained
1½ tablespoons Dijon mustard
1½ tablespoons white wine vinegar
125 ml (4 fl oz/½ cup) canola oil
2½ tablespoons olive oil
salt and freshly ground pepper

1 large purple onion, thinly sliced
12 teardrop tomatoes, halved lengthwise
12 cherry tomatoes, halved crosswise
4 Western Australian anchovy fillets or other high-quality anchovies in oil, cut into slivers
16 Kalamata olives

❧ Place the potatoes in a saucepan and add water to cover. Add salt to taste, bring to a boil and boil until half-cooked, about 10 minutes. Drain, let cool and then cut crosswise into slices 12 mm (½ in) thick.

❧ In a large frying pan over medium heat, warm 3 tablespoons of the oil. Add the potato slices and sauté, turning once, until crisp and just tender, about 10 minutes.

❧ Brush the tuna slices with oil. Heat a heavy frying pan over medium-high heat. Add the tuna and sear, turning once, until browned on the outside but still quite rare in the centre. The timing will depend upon the thickness of the tuna slices, but the cooking should take no more than a few minutes. Remove from the heat and set aside.

❧ Bring a saucepan three-quarters full of water to a boil. Add salt to taste and the beans and cook until tender-crisp, just a few minutes. Drain, refresh in iced water and drain again.

❧ To make the dressing, place the egg, mustard and vinegar in a blender and process to mix. With the motor running, add the canola and olive oils in a slow, thin, steady stream until thick and creamy. Season to taste with salt and pepper. If too thick, add a small amount of water; if too thin, add more oil and blend until thick.

❧ To assemble the salad, arrange the potatoes, tuna, beans, onion, tomatoes, anchovies and olives on 4 large flat plates. Drizzle the dressing over the top and serve at once.

SERVES 6

Clockwise from top: Warm Mediterranean-Style Potato Salad (recipe page 168), Moulded Vegetable Pasta (recipe page 164), Niçoise-Style Salad—photographed at Bondi, Sydney

WARM MEDITERRANEAN-STYLE POTATO SALAD

Pink-eye potatoes are grown in Tasmania and the mainlanders cannot get enough of them. They have brown skin and faint pinkish purple eyes. The flesh is pale yellow and the taste is superb. Anne Taylor, who owns one of Sydney's best restaurants, gave me this recipe. She says it can be made in advance, providing that the roasted tomatoes are folded in at the last moment. If the salad has been made in advance, it can be reheated in an oven or a microwave. Chopped fresh oregano, basil or parsley can be added after the dish has been reheated.

400 g (13 oz) cherry tomatoes
salt
1 teaspoon sugar
250 ml (8 fl oz/1 cup) extra-virgin olive oil
6 purple onions, halved and thinly sliced
1 kg (2 lb) small, uniform pink-eye potatoes, unpeeled
80 g (2½ oz/⅓ cup) thinly slivered sun-dried tomatoes
freshly ground pepper

❧ Preheat oven to 160°C (325°F).
❧ Pack the cherry tomatoes in a single layer in a small, heavy baking pan just large enough to hold them comfortably. Sprinkle with salt and the sugar and drizzle with 2 tablespoons of the oil. Roast for 1 hour.
❧ In a heavy, shallow pan over medium-high heat, warm 80 ml (3 fl oz/⅓ cup) of the oil. Add the onions and sauté, shaking the pan back and forth occasionally, until they are caramelised, about 5 minutes. Watch carefully and do not allow the onions to sweat or burn.
❧ Meanwhile, arrange the potatoes on a steamer rack over a pan of gently boiling water, cover and steam until just tender, about 20 minutes. Chop or slice the potatoes and place in a serving bowl.
❧ Add the remaining oil, the warm onions and both the cherry tomatoes and sun-dried tomatoes to the potatoes. Season to taste with pepper. Fold together gently and serve warm.

SERVES 6　　　　　　　　　　*Photograph page 167*

WARM BALMAIN BUG AND SPINACH SALAD

Balmain bugs are small shovel-nosed lobsters found in the cold waters of southern Australia. By contrast, the larger, and I think better, Moreton Bay bugs are from the warm waters in the northern half of the continent and are more plentiful on the east coast. The flesh of these marvellous crustaceans is sweet and succulent and must not be overcooked. Lobster tails can be substituted.

2 bunches spinach, carefully washed and stems removed
1 purple onion, finely chopped
2 tablespoons virgin olive oil
1 thick slice prosciutto, 250 g (½ lb), cut into small dice
1 clove garlic, crushed
1 kg (2 lb) green (raw) Balmain bugs, meat removed from tails in one piece

FOR THE WARM DRESSING:

1 egg
pinch of sugar
1 tablespoon tarragon-flavoured white wine vinegar

1 tablespoon red wine vinegar
salt and freshly ground pepper

❧ Pile the spinach leaves in a large bowl. Scatter the onion over the top.
❧ In a heavy frying pan over medium heat, warm the oil. Add the prosciutto and sauté until the fat is rendered. Add the garlic and sauté until soft, about 3 minutes. Add the bug meat and sauté until just opaque, 1–2 minutes. Set aside and cover to keep warm.
❧ To make the dressing, pour off any fat from the pan and wipe the pan out with a paper towel. In a small bowl, whisk together the egg, sugar and white and red wine vinegars. Pour the mixture into the frying pan and warm slowly, whisking constantly. Be careful not to allow the egg to set. Remove from the heat and season to taste with salt and pepper.
❧ Top the spinach with the warm Balmain bug mixture. Pour the warm dressing over the top. Serve immediately.

SERVES 8　　　　　　　*Photograph pages 154–155*

RAVIOLI WITH BALMAIN BUGS

Balmain bugs are readily available in the Sydney area. They are not as large as the Moreton Bay bugs caught in the warmer water off Brisbane.

FOR THE PASTA DOUGH:

750 g (1½ lb/4¾ cups) plain (all-purpose) flour
3 eggs
180 ml (6 fl oz/¾ cup) water

FOR THE FILLING:

200 g (6½ oz/¾ cup plus 1½ tablespoons) ricotta cheese
50 g (1½ oz/⅓ cup) finely grated parmesan cheese
80 ml (3 fl oz/⅓ cup) bottled demiglace (see glossary)
1 egg
4 tablespoons finely chopped fresh parsley
salt and freshly ground pepper

FOR THE SAUCE:

600 ml (19 fl oz/2⅓ cups) light (single) cream
250 ml (8 fl oz/1 cup) tomato juice
salt
1 bunch spinach, carefully washed and stems removed
2 teaspoons chopped fresh tarragon
2 drops Tabasco sauce or other hot-pepper sauce
freshly ground pepper

1½ unsalted butter
1 clove garlic, finely chopped
tail meat from 16 large green (raw) Balmain bugs (large crayfish)
1 tablespoon olive oil

❧ To make the pasta dough, mound the flour on a work surface. Make a well in the centre. Break the eggs into the well and then pour in the water; stir briefly with a fork. Using the fork, gradually pull the walls of flour into the liquid until all of the flour is incorporated. Then gather the dough into a ball and knead on a floured surface until smooth and elastic, 6–10 minutes.
❧ Divide the dough into 6 equal portions. Working with 1 portion at a time, pass it through the rollers of a hand-crank pasta machine, gradually reducing the setting of the rollers and dusting the dough each time, until it forms a long, thin pasta sheet. Set the sheet aside on a floured flat surface and cover

Ravioli with Balmain Bugs

with a cloth towel. Repeat with the remaining dough portions. Alternatively, roll out the dough by hand on a floured work surface to form thin sheets.

To make the filling, in a bowl, combine the ricotta and parmesan cheeses, demiglace, egg, parsley and salt and pepper to taste. Mix well.

Place 2 teaspoons of the filling at 5-cm (2-in) intervals on half of the pasta sheets. Top with the remaining pasta sheets and, using a round cutter 5 cm (2 in) in diameter, cut out the ravioli. Transfer to a floured tray and cover with a cloth towel.

To make the sauce, pour the cream into a saucepan and place over medium heat until reduced by half. Pour the tomato juice into a second pan and place it over medium heat until reduced by half.

While the liquids are reducing, fill a saucepan three-quarters full of water. Add salt to taste and the spinach and blanch for 30 seconds. Drain, refresh in iced water and drain again. Wring out excess water by hand and chop coarsely.

Pour half of the reduced cream into the reduced tomato juice and add the tarragon, Tabasco and salt and pepper to taste. Keep warm. Add the spinach to the remaining reduced cream and season to taste with salt and pepper. Keep warm.

To cook the ravioli, bring a large pot three-quarters full of water to a boil. While the water is reaching a boil, in a large frying pan over medium heat, melt the butter. Add the garlic and sauté for 2 minutes. Add the bugs and sauté until cooked through, 3–4 minutes; the timing will depend upon their size. Keep warm.

Add the oil and a light sprinkling of salt to the boiling water. Then add the ravioli and cook until they rise to the top and are al dente, 6–8 minutes. Drain the ravioli.

To serve, divide the ravioli among 6 pasta bowls. Ladle an equal portion of the spinach sauce on one side and an equal portion of the tomato sauce on the other side. Top the ravioli with equal amounts of the Balmain bugs. Serve immediately.

SERVES 6

SYDNEY

RAG PASTA WITH TOMATOES, FRIED LEEKS, CAPERS AND SHAVED PARMESAN

Stracci, also known as rag pasta, has become fashionable on Australian tables. It is simply uneven pieces of flat pasta.

2 tablespoons plus 100 ml (3½ fl oz/6½ tablespoons) olive oil
1 brown onion, chopped
350 g (11 oz) large Roma (plum) tomatoes, quartered lengthwise
1 tablespoon drained small capers
1–2 tablespoons finely shredded fresh basil or ½ teaspoon dried basil
250 ml (8 fl oz/1 cup) rich chicken stock
salt and freshly ground pepper
3 leek leaves, white part only, carefully washed and cut into julienne 5 cm (2 in) long
250 g (½ lb) dried rag pasta
80 g (2½ oz) parmesan cheese, cut into shavings with a vegetable peeler

In a large, heavy frying pan over medium heat, warm the 2 tablespoons oil. Add the onion and sauté until softened, about 5 minutes. Add the tomatoes, cover and cook slowly over very low heat until softened, about 20 minutes.

Add the capers, basil and stock and raise the heat to high. Simmer until the sauce is a good consistency, about 10 minutes. Season to taste with salt and pepper and cover to keep warm.

In another heavy frying pan over high heat, warm the 100 ml (3½ fl oz/6½ tablespoons) oil. Add the leek and cook until browned and crisp, about 1 minute. Using a slotted spoon, remove to paper towels to drain.

Meanwhile, bring a large pot three-quarters full of water to a boil. Add salt to taste and the pasta and cook until al dente; check package directions for timing. Drain the pasta and tip it into sauce. Gently toss the pasta in the sauce to coat thoroughly. Spoon onto warmed plates, top with the fried leek and parmesan and serve at once.

SERVES 6

SYDNEY

YABBY AND SPINACH GNOCCHI

Gnocchi is a typical Italian dish, combined here with one of Australia's indigenous freshwater crustaceans, the humble yabby. Stefano Manfredi, who gave me this recipe, is chef-owner of a successful restaurant in Sydney.

salt
500 g (1 lb) spinach, stems removed
2 large egg yolks
90 g (3 oz/¾ cup) freshly grated parmesan cheese
750 g (1½ lb/3 cups) ricotta, well drained
2 tablespoons plain (all-purpose) flour, or more as needed
1.5 kg (3 lb) yabbies (crayfish), cooked, tails removed and shelled
freshly ground pepper
pinch of freshly grated nutmeg
150 g (5 oz/⅔ cup) unsalted butter

Bring a saucepan three-quarters full of water to a boil. Add salt to taste and the spinach and cook for 5 minutes. Drain and allow to cool. Chop finely and squeeze to extract excess water. Place the spinach in a bowl and add the egg yolks, half of the

parmesan, the ricotta and the 2 tablespoons flour. Set aside 8 of the yabby tails and chop the remainder. Add the chopped tails to the bowl. Season to taste with salt and pepper and the nutmeg. Mix well with a wooden spoon, adding 1 or 2 tablespoons of flour if needed. Refrigerate for 30 minutes.

To shape the *gnocchi*, scoop up small pieces of the mixture about the size of a golf ball and roll each portion into a small sausage the length of your little finger. Set aside on a floured board.

To cook, bring a large pot three-quarters full of water to a boil. Add salt to taste and the *gnocchi* and simmer until they rise to surface, about 2–3 minutes. Remove the *gnocchi* with a slotted spoon.

In a saucepan over high heat, cook the butter, stirring constantly, until it turns a deep golden brown, 4–5 minutes.

Divide the gnocchi among 6 individual plates. Sprinkle with the remaining parmesan and top with the yabby tails. Drizzle with the hot butter and serve immediately.

SERVES 6

MELBOURNE

QUAIL AND PROSCIUTTO SALAD

This salad is the creation of food writer, author and cooking school owner–teacher Diane Holuigue. In Australia, she uses emu or kangaroo prosciutto.

4 quails
3 tablespoons unsalted butter
1 tablespoon oil
225 g (7 oz) mesclun (see glossary)
salt
100 g (3½ oz) shelled fresh broad (fava) beans

FOR THE DRESSING:

1 tablespoon red wine vinegar
3 tablespoons chicken stock
salt and freshly ground pepper
3 tablespoons olive oil

12 thin slices prosciutto
8 quail eggs, hard-boiled for 7 minutes, peeled and halved

Preheat an oven to 220°C (425°F).

Pin back the legs of the quails flat against the bodies with satay sticks (small bamboo skewers), then trim the sticks close to the skin so they do not prevent the quails from frying. In a frying pan over medium-high heat, melt the butter with the oil. Add the quail and brown well on all sides. Transfer to a baking pan and bake until tender, 8–10 minutes; the timing will depend upon the size of the quails.

Meanwhile, divide the salad greens among 4 plates. Bring a small saucepan three-quarters full of water to a boil and add salt to taste and the broad beans. Boil until just tender, about 1 minute. Drain and refresh in cold water. Drain again and remove the peel that covers each bean.

When the quails are ready, transfer to a board and keep warm. To make the dressing, place the baking pan used for the quails over medium heat and add the vinegar. Deglaze the pan, scraping up any browned-on bits. Then add the stock and stir in well. Season to taste with salt and pepper and stir in the oil. Set aside.

Discard the sticks from the quails and cut each quail into 4 or 5 small pieces. Scatter the quail pieces and broad beans throughout the mesclun. Arrange 3 prosciutto slices on each salad and then garnish with the eggs. Drizzle with the dressing and serve.

SERVES 4

Clockwise from top right: Quail and Prosciutto Salad, Yabby and Spinach Gnocchi, Rag Pasta with Tomatoes, Fried Leeks, Capers and Shaved Parmesan

THAI BEEF SALAD

Here is a classic of the Thai kitchen, and one that has been adopted with great gusto in Australia because of our excellent beef. Called yam nuea, *it makes a marvellous salad for a hot summer's day or evening. My favourite beef is pasture-fed Hereford, Murray Grey and Angus from the Darling Downs, southwest of Brisbane in Queensland.*

450 g (1 lb) eye of beef fillet
2 cloves garlic
6 fresh coriander (cilantro) leaves
2 tablespoons sugar
2 teaspoons light soy sauce
1 tablespoon fresh lime juice
½ teaspoon fish sauce (see glossary)
salt and freshly ground pepper
1¼ tablespoons vegetable oil
lettuce leaves

2 spring (green) onions, including tender green tops, thinly sliced
6 fresh red chillies, thinly sliced

❊ Preheat a broiler (griller) on high or prepare a fire in a barbecue. Place the beef fillet on a griller tray or barbecue rack and cook, turning once, until medium-rare, or as preferred. The timing will depend upon the thickness of the fillet. Cut the fillet into small, thin slices.

❊ Crush the garlic and finely chop 2 of the coriander leaves and place in a mortar. Add the sugar, soy sauce, lime juice, fish sauce and salt and pepper to taste. Pound with a pestle until a smooth paste forms.

❊ In a wok or deep frying pan over medium heat, warm the oil. Add the garlic paste and stir-fry for 30–60 seconds. Add the beef and toss to coat. Immediately remove from the heat and spoon onto a plate. Let cool completely.

❊ To serve, line a serving plate with the lettuce leaves. Top with the beef. Sprinkle the onions and chillies on top and garnish with the remaining 4 coriander leaves. Serve at once.

SERVES 6–8 *Photograph pages 154–155*

171

EGG SALAD WITH KALAMATA OLIVES

Fem Hawke lives in the beautiful countryside just outside of Orange in west-central New South Wales. She and her husband, Courtney, own a wonderful kitchen shop, and both are keen cooks. They serve this salad as a starter with lightly toasted pitta or warm crusty rolls and a locally produced crisp white wine.

4 Roma (plum) tomatoes, diced
1 white onion, thinly sliced
2 tablespoons capers, drained
2 tablespoons balsamic vinegar

FOR THE MAYONNAISE:

3 egg yolks
salt
300 ml (10 fl oz/1¼ cups) vegetable oil
1 tablespoon white wine vinegar
¼ teaspoon Worcestershire sauce
1 teaspoon hot mustard
2 tablespoons boiling water

5 hard-boiled eggs, roughly chopped
salt and freshly ground pepper
100 g (3½ oz/⅔ cup) South Australian Kalamata olives or other Kalamata olives

❧In a bowl, combine the tomatoes, onion and 1 tablespoon of the capers. Add the balsamic vinegar and toss gently. Let stand for about 1 hour.

Top to bottom: Egg Salad with Kalamata Olives, Rocket and Bocconcini Salad with Damper

❧To make the mayonnaise, in a bowl and using a fork, beat together the yolks and salt to taste until pale and thick. Slowly add the oil, drop by drop, beating constantly. When one-quarter of the oil has been added, add the remaining oil in a thin, steady stream, beating constantly. Add the wine vinegar, Worcestershire sauce and mustard and beat until well mixed. Add the boiling water (this helps to preserve the mayonnaise) and beat again.

❧Alternatively, in a blender, process the yolks and salt until thick. With the motor running, add the oil, drop by drop, until about one-quarter has been added and the mixture has emulsified. Then add the remaining oil in a thin, steady stream and blend until thick. Blend in the remaining ingredients.

❧Fold the chopped eggs and tomato mixture into the mayonnaise and season to taste with salt and pepper. Spoon the mixture into a shallow bowl and scatter the remaining 1 tablespoon capers and the olives over the top.

SERVES 6–8

ROCKET AND BOCCONCINI SALAD WITH DAMPER

Once damper was made with flour, water and salt in the coals of a camp fire, where it was the only bread the men ate on the long treks droving cattle. Today, it is a crisp-crusted, firm loaf, lightened with rising agents in the flour or with the addition of baking powder or bicarbonate of soda. This plain, very easy damper is from Penny Farrell, who tested many of the recipes in this book with me.

The damper works well, either freshly baked or grilled, with this salad. Bocconcini (literally, "little mouthfuls") are golf ball–sized cheeses made in Australia from cow's milk. At Paesanella in Marrickville, southwest of Sydney, bocconcini are made fresh every other day and are difficult to pass up.

FOR THE DAMPER:

520 g (17 oz/3¼ cups) self-raising flour
1 teaspoon salt
125 ml (4 fl oz/½ cup) plus 1 tablespoon buttermilk
125 ml (4 fl oz/½ cup) water

FOR THE SALAD:

2 bunches rocket (arugula), stems removed
6 *bocconcini,* thinly sliced
vinaigrette for radicchio, borlotti bean and grilled prosciutto salad (recipe on page 158)

❧To make the damper, position a rack in the upper part of an oven and preheat the oven to 200°C (400°F). Butter a baking tray (sheet).

❧In a large bowl sift together the flour and salt. Make a well in the centre and add the 125 ml (4 fl oz/½ cup) buttermilk and the water. Using a fork, mix the flour into the liquid. Turn out onto a lightly floured work surface and knead until smooth, 3–4 minutes.

❧Shape the dough into a round and place on the prepared tray. Using a sharp knife, cut a deep cross in the top of the bread. Brush with the 1 tablespoon buttermilk.

❧Bake until the damper sounds hollow when tapped on top, about 35 minutes.

❧Meanwhile, to make the salad, pile the rocket on the centres of 4 large flat plates. Arrange the *bocconcini* slices around the rocket salad and drizzle evenly with the vinaigrette. Serve at once with sliced damper.

SERVES 4

Warm Lamb Salad with Redcurrant Vinaigrette

Warm Lamb Salad with Redcurrant Vinaigrette

The main season for lamb is in the spring, when the animals are fattened on the lush winter pastures of clover and rye. The backstrap is the large strip of meat that comes from the loin. I've made this lamb salad many times in Australia, the United States and Canada, and everyone loves it. Be sure that the lamb is still warm when served.

100 g (3½ oz) snow peas (mangetouts)
1 bunch asparagus, 225–250 g (7–8 oz), trimmed and cut
    into 3-cm (1¼-in) lengths
1 tablespoon safflower oil
2 lamb backstraps, 180–200 g (6–6½ oz) each
salt and freshly ground pepper
6 cos (romaine) lettuce leaves
6 red mignonette (red-leaf) lettuce leaves
12 spinach leaves
1 small bunch rocket (arugula), stems removed
1 cucumber, sliced
6 cherry tomatoes, halved lengthwise
6 yellow teardrop tomatoes, halved lengthwise
1 carrot, peeled and cut into thin, narrow strips
3 baby yellow squash, sliced
4 white mushrooms, sliced

FOR THE DRESSING:

1½ tablespoons raspberry vinegar
2 teaspoons redcurrant jelly
100 ml (3½ oz/6½ tablespoons) olive oil
salt and freshly ground pepper

✿ Bring a saucepan three-quarters full of water to a boil. Add the snow peas and asparagus and cook for 3 minutes. Drain and refresh in iced water and drain again. Pat dry with paper towels.
✿ In a large, heavy frying pan over medium heat, warm the oil. Add the lamb and cook, turning to seal well on all sides. Season to taste with salt and pepper and then continue to cook until medium-rare, or until done to your liking. The timing will depend upon the thickness of the backstraps. Transfer to a warmed plate and cover. Reserve the pan juices.
✿ Arrange the lettuces, spinach and rocket in a pyramid on 6 large dinner plates. Scatter the cucumber, tomatoes, carrot, squash and mushrooms over the pyramid.
✿ To make the dressing, reheat the lamb cooking juice over medium heat. Deglaze the pan, scraping up any browned-on bits. Add the vinegar and jelly, mashing the jelly into the vinegar to melt it. Remove from the heat and whisk in the oil and salt and pepper to taste.
✿ Slice the lamb crosswise and arrange the medallions over the salad. Whisk the lamb juices that collected on the plate that held the lamb into the dressing. Drizzle the dressing over the salads and serve immediately.

SERVES 6

Clockwise from top right: Avocado, Orange and Purple Onion Salad, Mesclun Salad with Shaved Macadamias, Roasted Stuffed Yellow Capsicum Salad—photographed at Mosman, Sydney

MESCLUN SALAD WITH SHAVED MACADAMIAS

Macadamias are native to Australia and in the last few years, they have become readily available in several grades and styles. They are used extensively in cooking and, of course, are eaten on their own as a snack or with drinks, plain or unsalted.

200 g (6½ oz) mesclun (see glossary)

FOR THE DRESSING:

1 teaspoon sea salt
1 teaspoon West Australian Berry Farm raspberry vinegar or other high-quality raspberry vinegar

1 teaspoon balsamic vinegar
80 ml (3 fl oz/⅓ cup) virgin olive oil
freshly ground pepper

50 g (1¾ oz/⅓ cup) macadamia nuts

❧ Place the mesclun in a shallow salad bowl. Cover and refrigerate until ready to use.
❧ To make the dressing, in a small bowl, whisk together the salt, raspberry and balsamic vinegars, oil and pepper. Drizzle over the mesclun. If the bowl is shallow, there should be no need to toss the salad, as the dressing should reach all leaves.
❧ Place the macadamias in a food processor fitted with the metal blade or the grating disk. Process to form shavings. Alternatively, use a heavy chef's knife to cut the nuts into thin shavings. Scatter the nuts over the salad and serve at once.

SERVES 6

AVOCADO, ORANGE AND PURPLE ONION SALAD

Navel oranges are available most of the year, as our vast continent affords us several picking seasons. Oranges are used widely in the Australian kitchen. Serve this salad within 10 minutes of making it, before the avocado browns.

4 navel oranges
1 ripe but firm, large avocado
½ purple onion, cut into slices 1-cm (⅜-in) thick
pinch of salt
2 tablespoons light olive oil
¼ teaspoon dried mixed Italian herbs

Using a sharp knife, cut the skin and all the white pith off the oranges. Working over a small bowl to catch the juice, divide the oranges into segments, cutting on either side of each segment to release it from the membrane. Arrange attractively in a salad bowl.

Halve, pit and peel the avocado and cut crosswise into thin slices. Add to the salad bowl.

Separate the onion slices into rings. Arrange in the bowl with the orange segments and avocado slices.

In a small bowl, whisk together the salt, 1½ tablespoons of the reserved orange juice, the oil and the herbs. Immediately pour over the salad and serve at once.

SERVES 4

SEMOLINA GNOCCHI WITH ITALIAN TOMATO SAUCE AND PESTO

Now that good-quality fresh and dried pasta can be bought almost everywhere, it is seldom made at home. Nevertheless, I believe there are occasions when making your own is definitely worthwhile, and once you have mastered making pasta, the process is a true joy. Gnocchi can be made from potatoes, semolina or cornmeal (polenta). This particular gnocchi is made from semolina and is quite soft and therefore fragile, particularly when warm. Do not overheat the gnocchi or it will collapse. Store it warm rather than hot. Both sauces are staples of the Italian kitchen and have been adopted wholeheartedly into the Australian culinary repertoire.

FOR THE *GNOCCHI*:

800 ml (26 fl oz/3¼ cups) water
200 ml (6½ fl oz/¾ cup plus 1½ tablespoons) milk, or as needed
pinch of salt
120 g (4 oz/¾ cup) fine white semolina

FOR THE PESTO:

leaves from 1 bunch fresh basil
½ teaspoon sea salt
2 cloves garlic, bruised and halved
2 tablespoons pine nuts
2 tablespoons freshly grated parmesan cheese
80–100 ml (2½–3½ fl oz/5–7 tablespoons) virgin olive oil
freshly ground pepper

125 ml (4 fl oz/½ cup) tomato sauce, heated (see glossary)
100 g (3½ oz/¾ cup) freshly grated parmesan cheese

To make the *gnocchi,* in a saucepan, bring the water, milk and salt to a simmer. Pour in the semolina, in a thin, steady stream,

stirring constantly with a wooden spoon. Reduce the heat to low or remove the pan from the stove and continue to stir until the semolina is the consistency of medium-thick porridge. It should just be a thick dropping consistency. If the mixture is too thick, add more milk as needed to achieve the correct consistency. Dampen a Swiss (jelly) roll tin 26 by 37 cm (10 by 15 in) and pour the semolina mixture into it. Let stand until cold and set.

To make the pesto, place the basil leaves, salt and garlic in a food processor fitted with the metal blade or in a blender. Process until well chopped. Add the pine nuts and cheese and process until smooth. With the motor running, slowly add the virgin olive oil, a little at a time, and process until the mixture is smooth and creamy. Season to taste with pepper. If you will not be using the pesto right away, store it in an airtight container. Pour a thin layer of virgin olive oil on top before capping to keep the air out; this can be stirred into the pesto when you use it.

To serve, preheat an oven to 150°C (300°F). Run a knife around the edge of the sheet of *gnocchi* and then cut into 18 squares. Place in the oven and heat gently until warmed through, about 12 minutes. Do not overheat.

Spoon the pesto onto 6 warmed pasta plates. Arrange 3 pieces of *gnocchi* on top of each pool of pesto. Spoon a tablespoon of tomato sauce on each serving. (Refrigerate or freeze remaining tomato sauce.) Serve at once. Pass the parmesan at the table.

SERVES 6   *Photograph pages 8–9*

ROASTED STUFFED YELLOW CAPSICUM SALAD

Bright buttercup-yellow capsicums are my favourite. They are the sweetest and I always try to use them when they are in season, mostly in the summer and autumn. If unavailable, use red or green, but they will not taste the same. Use Australian black olives in this recipe, if possible.

8 small yellow capsicums (bell peppers)
8 small white onions
boiling water, as needed
8 oil-packed sun-dried tomatoes, drained, with oil reserved, and slivered
4 small cloves garlic, slivered
8 small fresh oregano sprigs or ¼ teaspoon dried oregano
30 g (1 oz) Italian sausage (pepperoni) or prosciutto, cut into narrow strips
90 g (3 oz/⅔ cup) ripe black olives, pitted

Position a rack in the upper part of an oven and preheat the oven to 200°C (400°F).

Stand the capsicums upright on a chopping board. Using a sharp knife, cut each capsicum into quarters from the stalk end through to the base. Discard the stems, seeds and ribs. Set aside.

Place the onions in a bowl and pour over boiling water to cover. Let stand for 2 minutes. Drain, and, when cool enough to handle, peel and quarter lengthwise.

Using a little of the oil reserved from the tomatoes, paint the base of 2 heavy baking trays (sheets). Arrange the capsicum quarters cut side up on the trays. Scatter the onions and garlic over them. Drizzle with the remaining tomato oil.

Place in the oven and roast for 10 minutes. Remove from the oven and evenly distribute the oregano and sausage or prosciutto over the capsicums. Return to the oven until the capsicums and onions are soft and beginning to brown, about 15 minutes longer. Let cool. Arrange on a large flat platter, scatter with the olives and serve.

SERVES 8

PASTA ROLL WITH FRESH TOMATO SAUCE AND BÉCHAMEL SAUCE

These rolls are simple to master once you've made them the first time. Best of all, they can be prepared ahead and cooked just before serving. Use a local ricotta because the cheese has a short shelf life and must be very fresh. This is my favourite tomato sauce, the one I make all the time.

FOR THE FILLING:

2 packages (250 g/8 oz each) frozen chopped English
    spinach, thawed
60 g (2 oz/¼ cup) unsalted butter, melted
250 g (8 oz/1 cup) very fresh ricotta cheese, sieved
100 g (3½ oz/¾ cup) freshly grated parmesan cheese
250 g (8 oz) prosciutto, finely minced
salt and freshly ground pepper

3 fresh spinach or plain lasagne sheets, 18 by 25 cm
    (7 by 10 in) each

FOR THE TOMATO SAUCE:

1 tablespoon olive oil
½ brown onion
1 can (800 g/26 oz) peeled Roma (plum) tomatoes, with
    their juice
salt and freshly ground pepper
1 teaspoon finely chopped fresh oregano, optional
1 teaspoon finely chopped fresh marjoram, optional
1½ tablespoons unsalted butter

FOR THE BÉCHAMEL SAUCE:

60 g (2 oz/¼ cup) unsalted butter
3 tablespoons plain (all-purpose) flour
500 ml (16 fl oz/2 cups) milk
salt and freshly ground white pepper

FOR SERVING:

freshly grated parmesan cheese

To make the filling, place the spinach in a sieve and press down to force out as much water as possible. (Save the water for adding to soup.) In a bowl combine the spinach, butter, ricotta and parmesan cheeses, prosciutto and salt and pepper to taste. Stir to make a smooth mixture.

Place the lasagne sheets on a work surface. Spread one-third of the filling over the surface of one sheet. Roll up the sheet loosely to form a cylinder. Repeat with the remaining sheets and filling. Wrap each roll in a clean kitchen towel and tie the ends of the towel closed with kitchen twine. (The rolls can be prepared to this point up to 1 day in advance and stored in an airtight container in the refrigerator. Bring back to room temperature before cooking.)

Select a pan large enough to hold the rolls easily and half fill the pan with salted water. Bring to a boil. Add the rolls, reduce the heat to medium and simmer until cooked through, 35–45 minutes. (If you do not have a pan large enough to hold all 3 rolls, cook them in separate pans; if they are cooked separately, they should take the lesser amount of time to cook.)

While the rolls are cooking, make the sauces. To make the tomato sauce, in a saucepan over medium heat, warm the oil. Add the onion and the tomatoes with their juice. Cook uncovered, breaking up the tomatoes with a wooden spoon and stirring from time to time, until thickened, about 45 minutes. Season to taste with salt and pepper and add the herbs (if using). Just prior to serving, remove the onion and discard and then stir in the butter.

To make the béchamel sauce, in a heavy saucepan over medium heat, melt the butter. Whisk in the flour and cook, whisking constantly, for 2 minutes. Slowly add the milk and cook, whisking, until the sauce thickens. Simmer gently, stirring occasionally, for 15 minutes. Season to taste with salt and white pepper.

Drain the pasta rolls and remove the towels. Ladle a little of each sauce onto 8 warmed dinner plates. Cut the pasta rolls into slices 2 cm (¾ in) thick and arrange on top of the sauces. Pass the parmesan at the table.

SERVES 8

LOBSTER AND LENTIL SALAD

There are times when a substantial salad like this plays the major role in a menu. I believe that it is best to concentrate on doing one dish very well and then let it carry the meal. This salad, followed by a bowl of perfectly ripe, seasonal fruits, preferably with lots of tropical varieties, makes an ideal lunch. If you want to extend the menu to three courses, add a platter featuring a trio of Australian cheeses.

2 tablespoons unsalted butter
2 shallots, finely chopped
1 clove garlic, finely chopped
500 g (1 lb) dried lentils
700 ml (22 fl oz/2¾ cups) chicken stock, or as needed
1 teaspoon balsamic vinegar
2½ tablespoons olive oil
250 ml (8 fl oz/1 cup) walnut oil
1 tablespoon finely chopped fresh basil leaves
1 purple onion, cut into 5 mm (¼ in) dice
1 tomato, cut into 5 mm (¼ in) dice
1 carrot, peeled and cut into 5 mm (¼ in) dice
1 tablespoon snipped fresh chives
salt and freshly ground pepper
500 ml (16 fl oz/2 cups) fish stock (see glossary)
1 kg (2 lb) lobster tail meat, cut into medallions 2 cm
    (¾ in) thick
heart of 1 radicchio, separated into leaves
1½ recipes vinaigrette for healthy salad (recipe on page 164)
leaves from 4 small tarragon sprigs, finely chopped

In a large heavy frying pan over medium heat, melt the butter. Add the shallots and garlic and sauté until softened, about 5 minutes. Add the lentils and chicken stock to cover. Bring to a simmer, cover and cook until the lentils are just cooked and the liquid is absorbed, 15–25 minutes. The cooking time will depend upon the age of the lentils. Remove from the heat and let cool.

In a large bowl, combine the cooled lentils, vinegar, olive and walnut oils, basil, onion, tomato, carrot and chives. Mix well and season to taste with salt and pepper. Set aside.

In a saucepan bring the fish stock to a boil. Reduce the heat to a gentle simmer and add the lobster. Poach gently until just cooked, about 3½ minutes. Using a slotted spoon, transfer the lobster to a warmed bowl and cover to keep warm. Reserve the stock for another use.

Arrange the radicchio leaves in a large bowl. Spoon the lentils on top of the lettuce. Add the vinaigrette and tarragon to the lobster and toss gently. Arrange on top of the lentils and serve at once.

SERVES 6   *Photograph pages 154–155*

*Pasta Roll with Fresh Tomato Sauce and Béchamel Sauce—
photographed at Bloodwood Estate, Orange, NSW*

NORTHERN TERRITORY

NORTHERN TERRITORY

THE TOP END

WHEREAS TOP END EUROPEANS roughly divide the year into two seasons, the Wet—the rainy season—and the Dry, Northern Territory Aborigines divide the year into six seasons, each of which conveys information about the weather and the available foods.

For the Aboriginal people of northeast Arnhem Land, *Dharratharramirri* (May through July) is the season for mud crabs and, later, turtle eggs. *Midawarr* (March and April, just after the rains), when the wind swings round to the southeast, is the time for bush fruits (such as black plums, native figs and the billygoat plum), roots (yams and waterlily roots) and the large game fish, barramundi. Towards the end of *Barra'mirri mayaltha,* during the northwest monsoon, the cycad nuts are in season.

These nuts, the fruit of the cycad palm (*Cycas armstrongonii*), are a major source of carbohydrate but are toxic in their raw state and require elaborate processing to be edible. Methods of removing the toxin vary, but usually involve soaking the roasted, crushed flesh of the nuts in a stream of running water for several days to leach out all the poison. In places like Yirrkala, the flesh is then pounded into a paste, wrapped in pandanus leaves and paperbark and baked in the embers of a fire.

Of all the states, the Northern Territory has the most Aborigines still living in nonurban, semitraditional style, attempting to keep their rich, complex and diverse cultures alive. If you are privileged to share bush foods with Aborigines in a traditional setting, where you sit is important. Women usually sit with women, and men with men. Depending upon which area you are in, the older women may divide up the food, while the younger women distribute it in a particular order in relation to a

Previous pages: The peaks of The Olgas offer a dramatic vantage on distant Uluru. Left: An Aboriginal girl collecting waterlilies bursts above the water with an armful of exquisite blossoms.

person's social position. It is only when eating with such communities that you may taste delicacies such as flying foxes—fruit bats—or dugong, a small sea mammal. Both are protected, but because they are traditional foods, Aborigines are allowed to hunt them.

An example of the diversity of Aboriginal cultures is found along the Northern Territory coast, between the Daly River and Yirrkala, a distance of some eight hundred kilometres (four hundred eighty miles). The area is home to an incredible density of Aboriginal languages—up to fifty different languages or dialects. It is said that tribes more than two removed from one another have difficulty understanding each other.

Despite these language differences, many words—up to one hundred—are common to them all. They are the result of contact with the Macassans (from what is now Sulawesi in Indonesia) hundreds of years before the arrival of Europeans. Among them are terms for imported goods introduced by the Macassans for which there would have been no local equivalent—rice, cloth, metal, glass—for items connected with boats and for money, which even today is the Indonesian, rupiah. The Top End Aborigines' word for white people is still *balanda,* a corruption of 'Hollander', the only Europeans then known to the Macassans. The Macassans also introduced the Aborigines to alcohol, tobacco and the dugout canoe. All this was as a result of Australia's first 'food industry'.

Hundreds of years ago, from November onwards, fleets of praus carrying up to two thousand men would arrive on the Northern Territory coast, borne down (from what is now Udjung Pandang) on the northwest monsoon. They came to harvest trepang. Trepang, also known as bêches-de-mer or sea slugs, sometimes wrongly as sea cucumbers, were, and are, highly prized as a delicacy by the Chinese. The Trepang Trade involved the harvest, boiling, curing, smoking and drying of these sea creatures.

Macassan sites have been found along the Northern Territory coast from the Gulf of Carpentaria, around the Coburg Peninsula, right down to the Kimberleys. The most obvious indications of these sites are the tamarind trees, the seeds of which the Macassans would have brought with them as a condiment for their rice. The sites are also recognisable from the remains of the big stone fireplaces used to support the huge wok-shaped metal cauldrons in which the trepang were boiled, and for the large amounts of charcoal.

Aborigines traded mother-of-pearl shell and tortoise-shell with the Macassans, and also worked alongside them, guiding them to the trepang and then helping in the harvest by diving for them. They even travelled to Macassar and back—Australian's first international tourism!

The dried and smoked trepang was transported thousands of kilometres back to Indonesia and then, it is thought, on to Singapore and China. This was Australia's first international export industry—and it was going on up to five hundred years before European settlement. It ceased in 1906, when the South Australian Government, in an effort to protect local trepangers, introduced regulations involving licensing and custom duties that they knew the Macassars would find impossible to observe.

European explorers of the sixteenth century knew of the existence of a Great South Land. The Dauphin Chart of 1530, considered by some to be the first map of Australia, described it as Java la Grande, supposing it to be separated from Java only by a river, the Rio Grande. The first recorded European landfall in what is now the Northern Territory was made by a Dutch ship, *Arnhem,* in

1623, which gave its name to Arnhem Land. (Captain Willem Jansz in the *Duyfken* had travelled up the west coast of the Gulf of Carpentaria in 1606.) By 1644, Abel Tasman had surveyed the coast of the Gulf of Carpentaria and named Groote Eylandt, although no further attempts to chart the northern coast were made until Matthew Flinders, who, on his way around Australia in 1803, bumped into a fleet of Macassan trepangers.

Although the British formally took possession of what is now the Northern Territory in 1824, over the next forty-five years, four different attempts at settlement were abandoned. Then finally, in 1869, Port Darwin was selected as the site of the chief town, Palmerston, now Darwin. By 1872, the Overland Telegraph had been brought through from Adelaide, a distance of nearly 3350 kilometres (2000 miles).

Once again it was gold that opened up the region. It had been discovered in the 1860s, but it wasn't until finds near Pine Creek in 1872 that any attempt was made to extract it. Even then, the climate made it difficult. Water was the stumbling block: too much in the Wet made transport impossible, and there was too little in the Dry.

In 1874, the South Australian Government (which controlled the Northern Territory until 1911) recruited two hundred Chinese labourers from Singapore to fill the labour shortage. Other Chinese followed, involving themselves in mining, as well as in growing fruit and vegetables and in fishing. By 1881, there were two thousand Chinese in the Northern Territory, outnumbering Europeans five to one, and by 1888, possibly as many as six thousand. Soon afterwards, however, immigration restrictions were imposed, and the numbers of Chinese declined.

Sheep and cattle—on the hoof—had accompanied the parties working on the Overland Telegraph; by 1872, properties were stocked with the livestock. In the end, the great distances between watering holes proved unsuitable for sheep. Cattle were better able to cope, and by the 1890s, there were a quarter of a million head.

The cattle industry was also important in opening up the Top End. Even as late as the 1950s, mobs of cattle were moved long distances overland. The Northern Territory Administration's droving programme for 1953—a timetable designed to keep different herds from getting mixed up—shows mobs as big as fifteen hundred being moved by drovers on horseback with largely English names (Richardson, Dollard, Lewis, Scobie) from Victoria River Downs Station and Newcastle Waters across to Queensland—a distance of about one thousand kilometres (six hundred miles)! Today, such mustering is done by helicopter.

Buffalo were first introduced from Timor in 1825, and again at the settlement at Port Essington when it was established in 1838. By the time Port Essington was abandoned, there were several herds. These animals went wild, multiplied and moved south to the Alligator Valley. Another shipment of buffalo, on its way to Sydney as a supply of meat for the goldfields, was shipwrecked near the Ord River. These animals also went wild and thrived. In time, buffalo became a major pest, and an eradication programme set up in the 1980s has seen their numbers decline. They are still a game meat associated with the Northern Territory, but are really only worth eating fresh.

Another introduced animal that has also gone wild and multiplied is the camel. Camels played an important role in expeditions like that of Burke and Wills, who made the first overland crossing of the continent from south to north. Later they served as mail carriers in the outback and as supply animals for Kimberley cattle stations and for the building of the railway from Adelaide to Alice Springs, which opened in 1929. Many have since gone wild. It was recently estimated that there are up to thirty thousand feral camels in central Australia, and camel meat is now being processed by an abattoir at Alice Springs.

More than half the people living in the Northern Territory live in its capital, Darwin, which is closer to Indonesia than to any of Australia's capital cities. It has become a fascinating Eurasian city, Australia's northern gateway to Asia. While some of the Chinese who stayed on after the gold rushes became market gardeners, and subsequently influential members of the community and its commerce, it is the new wave of migration, from Indochina—Vietnam, Cambodia, Laos—that has brought the most significant changes to Darwin's food choices. More recent migrants have come from other parts of Southeast Asia, such as Burma and Timor. All these communities have introduced foods from their home countries and a completely new range of fresh Asian produce.

Many early attempts at agriculture in the Northern Territory failed, such as a rice-growing experiment at Humpty Doo, when magpie geese ate the crop. As recently as the 1980s, Darwin was reliant on South Australia for much of its 'fresh' produce, such as lettuce, tomatoes and other vegetables. (You can imagine what effect a couple of days in transit had on freshness.) But in the last ten years there has been a horticultural revolution in the state. It is now practically self-sufficient in everything except temperate-climate vegetables and fruits like apples. Today refrigerated trucks ply up and down The Track—the Stuart Highway—most of the year, going back full instead of empty.

There are three main growing areas in the Northern Territory. Ti Tree, which lies about 150 kilometres (90 miles) north of Alice, produces the first of the country's new season's grapes and some of the last mangoes in March and April, as well as vegetables for southern markets. Near Katherine, 270 kilometres (160 miles) south of Darwin, vegetables are grown. This area is also home to one of the country's largest mango plantations, and many pawpaws (papayas) are harvested here as well. In the third area, the Litchfield Shire just south of Darwin, an enormous variety of tropical fruits—such as durians and rambutans—and many Asian vegetables are cultivated.

The Northern Territory also produces a myriad variety of melons—watermelons, honeydews and rockmelons (musk melons), all out of season with southern Australia—and boasts major plantings of such tropical citrus as red grapefruit, pomelos, lemons and limes, including the kaffir lime, the leaves and zest of which are used for flavouring Thai food. Recently there has been an explosion in the number and types of exotic tropical fruits being grown, among them black sapote (the chocolate pudding fruit), carambola (star fruit), jackfruit, guava, Amazon custard apple (also known as lemon meringue fruit), sapodilla and soursop. The Northern Territory also grows figs out of season with the rest of Australia, which are on the market from August to December.

These days Darwin has some of the most exciting produce markets in the country, particularly its Asian-style outdoor markets: Parap (Saturday mornings), Rapid Creek (Sundays) or, the most recent and by far the biggest, the evening market at Mindil Beach (Thursdays, only in the Dry). In addition to fresh produce, the vendors sell prepared dishes that range from *laksa* (Malaysian coconut noodle soup) to Thai fish cakes, green pawpaw (papaya) salad, satays and bowls of spicy noodles. Going

The same geologic forces that formed The Olgas and Uluru gave the ancient MacDonnell Ranges their dramatic gorges and chasms.

out to have Asian food or buy some exotic fresh fruit and vegetables has become the thing to do on Saturday mornings and Thursday nights in Darwin.

The waters of the Northern Territory offer all manner of tropical fish: gold band snapper, red jewfish, red emperor (red snapper), coral trout, spotted cod and mud crabs, as well as tuna, many different types of prawns (shrimp)—banana, endeavour, coral and king—bugs (the Moreton Bay variety) and that great game fish, the barramundi, which are fished commercially as well as by sportfishers.

The barramundi's life cycle is the reverse of that of the salmon. It goes out to sea to spawn and comes back upriver into fresh water to feed after the rainy season, when the rivers are swollen. The fish taste best on their way upriver; towards the Dry, when they are on their way back downriver, they tend to taste muddy. (They can be trapped upriver for years at a time.)

Despite the disappearance of much of its wonderful old tropical architecture in the cyclone of 1975, Darwin has the spirit of a frontier town. A palpable sense of excitement, of living on the edge, can be felt here—and not just because every time you go swimming in the sea you take your chances with the increased population of no-longer-protected, human-eating, saltwater crocodiles! Revenge is increasingly to be found on local menus, however. Farmed crocodile turns up on them, along with camel meat, buffalo and barramundi, the Northern Territory's other wild specialties.

VEGETABLES AND GRAINS

The vital Vietnamese community in the Richmond district of Melbourne ensures the availability of fresh Asian produce and ingredients.

VEGETABLES AND GRAINS

You could always tell the difference between a 'currency lass' and a 'sterling girl', observed German explorer Ludwig Leichhardt in 1843, because when offered a choice between pumpkins and potatoes, the Australian-born currency lass would choose pumpkins, whereas the English-born sterling girl would take potatoes. Pumpkins tasted good, were big and floury, and kept for a long time, whereas most other vegetables perished in the heat—an important consideration in the days before refrigeration.

Neither pumpkins or potatoes are indigenous, of course, but that is no surprise. The Australian diet is comprised almost entirely of crops that have been introduced since European settlement. Indeed, no culture on earth eats less of its indigenous plants. Even our native spinach, tetragonia, sometimes known as warrigal greens, is much more widely cultivated in France, and to a certain extent in England. Tetragonia is actually best known as New Zealand spinach: Captain Cook, aboard the *Endeavour,* stopped in New Zealand first and named it there before sailing on to Botany Bay.

Vegetables played a relatively small part in the diet of the early settlers. Only once the land had been tamed could anyone even think of putting in a vegetable patch, and even then it would probably have to be watered from the household's only supply—the rainwater tank. Worse still, droughts could last for years, even a decade.

The First Fleet had brought seeds for peas, beans, potatoes and turnips. Although the earliest attempts at cultivation were generally disappointing, there was one success: By the end of 1788, Reverend Johnson is reported to have had a flourishing vegetable garden. In 1794, twenty-two eleven-hectare (thirty-acre) farms were established alongside the upper reaches of the Hawkesbury River, which subsequently became a market gardening area, its produce being shipped out through Broken Bay down to Sydney.

A market in Norwood, a suburb of Adelaide, offers an eye-pleasing palette of grains.

Many of these early farms were discovered—too late—to be flood-prone, and new farms were established on higher ground. These flourished. Bucolic descriptions of the Hawkesbury area around Richmond in the 1820s noted fields of Indian corn (maize), orchards of peaches and a boy minding a herd of pigs in a field of (wheat) stubble. Also thriving were gooseberries, currants, lemons, oranges, melons, potatoes and pumpkins as big as buckets.

From the 1860s until the end of the century, the Chinese were responsible for a large share of the commercial vegetable growing. Most large towns had Chinese gardeners supplying their needs. It is said that Australia owes a debt to these gardeners for demonstrating what a wide range of vegetables could be grown using age-old furrow irrigation methods instead of hand watering.

What was generally available, of course, was what you grew yourself. Mrs Forster Rutledge, in her *Goulburn Cookery Book* of 1899, lists a mere fifteen vegetables, some of which are no longer so common or popular today: sea kale, turnips, Jerusalem artichokes and vegetable marrows (summer squash). Her cooking times were based on those of the English. She recommended boiling beetroots (beets) in winter—presumably when they were woody—for between five and seven hours! Asparagus was given up to twenty minutes and French beans up to twenty-five minutes. (You can tell where her priorities lay: only four pages were devoted to vegetable recipes, while nine were devoted to 'What to do with old meat', eleven to cakes and another ten to small cakes and buns!) Until the 1950s, there was likely to be a vegetable patch, even behind suburban houses—and, of course, the choko (chayote) vine growing over the backyard 'dunny', the loo (outhouse) at the bottom of the garden.

Today, few other countries are able to produce such a range of vegetables throughout the year. From durum wheat for pasta to corn for polenta, there is practically nothing that Australia doesn't grow, thanks to our great range of climates. Instead of the rather limited selection of largely British vegetables—swedes (rutabagas), cabbage, parsnips—available in the 1960s, there is now a much wider choice, from sugarsnap peas and snow peas to green or yellow zucchini (courgettes), acorn squash, okra, kumara (yellow sweet potato), fennel and borlotti (cranberry) beans, to name only a handful.

Thanks to our most recent migrants, there are also many Asian vegetables, including bok and pak choy, tiny cream-coloured and green eggplants (aubergines), bitter melon and Japanese radish (daikon), as well as flavourings like lemongrass, galangal, coriander (cilantro) and many different types of chilli.

Australia is also a major rice grower. Ninety percent of annual production—of around a million tonnes—is exported to between fifty and sixty countries, where it's generally considered premium grade. Both basic rice varieties—the medium- or short-grain Japonicas and the long-grain, tropical Indicas—are grown.

Almost all of Australia's rice is cultivated in the Riverina area of New South Wales. Rice growing didn't immediately catch on with Australian farmers, who couldn't see themselves wading in paddy fields in water up to their knees to plant individual seedlings. Thanks to the example of Jo Takasuka at Swan Hill in the early 1900s, who demonstrated that wheat-growing techniques—where the grain is dry sown and then the field is flooded—could be used, similar methods were adopted. Although these are still in use today, aerial sowing into an already flooded

A crop of plump artichokes grown in South Werribee, Victoria, is headed for market.

field has become increasingly popular since the late 1960s.

Few fertilisers or chemicals are needed because of the absence of rice pests and diseases, and the practice of an old-fashioned method of land-use rotation. The latter calls for fields to be used one year to grow rice and the next to grow wheat, rested for a year and then used for two years as sheep pasture, which naturally replenishes the nutrients in the soil. This method makes Australian rice almost organic and therefore some of the cleanest and 'greenest' in the world. The most popular and versatile variety is a Japonica—Amaroo—sold as Sunwhite Calrose, which represents about half of the market.

Obviously, the vegetables that are grown depend on the climate. Thus Victoria grows much of the country's asparagus, peas, broccoli, carrots, cauliflowers and potatoes, while Queensland produces the most beetroots, beans, capsicums (bell peppers), squash, zucchini and marrows, sweet corn and pumpkins.

Tasmania wins in the onion, turnip and mushroom stakes, and comes second to Queensland in beans, while Western Australia is the country's second biggest producer of carrots, and New South Wales grows the most avocados.

While it is preferable to eat locally grown poduce—and to follow the seasons—Australia is blessed with a range of climates that extends the seasons of many vegetables. What is available to the Australian cook is a veritable year-round cornucopia.

TASMANIA

Asparagus and Carrot Soufflé Tarts

The best time to enjoy Australian asparagus is in the spring, although they are available practically year-round. Heidi farmhouse cheese is ideal in this recipe because of its good melting qualities and mature flavour. It is made by Frank and Elizabeth Marchand in northern Tasmania.

2 sheets frozen shortcrust pastry, each 25 cm (10 in) square, thawed and cut into 4 equal squares
125 g (4 oz/½ cup) unsalted butter
3 tablespoons plain (all-purpose) flour
450 ml (14 fl oz/1¾ cups) milk
freshly grated nutmeg
6 egg yolks, lightly beaten
2 tablespoons grated Heidi Farm cheddar cheese or other high-quality cheddar cheese
1 teaspoon Dijon mustard
75 g (2½ oz) asparagus tips, boiled until tender-crisp
75 g (2½ oz) carrot, peeled, cut in thin, fine strips and boiled until tender-crisp
salt and freshly ground pepper
5 egg whites

Butter 8 regular muffin-tin wells each about 7 cm (2¾ in) in diameter at the top, 5 cm (2 in) in diameter at the bottom and 3¼ cm (1⅓ in) deep. Line each well with the pastry and trim level with the tops of the wells.

Position a rack in the middle of an oven and preheat the oven to 200°C (400°F). In a heavy pot over medium heat, melt the butter. Add the flour and cook, whisking constantly, for 2 minutes. Slowly add the milk, whisking constantly, and cook, continuing to whisk, until the sauce thickens slightly. Reduce the heat to low, season to taste with the nutmeg and cook, stirring often, for 10 minutes to form a good consistency. Remove from the heat and let cool slightly.

Whisk the egg yolks, cheese and mustard into the sauce. Fold in the asparagus and carrot and season to taste with salt and pepper.

In a bowl, beat the egg whites with a few grains of salt until they stand in stiff, glossy peaks. Using a large spoon, fold the egg white mixture into the vegetable mixture. Then spoon into the prepared muffin pans. Bake in the centre of the oven until puffed and golden on top, about 25 minutes.

Using an eggslice (metal spatula), ease the tarts out of the muffin-tin wells. Serve at once.

SERVES 8

ADELAIDE

Onions Stuffed with Mushroom and Prosciutto

White button mushrooms are the most common of our cultivated mushrooms. They can be bought at several stages of their production from the tiny tight, very white caps to cups (when the gills first show) to flats (when they open out flat).

3 brown onions, peeled but left whole

FOR THE STUFFING:

150 g (5 oz) thickly sliced lean prosciutto, minced
300 g (10 oz) white button mushrooms, minced
15 g (½ oz/5 tablespoons) chopped fresh parsley
salt and freshly ground pepper

1 tablespoon virgin olive oil
125 ml (4 fl oz/½ cup) chicken stock
5 fresh parsley sprigs

Position a rack in the centre of an oven and preheat the oven to 180°C (350°F). Butter a baking dish 12 by 18 cm (4½ by 7 in).

Bring a saucepan three-quarters full of water to a boil. Add the onions and simmer until tender, 15–20 minutes. Drain the onions well and let them cool until they can be handled. Cut down one side of each onion and remove the first 5 layers without breaking them. Spread the removed layers out on a work surface, concave side up. You will have 15 layers in all. Finely chop the remaining onion.

To make the stuffing, in a bowl, mix together the prosciutto, mushrooms, chopped onion, parsley and salt and pepper to taste. Divide the stuffing evenly among the onion layers; do not overfill. Fold the onion layers around the filling to enclose completely. When all are filled, arrange snugly, with the seam on the side, in the prepared dish.

Drizzle the oil and stock over the stuffed onions and tuck the parsley sprigs in among them. Cover with aluminium foil. Bake in the centre of the oven until bubbling and heated through, about 15 minutes. Serve immediately.

SERVES 3–4 *Photograph page 191*

SYDNEY

Spicy Vegetable Couscous

Couscous is to North Africans what pasta is to the Italians. It is tiny pellets made by rolling, sifting, steaming and drying semolina grains. Instant couscous is quick and easy; just follow the instructions on the packet.

3 tablespoons olive oil
1 brown onion, coarsely chopped
1 clove garlic, finely chopped
2 carrots, peeled and finely chopped
2 zucchini (courgettes), finely chopped
½ bunch snake beans (Chinese long beans), about 120 g (¼ lb), cut into pieces 1 cm (⅜ in) long (see glossary)
1 yellow summer squash, finely diced
60 g (2 oz/1 cup) small broccoli florets
80 g (3 oz/1 cup) small cauliflower florets
2 tomatoes, peeled, seeded and diced
¼ teaspoon ground cumin
1 fresh red chilli, sliced
250 ml (8 fl oz/1 cup) chicken stock
160 g (5 oz/1 cup) couscous (see glossary)
3 tablespoons unsalted butter
fresh coriander (cilantro) sprigs

In a large, heavy saucepan over medium heat, warm the oil. Add the onion and sauté gently until beginning to brown, about 10 minutes. Add the garlic and sauté for 2 minutes. Add the carrots, zucchini, snake beans, squash, broccoli, cauliflower, tomatoes, cumin, chilli and stock and bring to a boil. Simmer, uncovered, for 5 minutes.

Add the couscous and cook, stirring occasionally, until tender, about 5 minutes. Add the butter and fold through the mixture. Spoon into a warmed serving bowl, top with the coriander sprigs and serve.

SERVES 4 *Photograph page 190*

Asparagus and Carrot Soufflé Tarts

Clockwise from right: Spicy Vegetable Couscous (recipe page 188), Chargrilled Vegetables with Hommos, Baba Ghannouj

BABA GHANNOUJ

You will find baba ghannouj, a garlicky eggplant purée, on the menu of every Lebanese restaurant. It's easy to make at home and keeps well for at least 5 days in the refrigerator. Serve with pitta bread.

1 kg (2 lb) eggplants (aubergines), halved lengthwise
salt
2 cloves garlic, minced
250 ml (8 fl oz/1 cup) olive oil
1–2 tablespoons white wine vinegar
1–2 tablespoons fresh lemon juice
freshly ground pepper

FOR THE GARNISH:

4 spring (green) onions, including tender green tops, sliced
30 g (1 oz/¼ cup) black olives
2 firm ripe tomatoes, cut into eighths

❧ Preheat an oven to 200°C (400°F).
❧ Place the eggplants, cut side down, on an aluminium foil–lined baking pan. Bake for 20 minutes. Turn the eggplants over and roast until tender, 20–30 minutes. Remove from the oven and let cool.
❧ Scrape the flesh out of the eggplant halves into a colander and discard the skins. Sprinkle the flesh generously with salt, place a plate directly on top of the eggplant and let stand for 30 minutes to drain off the bitter juices.
❧ Wrap the eggplant flesh in a clean cloth and wring out every vestige of juice. Scrape the eggplant into a mixing bowl. Add the garlic and drizzle in the oil, drop by drop, beating vigorously with a wooden spoon until the oil and eggplant form a single mass. Beat in the vinegar, lemon juice and pepper to taste.
❧ Spoon into a serving bowl. Garnish with the spring onions and olives. Accompany with the tomatoes and serve.

SERVES 6

CHARGRILLED VEGETABLES WITH HOMMOS

Hommos is usually served with pitta bread. But it is delicious used in this way, as a topping for a variety of grilled seasonal vegetables. If you are pressed for time, use about 875 grams (28 ounces/4 cups) drained canned chickpeas, reserving some of the canning liquid to use in place of the cooking liquid.

FOR THE HOMMOS:

400 g (13 oz/1¾ cups) dried chickpeas, picked over and
    soaked in cold water to cover for 12 hours
3 cloves garlic
300 ml (10 fl oz/1¼ cups) tahini (see glossary)
salt to taste
juice of 2 lemons, or to taste
1 teaspoon ground cumin
½–1 teaspoon chilli flakes, optional

FOR THE VEGETABLES:

sea salt
3 carrots, peeled and halved lengthwise
2 kumaras or other sweet potatoes, peeled and cut
    lengthwise into quarters or eighths (see glossary)
3 leeks, carefully washed and halved lengthwise
1 ear of corn, cut crosswise into 6 pieces
6 brussels sprouts, halved lengthwise
80 ml (3 fl oz/⅓ cup) virgin olive oil
cracked black pepper

FOR SERVING THE HOMMOS:

1 teaspoon paprika
2 tablespoons olive oil
1½ tablespoons chopped fresh parsley

To make the hommos, place the chickpeas in a saucepan and add cold water to cover generously. Bring to a boil, skimming off any froth that forms. Reduce the heat to medium-low and simmer until tender, about 2 hours.

Drain the cooked chickpeas, reserving 80 ml (3 fl oz/⅓ cup) of the cooking liquid. Refresh the chickpeas in cold water and drain thoroughly.

Reserve 3 tablespoons of the chickpeas. Pass the remaining chickpeas through the fine disc of a food mill over a bowl, adding the reserved cooking liquid, 1 tablespoon at a time, to ease the passage. Do not make the purée too thin by adding too much liquid.

Working in batches, spoon the purée into a blender or a food processor fitted with the metal blade. Add the garlic, tahini and salt and purée until smooth. Add the lemon juice, cumin and chilli flakes (if using). Purée until the mixture is smooth and has a thick dropping consistency. Set aside.

To prepare the vegetables, preheat a griller (broiler) on high. Bring a saucepan three-quarters full of water to a boil. Salt lightly and add the carrots, kumaras, leeks, corn and brussels sprouts. Parboil until half cooked, 4–5 minutes. Drain, refresh in iced water and drain again. Pat dry on paper towels.

To finish the vegetables, arrange them on a griller tray (pan). Brush the vegetables with the oil, season to taste with salt and pepper, and cook, turning as needed, until crusty and golden on the outsides and tender in the centres. The timing will depend upon individual vegetables; pierce with a fork to make sure they are done.

While the vegetables are cooking, prepare the hommos for serving. Spoon into a shallow serving dish. Smooth the top with the back of a spoon, leaving spoon indentations. Sprinkle with the paprika. Drizzle with the oil and lemon juice. Scatter the parsley and reserved chickpeas over the top. Arrange the vegetables on the dish and serve.

SERVES 6

CARROT PURÉE WITH GINGER

This is one of my favourite vegetable dishes. My friend, lawyer Rupert Rosenblum, is a fabulous cook who makes this to accompany roast leg of pork. It's winter food fit for the gods— so easy and quick yet delectable.

500 g (1 lb) carrots, peeled and cut into chunky pieces
1 piece gingerroot, about 2 cm (¾ in) long
375–500 ml (12–16 fl oz/1½–2 cups) chicken stock
1½ tablespoons unsalted butter, optional
salt and freshly ground pepper

Place the carrots and gingerroot in a saucepan just large enough to hold them comfortably. Add stock to cover barely. Bring slowly to a boil, cover, reduce the heat and simmer until the carrots are tender, 15–20 minutes. Remove the lid and let cool for 10 minutes. Discard the ginger.

Using a slotted spoon, transfer the carrots to a food processor fitted with the metal blade and add 1–2 tablespoons of the cooking stock. Purée until smooth. Add the butter, if using, and just enough stock to make a thick dropping consistency. Season to taste with salt and pepper. Spoon into a warmed bowl and serve.

SERVES 4

Clockwise from top: Onions Stuffed with Mushroom and Prosciutto (recipe page 188), Carrot Purée with Ginger, Braised Zucchini with Ginger and Toasted Sesame Seeds (recipe page 192)

LAYERED EGGPLANT, TOMATOES AND PURPLE ONIONS

This is a lovely dish to make in the summer, when the garden is filled with bright red tomatoes and shiny eggplants.

2 medium-sized eggplants (aubergines), unpeeled, thinly sliced
salt
120 ml (4 fl oz/½ cup) plus 3 tablespoons olive oil
4 medium-sized purple onions, halved and thinly sliced
freshly ground black pepper
3 ripe tomatoes, cored and thickly sliced
1 tablespoon finely chopped fresh mixed herbs of choice
12 small fresh rosemary sprigs

❀ Layer the eggplant slices in a colander placed in a sink. Sprinkle each layer liberally with salt. Let stand for 30 minutes to drain off any bitter juices.

❀ In a large, heavy frying pan over medium heat, warm 60 ml (2 fl oz/¼ cup) of the olive oil. Add the onions and sauté until golden, about 10 minutes. Season to taste with salt and pepper, cover partially, reduce the heat to low and cook slowly, stirring from time to time until caramelised, about 20 minutes. Spoon into a 2-l (2-qt) baking dish and set aside.

❀ Preheat a griller (broiler) on high. Rinse the salt off the eggplant slices and, using your hands, press out any excess moisture. Dry very well on paper towels. Working in batches if necessary, arrange the slices on a griller tray (pan) and brush them on both sides with 60 ml (2 fl oz/¼ cup) of the olive oil. Grill (broil), turning once, until the slices begin to brown, just a minute or two on each side.

❀ Preheat an oven to 200°C (400°F). Arrange the eggplant slices in the baking dish, overlapping them on top of the layer of onions. Then arrange the tomato slices on top of the eggplant, again overlapping the slices. Sprinkle on the chopped herbs. Drizzle with the 3 tablespoons olive oil, season with salt and pepper and scatter the rosemary sprigs over the top. Bake until heated through, about 15 minutes. Slip unter the griller for 1 or 2 minutes to brown the top, then serve.

SERVES 6

JELLIED RATATOUILLE TERRINE

Ros Sweetapple is a good home cook who for years stocked the galley of her husband Bill's yacht, the Pippin, *for the Blue Water Classic, the Sydney–Hobart Yacht Race. Needless to say, the crew was one of the best fed in the fleet each year. This is Ros's terrine.*

3 red capsicums (bell peppers), roasted and peeled (see glossary)
6 large ripe tomatoes, peeled, seeded and chopped
3 tablespoons olive oil, plus olive oil for brushing on eggplant
4 brown onions, chopped
6 zucchini (courgettes), thinly sliced
2 eggplants (aubergines), thinly sliced

FOR THE ASPIC:

2 tablespoons unflavoured powdered gelatine
1 l (32 fl oz/4 cups) clear, defatted chicken stock
fresh basil sprigs

❀ Chop the capsicums and place in a colander to drain. Place the tomatoes in a sieve and leave to drain, then transfer to paper towels to dry further.

❀ In a heavy frying pan over medium heat, warm the 3 tablespoons oil. Add the onions and sauté until soft, about 5 minutes. Using a slotted spoon, transfer to paper towels to drain. Add the zucchini to the oil remaining in the pan and sauté until soft, about 5 minutes. Using a slotted spoon, transfer to paper towels to drain.

❀ Preheat a griller (broiler) on high. Paint the eggplant slices with oil and arrange on a griller tray (pan). Grill (broil), turning once, until just tender, 2–3 minutes on each side. Let cool.

❀ To make the aspic, in a small bowl stir the gelatine powder into 125 ml (4 fl oz/½ cup) of the stock until no lumps remain. Pour the remaining stock into a saucepan and bring to a simmer. Add the gelatine mixture and stir until dissolved. Place over a bowl of iced water and refrigerate until syrupy, about 20 minutes. Remove from the refrigerator.

❀ Rinse a 2-l (64-fl oz/2-qt) ring mould with water. Pour a thin layer of aspic into the mould and refrigerate until set. Arrange a layer of zucchini over the set aspic, pour in another thin layer and again refrigerate until set. Add a layer of red capsicum, add another layer of aspic and refrigerate until set. Then add a layer each of onions, tomatoes and eggplant, always adding a thin layer of aspic between the ingredients and waiting for it to set before adding the next layer. Repeat the layers until the mould is nearly full, then finish with a layer of zucchini and cover with aspic. Cover and refrigerate overnight.

❀ To unmould, dip the base of the mould in lukewarm water and invert onto a large flat plate, shaking the mould to release the terrine. Fill the centre of the terrine with the basil sprigs and serve.

SERVES 6–8

BRAISED ZUCCHINI WITH GINGER AND TOASTED SESAME SEEDS

Queensland grows more than twice the amount of zucchini of any other state. The most common zucchini has a shiny dark green skin, but any type of zucchini can be used here.

2 tablespoons olive oil
2 teaspoons Asian sesame oil (see glossary)
1 tablespoon sesame seeds
600 g (1¼ lb) zucchini (courgettes), sliced lengthwise
2 teaspoons grated, peeled gingerroot
80 ml (3 fl oz/⅓ cup) chicken stock

❀ In a heavy frying pan over medium heat, warm the olive and sesame oils. Add the sesame seeds and sauté until just beginning to colour, 1–2 minutes. Using a slotted spoon, transfer to paper towels to drain.

❀ Add the zucchini and gingerroot to the same pan and sauté over medium-high heat until beginning to colour, 2–3 minutes. Add the stock, cover partially and cook over low heat until al dente, about 2 minutes.

❀ Spoon into a warmed serving dish, scatter on the sesame seeds and serve.

SERVES 4   *Photograph page 191*

Left to right: Jellied Ratatouille Terrine, Layered Eggplant, Tomatoes and Purple Onions—photographed at Berry, on the south coast, NSW

GRILLED VEGETABLES WITH CORIANDER AIOLI AND SNOW PEA SPROUTS

The aioli can be made with any fresh herb that is in season and marries with the flavour of the grilled vegetables.

FOR THE CORIANDER AIOLI:

3 large cloves garlic
3 fresh coriander (cilantro) roots, chopped (see glossary)
leaves from fresh coriander (cilantro) sprigs
2 egg yolks
pinch of salt
200 ml (6½ fl oz/¾ cup plus 1½ tablespoons) olive oil

FOR THE VEGETABLES:

1 red capsicum (bell pepper), seeded, deribbed and cut into
    long strips 3 cm (1¼ in) wide
1 yellow capsicum (bell pepper), seeded, deribbed and cut
    into long strips 3 cm (1¼ in) wide
6 finger-sized eggplants (aubergines), halved lengthwise
6 small zucchini (courgettes), halved lengthwise
6 yellow (summer) squash, halved lengthwise
6 baby purple onions, halved
3 tablespoons peanut oil

snow pea (mangetout) sprouts (shoots) for garnish

To make the aioli, in a blender, combine the garlic and coriander roots and leaves. Blend until chopped. Add the egg yolks and salt and blend until thick. With the motor running, add the oil in a slow, thin, steady stream and process until thick and smooth. Spoon into a serving bowl.

To cook the vegetables, preheat a griller (broiler) on high. Cover the rack of a griller tray (pan) with aluminium foil. Arrange the vegetables on top of the foil and brush with the oil. Grill (broil) until just beginning to brown. Turn the vegetables over and grill until just tender. Total cooking time will be 4–8 minutes, depending upon the size and age of the vegetables.

Transfer to a platter and serve hot, garnished with snow pea sprouts. Pass the aioli.

SERVES 6–8

BRAISED OKRA AND TOMATOES

Many people don't like okra because of the slimy juices it weeps when cut. The trick is not to cut it before cooking. This is a simple way to cook okra and it goes superbly with grilled, barbecued or roasted lamb.

750 g (1½ lb) okra
125 ml (4 fl oz/½ cup) olive oil
1 brown onion, sliced
2 cloves garlic, finely chopped
6 Roma (plum) tomatoes, peeled and chopped
pinch of sugar
pinch of dried oregano
salt and freshly ground pepper
1 tablespoon finely chopped fresh flat-leaf (Italian) parsley

Trim the conical heads of the okra but do not expose the gelatinous juices within. Cover the okra with cold water, rinse and drain. Repeat the rinsing process until the water is crystal clear. Pat dry on paper towels.

In a heavy frying pan over medium heat, warm the oil. Add the onion and cook slowly until it caramelises, about 15 minutes. Add the garlic and sauté for 2 minutes. Add the okra and sauté gently, tossing the pods back and forth in the pan, until they begin to colour, about 5 minutes.

Add the tomatoes, sugar, oregano and salt and pepper to taste. Cover and cook very gently until the okra is tender, about 10 minutes. Strew with the parsley. Serve at once.

SERVES 6   *Photograph page 196*

TERRINE OF CHARGRILLED EGGPLANT

Tony and Di Sassi have a restaurant on the hill in Port Douglas, where they have a magnificent view of cane fields and mountains, a bay of mangroves and the Pacific Ocean. Tony is the chef and Di looks after the front of the house, where this terrine is on the menu.

Left to right: Terrine of Chargrilled Eggplant, Grilled Vegetables with Coriander Aioli and Snow Pea Sprouts

5 large eggplants (aubergines), about 1 kg (2 lb) total weight
salt
2 cloves garlic, finely chopped
2 tablespoons plus 125 ml (4 fl oz/½ cup) virgin olive oil
12 Roma (plum) tomatoes, quartered lengthwise
125 ml (4 fl oz/½ cup) vegetable oil
freshly ground pepper
4 or 5 red capsicums (bell peppers), roasted and peeled
    (see glossary)
6 fresh basil sprigs
375 ml (12 fl oz/1½ cups) high-quality commercial or
    homemade mayonnaise

Cut the eggplants crosswise into slices 1 cm (⅜ in) thick. Layer in a large colander placed over a sink, sprinkling each layer with salt. Let stand 30 minutes to drain off the bitter juices.

Preheat a griller (broiler) on high or prepare a fire in a barbecue. Preheat an oven to 170°C (350°F). In a small bowl, stir together the garlic and the 2 tablespoons olive oil. Line a springform pan 20 cm (8 in) in diameter with aluminium foil and brush with the garlic oil.

Meanwhile, oil a baking tray (sheet). Place the tomatoes on the tray and bake until soft, about 20 minutes. Let cool.

Rinse the eggplant slices in running cold water and pat dry with paper towels. Brush with the vegetable oil and grill (broil) or chargrill, turning once, until tender, about 3 minutes on each side. Transfer to a platter, let cool and then drizzle with one-third of the remaining olive oil. Sprinkle with salt and pepper.

To assemble the terrine, cut the capsicums into long, wide strips. Layer one-third of the eggplant slices, overlapping them, on the bottom of the prepared pan. Cover with a layer of half of the capsicum strips, followed by half of the tomatoes. Sprinkle with half of the remaining olive oil, salt and pepper to taste and 12–15 of the basil leaves. Repeat the layers, then finish with a layer of eggplant slices arranged in a neat circular pattern. Cover with plastic wrap.

Place a plate inside the pan directly on top of the vegetables. Place 2 or 3 cans of food on the plate to weight it down. Refrigerate for at least 2 hours, or preferably overnight.

To serve, place the mayonnaise in a bowl. Chop the remaining basil and stir into the mayonnaise. Remove the sides of the pan and cut the terrine into wedges. Serve with the basil mayonnaise.

SERVES 8

Top to bottom: Braised Okra and Tomatoes (recipe page 194), Red Capsicums Stuffed with Brown Rice and Vegetables

RED CAPSICUMS STUFFED WITH BROWN RICE AND VEGETABLES

In every cook's repertoire, there's always room for a vegetarian dish such as this one. Note that brown rice takes about twice as long to cook as white rice, approximately 40 minutes.

FOR THE STUFFING:

3 tablespoons olive oil
1 small eggplant (aubergine), finely diced
1 small zucchini (courgette), finely diced

½ green capsicum (bell pepper), seeded, deribbed and finely diced
1 large fresh white mushroom, finely diced
1 large tomato, peeled, seeded and finely diced
2 spring (green) onions, including tender green tops, finely chopped
100 g (3½ oz/½ cup) Australian short-grain brown rice, cooked
2 tablespoons finely chopped fresh parsley
1½ tablespoons unsalted butter, melted
salt and freshly ground pepper
1 egg
90 g (3 oz/¾ cup) grated Swiss-style cheese
1 tablespoon freshly grated parmesan cheese

4 red capsicums (bell peppers)
1 brown onion, chopped
1 clove garlic, crushed
3 tablespoons olive oil
1 fresh thyme sprig
1 fresh rosemary sprig

❦ To make the stuffing, in a large, heavy frying pan over medium heat, warm the oil. Add the eggplant, zucchini, green capsicum, mushroom, tomato and spring onions and cook, stirring occasionally, until the vegetables are tender, about 10 minutes. Remove from the heat and drain off the juices from the pan (they can go into a soup or into the stockpot). Add the rice, parsley, butter and salt and pepper to taste to the vegetables and mix well.

❦ In a bowl lightly beat the egg until blended and stir in the cheeses. Pour the egg mixture over the vegetables and fold together all the ingredients, mixing lightly.

❦ Preheat an oven to 350°F (180°C). Cut the tops off the red capsicums and reserve. Using a small, sharp knife, cut around the ribs inside the capsicums and remove. Shake out the seeds. Stuff the capsicums with the vegetable mixture, packing it down well with the back of a teaspoon. Re-cover with the tops.

❦ Place the capsicums on their sides in a small buttered baking dish just large enough to hold them snugly. Scatter the brown onion, garlic, oil and herb sprigs over the capsicums. Bake for 30 minutes. Carefully turn the capsicums over and bake until the stuffing is cooked, about 30 minutes longer.

❦ Remove the capsicums from the dish and let cool. Discard the caps. Cut crosswise into thick slices and serve.

SERVES 4

STUFFED BOK CHOY

Bok choy is the Cantonese name for a variety of Chinese cabbage. It has white stalks, green leaves and, sometimes, a flowering centre, and should be eaten while young and very small, preferably no more than 9–10 cm (3¾–4 in) long. Ketjap manis is sweet Indonesian soy sauce. It can be found in Asian food stores.

6 bok choy

FOR THE FILLING:

100 g (3½ oz) zucchini (courgettes), coarsely grated
100 g (3½ oz) carrots, peeled and coarsely grated
2 spring (green) onions, including tender green tops, chopped
30 g (1 oz) bean sprouts
½ fresh red chilli, finely chopped, or more to taste
1¼ teaspoons *ketjap manis*

❦ Using a small sharp knife, preferably a grapefruit knife, remove the heart of each bok choy. Chop the hearts finely and set aside. Open each bok choy out like a flower on a work surface.

❦ To make the filling, in a bowl, mix together the zucchini, carrots, spring onions, bean sprouts, chilli, chopped bok choy heart and *ketjap manis*. Stir well and spoon an equal portion into the centre of each bok choy. Do not overfill or they will be too heavy. Tie the tops together with kitchen twine.

❦ Stand each bok choy upright on a steaming rack set above boiling water. Cover and steam until tender, 10–15 minutes.

❦ To serve, cut each bok choy in half lengthwise and serve hot.

SERVES 6

Stuffed Bok Choy

DESIRÉE POTATOES PAN-COOKED WITH ROSEMARY AND GARLIC

These reddish pink-skinned potatoes are usually oval and have a cream-coloured, slightly waxy flesh.

750 g (1½ lb) desirée potatoes or other red potatoes, unpeeled, quartered lengthwise
sea salt
80 ml (3 fl oz/⅓ cup) virgin olive oil
10 large cloves garlic, unpeeled
2 tablespoons fresh rosemary

❧ Place the potatoes in a saucepan and add cold water to cover. Add salt to taste and bring to a simmer. Cook for 5 minutes. Drain thoroughly and let cool completely.
❧ In a heavy frying pan over medium-low heat, warm the oil. Add the garlic and sauté gently until just beginning to colour and soften, about 10 minutes. Using a slotted spoon, transfer to a plate and set aside.
❧ Increase the heat to high, add the potatoes and sauté, shaking the pan back and forth, until almost tender, about 12 minutes.

❧ Add the sautéed garlic, rosemary and salt to taste. Continue to sauté until the potatoes are crisp and golden, about 2 minutes longer.
❧ Transfer to a serving dish and serve at once. Guests squeeze the garlic cloves from their papery sheaths onto their own servings.

SERVES 4

BROCCOLI, SUN-DRIED CAPSICUM AND CHILLI PIZZAS

Australian sun-dried capsicums packed in canola oil are delicious. Keep a jar handy in the pantry for using in fritatas, sandwiches and salads and in these thin crisp pizzas.

FOR THE DOUGH:

200 g (6½ oz/1¼ cups) plain (all-purpose) flour
pinch of baking powder
1 tablespoon sugar

Broccoli, Sun-Dried Capsicum and Chilli Pizzas

Desirée Potatoes Pan-Cooked with Rosemary and Garlic—photographed at Woodbyne Park Gallery, Jasper's Brush, NSW

1 tablespoon salt
½ teaspoon active dry yeast
80 ml (3 fl oz/⅓ cup) water
1 teaspoon unsalted butter, melted

FOR THE TOPPING:

2 tablespoons olive oil
1 clove garlic, crushed
375 g (¾ lb) broccoli, cut into small florets, blanched in
    boiling water 1 minute and drained
1 or 2 fresh red chillies, seeded and sliced
60 g (2 oz) sun-dried capsicums (bell peppers) in canola oil,
    drained
60 g (2 oz/½ cup) grated mozzarella cheese
2 tablespoons sesame seeds

❧ To make the dough, in the bowl of an electric mixer, combine the flour, baking powder, sugar, salt and yeast and, using a wooden spoon, stir to mix. In a small bowl, stir together the water and melted butter and add to the bowl, stirring well. Attach the dough hook and mix on medium-low speed until the dough is silken and smooth, 4–5 minutes.

❧ To make the dough by hand, in a large bowl, stir together the dry ingredients as directed. In a small bowl, stir together the water and melted butter and add to the dry ingredients, stirring

well with a wooden spoon. When the dough pulls away from the sides of the bowl, turn out onto a floured work surface and knead until silken and smooth, 8–9 minutes.

❧ Gather the dough into a ball, place in an oiled bowl, turn to coat the surface of the dough with oil and cover the bowl with a cloth. Let stand in a warm corner away from drafts until doubled in size, about 45 minutes.

❧ Meanwhile, place a heavy baking tray (sheet) in the upper part of an oven and preheat the oven to 240°C (450°F). To make the topping, in a large, heavy frying pan over medium heat, warm the oil. Add the garlic and broccoli and sauté until the broccoli is almost tender, 3–4 minutes. Add the chillies and sauté for 1 minute. Remove from the heat.

❧ Punch down the dough and divide into 6 equal portions. On a lightly floured work surface roll out each portion into a round 1.5 cm (⅔ in) thick.

❧ Divide the broccoli mixture and capsicums among the dough rounds, pressing them down well into the centre of each. Cover the toppings with the mozzarella and then scatter the sesame seeds around the edges. Cover with a cloth and let stand in a warm corner to rise for 10 minutes.

❧ Transfer the pizzas to the heated baking tray and bake until puffed and golden, 12–15 minutes. Serve immediately.

SERVES 6

SYDNEY

MUSHROOM SALAD WITH BABY SPINACH LEAVES AND PARMESAN CHEESE

Gary Skelton is the chef at one of the best bistros in Sydney. His food is innovative and delicious, as this recipe testifies. Wild mushrooms are foraged from the Blue Mountains and farther west to Orange.

12 large fresh wild *matsutake* (pine) mushrooms
12 large fresh flat or field mushrooms
1 clove garlic, halved
1 fresh rosemary sprig
200 ml (6½ fl oz/¾ cup plus 1½ tablespoons) extra-virgin olive oil
250 g (½ lb) baby spinach, stems removed, carefully washed and dried
2 large tomatoes, peeled, seeded and cut into small dice
100 g (3½ oz) parmesan cheese, cut into shavings with a vegetable peeler
freshly ground pepper
2 lemons, halved lengthwise

❧ Preheat an oven to 180°C (350°F).
❧ Brush any dirt or fine needles from the mushrooms. Rub them with the cut side of the garlic and arrange, cap side up, in a roasting pan. Add the rosemary and drizzle with half of the olive oil. Bake until the mushrooms are just tender, 10–15 minutes; the timing will depend upon the size of the mushrooms. Remove from the oven and let cool to room temperature.
❧ Arrange the spinach leaves on 4 large flat plates in a sunburst pattern that radiates out from the centre. Place the roasted mushrooms on top of the spinach and sprinkle with the remaining oil and any juices from the roasting pan. Scatter on the tomato, then top with the parmesan and sprinkle with pepper to taste. Serve with the lemon halves.

SERVES 4

NEW SOUTH WALES

GREEN RISOTTO WITH SAUTÉED PRAWNS AND ASPARAGUS

Chef David Novak Piper makes this rich green risotto at the restaurant where he works in Sydney's eastern suburbs.

FOR THE *SALSA VERDE*:

¼ bunch fresh parsley
¼ bunch fresh chives
¼ bunch fresh basil
¼ bunch watercress
¼ bunch spinach (about 120 g/¼ lb)
½ small clove garlic
2 tablespoons well-drained capers
¼ medium gherkin
2½–3 tablespoons olive oil
salt and freshly ground pepper

100 g (3½ oz/6½ tablespoons) unsalted butter
100 g (3½ oz) brown onion, finely chopped
600 g (2⅔ cups) arborio rice (see glossary)
1.25 l (40 fl oz/5 cups) chicken stock, boiling
50 g (2 oz/½ cup) freshly grated parmesan cheese

TO FINISH:

80 ml (3 fl oz/⅓ cup) olive oil
1 kg (2 lb) green (raw) prawns (shrimp), peeled and deveined
750 g (1½ lb) asparagus, trimmed, parboiled 2 minutes, drained and cut into 5-cm (2-in) lengths
½ bunch fresh chives, snipped

freshly grated parmesan for serving

❧ To make the salsa, in a food processor fitted with the metal blade or in a blender, combine the parsley, chives, basil, watercress and spinach. Process until chopped. Add the garlic, capers and gherkin and process until smooth. With the motor running, slowly add enough oil to make a stiff or loose consistency and season to taste with salt and pepper. Set aside.
❧ In a heavy, shallow saucepan over medium heat, melt the butter. Add the onion and sauté until softened but without colouring, about 5 minutes. Add the rice and sauté gently, stirring occasionally, until the rice is golden and the grains are coated with the butter, 2–3 minutes. Add the boiling stock and season to taste with salt and pepper. Bring to a boil. Reduce the heat to low and cook gently, stirring occasionally with a wooden spoon, until the rice is tender and all the stock has been absorbed, about 25 minutes. Fold in the *salsa verde* and the 50 g (2 oz/½ cup) parmesan and taste and adjust the seasonings.
❧ To finish the dish, just before the rice is ready, in a large frying pan over medium-high heat, warm the oil. Add the prawns and sauté until almost cooked through, about 3 minutes. Then add the asparagus and sauté until tender-crisp, 1–2 minutes longer.
❧ Spoon the risotto into a serving dish and top with the prawn mixture. Sprinkle with the chives and parmesan.

SERVES 6   *Photograph pages 184–185*

QUEENSLAND

CARROT AND TOASTED CUMIN

Cumin is a small plant that bears elongated seeds used for flavouring in cooking. The seeds marry beautifully with carrots and the aromatic flavour of coriander. Serve this as a vegetable side dish or as part of an Asian antipasto.

2 tablespoons cumin seeds
3 tablespoons olive oil
650 g (1⅓ lb) carrots, peeled and cut on the diagonal into slices 12 mm (½ in) thick
2 teaspoons brown sugar
1 tablespoon light soy sauce
250 ml (8 fl oz/1 cup) chicken stock
1 tablespoon finely chopped fresh coriander (cilantro)

❧ Place the cumin seeds in a dry, heavy frying pan over medium heat. Toast, shaking the pan back and forth over the heat, until aromatic, 2–3 minutes. Remove to a plate.
❧ Add the oil to the same pan and place over medium heat. When the oil is warm, add the carrots and sauté until they begin to soften, 2–3 minutes. Add the cumin seeds, sugar, soy sauce and stock, stir well and bring to a simmer. Cook until the stock has almost evaporated and the carrots are just tender, about 4 minutes.
❧ Transfer to a serving dish and scatter the coriander over the top. Serve hot.

SERVES 4   *Photograph page 202*

Mushroom Salad with Baby Spinach Leaves and Parmesan Cheese— photographed at Orange, NSW

Clockwise from right: Braised Winter Vegetables with Brown Lentils, Rosemary and Garlic, Carrot and Toasted Cumin (recipe page 200), Potato Gratin

BRAISED WINTER VEGETABLES WITH BROWN LENTILS, ROSEMARY AND GARLIC

When I'm overwined and overdined and tired, this is the kind of dish I yearn for. This is another of Sydney chef Gary Skelton's recipes.

FOR THE LENTILS:

2 tablespoons olive oil
1 brown onion, diced
1 large carrot, peeled and diced
1 clove garlic, chopped
2 large ripe tomatoes, diced
100 g (3½ oz/½ cup) brown lentils, rinsed and picked over
1 l (32 fl oz/4 cups) chicken stock
1 fresh rosemary sprig
salt and freshly ground pepper

FOR THE VEGETABLES:

1 l (32 fl oz/4 cups) chicken stock
800 g (1⅔ lb) kumaras, peeled and quartered lengthwise (see glossary)

2 heads fennel, tough outer leaves removed and bulbs quartered lengthwise
2 celeriacs (celery roots), peeled and quartered
4 pink-eye potatoes or other potatoes, halved
4 small carrots, peeled
4 leeks, carefully washed and halved lengthwise

FOR THE GARLIC MAYONNAISE:

2 cloves garlic
½ teaspoon Dijon mustard
salt
1 egg yolk, plus 1 whole egg
250 ml (8 fl oz/1 cup) olive oil
dash of red wine vinegar
freshly ground pepper

FOR SERVING:

1 tablespoon chopped fresh parsley

To cook the lentils, in a large, heavy frying pan over medium heat, warm the oil. Add the onion, carrot and garlic and sauté until softened without colouring, about 10 minutes. Add the tomatoes, lentils and stock. Bring to a boil, reduce the heat and simmer until the lentils are soft and cooked, about 30 minutes; the timing will depend upon the freshness of the lentils. Remove from the heat and add the rosemary and salt and pepper to taste.

202

To cook the vegetables, preheat an oven to 190°C (375°F). In a saucepan bring the stock to a boil. Lay the vegetables in a large roasting pan. Pour in the stock to half-cover the vegetables. Cover with aluminium foil and bake until just tender, 20–30 minutes; the timing will depend upon the size and age of the vegetables.

Meanwhile, to make the mayonnaise, in a blender, combine the garlic, mustard, salt to taste, egg yolk and whole egg. Blend until thick and creamy. With the motor running, add the oil in a slow, thin, steady stream and blend until thick. Add the vinegar and season to taste with pepper. If too thick, add 1–2 tablespoons boiling water. It should be pouring consistency.

Arrange the warm lentils on large warmed plates. Add the vegetables in piles around the lentils. Drizzle the mayonnaise over the top. Scatter with the parsley and serve at once.

SERVES 4

NEW SOUTH WALES

POTATO GRATIN

Robin Howard has a restaurant in Goulburn in New South Wales. She says this is her favourite potato dish and her customers love it. Pontiac potatoes are more often than not mistakenly called pink-eye potatoes because they have a pink skin and they do have pink eyes. But their flesh is white, rather than pink like that of the Tasmanian pink-eyes. Sebago potatoes grow in the colder reaches of Tasmania. They are one of the most common potatoes in Australia and are excellent for baking.

1 kg (2 lb) pontiac or sebago potatoes, peeled and thinly sliced
2 cloves garlic, minced
salt and freshly ground pepper
about 600 ml (20 fl oz/2½ cups) thickened (double/heavy) cream

Preheat an oven to 180°C (350°F).

Place the potatoes, garlic and salt and pepper to taste in a bowl. Rub the potatoes between your palms to make sure the minced garlic is evenly spread throughout the potato slices.

Transfer to a baking dish and pat down firmly. Pour the cream evenly over the potatoes. Bake until golden brown, about 35 minutes. Serve hot.

SERVES 6

NEW SOUTH WALES

DOUBLE TOMATO RISOTTO WITH MINT

Australian Calrose rice is grown in the Leeton district of New South Wales and, like the arborio rice imported from northern Italy, has great absorption qualities. Generally, this short-grain rice will absorb three times its weight in liquid, which is helpful to know when making a pilaf (rice cooked with twice its volume in liquid, undisturbed in a lidded vessel in the oven) or a risotto, as is the case in this recipe. Australian Calrose rice is infinitely less expensive than most of the rice imported for making risotto.

about 350 ml (11 fl oz/1½ cups) chicken stock
3 tablespoons unsalted butter
2 tablespoons olive oil
1 brown onion, chopped
2 cloves garlic, finely chopped
200 g (6½ oz/1 cup) Australian Calrose rice or other short-grain white rice

1 can (400 g/13 oz) Roma (plum) tomatoes, puréed with their juices
50 g (1½–2 oz) drained oil-packed sun-dried tomatoes, chopped
1½ tablespoons chopped fresh mint
2 tablespoons freshly grated parmesan cheese, plus 45 g (1½ oz) parmesan cheese, cut into shavings with a vegetable peeler
salt and freshly ground pepper

Pour the stock into a saucepan and bring just to a simmer. In a heavy pot over medium heat, melt 2 tablespoons of the butter with the oil. Add the onion and cook, stirring, until it begins to caramelise, about 12 minutes. Add the garlic and sauté for 2 minutes. Add the rice and stir until golden and each grain is coated with the oil and butter, 2–3 minutes.

Add the puréed tomatoes and sun-dried tomatoes and stir well. Cook, stirring, until the purée is absorbed. Ladle in just enough of the stock almost to cover the rice and stir over medium heat until the stock is absorbed. Add more stock nearly to cover and continue stirring and cooking until the stock is absorbed. Never cover the rice with stock and never add more stock until the previously added stock has been absorbed. Cook until the rice is al dente; this will take about 20 minutes from start to finish. You may not need all of the stock; add stock only until the rice is al dente.

Add the remaining 1 tablespoon butter, mint, grated parmesan and salt and pepper to taste and stir to mix. Place a tight lid on the risotto, remove from the heat and let stand for 1 minute.

Sprinkle the parmesan shavings over the top and serve at once.

SERVES 6

Double Tomato Risotto with Mint

POTATO-CHILLI STRAW CAKES

Chillies have been popular in Australia since the late 1980s. The popularity of Thai food has probably been the main reason. There are more chilli varieties being grown, but the naming of them is inconsistent, so there's likely to be a lot of misunderstanding. The most common chillies are those that are 6–7 cm (2½–2¾ in) long and green (unripened and very hot) and the sweeter but still fiery red chilli. Small birdseye chillies, the next most common, are hotter than the longer ones.

750 g (1½ lb) old (mature baking) potatoes, peeled
1 or 2 small fresh red chillies, finely sliced
60 g (2 oz/¼ cup) unsalted butter
3–4 tablespoons olive oil
salt and freshly ground pepper

❧ Coarsely grate the potatoes and place in a bowl. Add cold water to cover. Drain in a colander and again place in a bowl with cold water to cover. Drain again in a colander. (Rinsing the potatoes helps to remove the starch.) Spread the potatoes out on a clean cloth and roll up, pressing out as much moisture as possible. Unroll and place in a bowl. Add the chillies and mix well.

❧ In a large, heavy frying pan over medium heat, place half each of the butter and oil and heat until sizzling. Spoon half of the potato mixture into the pan to form 3 large cakes. Pack down the cakes with the back of a fork. Sprinkle with salt and pepper and spoon the butter-oil mixture over the top. Cook until golden on the underside, about 8 minutes. Flip the cakes over and cook on the second side until crisp and golden, 4–5 minutes longer.

❧ Remove to a plate lined with crumpled paper towels and keep warm. Cook 3 more cakes in the same way. Serve immediately.

SERVES 6

CHINESE EGGPLANT

The most interesting treatments of eggplant come from the Mediterranean countries and from Asia. This Chinese recipe is a good example.

1 large eggplant (aubergine), about 600 g (1¼ lb), cut
    lengthwise into slices 1 cm (⅜ in) thick
salt
500 ml (16 fl oz/2 cups) peanut oil
1 tablespoon chilli-garlic sauce (see glossary)
1 teaspoon rice vinegar
1 small fresh red chilli, thinly sliced
1 celery stalk, finely chopped
1 coriander (cilantro) root, sliced (see glossary)
1 teaspoon grated, peeled gingerroot
2 shallots, finely sliced
125 ml (4 oz/½ cup) chicken stock
freshly ground pepper
2 spring (green) onions, including tender green tops,
    thinly sliced crosswise

❧ Cut the eggplant slices into strips 1 cm (⅜ in) wide. Place the eggplant in a colander over a bowl. Salt liberally, turning the eggplant pieces to coat all surfaces. Let stand for 15 minutes, to allow bitter juices to drain. Rinse under running cold water, drain well and pat dry on paper towels.

❧ In a wok or deep frying pan, heat the oil until very hot. To test, drop a piece of dry crust into the oil; the oil is ready when the crust sizzles and rises to the surface immediately. Working

in batches, add the eggplant and cook until it begins to colour, about 2 minutes. Using a slotted spoon, remove to paper towels to drain.

❧ Pour off all but 2 tablespoons of oil from the pan. Reheat the oil until very hot and add the chilli-garlic sauce, vinegar, chilli, celery, coriander root, gingerroot and shallots. Stir-fry for 2 minutes. Add the stock and bring to a boil. Return the eggplant to the pan and stir over high heat until the sauce is reduced by half, about 2 minutes. Season to taste with salt and pepper.

❧ Spoon into a serving dish, sprinkle with the spring onions and serve at once.

SERVES 4–6

KUMARA-CORIANDER CAKES

Kumaras are available year-round. Buy the smaller, younger ones with unblemished skins. These flavoursome cakes are wonderful served as a simple side dish, or they make an excellent base for other vegetables, such as grilled eggplant (aubergine) or sautéed capsicums (bell peppers) and mushrooms.

250 g (½ lb) kumaras, peeled and coarsely grated
    (see glossary)
1 small brown onion, finely chopped
2 eggs
2 tablespoons plain (all-purpose) flour
⅛ teaspoon ground cumin
2 tablespoons chopped fresh coriander (cilantro) leaves
salt and freshly ground pepper
3 tablespoons vegetable oil

❧ Wrap the grated kumara in a clean cloth. Wring out tightly to eliminate any excess moisture. Place in a mixing bowl with the onion.

❧ In another bowl, beat together the eggs, flour, cumin, coriander and salt and pepper to taste. Pour over the kumara mixture and mix well.

❧ In a large, heavy frying pan over medium heat, warm the oil. Working in batches, drop the mixture by tablespoonfuls into the pan. Cook until lightly browned on the first side, about 1 minute. Turn and cook on the second side until lightly browned, about 1 minute longer. You should have 6 cakes in all. Serve immediately.

SERVES 6

CHOKO AND BEAN CURD IN SPICY COCONUT CREAM

Many Australian backyards have a rampant choko vine climbing fences and garage roofs. They bear prolifically, and everyone thinks up different ways to use the squashes. This is my favourite way. Called orem-orem, this dish is eaten in most Indonesian households at least once a week. Candlenuts, the seeds of a tropical tree that are typically used in Indonesian dishes, can be found in shops selling Asian foods. So, too, can the aromatic salam leaf. Serve this spicy preparation with a fish dish and fragrant steamed rice.

500 g (1 lb) chokos (chayotes)
¼ teaspoon salt, plus salt to taste
400 ml (13 fl oz/1⅔ cups) peanut oil
500 g (1 lb) bean curd, cut into 2-cm (¾-in) cubes
75 g (2½ oz) fresh sweet red chillies, thickly sliced
2 candlenuts or macadamia nuts, crushed

Clockwise from top: Choko and Bean Curd in Spicy Coconut Cream, Kumara-Coriander Cakes, Potato-Chilli Straw Cakes, Chinese Eggplant

½ small brown onion, coarsely chopped
1 clove garlic, thickly sliced
⅛ teaspoon coriander seeds
1 piece fresh kaffir lime leaf, about 1 cm (⅜ in) wide
    (see glossary)
500 ml (16 fl oz/2 cups) chicken stock
½ teaspoon raw sugar
⅛ teaspoon grated fresh galangal (see glossary)
⅛ teaspoon ground turmeric
1 salam leaf
375 ml (12 fl oz/1½ cups) thick coconut cream (see glossary)
3 spring (green) onions, including tender green tops, chopped
1 or 2 fresh sweet green chillies, seeded and thinly sliced

To prepare the chokos, cut each one in half lengthwise and rub the cut surfaces together until a thick, white resin appears. Scrape off the resin with a knife and discard with the seeds. Peel the choko and cut into 2-cm (¾-in) cubes. Place in a bowl, sprinkle with the salt and let stand for 5 minutes. Rinse in cold running water and drain.

Pour the oil into a wok and place over high heat. When the oil is hot, add the bean curd and fry until puffed and golden brown, 3–5 minutes. Using a slotted spoon, transfer to crumpled paper towels to drain. Reserve 1 tablespoon of the oil.

Place the red chillies, candlenuts or macadamia nuts, brown onion, garlic, coriander seeds, lime leaf and 3 tablespoons of the stock in a blender. Blend until smooth.

Place the reserved 1 tablespoon oil in a saucepan and add the blended ingredients. Add the sugar, galangal and turmeric and cook over medium heat, stirring frequently, until aromatic, about 4 minutes. Remove from the heat and set aside.

Bring the remaining stock to a boil. Add the choko and salam leaf and cook gently for 5 minutes. Add the bean curd, aromatic spice mixture, coconut cream, spring onions and green chillies. Season to taste with salt and stir well. Cook, uncovered, over gentle heat, stirring frequently, for 30 minutes, to blend the flavours. Taste and adjust the seasoning.

Transfer to a deep serving dish and serve at once.

SERVES 6

WARM TIGER PRAWN SALAD WITH BURGHUL AND HERBS

I was given the recipe for this delightful salad when I stayed at Hayman Island Resort and have regularly made it at home for my family and friends with great success.

200 g (6½ oz/1 cup) coarse or medium burghul (bulgur)
625 ml (20 fl oz/2½ cups) water
2 large ripe tomatoes, skinned, seeded and finely diced
40 g (1⅓ oz/1 cup) fresh coriander (cilantro) leaves, chopped, plus 4 fresh coriander sprigs for garnish
40 g (1⅓ oz/1 cup) fresh mint leaves, chopped
40 g (1⅓ oz/1 cup) fresh parsley leaves, chopped
1 small brown onion, finely diced
90 ml (3 fl oz/6 tablespoons) extra-virgin olive oil
1 tablespoon fresh lemon juice
salt and freshly ground pepper
1 tablespoon curry powder
20 tiger prawns (shrimp), each about 7 cm (2¾ in) long, cooked, peeled and deveined

❧ In a heavy saucepan, combine the burghul and water. Bring to a simmer, reduce the heat to low, cover and cook until the water is completely absorbed, 20–25 minutes. Remove the pan from the heat and set aside, covered, for 10 minutes to allow the grains to dry out. Uncover and fluff the burghul with a fork. Let cool.

❧ In a bowl, combine the tomatoes, chopped coriander, mint, parsley, onion and 2 tablespoons of the olive oil. Add the cooled burghul and mix well. In another bowl, whisk together the lemon juice, salt and pepper to taste, the remaining olive oil and the curry powder to make a dressing. Taste and adjust the seasonings.

❧ Spoon the burghul mixture onto 4 flat plates. Arrange the prawns on top and drizzle each salad with some of the dressing. Garnish with the coriander sprigs and serve immediately.

SERVES 4

ROASTED ROMA TOMATOES

Roma tomatoes are my favourite because they are fleshy and keep well. Never refrigerate tomatoes unless they are getting too ripe, in which case it is better to stew them with some fresh herbs, a fruity olive oil, a little sea salt and lots of freshly cracked black pepper. Nothing could be easier than this recipe. The trick is to have all the tomatoes the same size and line them up so each points the same way in the dish.

9 Roma (plum) tomatoes, halved lengthwise
4 fresh thyme sprigs
2 tablespoons olive oil
freshly ground pepper
sea salt

❧ Position a rack in the upper part of an oven and preheat the oven to 180°C (350°F). Lightly oil a flameproof baking dish. Arrange the tomato halves, cut side up and all facing the same way, in the dish. Strew with the thyme sprigs, drizzle with the oil and season with pepper.

❧ Cook in the hottest part of the oven until just tender, about 15 minutes. Scatter salt to taste over the tomatoes and slip under a preheated griller (broiler) long enough to brown the edges. Serve warm.

SERVES 6   *Photograph page 211*

ROASTED CAPSICUMS AND TOMATOES

Restaurateur and chef Anne Taylor says this dish can be made in advance and reheated in the microwave oven, which is good news when you have no time to wait for the oven to heat. Serve with grilled polenta.

2 red capsicums (bell peppers), roasted and peeled (see glossary)

Left to right: Warm Tiger Prawn Salad with Burghul and Herbs, Roasted Capsicums and Tomatoes—photographed at Vaucluse House, Sydney

2 yellow capsicums (bell peppers), roasted and peeled (see glossary)
6 large Roma (plum) tomatoes, peeled, seeded and roughly chopped
2 garlic cloves, sliced lengthwise paper-thin
4 anchovy fillets in oil, drained and cut into small pieces
1 tablespoon finely chopped fresh parsley
1 tablespoon finely chopped fresh basil
chilli flakes
salt and freshly ground pepper
3–4 tablespoons olive oil

❧ Position a rack in the top third of an oven and preheat the oven to 190°C (375°F). Oil a 23-cm (9-in) oval baking dish.

❧ Slice the capsicums into long strips 2 cm (¾ in) wide. Layer one-third of the capsicums in the prepared dish. Top with half of the tomatoes, garlic, anchovies, parsley and basil and then chilli flakes and salt and pepper to taste. Repeat the layers, using half of the remaining capsicums, then top with a layer of capsicums. Drizzle with the oil.

❧ Bake in the upper part of the oven until the capsicums are very tender and the top is slightly browned, about 20 minutes. Serve hot.

SERVES 6

Mixed Rice Pikelets with Ratatouille

VICTORIA

MIXED RICE PIKELETS WITH RATATOUILLE

Pikelets, which are also known as drop scones, are usually sweet and served buttered or with jam and cream. Made from a batter, they are literally dropped by the spoonful into a hot pan where they form irregular shapes. When the batter is mixed with cooked rice or other cooked grains, the pikelets offer an interesting change from those most Australians associate with breakfast and afternoon tea. There are several excellent rice blends on the market, one of which is used in this recipe.

FOR THE RATATOUILLE:

1 eggplant (aubergine), cut into 1-cm (⅜-in) dice
salt
100 ml (3½ fl oz/6½ tablespoons) olive oil
1 large brown onion, thinly sliced
1 large red capsicum (bell pepper), seeded, deribbed and
    sliced lengthwise
1 green capsicum (bell pepper), seeded, deribbed and sliced
    lengthwise
6 small zucchini (courgettes), cut into slices 6 mm (¼ in) thick
6 Roma (plum) tomatoes, peeled, seeded and chopped
3 cloves garlic, finely chopped
200 ml (6½ fl oz/¾ cup plus 1½ tablespoons) chicken stock
salt and freshly ground pepper

FOR THE PIKELETS:

salt
100 g (½ cup) Sunlong long-grain brown rice and wild rice
    blend or other rice blend
130 g (4 oz/¾ cup) plain (all-purpose) flour
2 teaspoons cream of tartar
1 teaspoon bicarbonate of soda (baking soda)
1 egg
200 ml (6½ fl oz/¾ cup plus 1½ tablespoons) milk
2½ tablespoons unsalted butter

To make the ratatouille, place the eggplant in a colander and sprinkle with salt to coat all surfaces. Let stand for 15 minutes, to allow the bitter juices to drain. Rinse in running cold water and dry on paper towels.

In a large pan over medium-low heat, warm the oil. Add the onion and sauté until soft, about 5 minutes. Add the capsicums, cover and cook over low heat, stirring occasionally, until soft, 5–8 minutes. Add the zucchini, tomatoes and garlic and stir to mix. Add the eggplant and chicken stock, cover and cook for 30 minutes. Season to taste with salt and pepper. Re-cover and continue to cook over low heat, stirring occasionally, until all the vegetables are very tender, about 1 hour. Keep warm.

Meanwhile, to make the pikelets, half fill a medium-sized saucepan with water, salt lightly and bring to a boil. Add the rice, stir and simmer until the rice is tender, about 25 minutes. The timing will depend upon the blend used. Drain in a sieve and refresh under running cold water. Leave in the sieve to drain.

In a bowl, sift together the flour, a pinch of salt, the cream of tartar and the bicarbonate of soda. Add the egg and milk and beat until the batter is smooth. Fold in the cooked rice. Let stand for 30 minutes before cooking.

To cook, place a large nonstick frying pan over medium heat and melt half of the butter in it. Working in batches, add the batter by tablespoonfuls and cook until just set on the underside, 3–4 minutes. Flip the pikelets over and cook until golden on the second side, about 2 minutes. Transfer to a platter and keep warm while cooking the remaining pikelets, adding the remaining butter as needed.

To serve, arrange the pikelets on 6 warmed individual plates. Spoon the warm ratatouille alongside the pikelets and serve at once.

SERVES 6

VICTORIA

TOASTED CHICKPEA SALAD

This delightful vegetarian salad is ideal for when you are short of time. Mesclun is the perfect bed for the simple mix of chickpeas and carrots.

1 can (450 g/14 oz) chickpeas, thoroughly drained and
    dried on paper towels
1 tablespoon olive oil
1 carrot, peeled and cut into thin, fine strips

FOR THE DRESSING:

sea salt and freshly ground pepper
1 tablespoon fresh lemon juice
2 tablespoons virgin olive oil
1 teaspoon finely chopped fresh mint

200 g (6½ oz) mesclun (see glossary)
1 teaspoon paprika

Discard any loose skins from the chickpeas. Place the chickpeas in a large, heavy frying pan over medium heat and toast, frequently rolling them around in the pan, until evenly coloured, about 10 minutes. Set aside to cool.

In a small frying pan over medium heat, warm the oil. Add the carrot and sauté until tender, about 3 minutes. Remove from the heat and let cool.

To make the dressing, in a small bowl, whisk together the salt and pepper to taste, lemon juice, olive oil and mint.

Mound the mesclun in a large, shallow bowl. Scatter the chickpeas and carrot over the top.

Drizzle the dressing over the salad and dust with the paprika. Serve at once.

SERVES 4

QUEENSLAND

Burghul, Tomato and Zucchini Salad

Chefol peanut oil is a triple-refined oil produced in Australia. It is excellent for many cooking purposes.

180 g (1 cup) burghul (bulgur)
1 l (32 fl oz/4 cups) water
2 tablespoons chilli flakes

FOR THE HERB VINAIGRETTE:

2 tablespoons red wine vinegar
125 ml (4 fl oz/½ cup) Chefol peanut oil or other high-quality peanut oil
3 tablespoons snipped fresh chives
2 tablespoons finely chopped fresh parsley
salt and freshly ground pepper

2 Roma (plum) tomatoes, diced
4 baby zucchini (courgettes), cut into slices 6 mm (¼ in) thick, blanched in boiling water 2 minutes and drained
12 small cos (romaine) lettuce leaves

Place the burghul in a bowl and add the water. Let stand for 2–3 hours. Drain well, place in a clean cloth and wring out all excess water. Scrape into a dry bowl and add the chilli flakes.

To make the vinaigrette, in a small bowl, whisk together the vinegar, oil, chives, parsley and salt and pepper to taste.

Pour half of the vinaigrette over the burghul mixture and mix well. Add the tomatoes and zucchini and gently fold into the burghul. Season to taste with salt and pepper.

Arrange the lettuce leaves on individual flat plates. Top with the burghul mixture. Pour the remaining vinaigrette over the salads and serve at once.

SERVES 4

SYDNEY

Snow Peas and Green Beans with Piquant Avocado Dressing

I always believe that you can judge a cook by the way he or she cooks vegetables. Sydney chef Anne Taylor is a master of vegetable dishes. This is her recipe. Beanettes are small, green, stringless runner beans about 10 centimetres (4 inches) long. Any young, tender green beans can be used in their place.

FOR THE AVOCADO DRESSING:

2 avocados, pitted, peeled and chopped into small pieces
juice of 1 lime or lemon
1 small purple onion, finely diced
pinch of chopped fresh red or green chilli
2 tablespoons extra-virgin olive oil
2 teaspoons finely chopped fresh coriander (cilantro) or 2 tablespoons finely diced red capsicum (bell pepper)

250 g (½ lb) young, tender snow peas (mangetouts) or sugar snap peas
250 g (½ lb) beanettes

To make the dressing, in a bowl, gently stir together the avocados, lime or lemon juice, onion, chilli, oil and coriander or capsicum. Adjust with additional lime juice and chilli, if desired. Cover and refrigerate until serving.

Bring a saucepan three-quarters full of water to a boil and add the snow peas or sugar snap peas and the beanettes. Boil until barely cooked, about 2 minutes; the timing will depend upon the size and age of the vegetables. Drain well, shaking out excess water. Place in a serving bowl. Add the dressing, toss well and serve.

SERVES 6

Top to bottom: Toasted Chickpea Salad, Snow Peas and Green Beans with Piquant Avocado Dressing, Burghul, Tomato and Zucchini Salad

SPICED COUSCOUS WITH YAMBA PRAWNS

Chef Megan Brown uses Yamba prawns (eastern king prawns) in this couscous. They are caught from Newcastle, north of Sydney, all the way up the east coast to Mooloolaba in southern Queensland.

FOR THE COUSCOUS:

375 g (12 oz/2½ cups) couscous (see glossary)
375 ml (12 fl oz/1½ cups) boiling salted water
salt
½ teaspoon coriander seeds, roasted in a dry pan until fragrant, then ground
¼ teaspoon cumin seeds, roasted in a dry pan until fragrant, then ground
2 tablespoons virgin olive oil
1 tablespoon finely chopped fresh coriander (cilantro) leaves

FOR THE SALAD:

½ small Spanish (red) onion, finely diced
1 small tomato, peeled, seeded and finely diced
⅓ small cucumber, peeled and finely diced
20 fresh basil leaves

FOR THE GINGER VINAIGRETTE:

1 piece gingerroot, 5 cm (2 in) long, peeled and finely grated
250 ml (8 fl oz/1 cup) vegetable oil
finely grated zest of 2 limes
2 tablespoons fresh lime juice
finely grated zest of 1 lemon
juice of 1 lemon
finely grated zest of 1 orange
juice of 1 orange
1 teaspoon sherry vinegar
salt and freshly ground pepper

FOR THE PRAWNS:

12 green (raw) Yamba prawns (shrimp) or other large prawns
salt and freshly ground pepper
olive oil for sautéing

FOR THE PRAWN OIL:

1 tablespoon vegetable oil
120 g (4 oz/1 cup) roughly chopped onion, carrot, fennel or celery
1½ tablespoons brandy
4 cloves garlic, finely chopped
1 piece gingerroot, about 2 cm (¾ in) long, finely chopped
1 bay leaf
1 teaspoon paprika
250 ml (8 fl oz/1 cup) vegetable oil
salt and freshly ground pepper

✂ To cook the couscous, place the couscous in a bowl and pour the boiling water over it. Let stand until the liquid is absorbed and the couscous is fluffy, about 5 minutes. Mix in salt to taste and the ground coriander and cumin seeds, oil and fresh coriander. Set aside.
✂ To make the salad, in a small bowl, mix together the onion, tomato, cucumber and basil leaves. Set aside.
✂ To make the vinaigrette, place the gingerroot in a heat-resistant bowl. In a small pan, heat the oil until just before it starts to smoke. Pour over the ginger and let cool. Mix in the citrus zests and juices and the sherry vinegar. Season to taste with salt and pepper. Set aside.
✂ Remove the heads and shells from the prawns and reserve for making the prawn oil. Set the prawns aside.
✂ To make the prawn oil, in a heavy frying pan over medium heat, warm the vegetable oil. Add the vegetable of choice and sauté until softened, about 8 minutes. Add the reserved prawn heads and shells and sauté until they change colour. Add the brandy and deglaze the pan by scraping up any browned-on

bits. Add the garlic, gingerroot, bay leaf and paprika and cook over medium heat until most of the liquid evaporates, about 10 minutes. Add the oil and salt and pepper to taste and simmer gently for 15 minutes to blend the flavours. Strain through a fine-mesh sieve (twice, if necessary, to remove any sediment) into a small jug.
✂ To cook the prawns, lightly season them with salt and pepper. In a frying pan over medium-high heat, warm the olive oil, add the prawns and sauté until just cooked, 2–3 minutes.
✂ To assemble the dish, mound the couscous in a serving dish. Mix together the salad, prawns, and ginger vinaigrette and pile on top of the couscous. Drizzle the prawn oil around the couscous and serve.

SERVES 4

BURGHUL WITH THREE BEANS AND SPICY DRESSING

Red radicchio, a member of the chicory family, has a compact head of dark red leaves and is popular for its slightly bitter flavour and beautiful colouring. It originated in Italy around Treviso and Verona, but grows very well in Australia.

100 g (3½ oz/½ cup) dried black beans, soaked in cold water to cover overnight
250 ml (8 fl oz/1 cup) chicken stock
90 g (3 oz/½ cup) burghul (bulgur), soaked in cold water to cover for 30 minutes
salt
80 g (2½ oz) snake beans (Chinese long beans), cut into 3-cm (1¼-in) lengths (see glossary)
150 g (5 oz) shelled broad (fava) beans

FOR THE DRESSING:

1 clove garlic, finely chopped
1 tablespoon finely chopped fresh parsley
1½ tablespoons fresh lemon juice
100 ml (3½ fl oz/6½ tablespoons) olive oil
pinch of chilli flakes
salt and freshly ground pepper

4–6 red radicchio leaves

✂ Drain the black beans and place in a small saucepan. Add the stock and bring to a boil. Cover, reduce the heat to a simmer and cook until tender, about 1½ hours. Remove from the heat and let cool in the stock.
✂ Drain the burghul, wrap in a clean cloth and wring out all excess water. Transfer to a bowl.
✂ Bring a saucepan three-quarters full of water to a boil. Add salt to taste and the snake beans and boil until tender-crisp, about 4 minutes. Drain and refresh in iced water. Drain again. Cook the broad beans in the same way; they should take 2–3 minutes. Drain the broad beans and, once cold, peel off the skins and discard.
✂ Drain the black beans (reserve the stock for another use) and place in a bowl. Add the snake beans and broad beans and mix well, then add to the bowl holding the burghul.
✂ To make the dressing, in a small bowl, whisk together the garlic, parsley, lemon juice, oil, chilli flakes and salt and pepper to taste. Mix into bean mixture. Taste and adjust the seasonings.
✂ Arrange the radicchio leaves around the sides of a salad bowl and add the bean mixture. Serve at once.

SERVES 4

Clockwise from top right: Burghul with Three Beans and Spicy Dressing, Roasted Roma Tomatoes (recipe page 206), Spiced Couscous with Yamba Prawns—photographed at Sydney Harbour

QUEENSLAND

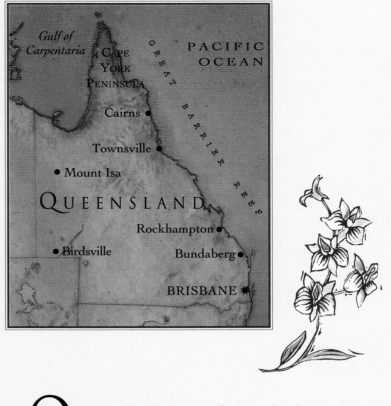

QUEENSLAND

T R O P I C A L   B O U N T Y

Durians, sapodillas and mangosteens are just some of the tropical fruits being grown in Far North Queensland these days, along with the even more exotic black persimmons, casimiroas and japoticabas. Lychees, rambutans and babacos begin to seem rather ordinary by comparison. But such fruits are only one of the things that set northern Queensland apart from the rest of Australia.

Driving through its corridors of sugarcane, you could believe you were in another country, and in fact Far North Queensland—or FNQ as it is known—nearly was another state. There were moves during the last century to split Queensland into three; in the north this was due in part to disputes over the Kanaka cane cutters.

Although cane is grown as far south in Queensland as Nambour and Bundaberg—a town famous for its sugar by-product, rum—it was particularly significant in the settlement of these northern humid tropics, which were slow to develop. New South Wales was nearly a hundred years old before the Far North was opened up.

Stretching from the crystal waters of the Coral Sea and the islands of the Great Barrier Reef in the east, over the Great Dividing Range to The Big Empty in the west, Queensland is so big that if you ask how far away somewhere is, you are told not in kilometres, but in hours. With its capital, Brisbane, tucked in its southeastern corner, Queensland comprises nearly a quarter of Australia. Only Western Australia is larger. More than half of the state is in the tropics: its tip, Cape York, is only eleven degrees south of the equator.

There is some evidence that the Portuguese sailed down the east coast of the Cape York Peninsula as early as 1524—a mere thirty-two years after Columbus crossed the

Previous pages: Australia's largest virgin tropical rainforest is preserved in Daintree National Park. Left: Outback hotels and mining towns are interspersed throughout the remote Channel Country.

Atlantic—but it is certain that the Dutch captain, Willem Jansz (in the *Duyfken*), travelled up the west coast of Cape York in 1606. Nevertheless, Queensland wasn't settled until September 1824. Initially established as a British penal settlement, Brisbane lies on the hills on either side of the river with which it shares its name, twenty kilometres (twelve miles) inland from the river mouth that empties into Moreton Bay (from which the famous shellfish, Moreton Bay bugs, take their name).

Part of New South Wales until 1859, the colony had gold rushes during the sixties, seventies and eighties that helped establish coastal and inland centres to its north—both Gympie (1867) and Charters Towers (1872) began as 'rush' towns—although some no longer appear on the map. The ports of Rockhampton, Cairns and Cooktown were developed to supply goldfields in their respective hinterlands.

Everything about Queensland is big. It is the country's biggest beef producer, producing well over 40 percent of the country's total, 80 percent of which is exported. Queensland also produces one-third of Australia's vegetables and, in the winter months, provides vegetables and much of the fruit—melons, even strawberries—for the rest of the eastern states. Simply put, just about anything will—and does—grow in Queensland.

The state produces lamb and venison, and there is also dairying and cheese making. A small amount of wine comes from Stanthorpe in the Granite Belt west of Brisbane, where a Bald Mountain Chardonnay is made. Queensland's warm waters offer tropical and reef fish, and an abundance of prawns (shrimp), which these days are also being farmed to maintain a consistent supply.

There are major climatic differences between Queensland's coast and its much drier inland. All manner of tropical fruits grow on its fertile coastal plains, while its cooler climate tablelands—because of their higher altitude and being farther inland—also produce more temperate crops. Citrus fruits are grown northwest of Brisbane and much farther north on the sandy soil of the Atherton Tableland. Also from here come avocados, mangoes, macadamias and custard apples as well as potatoes and peanuts. This is the main peanut-growing area of the north, as Kingaroy is of the south, and roasted peanuts are a traditional Queensland snack.

Inland from the beaches of the Sunshine Coast are plantations of sugarcane and fragrant tropical fruits like pineapple.

From this same area—somewhat surprisingly as it is so far north—comes Malanda milk. Said to be the biggest 'milk run' in the world, Malanda supplies milk for most of northern Australia (certainly as far west as Darwin). Malanda also makes cheese—cheddar, mozzarella and havarti—as well as yoghurt and butter.

From Mareeba come watermelons, pumpkins, capsicums (peppers) and tomatoes. Farther south, in the area around Cardwell and Innisfail on the coast, grow bananas and pineapples, some near the charmingly named Rolling Stone. Even farther south, near Ingham, with its Italian community, are found the more exotic rambutans and lychees. From Bowen come tomatoes, zucchini (courgettes), cabbages, melons—honeydew, watermelons and rockmelons (musk melons)—cauliflower, potatoes and, most importantly, mangoes.

Mangoes thrive in the dry tropics around Bowen—particularly the Kensington Pride, an Australian variety often known as the Bowen mango. Luscious and less stringy than many other varieties, the Bowen comes into season slightly later than other mangoes (October to December) and peaks, luckily for southerners, around Christmas.

The Granite Belt west of Brisbane has long produced large quantities of vegetables, but the most recently developed growing area for fruit and vegetables is the Burdekin Basin. Since the creation of the Burdekin Dam—four times the size of Sydney Harbour—at the end of the 1980s, it is said that enough food could be grown in the Burdekin to feed the whole of Australia!

The Burdekin region is southwest of Townsville, the main port of the far north. Founded in the 1860s, Townsville boomed as the port for Charters Towers during its gold rush. Townsville's early prosperity can be glimpsed in its nineteenth-century architecture, in its grand Edwardian facades painted in pastel shades and in its charming pubs with verandas along the harbour. It is the biggest city in Australia north of Brisbane, twice the size of its glitzier northern neighbour, Cairns.

Traditionally, Townsville is also a strong pastoral town, and its meatworks handle much of the beef from the hinterland. A large proportion of Australia's prawn (shrimp) catch also comes through the port from as far away as the Kimberleys in the west, as well as from Papua New Guinea and the Solomon Islands. The region is unusually dry for the coastal tropics. Here, the Great Dividing Range is farther inland, leaving Townsville in a rain shadow. Often described as the 'dry tropics', it has a wet season that lasts for only six weeks. Sugarcane, which needs high rainfall, grows both to its north and to its south.

Driving north up the coast from the border of New South Wales—even south of Brisbane—you hit pockets of cane. Even though it has lost its formerly important European market, sugar is still one of Queensland's main crops, particularly around Innisfail and north past Cairns to Port Douglas and Mossman.

The Palmer River gold rush inland in 1873 brought about the establishment of Cooktown as its port. By 1876, Cooktown had a population of twenty-six thousand, one-third of whom were said to be Chinese. Even five years later, when there were only three hundred Europeans, five thousand Chinese remained. By 1886, Chinese represented nearly two-thirds of the population of the fertile agricultural districts of the Far North.

The Chinese were granted five-year licences to farm the land and were largely responsible for clearing the rainforest and developing tropical crops like bananas around Cairns. By moving every five years and clearing more and more land, they subsequently made possible the establishment of the sugar industry. It was said in the Queensland Parliament in 1913 that the north would be a perfect wilderness had the Chinese not opened it up. Due to the White Australia Policy, however, from the 1890s onwards the numbers of Chinese dwindled.

Also significant in the development of the sugar industry were the Kanakas—men brought from their Melanesian island homes on three-year terms, in a process known as blackbirding. They were described in the *Bulletin* in 1893, as 'South Sea slaves'. At that time there were nearly eight thousand of them, working in extremely harsh conditions. By 1900, more than half the sugar crop was being grown by such labourers, but following Federation, blackbirding was forbidden. With the passage of the Pacific Islanders Labourers Act of 1902, most of the Kanakas were deported or returned home by 1906.

More recent horticultural developments set tropical Queensland apart. Small plantations of coffee and tea have been established and green peppercorns are now being raised near Silkwood. Also being cultivated, on a small scale, are fruits like mangosteens (the trees can take up to fifteen years to fruit); rollinias (similar to custard apples but no relation); Brazilian japoticabas, which are like black grapes—purply black when ripe, although thicker-skinned and with more tangy flesh—and the abiu. The abiu, similar in size and colour to a small grapefruit, has soft, smooth skin that bruises easily and delicious, moist, sweet flesh that can be scooped out with a spoon.

There is also black sapote—chocolate pudding fruit—which is actually a black persimmon. When it is ready to eat, its flesh is the colour of axle grease. A native of Mexico, it undergoes a dramatic ripening process—overnight the fruit turns from dark green to brown-black. Its sweet flesh has a slightly gelatinous quality that is delicious on its own, mixed with cream or used in baking, for instance, to moisten a chocolate cake. Other fruits with equally exotic credentials—casimiroa (sometimes wrongly called white sapote), grumichama (a tropical cherry) and guanabana (formerly the soursop)—are being grown, although not yet in great quantities.

Since the 1960s, that Queensland native, the macadamia nut—sometimes called the bauple nut—has been more and more widely cultivated. Its oil, rich in monounsaturates (85 percent compared with olive oil's 76 percent), is delicious and versatile, and the nut's unique flavour and texture are wonderful in cakes and confectionery. Although first established commercially in Hawaii, this Australian rainforest tree is the sole indigenous plant cultivated on a large scale, and is second only to table grapes as a fruit and nut export. It is now being grown from the northern New South Wales coast to the Atherton Tableland in the north, and particularly on the Sunshine Coast, near Noosa.

Also from the Sunshine Coast comes the justifiably famous Buderim ginger, grown on the black volcanic soil of the hinterland behind Mooloolaba and at Yandina. A long-standing industry, the ginger is reputedly among the best in the world. Cheese, too, is produced near here at Kenilworth, as well as at Murgon, out past Ipswich. Both produce largely cheddars. From Warwick comes brie and camembert, while Queensland's best-known blue cheese, Unity Blue, comes from around Toowoomba.

Wonderful fish are available up and down the state's long coastline. The king of crustaceans, the sensational sweet-fleshed Queensland mud crab, thrives in the mangroves. There are slipper lobsters, the large painted

A diver in the Great Barrier Reef encounters a potato cod, one of 1500 species of fish that live in the world's largest reef environment.

crayfish of the north (found up to the Torres Strait); spanner crabs; Moreton Bay bugs; myriad types of prawns; and beautiful white scallops. These scallops are the warm-water *Amusium balloti,* as opposed to the cold-water *Pecten fumata* that are found in Tasmania.

Queensland's major fish include red emperor (red snapper), coral trout, Spanish mackerel, mangrove jack (like a big morwong), red jewfish, squire or baby snapper, sampson, black kingfish, king snapper, barramundi, threadfin salmon, surgeon fish, mahi mahi, tuna, grey mackerel and spotted mackerel. There are numerous aquaculture projects, including the farming of barramundi, red claw crayfish and prawns (shrimp). The two biggest farms are at Cardwell and Mossman.

Up in the north, the local chefs are increasingly making use of native ingredients, from the blue quandong fruit (a different species from the desert quandong of South Australia, which is red and a member of the sandalwood family) to wattleseeds, which come from a native acacia and are sometimes used in breads and ice cream. Other indigenous plants being used include a hibiscus, of which the roots, shoots and brilliant yellow flowers are all edible; a native ginger; a fern with young shoots that taste a bit like asparagus; and the beach bean, which grows on the beaches near Port Douglas and has a purple or pink flower. Information about edible native plants is often sought from the local Aborigines. Queensland has the largest population of Aboriginal people, some forty-eight thousand, outside the Northern Territory.

One of the most engaging experiences of the Far North is the Sunday morning market at Port Douglas, in front of the Court House Hotel. In the Dry there are some tropical fruits on sale, but there are many more available in the Wet, outside the tourist season.

After shopping, you can sit under a palm tree where the grass meets the beach and, in its season, eat that most heavenly of fruit, a mangosteen, while looking out across the bay towards Mossman. Strains of songs of praise might drift across from the morning service in the tiny white wooden church that stands at the water's edge. There's much indeed to be thankful for in this piece of paradise on earth.

DESSERTS AND BAKING

Kuchen is among the German specialities made at the Apex Bakery in Tanunda, South Australia.

DESSERTS AND BAKING

ONE EMU EGG, so bush cooks claim, was the equivalent of a dozen chicken eggs. A bit hard to come by these days, emu eggs were once a bush standby and, it is said, turned out a light, fluffy sponge.

Although baking developed slowly due to a lack of equipment, it became one of Australia's great culinary traditions, particularly in the bush. It began in a camp fire, the origin of the famed Australian bread, damper, baked in the raked embers. An early settler, Louisa Meredith, wasn't impressed. She called it 'a stiff dough, made of flour, water and salt, kneaded into a flat cake two or three inches thick, and from twelve to eighteen broad . . . when cut into, it exceeds in closeness or hard heaviness to the worst bread or pudding I have ever tasted'. There is no question that damper has improved since then—thanks to leavening agents such as bicarbonate of soda (baking soda)!

Nevertheless, in the bush, where food was a moveable feast, damper became Australia's traditional bread and was accompanied by billy tea, which even until recently—when factory-made billies appeared—was brewed in a large, wire-handled jam tin precariously balanced on the fire. Tea was once the Australian national drink: at the beginning of the 1900s, we were the world's greatest tea drinkers.

Baking became a ritual, particularly for Sunday afternoon teas. Time was when it was a deeply competitive activity, too: branches of the Country Women's Association ran competitions for the best sponges or the best scones, for cake decorating or for the best fruitcake.

Along with lamingtons—squares of sponge dipped in chocolate sauce and coated in dessicated coconut—another of Australia's culinary icons is the pavlova, a soft-centred meringue, usually topped with passionfruit and whipped cream. Named after the Russian ballerina, Anna Pavlova, its creation is usually credited to a chef named Sachse at the Esplanade Hotel in Perth in 1935, although some controversy surrounds its origin. In fact, the New Zealanders claim it as their invention. Its popularity became so widespread probably because the ingredients for it were close at hand—in the backyard. There, one could find the hens for the egg whites and the passionfruit from the vine on the back fence.

Regional differences defined baking, too, since cooks had access to various ingredients depending on where they lived. In Queensland, there was probably a mango tree in the backyard; in Sydney, a lemon tree; and in Tasmania, a walnut tree. In Queensland, where pumpkins were easily grown, they turned up in that Queensland classic, the pumpkin scone. These days, with the increasing availability of tropical fruits like pawpaw (papaya), scones have been given a whole new identity.

Although no one who lived through the 1950s could forget sago, or even junket, these days desserts are likely to make use of our multitude of wonderful fresh fruits, whether it's a guava sorbet or a custard apple ice cream.

Australia's early baking traditions were drawn largely from the English—flour-based and stodgy.

Previous pages: Pavlova with Raspberries, Passionfruit and Glass Bark (recipe page 231)

Certainly at Christmas there have always been mince pies—individual tartlets made with citrus peel and dried fruits in a short pastry crust—and plum puddings, even in the Queensland heat. Although there has been a nostalgic return to some traditional puddings, as a general rule desserts have become much lighter. Rarely seen are those relics of English fare like jam roly-poly, or spotted dick, that in earlier times were a credit to the cook's ingenuity in turning out something filling and sweet to conclude the meal.

Another of Australia's culinary icons is the Anzac biscuit. As the name implies, the biscuits date to World War I, when they were baked to be shipped over to the troops in the trenches at Gallipoli. They were made from coconut, rolled oats and flour, bicarbonate of soda, golden syrup and dripping. Dripping, or suet, was used so the biscuits wouldn't go rancid during the long sea voyage.

Dripping was a baking stand-by before the days of refrigeration allowed even salted butter to be kept for long. Certainly in Queensland and western New South Wales you will hear a sigh of nostalgia when you mention puftaloons to anyone aged fifty or over. They were basically a scone mixture that was deep-fried in beef dripping, a technique not dissimilar to that used for making doughnuts. Now even the trifle—a way of using up stale sponge cake by spreading it with jam, sprinkling it with sherry and topping it with whipped cream and almond slivers—is a nostalgia food.

These days we are putting more of an Australian stamp on our desserts. Australia's native bush fruits and berries are increasingly being used as flavourings. Their potential has been recognized only relatively recently, thanks to the efforts of people like Vic Cherikoff, whose company, Bush Tucker Supply Australia, organises gatherers. He has a network of well over a thousand foragers around the country. Because bush fruits are small and are found in such limited quantities, usually in remote areas, they are largely suitable only for use as flavourings—in combination with other fruits to extend them, for instance—rather than as a major component of a dish.

The only Australian native that is widely available and commercially cultivated is the macadamia nut, but wattleseeds from a native acacia, which, once toasted, give a particularly wonderful flavour to ice cream, are growing in popularity. They taste like roasted hazelnuts but with the texture of coffee grounds, and their applications are many, with one of the most successful their use in Anzac biscuits.

The quandong, a native peach, is now being farmed in South Australia. One of the more common bush fruits is the Kakadu plum (*Terminalia ferdinandiana*), also known as the billygoat plum, which boasts fifty times the vitamin C by weight of an orange! There are Illawarra plums, which have a slightly resinous flavour, and muntharies, which are the size of peas but taste like Granny Smith apples.

Lemon myrtle can flavour a custard or a tart, or you might find a bush berry *crème brûlée*. The leaf of the pepperberry sometimes turns up in a savoury piecrust, or tiny bush tomatoes can be used in a croissant.

This unique bush harvest is also added to spreads for breads, such as lemon myrtle, eucalypt, native pepper or akudjura butter (the latter an Aboriginal name for the bush tomato, in this case, ground). Or you might come across a bread flavoured with wattleseed, akudjura or the ground leaf of the native pepper.

Australian chefs are also using Asian spices in desserts. They might turn up in a baked custard flavoured with cardamom or in a tropical sweet fruit soup. With such an array of fruits and flavours available, the creation of desserts is limited only by the imagination of the cook.

A sidewalk café along Adelaide's busy Rundle Street lets patrons watch the parade of shoppers while enjoying a cool refreshment.

GOLDEN SYRUP PUDDING

Maureen Simpson has been food editor of one of Australia's best-known magazines for two decades and has a national radio program on Sunday mornings. Her golden syrup pudding is my idea of a perfect warm pudding for a cold winter's day. Serve it with Maureen's boiled custard.

3 tablespoons golden syrup
125 g (4 oz/½ cup) butter, at room temperature
100 g (3½ oz/½ cup) caster (superfine) sugar
1 teaspoon vanilla essence (extract)
2 eggs
195 g (6½ oz/1¼ cups) self-raising flour, sifted
125 ml (4 fl oz/½ cup) milk
boiled custard (recipe below)

❧ Butter a 1¼–1½-l (40–48-fl oz/5–6-cup) pudding basin. Pour the golden syrup into the bottom. Set aside.
❧ In a bowl, beat together the butter and sugar until light and creamy. Then beat in the vanilla. Add the eggs, one at a time, beating well after each addition. Fold in the sifted flour and then stir in the milk. Spoon the pudding mixture on top of the golden syrup in the basin. Cover the basin with 2 sheets of aluminium foil or baking (parchment) paper, buttering the layer next to the pudding so it does not stick. Tie the foil or paper in place with kitchen twine.
❧ Pour enough water into a large saucepan for it to reach halfway up the sides of the basin once it is placed in the pan. Bring the water to a boil and lower the basin into the pan. Cover and simmer gently for 1¼ hours. Remove the basin and let stand for 5 minutes, then remove the cover and invert onto a flat plate to unmould. Serve with the boiled custard.

SERVES 6

BOILED CUSTARD

This version of a traditional accompaniment for puddings, pies and pastries is from Maureen Simpson, well-known cookbook writer.

500 ml (16 fl oz/2 cups) plus 3 tablespoons milk
2–3 tablespoons sugar
2 thin lemon peel strips, optional
2 tablespoons custard powder (cornstarch)
2 egg yolks
1 teaspoon vanilla essence (extract)
cream

❧ In a saucepan, combine the 500 ml (16 fl oz/2 cups) milk, sugar and lemon peel (if using). Bring to a boil. In a small bowl, stir together the custard powder and the 3 tablespoons milk until smooth. Add to the saucepan and stir constantly over moderate heat until the custard thickens, about 5–7 minutes.
❧ In a bowl, whisk together the egg yolks and vanilla. Tip a little of the hot custard onto the yolks and quickly whisk it in. Then pour the yolk mixture into the saucepan. Return to very low heat and stir without boiling to cook the yolks (the heat of custard is usually sufficient), 1–2 minutes.
❧ Remove and discard the lemon peel (if used) and serve hot. If serving cold, pour into a bowl and cover tightly with plastic wrap, pressing it directly onto the surface to prevent a skin from forming. Refrigerate until well chilled. It will have the consistency of softly whipped cream; thin with a little cream, if necessary.

SERVES 6

QUEEN PUDDING

Many Australians treasure this pudding, which recalls their Anglo-Saxon heritage.

600 ml (20 fl oz/2½ cups) milk
30 g (1 oz/½ cup) fresh white breadcrumbs
4 eggs, separated
2 teaspoons granulated sugar
2 tablespoons raspberry jam
2 tablespoons caster (superfine) sugar

❧ Position a rack in the centre of an oven and preheat the oven to 170°C (325°F). Butter a 1.5-l (48-fl oz/6-cup) baking dish.
❧ In a small pan, heat the milk until hot. Place the breadcrumbs in a bowl and pour the milk over them. In another bowl, beat together the egg yolks and granulated sugar until light and stir into the breadcrumbs. Pour into the prepared dish and place in a baking pan. Pour hot water into the pan to reach halfway up the sides of the dish.
❧ Bake in the centre of the oven until set, about 30 minutes. Remove from the oven and spread the jam over the top.
❧ In a bowl, whip the egg whites until soft peaks form. Add half of the caster sugar and beat until stiff, shiny peaks form. Fold in the remaining caster sugar. Pile the egg whites on top of the pudding.
❧ Return the pudding to the oven and bake until the meringue is set and a pale fawn colour, about 10 minutes. Serve warm.

SERVES 4–6

FEIJOA JELLY

Feijoa, also known as pineapple guava, is a native of South America. It grows well in subtropical warmth and fruits in the autumn. The fruit is oval and has medium green skin and crunchy, creamy white flesh. Jelly made from feijoas has the fragrance of pineapple and is a lovely rose pink. It is delicious with scones, cold lamb, pork or ham.

sound, just ripe feijoas
sugar
fresh lemon juice

❧ Wipe the fruit with a damp cloth. Cut into quarters and place in a heavy pot with just enough water to cover. Bring slowly to a boil and simmer until the fruit is tender, about 15 minutes. Mash the fruit when it is soft and continue to simmer gently, stirring from time to time, until the fruit is well coloured and mushy, about 2 hours.
❧ Transfer the fruit to a jelly bag placed over a bowl and let drip overnight. (Do not press the pulp through the bag or the jelly will be cloudy.)
❧ Preheat an oven to 180°C (350°F). Measure the liquid. For each litre (32 fl oz/4 cups) of liquid, measure out 750 g (1½ lb/ 3 cups) sugar and 2¼ tablespoons fresh lemon juice.
❧ Place the sugar in a shallow pan and place in the oven until warm, about 10 minutes. Pour the feijoa liquid into a large, heavy pot. Add the lemon juice and bring to the boil over medium-high heat. Add the sugar and stir until it dissolves. Boil hard until the mixture reaches the jell point, 150°C (220°F) on a sugar (candy) thermometer. Watch carefully, in case it boils up over the top of the pot.
❧ Ladle into hot, sterilized jars and let cool. Cover with self-sealing canning jar lids and label when cold. Store in a cool, dry cupboard for up to 1 year.

Photograph pages 226–227

Clockwise from top: Boiled Custard, Queen Pudding, Golden Syrup Pudding—photographed at Blackheath, in the Blue Mountains, NSW

Nashi Nut Cake—photographed at the Bathers Pavilion, Balmoral, Sydney

NASHI NUT CAKE

Nashi fruits were originally known in Australia as Chinese pears because they were planted here by Chinese miners in the mid-1800s. In Japan, the same pears had long been cultivated solely for the table of the emperor. Eventually, Australians began calling the pears by their Japanese name, as it was widely used internationally. Nashis are grown in the Goulburn Valley in Victoria. They are round and have a crisp applelike texture. This delicious tea cake has a crunchy consistency, which is enhanced by the moistness contributed by the nashis. Accompany the cake with King Island cream or other thick cream.

260 g (8½ oz/1⅔ cups) self-raising flour
½ teaspoon mixed spice (pumpkin-pie spice)
300 g (10 oz/1⅓ cups) caster (superfine) sugar
125 g (4 oz/½ cup) unsalted butter, at room temperature, cut into small pieces
2 eggs
125 g (4 oz/¾ cup plus 1 tablespoon) macadamia nuts
3 nashi fruits, cored and thinly sliced

Position a rack in the centre of an oven and preheat the oven to 180°C (350°F). Butter a 26-cm (10-in) round cake pan.

In a food processor fitted with the metal blade, combine the flour, mixed spice and sugar. Pulse to mix. With the motor running, add the butter and then the eggs. Process until combined. Stir in the nuts.

To make the batter by hand, in a bowl, stir together the flour and mixed spice. In another bowl, using a wooden spoon or an electric mixer, beat together the sugar and butter until light and creamy. Beat in the eggs, one at a time, beating well after each addition. Stir in the flour until fully incorporated and then stir in the nuts.

Spoon half of the batter into the prepared pan. Arrange the nashi slices over the top. Cover with the remaining cake mixture.

Bake in the centre of the oven until the cake recedes from pan sides and is golden on top, about 1 hour. Let stand for 5 minutes before turning out of pan onto a wire rack.

Serve warm, cut into wedges.

SERVES 12

NEIL PERRY'S FRESH DATE TART

This is one of the most talked-about desserts in Australia. It is a signature dish of Neil Perry, who operates a well-known seafood restaurant in The Rocks in Sydney. Pass a jug of King Island or Tarago River cream at the table for guests to pour over each serving.

FOR THE PASTRY:

180 g (6 oz/¾ cup) unsalted butter, chilled, cut into small cubes
1½ tablespoons sugar
1 egg
1 tablespoon milk
250 g (8 oz/1⅔ cups) plain (all-purpose) flour

FOR THE FILLING:

18–20 dates, halved and pitted
7 egg yolks
80 g (2½ oz/5 tablespoons) sugar
½ vanilla bean, split lengthwise
700 ml (22 fl oz/2¾ cups) thickened (double/heavy) cream

❧ Position a rack in the centre of an oven and preheat the oven to 200°C (400°F). Butter a deep 26-cm (10-in) tart pan with a removable bottom.

❧ To make the pastry, in a food processor fitted with the metal blade, combine the butter, sugar, egg and milk. Process until the butter is in small pieces. Add the flour and process until the mixture gathers around the blade. Remove from the processor to a floured work surface and work the dough briefly until it forms a smooth ball. Wrap in plastic wrap and refrigerate for 2 hours.

❧ On a lightly floured surface, roll out the dough thinly into a round large enough to fit the tart pan. Carefully transfer the dough round to the pan. Trim off the overhang even with the pan rim. Cover and refrigerate for 30 minutes.

❧ To make the pastry by hand, place the flour and sugar in a bowl. Add the butter and, using fingertips, 2 knives or a pastry blender, work it into the flour until the mixture is the consistency of rolled oats. Add the egg and milk and stir together to form a dough. Turn out onto a floured board and proceed as directed for dough made in a processor.

❧ Line the pastry with baking (parchment) paper and fill with pie weights. Bake in the centre of the oven until golden, about 20 minutes. Remove the weights and paper and return the tart shell to the oven for 5 minutes until dry to the touch. Remove from the oven. Reduce the oven temperature to 180°C (350°F).

❧ To make the filling, arrange the dates in the pastry shell in 2 circles, one inside the other, with the tips pointing towards the centre. In a bowl, beat together the yolks and sugar until light and fluffy. Scrape the seeds out of the vanilla bean into the mixture and then stir in the cream, mixing well. Carefully pour the cream filling over the dates.

❧ Bake in the centre of the oven until the custard is just set, 75–80 minutes. Be careful not to overcook the tart, as its charm is its lightness. Let cool on a wire rack. Serve the tart at room temperature.

MAKES ONE 26-CM (10-IN) TART; SERVES 8

LIME-AND-ORANGE POPPY SEED CAKE

I first tasted this cake in the boardroom of one of Australia's top food magazines. The assistant food editor of the magazine, Anneka Mitchell, made it for the meeting I attended there. She says that orange zest and juice can be substituted for the lime zest and juice.

185 g (6 oz/¾ cup) unsalted butter, at room temperature
200 g (6½ oz/¾ cup plus 2 tablespoons) granulated sugar
finely grated zest of 2 limes
finely grated zest of 1 orange
2 tablespoons fresh lime juice
3 eggs
85 g (2¾ oz/½ cup) poppy seeds
290 g (9 oz/1¾ cups) self-raising flour
½ teaspoon bicarbonate of soda (baking soda)
175 ml (6 fl oz/¾ cup) buttermilk

FOR THE CANDIED CITRUS PEELS:

250 ml (8 fl oz/1 cup) water
200 g (6½ oz/¾ cup plus 1 tablespoon) granulated sugar
peel of 2 limes, cut into fine strips
peel of 1 orange, cut into fine strips

2 tablespoons icing (confectioners') sugar

❧ Position a rack in the centre of an oven and preheat the oven to 180°C (350°F). Butter and line a 12-by-22-cm (5-by-9-in) loaf pan.

❧ In a bowl, beat together the butter, sugar, lime and orange zests and lime juice until light and creamy. Add the eggs, one at a time, beating well after each addition. Stir in the poppy seeds.

❧ In another bowl, sift together the flour and bicarbonate of soda. Fold the flour mixture into the butter mixture alternately with the buttermilk. Pour into the prepared pan.

❧ Bake in the centre of the oven until a toothpick inserted in the centre comes out clean, 50–55 minutes. Let stand in the pan on a wire rack for 5 minutes, then turn out onto the rack to cool.

❧ To candy the citrus peels, in a small pan over medium heat, stir together the water and sugar until the sugar dissolves. Bring to a boil, add the lime and orange peels and cook until the syrup is thick, 10–15 minutes. Using a slotted spoon, remove the peels from the syrup and drain on a wire rack placed over the sink. (If preparing the candied peels in advance, store them in an airtight container at room temperature until needed.)

❧ To serve, decorate the cake with the candied citrus peels and sift the icing sugar over the top.

MAKES ONE LOAF CAKE; SERVES 8

Left to right: Lime-and-Orange Poppy Seed Cake, Neil Perry's Fresh Date Tart

QUEENSLAND

PUMPKIN SCONES WITH FEIJOA JELLY

Scones are part of our English heritage. They are mostly served at afternoon tea with butter and jam or with jam and whipped cream. Pumpkin scones are better known in Queensland than in any of the other states, and are best when made with a richly coloured pumpkin or other winter squash, such as butternut. Also from sunny Queensland's Coral Coast come pawpaw (papaya) scones. They can be made following the same method, substituting 110 grams (3½ ounces/⅓ cup) mashed ripe pawpaw for the pumpkin and increasing the sugar by 1 tablespoon.

1½ tablespoons unsalted butter, at room temperature,
   plus unsalted butter for serving
1 tablespoon sugar
1 egg, well beaten
60 g (2 oz/¼ cup) mashed cooked pumpkin
60 ml (2 fl oz/¼ cup) milk, plus 1 teaspoon milk
260 g (8½ oz/1⅔ cups) self-raising flour, sifted twice
feijoa jelly (recipe on page 222)

❧ Position a rack in the upper part of an oven and preheat the oven to 220°C (425°F). Place a baking tray (sheet) in the oven to heat.
❧ In a bowl, beat together the 1½ tablespoons butter and the sugar until light and fluffy. Set aside 2 teaspoons of the egg, then beat the remaining egg, the pumpkin and the 60 ml (2 fl oz/¼ cup) milk into the butter mixture alternately with the flour. Using a fork, quickly mix to a soft dough.
❧ Turn out onto a floured work surface and knead lightly— the less the better. With floured hands, press out into a rectangle 20 cm (8 in) long by 15 cm (6 in) wide by 2 cm (¾ in) thick. Mark in 12 squares with a floured knife. Remove the tray from the oven and either butter it or spray it with nonstick cooking spray. Place the scones, still joined, on the hot tray. Stir the 1 teaspoon milk into the reserved egg and brush over the tops of the scones.
❧ Bake at once in the upper part of the oven until golden on top and cooked through, about 20 minutes. Serve warm or at room temperature with butter and feijoa jelly.

MAKES 12

QUEENSLAND

LAMINGTONS

Named after a Queensland governor, Barron Lamington, who served at the turn of this century, these small cakes have been part of the Australian kitchen since just after World War I. They are rather messy to bake at home, but nevertheless great fun for the whole family to make together. Every suburban bakery sells them also. Sometimes they are filled with whipped cream and jam. The mixture can also be made as a large cake, in which case it is split and filled with cream and jam. Plain lamingtons are the most popular.

FOR THE CAKE:

225 g (7 oz/1⅓ cups) self-raising flour
125 g (4 oz/½ cup) unsalted butter, at room temperature
150 g (5 oz/⅔ cup) caster (superfine) sugar
1 teaspoon vanilla essence (extract), or to taste
2 eggs
150 ml (5 fl oz/⅔ cup) milk

FOR THE COATING:

about 150 ml (5 fl oz/⅔ cup) water
3 tablespoons cocoa powder
2 tablespoons unsalted butter

1 teaspoon vanilla essence (extract), or to taste
450 g (14 oz/3½ cups) icing (confectioners') sugar, sifted
150 g (5 oz/1¼ cups) desiccated coconut

❧ Position a rack in the centre of the oven and preheat the oven to 180°C (350°F). Butter a 26-by-30-cm (10½-by-12-in) lamington or Swiss (jelly) roll tin.
❧ To make the cake, sift the flour into a bowl. In another bowl, beat together the butter and sugar until light and creamy. Beat in the vanilla and then beat in the eggs, one at a time, beating well after each addition. Fold the flour into the butter

Clockwise from top right: Ginger Sponge (recipe page 228), Pumpkin Scones with Feijoa Jelly, Lamingtons—photographed at Vaucluse House, Sydney

mixture alternately with the milk, mixing until fully combined.
⁂ Pour into the prepared pan. Bake in the centre of the oven until the cake recedes from the sides of the pan and is golden on top, about 25 minutes.
⁂ Let cool in the pan on a wire rack for 5 minutes. Turn out onto the rack and let cool completely.
⁂ To make the coating, combine the water and cocoa in a large pot placed over medium heat. Add the butter and stir until melted. Add the vanilla and icing sugar and stir until smooth and shiny. Place half of the coconut into a large bowl. Stand the pot in a bowl of hot water to keep the mixture liquid.

⁂ To finish, cut the cooled cake into 16 squares. Using 2 skewers to hold each square, dip the squares, one at a time, into the warm coating. Allow the excess coating to drip back into pot, then dip the square into the coconut. Place on a rack covered with baking (parchment) paper to dry. Continue coating, adding the remaining coconut to the bowl as needed.
⁂ Let the coating set, then serve. Lamingtons are best eaten the day they are made, but leftovers can be stored in an airtight container at room temperature for up to 4 days.

MAKES 16 SQUARES

BAKED CARDAMOM CUSTARD WITH WHISKY FIGS AND ALMONDS

The exotic flavour of the cardamom perfumes the baked custard, lifting it out of the ordinary.

FOR THE CUSTARD:

600 ml (19 fl oz/2⅓ cups) milk
100 g (3½ oz/½ cup) caster (superfine) sugar
4 eggs
1 teaspoon ground cardamom

FOR THE FIGS:

200 ml (6½ fl oz/¾ cup plus 1½ tablespoons) water
50 ml (1¾ fl oz/3½ tablespoons) whisky
3 tablespoons caster (superfine) sugar, or to taste
1 orange zest strip
8 new season's dried figs
12 blanched whole almonds

⚘ Position a rack in the centre of an oven and preheat the oven to 160°C (325°F). Butter a deep 1-l (32-fl oz/4-cup) baking dish.
⚘ To make the custard, rinse a saucepan with cold water. (This prevents the milk solids from sticking, making the pan easier to clean.) Pour the milk into the pan and heat slowly until small bubbles form along the edge of the pan.
⚘ Meanwhile, in a bowl, beat together the sugar, eggs and cardamom. Slowly pour the hot milk over the egg mixture, beating until well blended.
⚘ Pour the custard into the prepared dish. Place the dish in a baking pan and pour hot water into the pan to reach halfway up the sides of the dish. Bake in the centre of the oven until just set, about 1 hour. The custard should still be a little wobbly in the centre, as it will cook in its own heat after removing it from the oven.
⚘ Meanwhile, to cook the figs, in a saucepan over medium heat, stir together the water, whisky and sugar until the sugar dissolves. Bring to a boil, add the orange zest and figs and stew gently until the figs are plump and tender, about 10 minutes. Add the almonds and let the figs cool in the syrup.
⚘ To serve, spoon the warm custard onto individual plates and spoon the figs and almonds and their syrup alongside.

SERVES 4

Left to right: Russian Cream with Raspberries Cooked in Their Own Syrup, Baked Cardamom Custard with Whisky Figs and Almonds

RUSSIAN CREAM WITH RASPBERRIES COOKED IN THEIR OWN SYRUP

Damien Pignolet is an exceptionally talented chef and a successful restaurateur. He shares this delightful dessert, which has been copied many times. The balance of sweetness and acidity and the silky smooth texture make it special. It's the perfect example of both good bistro food and home cooking, as it is simple and inexpensive, can be made in advance and can be dressed up or down, according to the occasion and your pocket. In winter, quinces cooked in a slow oven can be used in place of the berries.

3 gelatine leaves or 2½ teaspoons unflavoured powdered gelatine
½ vanilla bean, split lengthwise
90 g (3 oz/scant ½ cup) caster (superfine) sugar
65 ml (2 fl oz/¼ cup) thickened (double/heavy) cream
400 ml (13 fl oz/1¾ cups plus 1 tablespoon) buttermilk
70 ml (2⅓ fl oz/4½ tablespoons) whipping (double) cream

FOR THE BERRIES:

250 g (8 oz) fresh raspberries
3 tablespoons caster (superfine) sugar, or to taste

⚘ Soften the gelatine leaves in cold water to cover for 5 minutes. Squeeze the water out of the leaves by hand. If using powdered gelatine, in a bowl dissolve the gelatine in 1 tablespoon hot water for 5 minutes. Set aside.
⚘ Using the tip of a paring knife, scrape the vanilla seeds out of bean into a small pan. Add the sugar and thickened cream and heat over medium heat until the sugar dissolves. Add the squeezed gelatine or dissolved powdered gelatine and stir until melted. Let cool.
⚘ Stir the buttermilk into the cooled mixture. In a bowl, whip the whipping cream until soft peaks form. Using a rubber spatula, fold the whipped cream into the buttermilk mixture. Rinse four 150-ml (5-fl oz/⅔-cup) moulds with cold water. Divide the buttermilk mixture evenly among the moulds, cover and refrigerate for 4 hours.
⚘ To prepare the berries, crush a few with a fork in a small pan and add the sugar. Cook over medium heat, stirring, until the sugar dissolves. When bubbling, add the remaining raspberries and immediately remove from the heat. Stir to distribute the juices evenly, then let cool to room temperature.
⚘ To serve, unmould each cream by dipping the base of the mould into warm (not hot) water briefly and then inverting it onto a flat dessert plate. Spoon the berries and their juices around each cream. Serve at once.

SERVES 4

GINGER SPONGE

This cake could be called the all-Australian cake, as every Australian who grew up in this country will have had a sponge at one time or another. Sponges make great birthday cakes, and many an Australian cook has been judged on the ability to make a perfect sponge. Ginger is grown at Yandina in southeastern Queensland on the Sunshine Coast and is processed at Yandina's ginger factory, the only one in the Southern Hemisphere.

1½ tablespoons unsalted butter
1 tablespoon golden syrup
3 tablespoons hot water
4 eggs

Cheese Scones—photographed at Berry, on the south coast, NSW

200 g (6½ oz/¾ cup plus 2 tablespoons) caster (superfine)
  sugar
160 g (5½ oz/rounded 1 cup) self-raising flour
2 tablespoons cornflour (cornstarch)
1 tablespoon ground ginger
1 teaspoon ground cinnamon

FOR THE FILLING:

200 ml (6½ fl oz/¾ cup plus 2 tablespoons) whipping
  (double) cream, whipped
2 tablespoons crystallised ginger, chopped

icing (confectioners') sugar for dusting

❧ Position a rack in the centre of an oven and preheat the oven
to 180°C (350°F). Line the bottoms of two sponge pans, each
20 cm (8 in) in diameter, with baking (parchment) paper. Butter
and flour the paper and the pans' sides.
❧ In a small saucepan, combine the butter, golden syrup and
water and bring to a boil. Remove from the heat and let cool.
In a bowl, beat together the eggs and sugar until thick and
creamy. In another bowl, sift together the flour, cornflour,
ginger and cinnamon three times. Using a rubber spatula, fold
the flour mixture into the creamed mixture. Add the cooled
butter mixture and fold into the batter. Divide the mixture
between the prepared pans.
❧ Bake in the centre of the oven until the cakes recede from the
pan sides and the tops are golden, 25–30 minutes. Let cool in
the pans on wire racks for 5 minutes, then turn them out onto
the racks to cool completely.
❧ To fill the cake, place 1 cake layer on a serving plate. Spread
the cream over the top and then sprinkle with the ginger. Place
the second layer on top. Sift icing sugar over the top and serve.

SERVES 8   *Photograph pages 226–227*

CHEESE SCONES

*You can make this recipe as one large scone (it's quicker) and
break or cut it into wedges as you need it. Or the dough can be
cut into squares or stamped out in rounds with scone cutters. The
scones are best eaten the day they are made. Serve them with
pâtés, sliced tomatoes and black olives or with apricot preserves.*

250 g (8 oz/1⅔ cups) self-raising flour
½ teaspoon salt
few grains of cayenne pepper
2 tablespoons unsalted butter
100 g (3½ oz) well-aged cheddar cheese, coarsely grated
about 110 ml (3½ fl oz/7 tablespoons) milk, plus 2
  tablespoons milk for brushing on top
1 egg

❧ Position a rack in the upper part of an oven and preheat the
oven to 220°C (425°F). Butter and flour a baking tray (sheet).
❧ In a bowl, sift together the flour, salt and cayenne pepper.
Using your fingertips, lightly rub in the butter until the mixture
resembles coarse crumbs.
❧ Stir in the cheese and make a well in the centre. In a small bowl,
whisk together the 110 ml (3½ fl oz/7 tablespoons) milk and
egg. Pour into the well and stir the dry ingredients into the wet
ingredients, mixing quickly and lightly to form a soft dough. If the
dough seems too dry, add a few more drops of milk as needed.
❧ On a lightly floured board, roll out the dough into a square
about 2.5 cm (1 in) thick. Cut into 8 squares and place on the
prepared tray. Brush the tops with the 2 tablespoons milk. Bake
in the upper part of the oven until golden and crisp, 12–15
minutes. Serve warm or at room temperature.

MAKES 8

Bush Berry Custards—photographed at Mount Canobolas, NSW

BUSH BERRY CUSTARDS

In these flavoursome custards, chef Hugh Longstaff uses three indigenous ingredients, lilly pillies, munthari berries and rosella flowers.

1½ tablespoons raspberries
3 tablespoons water
1 cinnamon stick, about 5 cm (2 in) long
2 tablespoons Grand Marnier
40 g (1½ oz) lilly pillies (see glossary)
20 g (¾ oz) munthari berries (see glossary)
10 g (⅓ oz) rosella flowers (see glossary)
100 ml (3½ fl oz/6½ tablespoons) milk
2 vanilla beans, split lengthwise
5 egg yolks
95 g (3 oz/6 tablespoons) caster (superfine) sugar
400 ml (13 fl oz/1⅔ cups) thickened (double/heavy) cream

FOR THE CRÈME ANGLAISE:

4 egg yolks
3 tablespoons sugar
60 ml (2 fl oz/¼ cup) milk
80 ml (3 fl oz/⅓ cup) thickened (double/heavy) cream
4 tablespoons fresh lime juice
2 teaspoons crème de menthe

FOR THE NUTS:

120 g (4 oz/¾ cup) whole macadamia nuts
70 g (2⅓ oz/4½ tablespoons) sugar
3 tablespoons water
2 tablespoons butter

In a small saucepan, combine the raspberries, water, cinnamon and Grand Marnier. Place over medium-low heat, bring to a gentle simmer and cook, stirring occasionally, for 5 minutes. Discard the cinnamon and stir the raspberry mixture until smooth. While still hot, add the lilly pillies, munthari berries and rosella flowers. Stir well, cover and let stand for 1 hour in a warm spot to infuse the ingredients with flavour.

Place the milk in a wide, shallow bowl. Scrape the seeds out of the vanilla beans into the milk and add the pods to the milk. Cover and let stand to infuse for 1 hour.

Preheat an oven to 150°C (300°F). Butter six 100-ml (3½-fl oz/ ½-cup) soufflé dishes.

In a bowl, beat together the egg yolks and sugar until pale and light. Strain the milk into the bowl holding the egg yolk mixture and whisk well. Add the cream and again whisk thoroughly. Fold the cooled berry mixture into the cream mixture.

Pour the berry-cream mixture into the prepared moulds, ensuring that the bush berries are evenly distributed. Place the moulds in a large roasting pan and pour in water to reach halfway up the sides of the moulds. Bake until just set, about 40 minutes. Let cool, then cover and refrigerate.

To make the crème anglaise, in a metal bowl, beat together the egg yolks and sugar until pale and fluffy. In a saucepan, combine the milk and cream and bring to a boil. Slowly stir the milk mixture into the egg mixture. Add the lime juice and crème de menthe. Place over a pan of barely simmering water and cook, stirring constantly, until it thickens enough to coat the back of a spoon, 7–10 minutes. Set aside to cool.

To prepare the nuts, place them on a wire rack set over baking (parchment) paper. In a small pan, combine the sugar and water. Bring to a boil, stirring to dissolve the sugar. Cook over high heat without stirring again until the mixture turns brown and caramelises, about 7–10 minutes. Add the butter and remove from the heat. Pour the hot caramelised sugar evenly over the nuts. Let stand until set.

❧ To serve, ladle the crème anglaise onto individual plates. Invert a custard in the centre of each plate. Arrange the nuts around the custards. Serve at once.

SERVES 6

PERTH

PAVLOVA WITH RASPBERRIES, PASSIONFRUIT AND GLASS BARK

There are varying accounts as to the origins of the pavlova. One is that it was created by a hotel chef in Perth in Western Australia in 1935, to honour the Russian prima ballerina, Anna Pavlova. The chef made the dessert to resemble the ballerina's tutu, a crisp, snowy white, light-as-air creation. It has been popular ever since—especially in the home kitchen. Its origin is also often attributed to New Zealand, where some records show that it was being made there a decade earlier than in Perth. Raspberries grow well in the colder states, Tasmania and Victoria.

FOR THE MERINGUE:

6 egg whites
pinch of salt
400 g (13 oz/1¾ cups) caster (superfine) sugar
2 teaspoons distilled white vinegar
1 teaspoon vanilla essence (extract), or to taste

FOR THE FILLING:

300 ml (9½ fl oz/1¼ cups) thickened (double/heavy) cream
4 passionfruits, flesh scooped out
250 g (8 oz/2 cups) raspberries

FOR THE GLASS BARK:

100 g (3½ oz/½ cup) caster (superfine) sugar

❧ Preheat an oven to 120°C (250°F). To make the meringue, in a bowl, combine the egg whites and salt and beat until firm, shiny peaks form. Gradually beat in about three-quarters of the sugar and then continue to beat until stiff and glossy. Fold in the vinegar, vanilla and remaining sugar.

❧ Cut out a 30-cm (12-in) circle of brown or baking (parchment) paper. Wet on one side under the tap. Shake off the excess water. Place the paper, damp side up, on a heavy baking tray (sheet). Spoon the egg white mixture onto the paper, smoothing it out to a 25-cm (10-in) round. Using a spatula, shape the mixture so the sides and top are straight and level.

❧ Bake in the centre of the oven until crisp on the outside and just set in the centre, 1¼–1½ hours. Remove from the oven and invert onto a serving platter. Carefully remove the paper and let cool.

❧ To make the filling, in a bowl, beat the cream until soft peaks form. Spoon the cream on top of the meringue and spread it with a spatula. Push the passionfruit flesh through a fine-mesh sieve and stir half of the seeds back into the resulting juice. Drizzle over the top of the pavlova and then scatter the raspberries over the top.

❧ To make the glass bark, preheat a griller (broiler) on high. Using a flavourless oil, lightly oil the back of a baking tray. Lightly wipe off the oil with a tissue. Sieve the sugar over the back of the tray. Place in the griller and grill (broil) until melted and golden. Watch the sugar carefully as it burns quickly. Remove from the griller and let stand until completely cool.

❧ Spread a sheet of baking paper on a work surface. Tap the baking tray hard over paper, so that the glass bark falls off in shards. Break into appropriately sized pieces and stick into the top of the pavlova. Cut into wedges and serve.

SERVES 8   *Photograph pages 218–219*

QUEENSLAND

TAMARILLO AND KAKADU PLUM TARTLETS WITH CUMQUAT CREAM

Tamarillos are the size of large eggs and have red or sometimes yellow flesh and tart seeds. Cumquats are tiny, oval orange fruits with an edible skin and tangy flesh. Kakadu plums look like oversized green olives and have a mild apricot flavour. This recipe is from Hugh Longstaff.

FOR THE FRUIT COMPOTE:

750 ml (24 fl oz/3 cups) water
200 g (6½ oz/¾ cup plus 1½ tablespoons) caster (superfine) sugar
8 tamarillos
15 Kakadu plums
1 lemon zest strip
2 tablespoons cognac

shortcrust pastry dough for sour cream and mixed berry tart (recipe on page 233), refrigerated for 30 minutes
1 teaspoon brown sugar

FOR THE CREAM:

10 cumquats (kumquats), quartered
1½ tablespoons sugar
60 ml (2 fl oz/¼ cup) dry white wine
300 ml (10 fl oz/1¼ cups) whipping (double) cream
2 teaspoons ground cinnamon

❧ To make the compote, in a small saucepan over medium heat, combine the water and sugar, stirring until the sugar dissolves. Add the tamarillos and poach gently over medium-low heat for 3 minutes. Remove from the heat and let stand for 20 minutes. Using a slotted spoon, remove the tamarillos from the syrup and peel them. Cut 6 of the tamarillos into walnut-sized pieces. Pit 10 of the Kakadu plums and cut them into the same-sized pieces.

❧ Discard half of the sugar syrup and reduce the remainder over high heat to one-quarter of its original volume. Add the cut-up tamarillos and plums and the lemon zest to the reduced sugar syrup and reduce over high heat until thickened. Remove from the heat, stir in the cognac and let cool.

❧ Preheat an oven to 160°C (325°F). Butter six 7.5-cm (3-in) tartlet moulds.

❧ Roll out the pastry about 3 mm (1/8 in) thick. Cut out 6 rounds each about 2 cm (3/4 in) larger in diameter than the prepared moulds. Carefully transfer each round to a mould and press in gently. Let rest 10 minutes, then line each mould with baking (parchment) paper and fill with pie weights. Bake until the pastry is set, about 10 minutes. Remove from the oven and remove the weights and paper. Increase the oven temperature to 170°C (340°F).

❧ Fill the tartlet moulds with the fruit compote. Pit the remaining plums and slice the plums and the remaining tamarillos. Arrange the fruit slices on top of the compote. Sprinkle with the brown sugar. Bake until the pastry is golden, 15–20 minutes. Remove from the oven and let cool completely on a wire rack.

❧ While the tarts are baking, make the cream. In a small saucepan, combine the cumquats, sugar and wine. Place over high heat, stirring to dissolve the sugar. Continue to cook until there are only 2 tablespoons syrup remaining. Remove from the heat and let cool completely.

❧ Place the cream in a bowl and beat until stiff peaks form. Sprinkle on the cinnamon. Using a rubber spatula, fold the cumquat mixture into the cream. Cover and refrigerate until serving time.

❧ To serve, carefully remove each tart from its mould. Serve with the cream spooned on top.

SERVES 6   *Photograph page 10*

CANBERRA

RAISIN AND ALMOND ANZACS

Anzac stands for Australian and New Zealand Army Corps. These biscuits (cookies) are named in tribute to our soldiers who fought in World War I. The raisins are a nontraditional addition. Once the wet and dry ingredients have been combined, the biscuits must be formed and baked immediately, or the oats will soak up too much moisture and the biscuits will be dry.

80 g (2¾ oz/scant 1 cup) rolled oats
80 g (2¾ oz/¾ cup) desiccated coconut
150 g (5 oz/1 cup) plain (all-purpose) flour
180 g (6 oz/¾ cup) sugar
100 g (3½ oz/⅔ cup) raisins
60 g (2 oz/⅓ cup) almonds, chopped
1 teaspoon bicarbonate of soda (baking soda)
80 ml (3 fl oz/⅓ cup) water
125 g (4 oz/½ cup) unsalted butter
2 tablespoons golden syrup

❧ Preheat an oven to 140°C (290°F). Butter 4 baking trays (sheets).
❧ Place the oats, coconut, flour, sugar, raisins and almonds in a large bowl. Place the bicarbonate of soda, water, butter and golden syrup in a small pan and heat until the butter melts. Stir the butter mixture into the dry ingredients, mixing thoroughly.

❧ Form 3-cm (1¼-in) mounds on the prepared trays, spacing them 5 cm (2 in) apart. Flatten each mound with a rubber spatula. Place 2 trays in the oven and bake until evenly golden brown, 17–20 minutes. Remove the trays from the oven and immediately bake the remaining biscuits.
❧ Let cool on the trays for 2 minutes; then, using an eggslice (metal spatula), transfer to wire racks to cool completely. Once cool, store in an airtight container for up to 1 week.

MAKES ABOUT 30

TASMANIA

LEATHERWOOD HONEY BAVAROIS WITH LIME-CHAMPAGNE SYRUP

Leigh Stone-Herbert is a peripatetic cook who combines his traditional English background, classical French training and modern Australian sense of culinary adventure to create individual food for the demanding palates of the Sydney cognoscenti. Leatherwood honey is gathered in the mountain wilderness in Tasmania. It has a distinctive aroma and full flavour. If you cannot locate it, use any high-quality, full-bodied honey.

Raisin and Almond Anzacs—photographed at Woodbyne Park Gallery, Jasper's Brush, NSW

FOR THE BAVAROIS:

100 g (3½ oz/⅓ cup) Tasmanian Leatherwood honey
3 gelatine leaves or 2½ teaspoons unflavoured powdered
  gelatine
330 ml (11 fl oz/1⅓ cups) milk
4 large egg yolks
1½ tablespoons caster (superfine) sugar
300 ml (10 fl oz/1¼ cups) thickened (double/heavy) cream

FOR THE LIME-CHAMPAGNE SYRUP:

250 ml (8 fl oz/1 cup) sparkling white wine
150 g (5 oz/⅔ cup) caster (superfine) sugar
zest of 2 limes, finely julienned, blanched 1 minute and drained
fresh lime juice

fresh pesticide-free edible flowers for garnish

❧ To make the bavarois, in a small saucepan, warm the honey gently and then set aside. Soak the gelatine leaves in cold water to cover for 5 minutes. Squeeze the water out of the leaves by hand. If using powdered gelatine, in a bowl, dissolve the gelatine in 1 tablespoon hot water for 5 minutes. Combine the gelatine leaves or dissolved powdered gelatine and milk in the top pan of a double boiler placed over hot water. Stir to disslove the gelatine completely. Set aside.

❧ In a bowl, using an electric mixer or a wooden spoon, beat together the yolks and sugar until the mixture is thick and falls in 'ribbons' from the beaters or spoon. Slowly add the milk-gelatine mixture and then the honey to the egg mixture, whisking constantly. Transfer the mixture to the top pan of the double boiler placed over simmering water and cook, whisking constantly, until thick enough to coat the back of a wooden spoon, about 10 minutes. Remove from the heat and place over a bowl of iced water to cool, whisking from time to time to prevent a skin from forming.

❧ In a bowl, beat the cream until it forms soft peaks. Fold it into the cooled egg yolk mixture.

❧ Rinse a 1-l (32-fl oz/4-cup) terrine with cold water and pour the mixture into it. Cover with plastic wrap and refrigerate until set, about 12 hours.

❧ To make the sauce, in a pan, combine the wine and sugar and bring to a boil, stirring until the sugar dissolves. Remove from the heat and let cool over ice water. Stir in the lime zest and lime juice to taste. Chill for 2 hours before serving.

❧ To serve, dip the base of the terrine in warm water and immediately invert onto a flat plate. Lift off the terrine, shaking it to release the bavarois. Cut the bavarois into slices. Spoon a little of the sauce onto each individual plate. Place a slice of bavarois to one side of each plate and decorate with a fresh flower.

SERVES 6–8

S Y D N E Y

SOUR CREAM AND MIXED BERRY TART

Berries grow in the colder states of Australia; the best come from Tasmania, Victoria and central-west New South Wales. Such exotic varieties as white currants, black raspberries and beautifully aromatic wild strawberries, both red and white, are now being cultivated. These special berries are available in small commercial quantities. The recipe for this delicious tart was given to me by Stephen Neale, who is the chef at a café near where I live in Sydney.

FOR THE SHORTCRUST PASTRY:

250 g (8 oz/1⅔ cups) plain (all-purpose) flour, sifted
75 g (2½ oz/⅓ cup) caster (superfine) sugar
finely grated zest of 1 lemon
175 g (6 oz/¾ cup) unsalted butter, chilled, cut into small pieces
2 tablespoons ice water

*Top to bottom: Sour Cream and Mixed Berry Tart,
Leatherwood Honey Bavarois with Lime-Champagne Syrup*

FOR THE FILLING:

7 egg yolks
150 g (5 oz/⅔ cup) caster (superfine) sugar
1 teaspoon vanilla essence (extract), or to taste
500 g (1 lb/2 cups) sour cream
250 g (8 oz) mixed berries

❧ To make the pastry, in a large bowl, stir together the flour, sugar and lemon zest. Add the butter and, using fingertips, 2 knives or a pastry blender, work it in until the mixture is the consistency of rolled oats. Add half of the water and mix with a fork until the dough feels damp and workable. Add the remaining water, if you need it to achieve the proper consistency. Mix the dough until it comes together in a ball. Wrap in plastic wrap and refrigerate for 30 minutes.

❧ Position a rack in the centre of an oven and preheat the oven to 180°C (350°F). Butter a deep 25-cm (10-in) tart pan with a removable bottom. On a lightly floured work surface, roll out the dough thinly into a round large enough to fit the prepared pan. Carefully transfer the round to the pan. Refrigerate for 1 hour.

❧ Line the pastry with baking (parchment) paper and fill with pie weights. Cook in the centre of the oven until golden around the edges, 15–20 minutes. Remove the weights and baking paper and return to the oven until the pastry is golden, about 5 minutes longer. Let cool on a wire rack. Reduce the oven temperature to 150°C (300°F).

❧ To make the filling, in a bowl, whisk together the egg yolks and sugar until pale, light and fluffy. Add the vanilla and sour cream and mix well.

❧ Arrange the berries in the cooled tart shell. Pour the sour cream mixture evenly over the top. Bake in the centre of the oven until the mixture is firm but not set solidly, 20–30 minutes.

❧ Let cool, then cover and refrigerate for at least 3–4 hours or as long as overnight. To serve, using a hot knife, cut into wedges.

MAKES ONE 25-CM (10-IN) TART; SERVES 8

Top to bottom: Linseed and Sesame Bread, Lavash with Gruyère, Ported Raisins and Walnuts—photographed on board the Green Parrot *at Sydney Harbour*

LINSEED AND SESAME BREAD

Narsai David, a San Francisco–based food importer, raconteur, broadcaster, food writer and friend to the food community, enjoys visiting Australia immensely. He collected this bread recipe from the Lyndoch Bakery in South Australia's Barossa Valley and has baked it several times for me when I have visited him at his home.

60 g (2 oz/¼ cup) wheat berries (unprocessed wheat kernels)
580 ml (19 fl oz/2⅓ cups) lukewarm water
1 tablespoon active dry yeast
130 g (4 oz/¾ cup) wholemeal (whole-wheat) flour
520 g (17 oz/3¾ cups) bread flour or plain (all-purpose) flour
2 tablespoons oil
2 tablespoons malt powder or 1 tablespoon molasses
1½ teaspoons salt
45 g (1½ oz/⅓ cup) linseeds (flaxseeds), toasted
60 g (2 oz/½ cup) sesame seeds
cornmeal for dusting

❧ In a small saucepan, combine the wheat berries and 80 ml (3 fl oz/⅓ cup) of the water and place over medium heat until the water is absorbed, 3–5 minutes. Set aside to cool.
❧ In a large mixing bowl, dissolve the yeast in the remaining 500 ml (16 fl oz/2 cups) water. Let stand until creamy, about 5 minutes. Add the flours, oil, malt or molasses, salt, linseeds and wheat berries and mix, using a wooden spoon or the paddle attachment on a heavy-duty electric mixer, until the mixture comes together in a dough. If making by hand, turn out onto a floured work surface and knead the dough until it is smooth and elastic, about 10 minutes. If using a dough hook on an electric mixer, knead the dough at the slowest speed for about 5 minutes until smooth and elastic.
❧ Pat the dough into a ball and place in a lightly oiled bowl. Turn the ball to coat it with the oil. Cover the bowl with a kitchen towel and set it in a warm, draft-free place. Let the dough rise until doubled in bulk, 1–1¼ hours. (A perfect place is a gas oven with only the slight heat given off by the pilot light; an electric oven, turned on low for no more than 2 minutes, then turned off, works equally well.)
❧ Turn out the dough onto a well-floured work surface, punch it down and knead until no air bubbles remain. Divide the dough in half and shape each half into 2 round loaves.
❧ To coat the loaves with sesame seeds, prepare 2 bowls each large enough to hold one loaf easily. Fill one bowl partly with water; put the sesame seeds in the other bowl. Hold 1 loaf gently in both hands and dip it into the water just enough to dampen it on all surfaces. Immediately set the dampened loaf in the bowl of seeds, jiggling the bowl until the seeds coat the loaf evenly. Place the loaf on the work surface and cover

234

with a towel. Repeat with the second loaf. Let the loaves rise until almost doubled in size, 15–30 minutes.

Using a razor blade, cut 3 deep parallel gashes in a pattern in the top of each loaf. Cover the loaves with a towel and let rise again 20–25 minutes.

While the loaves are rising, preheat an oven to 400°C (200°F). Place a pie tin half-filled with water on the bottom rack of the oven. Position an oven rack just above the bottom rack. Dust a baking tray (sheet) with cornmeal.

Gently pick up the loaves and transfer them to the baking tray. Place in the oven on the rack just above the bottom rack. Bake until the crust is golden brown, 40–45 minutes. To test, tap on the bottom with your knuckles. The loaf should feel firm and make a hollow sound. Let cool on a wire rack. To serve, cut into slices.

MAKES 2 LOAVES

TASMANIA

LAVASH WITH GRUYÈRE, PORTED RAISINS AND WALNUTS

There's nothing quite like having a pot of ported raisins on hand. All you need is the new season's seedless raisins, an Australian port and a cupboard in which to hide the pot until the raisins are ready to use five weeks later. We make so many good cheeses in Australia that it's difficult to single out one. But knowing the taste and texture of homemade lavash, a cracker-style bread that is believed to have originated in Assyria, and ported raisins, I suggest Tasmania's Heidi Farm gruyère as the perfect cheese to marry with the other components. Thin mango slices are also a good accompaniment.

FOR THE PORTED RAISINS:

500 g (1 lb) sun-dried raisins
300 ml (10 fl oz/1¼ cups) port

FOR THE LAVASH:

500 g (1 lb/3 cups) plain (all-purpose) flour
60 g (2 oz/¼ cup) caster (superfine) sugar
1 teaspoon salt
60 g (2 oz/¼ cup) unsalted butter, at room temperature
2 eggs
about 240 ml (8 fl oz/1 cup) milk
2 tablespoons sesame seeds
2 tablespoons poppy seeds

Heidi Farm gruyère cheese or other high-quality gruyère
   cheese
1 kg (2 lb) walnuts in the shell
6 olive branch twigs

To prepare the raisins, place them in a glass-topped jar. Pour in the port and cover the jar. Shake each day for the first week to ensure that the raisins steep evenly. Leave in a cupboard for 5 weeks.

Preheat an oven to 180°C (350°F). Butter 2 baking trays (sheets).

To make the lavash, in a food processor fitted with the metal blade, combine the flour, sugar and salt. Pulse to mix. Add the butter and process until the mixture is crumbly. Then add the eggs and as much of the milk as needed for the mixture to gather in a rough mass around the blades. Alternatively, to make the dough by hand, sift together the dry ingredients. Add the butter and, using your fingertips, 2 knives or a pastry blender, work it in until the mixture is crumbly. Add the eggs and, while stirring with a fork, as much of the milk as needed until the mixture comes together in a ball.

Transfer the dough to a lightly floured work surface and knead until smooth, just a few minutes. Divide the dough in half and roll out each half into a free-form sheet about 3 mm (⅛ in) thick. Transfer 1 sheet to each prepared tray. Dampen the tops using a pastry brush dipped in water. Scatter with the sesame and poppy seeds and press in lightly with a rolling pin.

Bake in the oven until dry, golden and crisp, 30–40 minutes. Let cool completely on a wire rack.

To serve, break the lavash into barklike pieces and arrange on a serving plate. Accompany with the cheese and garnish with the nuts and olive twigs. Serve the ported raisins in a bowl.

SERVES 6

QUEENSLAND

TROPICAL FRUIT SOUP WITH ASIAN SPICES

Lemongrass was first brought to Australia in 1778 by botanist Joseph Banks. Mangosteens are native to the tropical jungles of Malaysia and also Sumatra. The fruit has purple-black skin, is round and contains four to eight delicate white-fleshed segments with one or two light brown seeds. They are grown in the tropics of Far North Queensland. The rambutan, a hairy lychee-type fruit, is also native to Malaysia and Sumatra. The name is derived from the Malay word rambut, *meaning 'hair of the head'. The fruit is covered with hairy soft spines that range from red to pink and yellow, and the translucent white flesh is sweet, with a mild acid flavour and a single seed at its centre. They are grown in the wet tropical areas of Queensland and are available from January until August, with peak supplies in autumn.*

Peak-of-season fruits from Queensland are the best choice for this dessert. Although I call it a soup, it should be served after a flavoursome main course such as curry or another fiery-hot Asian dish. It is a refreshing, palate-cleansing finale.

FOR THE SYRUP:

zest and juice of 1 lime
180 g (6 oz/¾ cup) caster (superfine) sugar
750 ml (24 fl oz/3 cups) water
1 lemongrass stalk, tender part only, finely chopped
   (see glossary)
3 whole cloves
1 cinnamon stick, about 5 cm (2 in) long
½ vanilla bean, split lengthwise
1 star anise
1 teaspoon coriander seeds, cracked with a mallet
1 piece gingerroot, about 3 cm (1¼ in) long, peeled and
   finely sliced
100 ml (3½ fl oz/6½ tablespoons) late-picked Rhine
Riesling wine

FOR THE FRUITS:

1 mango, peeled, pitted and diced
½ small pineapple, peeled and finely diced
4 rambutans, peeled, pitted and quartered
2 mangosteens, peeled, pitted and quartered

6 fresh mint sprigs

To make the syrup, in a large, heavy pan, combine all the syrup ingredients and bring slowly to a boil. Reduce the heat and simmer gently for 5 minutes. Remove from the heat and let cool. Pour through a sieve and discard the spices. Cover and refrigerate the syrup until well chilled.

Arrange the fruits in a serving bowl. Ladle the chilled syrup over the top, garnish with the mint and serve cold.

SERVES 4   *Photograph page 10*

Genoa Cake—photographed at Sydney Harbour

AUSTRALIA

GENOA CAKE

I don't know the origins of this cake, but it's one that I grew up with in Adelaide, and my husband, John Kelly, also remembers it from when he was a boy in Tasmania. The triple layer of newspaper that covers the outside of the pan helps the cake to cook more evenly. This is a great cake for morning tea, school lunches and picnics.

250 g (8 oz/1 cup) unsalted butter, at room temperature
250 g (8 oz/1 cup) sugar
5 eggs
300 g (9½ oz/scant 2 cups) plain (all-purpose) flour
1 teaspoon baking powder
240 g (8 oz/1⅓ cups) sultanas (golden raisins)
120 g (4 oz/⅔ cup) glacé cherries
120 g (4 oz/¾ cup) almonds
2 tablespoons milk
120 g (4 oz/⅔ cup) mixed candied citrus peel

Position a rack in the centre of an oven and preheat the oven to 190°C (375°F). Line a 20-cm (8-in) round cake pan with a double layer of newspaper that stands twice as high as the height of the pan. Then top with a layer of well-buttered brown paper, buttered side up, again with the sides standing twice the height of the pan.

In a bowl, beat together the butter and sugar until light and creamy. Beat in the eggs, one at a time, beating well after each addition. In another bowl, sift together the flour and baking powder. Fold the flour mixture into the butter mixture alternately with the sultanas, cherries and almonds, mixing until fully combined.

Spoon into the prepared pan, brush with the 2 tablespoons milk and top with the citrus peel. Using kitchen twine, tie a triple layer of newspaper around the outside of the pan.

Bake in the centre of the oven until the cake recedes from the sides of the pan and is golden on top, about 1¼ hours. Let cool completely in the pan on a wire rack, then invert, lift off the pan and pull off the paper. Cut into slices and serve.

MAKES ONE 20-CM (8-IN) CAKE; SERVES 6–8

MACADAMIA NUT ICE CREAM

Australians love ice cream. In fact, we boast one of the largest per capita consumption rates in the world. Although much of it is bought, there are still many people who prefer to make ice cream at home.

6 eggs, separated
100 g (3½ oz/½ cup) caster (superfine) sugar
250 ml (8 fl oz/1 cup) milk
500 ml (16 fl oz/2 cups) thickened (double/heavy) cream
125 g (4 oz/¾ cup) macadamia nuts, lightly toasted and
    finely chopped

In a bowl, beat together the egg yolks and sugar until pale and fluffy. In a saucepan over medium heat, combine the milk and half of the cream and cook until bubbles form along the sides of the pan. Pour a little of the hot milk mixture onto the yolk mixture, whisking well. Whisk the milk-yolk mixture into the saucepan and cook over medium-low heat, whisking constantly, until the mixture thickens enough to coat the back of a wooden spoon, 5–8 minutes. Do not allow the mixture to boil. Remove from the heat and place the pan in a sink of ice water to cool, stirring from time to time to prevent a skin from forming.

In a bowl, beat the remaining cream until soft peaks form. Fold the whipped cream into the cooled cream mixture. Stir in the macadamia nuts. Pour into an ice cream maker and freeze according to the manufacturer's directions.

Serve at once or transfer to a covered container and place in the freezer until ready to serve.

MAKES ABOUT 750 ML (24 FL OZ/1½ PT)

BLACKBERRY SORBET AND ICE CREAM CAKE

Genevieve Harris spent 18 months cooking at a famous resort in Bali. Now that she's back in Sydney as chef at a restaurant on Balmoral Beach, her followers are feasting on her sophisticated food, much of which has an Asian accent. Although this dessert is not Asian, it is one of the most attractive ice cream dishes I have ever tasted. In Australia, blackberries are rarely picked in the wild as they are in England and Europe; for the most part they are bought in markets during their brief summer season. There are excellent frozen ones available all year long, however, and they can be substituted when fresh ones are out of season.

FOR THE VANILLA ICE CREAM:

80 ml (3 fl oz/⅓ cup) milk
170 ml (6 fl oz/¾ cup) thickened (double/heavy) cream
⅓ vanilla bean, split lengthwise
2 egg yolks
3½ tablespoons vanilla sugar (see glossary)

FOR THE BLACKBERRY ICE CREAM:

200 g (6½ oz/scant 1 cup) caster (superfine) sugar
330 ml (11 fl oz/1⅓ cups) puréed blackberries
1½ teaspoons fresh lime juice
330 ml (11 fl oz/1⅓ cups) thickened (double/heavy) cream

FOR THE BLACKBERRY SORBET:

3½ tablespoons caster (superfine) sugar
350 ml (11 fl oz/1⅓ cups) puréed blackberries
1½ teaspoons fresh lime juice
70 g (2⅓ oz/1¼ cups) liquid glucose

FOR THE BLACKBERRY SYRUP:

370 g (12 oz/1½ cups) granulated sugar
350 ml (11½ fl oz/1⅓ cups) water
150 ml (5 fl oz/⅔ cup) puréed blackberries

To make the vanilla ice cream, in a saucepan over medium heat, combine the milk, cream and vanilla bean and heat until small bubbles form along the edge of the pan. Meanwhile, in a bowl, whisk together the yolks and sugar until pale and creamy. Pour the hot milk mixture over the eggs, whisking well. Return the mixture to the pan and cook, stirring, until the mixture thickens to a custard consistency and coats the back of a spoon, 5–8 minutes. Strain through a fine-mesh sieve into a bowl and let cool. Pour into an ice cream maker and freeze to soft-serve stage according to the manufacturer's directions. Transfer to a container and place in the refrigerator.

To make the blackberry ice cream, in a bowl, stir together the sugar, blackberry purée and lime juice until the sugar dissolves. Stir in the cream. Pour into an ice cream maker and freeze to soft-serve stage according to the manufacturer's directions. Transfer to a container and place in the refrigerator.

To make the sorbet, in a bowl, stir together the sugar, blackberry purée and lime juice until the sugar dissolves. Place the glucose in a bowl over a saucepan of water and heat over medium heat. Add the glucose to the blackberry mixture and stir well. Strain through a fine-mesh sieve into a bowl. Pour into an ice cream maker and freeze to soft-serve stage according to the manufacturer's directions. Transfer to a container and place in the refrigerator.

To make the syrup, in a small saucepan, stir together the sugar and water and place over medium heat, stirring until the sugar dissolves. Bring to a simmer and cook gently for 20 minutes. Add the blackberry purée and simmer for 10 minutes. Remove from the heat and let cool. Cover and refrigerate until ready to use.

To assemble the cake, line a rectangular cake pan measuring 30 by 15 cm (12 by 6 in) with baking (parchment) paper. Spoon large tablespoons of the 2 ice creams and the sorbet into the pan. Using a chopstick, swirl together the ice creams and sorbet to create a marbled pattern. Repeat the process until the pan is full.

Tap the pan on the work surface to release any air bubbles. Using an eggslice (metal spatula), level the top of cake. Cover and freeze until solid, preferably overnight.

To unmould, invert onto a cutting board and wrap a hot cloth over the pan bottom. Shake the pan until the cake slips out. Slice with a knife dipped in hot water and arrange on flat plates. Drizzle with the blackberry syrup and serve at once.

SERVES 12–14

Clockwise from top: Iced Pineapple Soufflés with Tropical Fruits (recipe page 238), Macadamia Nut Ice Cream, Blackberry Sorbet and Ice Cream Cake

CUSTARD APPLE AND GRANNY SMITH CRISP

Thomas and Maria Ann Smith arrived from England in 1838 and settled in the Ryde district of Sydney. Granny Smith, as she was known to her children, had an orchard and took her produce to the Sydney markets. According to legend, she brought back cases with some rotting Tasmanian apples, which she threw away. Years later, where she had tipped the cases, she discovered a seedling bearing magnificent green-skinned apples. This seedling, apparently a crossbreed, was later named after Granny Smith.

Custard apples, with their green knobbly skin and smooth custard-like flesh, must be ripe before using. They are extremely sweet and therefore marry well with the acidity of the Granny Smiths.

FOR THE FILLING:

2 Granny Smith apples, peeled, halved, cored and thinly sliced
1 large ripe custard apple, flesh scooped out and seeds discarded
90 g (3 oz/½ cup) sultanas (golden raisins) or halved, pitted dates
90 ml (3 fl oz/6 tablespoons) water
3 tablespoons unsalted butter, cut into pieces
¼ teaspoon ground cinnamon

FOR THE TOPPING:

60 g (2 oz/⅓ cup) plain (all-purpose) flour
3 tablespoons sugar
¼ teaspoon ground cinnamon
3 tablespoons unsalted butter, cut in small pieces

Position a rack in the centre of an oven and preheat the oven to 180°C (350°F). Butter an 800-ml (26-fl oz/3¼-cup) baking dish.

To make the filling, arrange the apple slices and custard apple pieces in the baking dish, overlapping the pieces. Scatter the sultanas or dates and the water evenly over the top. Dot with the butter and sprinkle the cinnamon over the top.

To make the topping, place the flour, sugar and cinnamon in a bowl. Add the butter and, using your fingertips, work in until the mixture is crumbly. Spoon over the apples.

Bake in the centre of the oven until the apples are tender and the top is golden and crisp, about 35 minutes. Serve warm.

SERVES 4

APPLE SNOW WITH SPONGE KISSES

This thoroughly old-fashioned dessert is fabulous made with lovely pale yellow Golden Delicious apples. Sponge kisses were one of my favourites when I was growing up in Adelaide.

FOR THE SPONGE KISSES:

75 g (2½ oz/⅓ cup) caster (superfine) sugar
1 tablespoon boiling water
2 eggs
½ teaspoon vanilla essence (extract), or to taste
85 g (2¾ oz/½ cup plus 1 tablespoon) self-raising flour

FOR THE SNOW:

6 large Golden Delicious apples, peeled, cored and cut into eighths
125 g (4 oz/½ cup) granulated sugar
4 whole cloves
60 ml (2 fl oz/¼ cup) water
1 tablespoon fresh lemon juice

finely grated zest of 1 lemon
2 egg whites

200 ml (6½ fl oz/¾ cup plus 1½ tablespoons) whipping (double) cream, whipped until stiff
1 tablespoon icing (confectioners') sugar
ground cinnamon or additional finely grated lemon zest

Preheat an oven to 190°C (375°F). Butter and flour 2 baking trays (sheets).

To make the kisses, place the caster sugar in a bowl. Pour the boiling water over it, stir and let cool. Add the eggs and vanilla and beat until pale and light.

Sift the flour into the bowl and, using a rubber spatula, fold it into the egg mixture. Drop the batter onto the prepared trays, forming 6 mounds on each tray and spacing them at least 5 cm (2 in) apart to allow for spreading. Bake until golden and crusty on top, about 8 minutes. Remove from the oven and let cool completely in a warm corner away from drafts.

While the kisses are cooling, make the snow. In a large saucepan, combine the apples, granulated sugar, cloves, water and lemon juice. Bring to a boil, stirring to dissolve the sugar. Reduce the heat to low and simmer, uncovered, until the apples are very tender, 15–20 minutes. Let cool.

Using a fork, mash the apples. Alternatively, transfer to a food processor fitted with the metal blade or to a blender and purée until smooth. Fold in the lemon zest.

In a bowl, beat the egg whites until they stand in firm, shiny peaks. Fold the egg whites into the apple mixture.

Using an eggslice (metal spatula), remove the kisses from the trays. Spread the flat side of half of them with whipped cream. Then press the flat side of the remaining kisses onto the whipped cream, to form sandwiches. Arrange on a plate and sift the icing sugar over the tops. Pile the apple mixture into glass dishes or glasses. Dust with cinnamon just before serving, or top with lemon zest. Serve with the sponge kisses.

SERVES 6

ICED PINEAPPLE SOUFFLÉS WITH TROPICAL FRUITS

Pineapples are plentiful year-round, but are at their best during the warmer months. Strawberry pawpaw, often called Fijian pawpaw, has salmon-pink flesh and is much sweeter than golden pawpaw.

FOR THE SOUFFLÉS:

5 eggs, separated
175 g (5½ oz/scant ¾ cup) caster (superfine) sugar
250 ml (8 fl oz/1 cup) puréed ripe pineapple
juice of 1 lime, strained, or to taste

FOR THE FRUITS:

6 rambutans, halved and tops removed to expose the flesh
1 large star fruit, cut crosswise into 6 slices
1 mango, peeled, pitted and sliced
1 small strawberry pawpaw (papaya), peeled, seeded and sliced

Select six 150 ml (5 fl oz/⅔ cup) soufflé dishes. Cut 6 strips of aluminium foil long enough to encircle the dishes and fold each strip in half lengthwise. Wrap a strip around the outside of each dish so that it rises about 2.5 cm (1 in) above the rim and secure in place with kitchen twine.

To make the soufflés, in a bowl, using an electric mixer set on medium speed, beat together the egg yolks and sugar until pale and light and doubled in volume. Gradually beat in the pineapple purée, then add the lime juice to taste.

In another bowl, beat the whites until they form soft peaks. Fold one-third of the egg whites into the pineapple mixture to

Clockwise from top right: Sponge-Topped Rhubarb and Strawberries with Sheep's Milk Yoghurt, Custard Apple and Granny Smith Crisp, Apple Snow with Sponge Kisses—photographed at Vaucluse House, Sydney

lighten it, then carefully fold in the remaining egg whites. Spoon the mixture into the prepared soufflé dishes and place the dishes on a tray. Freeze until set, 2–4 hours.

℀ To serve, remove the collars and stand the soufflés on the bottom shelf of the refrigerator for 30 minutes to soften slightly. Transfer the soufflés to large flat plates and surround with the prepared fruits. Serve at once.

SERVES 6 *Photograph page 237*

VICTORIA

SPONGE-TOPPED RHUBARB AND STRAWBERRIES WITH SHEEP'S MILK YOGHURT

In the past, rhubarb was grown in many backyards, but now people more often buy it at the fruiterer, where it is available year-round. Meredith brand sheep's milk yoghurt was developed by Richard Thomas at Meredith Farm, southeast of Melbourne, where it is made by the owners of the farm, Julie and Sandy Cameron.

500 ml (16 fl oz/2 cups) water
200 g (6½ oz/¾ cup plus 2 tablespoons) caster (superfine) sugar
3 cardamom pods

FOR THE SPONGE:

2 tablespoons unsalted butter, at room temperature
1½ tablespoons caster (superfine) sugar
1 egg
70 g (2½ oz/½ cup) self-raising flour
about 1 tablespoon milk

1 bunch rhubarb, trimmed and cut into 4-cm (1½-in) lengths
250 g (8 oz/2 cups) ripe strawberries, stems removed
500 g (1 lb/2 cups) Meredith Farm sheep's milk yoghurt or other high-quality plain yoghurt

℀ In a large saucepan over medium heat, stir together the water and sugar until the sugar dissolves and the mixture forms a syrup. Add the cardamom and bring to a simmer; keep hot over low heat. Preheat an oven to 190°C (375°F).

℀ To make the sponge, in a bowl, beat together the butter and sugar until light and creamy. Beat in the egg and fold in the flour. Add just enough milk to make a light dropping consistency.

℀ Place the rhubarb in a shallow 750-ml (24-fl oz/3-cup) baking dish. Pour the hot syrup over the rhubarb. Bake until the rhubarb is just tender, about 10 minutes. Remove from the oven and stir in the strawberries.

℀ Drop the sponge mixture by tablespoonfuls onto the hot fruit, leaving gaps between the sponge so the fruit can be seen. Return to the centre of the oven and bake until the sponge is puffed and golden, 10–15 minutes longer. Serve warm with the yoghurt.

SERVES 6

239

BUSH BREADS WITH WILD BUTTER

Vic Cherikoff, an authority on Australia's native foods, offers this recipe for breads that call for some of the most intriguing native ingredients. The basic bread serves as the foundation for three different breads. The recipe makes two loaves that can be stored at room temperature in a bread box for up to 1 week or can be sliced, wrapped in plastic wrap and then frozen for up to 6 months.

FOR THE BASIC BREAD:

200 ml (6½ fl oz/¾ cup plus 1½ tablespoons) warm
    water
400 ml (13 fl oz/1⅔ cups) warm skim milk
2 tablespoons active dry yeast
650 g (1⅓ lb/scant 4¼ cups) unbleached plain (all-purpose)
    flour, plus additional plain flour for kneading
125 ml (4 fl oz/½ cup) macadamia nut oil

FOR THE PEPPERLEAF BREAD:

1 tablespoon ground pepperleaf (see glossary)

FOR THE AKUDJURA BREAD:

1 heaped tablespoon dried akudjura, soaked in 3 tablespoons
    water (see glossary)
30 g (1 oz/¼ cup) grated cheddar cheese
1 small brown onion, finely chopped and sautéed in
    1 tablespoon macadamia oil until translucent

FOR THE WATTLESEED BREAD:

1 tablespoon wattleseeds (see glossary)
375 ml (12 fl oz/1½ cups) golden syrup
2 bananas, mashed

FOR THE WILD BUTTER:

250 g (8 oz/1 cup) unsalted butter, at room temperature
15–20 drops food-grade eucalyptus oil, or to taste, or ½
    teaspoon ground pepperleaf (see glossary)

First, prepare the ingredients for the basic bread. To make pepperleaf bread, in a small bowl combine the warm water and milk and dissolve the yeast in it. Let stand until foamy, 15 minutes. Sift the flour into a large bowl and add the ground pepperleaf. Stir in the yeast-milk mixture and macadamia nut oil and mix well. Turn the dough onto a floured work surface and knead briefly to form a round ball. Return to the bowl, cover with a towel and let rise in a warm place until doubled in bulk, about 1 hour.

Preheat an oven to 180°C (350°F). Line 2 loaf pans each 20 cm (8 in) long with baking (parchment) paper.

Turn the dough onto a well-floured work surface. Knead very gently for only 30 seconds or so to release the fermentation gases and to reduce the stickiness. Divide the dough in half and shape each half into a rectangular loaf. Place a loaf into each prepared pan.

Bake until the loaves are golden and sound hollow when the tops are tapped, 30–40 minutes. Leave to cool for 10 minutes and remove from the pans.

To make the akudjura bread, in a small bowl, combine the warm water and milk and dissolve the yeast in it. Let stand until foamy, 15 minutes. Sift the flour into a large bowl. Stir in the yeast-milk mixture, macadamia nut oil, akudjura, cheddar cheese and sautéed onion and mix well. Turn the dough onto a floured work surface and knead briefly to form a round ball. Return to the bowl, cover with a towel and let rise in a warm place until doubled in bulk, about 1 hour. Knead and bake as for the pepperleaf bread.

To make the wattleseed bread, in a small bowl, combine 80 ml (3 fl oz/⅓ cup) of the warm water and the warm milk and

*Bush Breads with Wild Butter—
photographed at Bloodwood Estate, Orange, NSW*

dissolve the yeast in it. Let stand until foamy, 15 minutes. Place the remaining warm water in a small saucepan, add the wattleseeds and bring to a boil. Remove from the heat and let stand 10 minutes. Sift the flour into a large bowl. Stir in the yeast-milk mixture, wattleseeds and their water, macadamia nut oil, golden syrup and mashed bananas and mix well. Turn the dough onto a floured work surface and knead briefly to form a round ball. Return to the bowl, cover with a towel and let rise in a warm place until doubled in bulk, about 1 hour. Knead and bake as for the pepperleaf bread.

Meanwhile to make the wild butter, place the butter in a bowl. If you have made the wattleseed bread, add the eucalyptus oil and whip until light and smooth. If you have made the akudjura bread, add the ground pepperleaf and whip until light and smooth. If you have made the pepperleaf bread, leave the butter plain. Slice the bread and serve with the butter.

MAKES 2 LOAVES

SULTANA SLICE

Fruit slices were popular when I was growing up, particularly this one made with sultanas. It's a versatile recipe that can be made with dried apricots or other dried fruits as well. The slice packs well for lunch boxes and picnics and is delicious served warm with custard or cream.

FOR THE SHORTCRUST PASTRY:

130 g (4 oz/¾ cup) plain (all-purpose) flour
1 tablespoon caster (superfine) sugar
125 g (4 oz/½ cup) unsalted butter, at room temperature,
    cut into small pieces
1 egg yolk
2–4 teaspoons fresh lemon juice

FOR THE FILLING:

125 g (4 oz/⅔ cup) sultanas (golden raisins)
1½ tablespoons caster (superfine) sugar
1 teaspoon mixed spice (pumpkin-pie spice)
1 tablespoon warm water
4 drops lemon essence (extract), or to taste

1 tablespoon milk
2 tablespoons caster (superfine) sugar

To make the pastry, in a large bowl, stir together the flour and sugar. Add the butter and, using your fingertips, 2 knives or a pastry blender, work it in until the mixture is the consistency of rolled oats. Using a fork, mix in the egg yolk and enough of the lemon juice to bring the dough together in a rough mass. Knead lightly on a lightly floured work surface until smooth. Shape the dough into a ball, wrap in plastic wrap and refrigerate for 30 minutes.

Position a rack in the centre of an oven and preheat the oven to 190°C (375°F). Butter an 18-by-27-by-3-cm (7-by-11-by-1¼-in) baking tray (sheet).

Divide the dough in half. On a lightly floured work surface, roll out each half to fit the bottom of the baking tray. Place one sheet of the dough in the tray and the other on the back of another baking tray. Cover and refrigerate.

To make the filling, in a bowl, stir together the sultanas, sugar, mixed spice, water and lemon extract. Prick the pastry in the tray in several places and sprinkle the filling on top. Top with the other dough sheet. Brush with the milk and scatter with the sugar.

Bake in the centre of the oven until golden, about 25 minutes. Let cool completely on a wire rack. To serve, cut into slices about 6 by 9 cm (2⅓ by 3¾ in).

MAKES 9 LARGE PIECES   *Photograph pages 244–245*

Left to right: Macadamia Nut Cake with Caramel Sauce, Snap-Freeze Indulgence Chocolate Cake, Passionfruit-Lime Delicious Pudding—photographed at Middle Harbour, Sydney

PASSIONFRUIT-LIME DELICIOUS PUDDING

Passionfruits grow prolifically in temperate climates. At one time or another, most Australian backyards have had a passionfruit vine climbing unchecked over fences and garages. During the peak season, they are prized for their sharply acidic yet sweet taste. Some people like to sieve out the seeds, leaving the residual juice; this seems to me a terrible waste, as the seeds add both texture and fibre. The best and most Australian way to eat a passionfruit is to spoon the flesh right out of the skin. Even better, cut off the top, pour in some cream and savour the two together. The heaviest fruits are the best value, and the flesh should be purple and just beginning to dimple. If you like, serve King Island cream for pouring over the pudding at the table.

60 g (2 oz/¼ cup) unsalted butter
150 g (5 oz/⅔ cup) caster (superfine) sugar
finely grated zest of 2 limes
2 tablespoons fresh lime juice
80 ml (3 fl oz/⅓ cup) passionfruit pulp
2 eggs, separated
60 g (2 oz/½ cup) self-raising flour
250 ml (8 fl oz/1 cup) milk

❦ Position a rack in the centre of an oven and preheat the oven to 190°C (375°F). Butter six 150 ml (5 fl oz/⅔ cup) soufflé dishes.
❦ In a bowl, combine the butter and sugar and beat until light and creamy. Beat in the lime zest and juice and the passionfruit. Beat in the egg yolks, one at a time, beating well after each addition. Fold the flour into the butter mixture alternately with the milk, mixing until just combined.

❦ In another bowl, beat the egg whites until they hold firm, shiny peaks. Using a rubber spatula, fold one-quarter of the whites into the butter-flour mixture to lighten it. Then gently fold in the remaining whites. Spoon the mixture into the prepared dishes. Place the dishes in a large baking pan and pour hot water into the pan to reach halfway up the sides of the dishes.
❦ Bake in the centre of the oven until just set, 20–25 minutes.

SERVES 6

SNAP-FREEZE INDULGENCE CHOCOLATE CAKE

Penny Farrell was part of the recipe-testing team for this book and we spent many long hours talking about food, cooking up recipes and enjoying the results. She says this cake is her major stand-by for spur-of-the-moment entertaining. Freezing this dessert firms it and makes it more of a cake than a mousse.

500 g (1 lb) dark couverture chocolate
125 g (4 oz/½ cup) unsalted butter
6 eggs
2 tablespoons plain (all-purpose) flour

❦ Position a rack in the centre of an oven and preheat the oven to 200°C (400°F). Line a 22-cm (9-in) round cake pan with aluminium foil and butter it.
❦ In a large bowl, combine the chocolate and butter and place

over a pan of hot water. Stir occasionally until melted and smooth. Do not allow the water to boil. Set aside to cool.

❧ Break the eggs into the top pan of a double boiler. Place over the lower pan of barely simmering water. Using an electric mixer, beat until the eggs form a white, thick foam, about 15 minutes. Fold in the melted chocolate and the flour.

❧ Spoon the chocolate mixture into the prepared pan. Bake in the centre of the oven for about 15 minutes. The top of the cake will have a crust, and the inside will be runny. Remove from the oven and let cool in the pan.

❧ Cover the cake and freeze overnight, for at least 12 hours. Move the cake into the refrigerator 1 day before serving, then remove it from the refrigerator 1 hour before serving. To serve, invert the cake onto a serving plate and remove the foil.

MAKES ONE 22-CM (9-IN) CAKE; SERVES 12

MACADAMIA NUT CAKE WITH CARAMEL SAUCE

Macadamias are indigenous to Australia. The Europeans first discovered them in the rainforests along the east coast of Queensland in the 1820s, although they were obviously known to local Aborigines long before that. They were originally called bush nuts, Queensland nuts or bauple nuts. They were later named after Dr John Macadam, a noted forensic scientist. If stored cool in an airtight container, they will keep for a year without going rancid. I always have a supply in the freezer.

FOR THE CAKE:

200 g (6½ oz/1⅓ cups) macadamia nuts
70 g (2½ oz/scant ½ cup) plain (all-purpose) flour
1 teaspoon baking powder
6 eggs, separated
200 g (6½ oz/¾ cup plus 1½ tablespoons) caster (superfine) sugar
1 teaspoon vanilla essence (extract)

FOR THE CARAMEL SAUCE:

230 g (7½ oz/generous 1 cup) dark brown sugar
250 ml (8 fl oz/1 cup) thickened (double/heavy) cream
4 teaspoons unsalted butter

300 ml (10 fl oz/1¼ cups) whipping (double) cream, whipped

❧ Preheat an oven to 180°C (350°F). Butter a 25-cm (10-in) ring pan.

❧ To make the cake, in a food processor fitted with the metal blade, combine the nuts, flour and baking powder. Pulse to chop the nuts finely. Set aside.

❧ In a large bowl, beat together the egg yolks and sugar until pale and light. In another bowl, beat the egg whites until they form stiff, shiny peaks. Using a rubber spatula, fold the whites into the yolk mixture. Sprinkle half of the nut mixture over the top and fold in gently. Sprinkle the remaining nut mixture over the top and fold in with the vanilla.

❧ Spoon into the prepared pan. Bake on the second lowest shelf of the oven until the cake recedes from the pan sides and is puffed and golden on top, 30–35 minutes.

❧ Let cool completely in the pan on a wire rack. Run a knife around the pan edge and invert the cake onto a serving plate.

❧ While the cake is cooling, make the sauce. In a saucepan over medium heat, stir together the sugar and cream until the sugar dissolves. Simmer gently without stirring until caramelised, about 20 minutes. Remove from the heat and stir in the butter. Let cool. Serve the cake at room temperature. Pass the sauce and the whipped cream.

MAKES ONE 25-CM (10-IN) CAKE; SERVES 8

DRIED-FRUIT CHOCOLATES

Australia's dried-fruit industry is second to none. We are fortunate to have such variety and quality. Most of the tree fruits for drying come from South Australia's Riverland, while the vine fruits— sultanas, raisins, currants—are principally grown in the Sunraysia district around Mildura. Ditter's, a well-known Adelaide company, also produces high-quality dried and glacé fruits and nuts. Plaistowes is an award-winning chocolate that contains just over 28 percent cocoa fat. It is available in supermarkets and delicatessens the length and breadth of the nation.

400 g (13 oz) Plaistowes dark chocolate or other high-quality dark chocolate, broken into squares
36 dried apricots
18 glacé cherries, halved
36 flaked (sliced) almonds, toasted
36 raisins
36 sultanas (golden raisins)

❧ Cover 3 baking trays (sheets) with baking (parchment) paper, sticking it down at the corners with a little butter.

❧ Place the chocolate in the top pan of a double boiler placed over hot water. Stir the chocolate from time to time with a wooden spoon until smooth. It will take about 10 minutes. Do not allow the water to boil.

❧ Drop the chocolate by teaspoonfuls onto the trays, leaving room for it to spread. Smooth the chocolate with the back of a teaspoon, making each round about 4 cm (1½ in) in diameter. You should have 36 rounds in all. Working quickly, stick 1 piece of each fruit and 1 piece of almond into each chocolate. When all are assembled, refrigerate until set.

❧ Using an eggslice (metal spatula), carefully remove each chocolate. Store in an airtight container in a cool place for up to 1 week.

MAKES 36

Dried-Fruit Chocolates—photographed at Bondi, Sydney

AUSTRALIA

MELTING MOMENTS

These are old Australian favourites that, when made with a light hand, simply melt away in the mouth.

FOR THE BISCUITS:

250 g (8 oz/1 cup) unsalted butter, at room temperature
60 g (2 oz/½ cup) icing (confectioners') sugar
210 g (6½ oz/1¼ cups) plain (all-purpose) flour
60 g (2 oz/½ cup) cornflour (cornstarch)

FOR THE ICING:

220 g (7 oz/1¾ cups) icing (confectioners') sugar
1 tablespoon unsalted butter, at room temperature
about 1 tablespoon passionfruit flesh

Position a rack in the centre of an oven and preheat the oven to 200°C (400°F). Lightly butter 2 baking trays (sheets).

To make the biscuits, in a bowl, beat together the butter and sugar until light and creamy. Sift together the plain flour and cornflour over the top. Using a rubber spatula, fold the flours in gently, mixing until fully combined. Cover and refrigerate for up to 30 minutes.

Dust your hands with flour and roll the biscuit dough into 18 equal-sized balls between your palms. Arrange on 2 lightly buttered baking trays, spacing them well apart as they spread during baking. Mark the tops once with a fork. (If the fork sticks, dip it in icing sugar.)

Bake in the centre of the oven until just beginning to colour underneath, about 15 minutes. Cool for 2 minutes on the trays, then, using an eggslice (metal spatula), carefully remove to a wire rack. (They are very fragile, so handle carefully.) Let cool completely.

To make the icing, in a bowl, beat together the icing sugar and butter. Beat in just enough passionfruit to form a smooth, thick spreadable consistency. If necessary, add a few drops of water to achieve a good spreading consistency.

Spread the flat side of half of the biscuits with the icing. Then press the flat side of the remaining biscuits onto the icing, to form sandwiches. Let set for 20–30 minutes before serving.

MAKES 9 BISCUITS

BRISBANE

FRUIT CAKE TOPPED WITH DRIED FRUITS AND NUTS

Australian cooks enter their fruit jellies and preserves, dark fruit cakes, lamingtons, scones, sponges and other traditional dishes in award competitions in fairs and shows such as the Royal Queensland Agriculture Show and Sydney's Royal Easter Show. Dark fruit cakes are still traditional at Christmas time for many Australian families, no matter how unsuitable in our hot climate, and they are still popular for family weddings and christenings. This cake, with its colourful fruit topping, makes a great Christmas dessert; if you want to make it for other celebrations, omit the topping and cover the cake with a simple icing. You will need to start making this cake at least 2 days in advance of serving.

FOR THE CAKE:

250 g (8 oz/1⅓ cups) raisins
250 g (8 oz/1⅓ cups) sultanas (golden raisins)
250 g (8 oz/1⅓ cups) dried currants
100 g (3½ oz/⅔ cup) chopped mixed candied citrus peel
100 g (3½ oz/⅔ cup) glacé cherries, halved
125 g (4 oz/¾ cup) almonds, chopped
125 ml (4 fl oz/½ cup) brandy or fresh orange juice, plus
    additional 60 ml (2 fl oz/¼ cup) brandy

300 g (9½ oz/1¾ cups plus 1 tablespoon) plain (all-purpose)
    flour
60 g (2 oz/⅓ cup) self-raising flour
⅛ teaspoon salt
1 teaspoon mixed spice (pumpkin-pie spice)
½ teaspoon ground nutmeg
½ teaspoon ground cinnamon
250 g (8 oz/1 cup) butter, at room temperature
250 g (8 oz/1 cup plus 2 tablespoons) dark brown sugar
2 tablespoons marmalade
1 teaspoon vanilla essence (extract)
4 eggs

FOR THE TOPPING:

250 g (8 oz) mixed whole glacé fruits, such as pears,
    apricots, peaches, figs and pineapple slices and including
    glacé cherries
125 g (4 oz/¾–1 cup) mixed whole almonds, brazil nuts,
    hazelnuts (filberts) and walnuts or pecans

Clockwise from right: Melting Moments, Sultana Slice (recipe page 241), Fruit Cake Topped with Dried Fruits and Nuts—photographed at Blackheath, in the Blue Mountains, NSW

FOR THE GLAZE:

100 g (3½ oz/½ cup) caster (superfine) sugar
125 ml (4 fl oz/½ cup) water
125 g (4 oz/⅓ cup) apricot jam

❧ To make the cake, in a bowl, mix together the raisins, sultanas, currants, candied peel, cherries and almonds. Add the 125 ml (4 fl oz/½ cup) brandy or orange juice and mix well. Cover and let stand at room temperature overnight.

❧ Position a rack in the lowest part of an oven and preheat the oven to 130°C (275°F). Line a 20-cm (8-in) round cake pan with 2 layers of brown paper and then 2 layers of baking (parchment) paper, buttering each of the baking paper layers. In a bowl, sift together the plain and self-raising flours, salt, mixed spice, nutmeg and cinnamon. In another bowl, beat together the butter and sugar until pale and creamy. Add the marmalade and vanilla to the butter mixture and mix well. Beat in the eggs, one at a time, beating well after each addition.

❧ Add one-third of the fruit mixture and one-third of the flour mixture to the butter mixture, folding them in with a rubber spatula. Fold in the remaining fruit and flour mixtures, one-third of each at a time. Spoon the mixture into the prepared pan. Level the top.

❧ Bake on the lowest shelf of the oven until a skewer inserted in the centre comes out clean, 5–6 hours. Remove from the oven and let cool completely in the pan.

❧ Remove the cooled cake from the pan, leaving the papers in place on the cake. Using a skewer, make 9 holes in the top of the cake. Slowly pour the 60 ml (2 fl oz/¼ cup) brandy over the cake. (The cake can be left like this until ready for finishing.)

❧ The day before you serve the cake, cut the topping fruits, except the cherries, into eighths. Arrange all the fruits on top of the cake with the nuts. In a small pan, mix together the sugar, water and jam for the glaze. Bring to a boil, stirring to dissolve the sugar. Simmer for 5 minutes, then let cool. Spoon the glaze over the fruits and nuts and leave to set 24 hours before serving.

MAKES ONE 20-CM (8-IN) ROUND CAKE; SERVES 16–20

Sticky Toffee Pudding

HUNTER VALLEY

STICKY TOFFEE PUDDING

Sticky toffee pudding is sinfully rich and marvellously irresistible. One of the best versions comes from Ian and Jenny Morphy, who operate a wonderful restaurant in the Upper Hunter Valley. Tarago River cream, which is 55 percent butterfat, is from Gippsland in Victoria. It thickens as it matures, so that you can spoon it out of the container like ice cream.

FOR THE TOFFEE SAUCE:

3 tablespoons soft brown sugar
50 g (1⅔ oz/3½ tablespoons) caster (superfine) sugar
3½ tablespoons unsalted butter
250 ml (8 fl oz/1 cup) golden syrup
100 ml (3½ fl oz/6½ tablespoons) thickened (double/heavy) cream

FOR THE PUDDING:

100 g (3½ oz/6½ tablespoons) unsalted butter, at room temperature
175 g (5½ oz/⅔ cup plus 1 tablespoon) soft brown sugar
4 eggs, lightly beaten
225 g (7 oz/scant 1½ cups) self-raising flour
225 g (7 oz) pitted dates, coarsely chopped
300 ml (10 fl oz/1¼ cups) water, boiling
1 teaspoon bicarbonate of soda (baking soda)
3 tablespoons coffee chicory essence (extract)
100 g (3½ oz/rounded ¾ cup) coarsely chopped walnuts

Tarago River cream or other thick, rich cream for serving

To make the sauce, stir together the brown and caster sugars and butter in a heavy saucepan over medium heat, stirring until the sugars dissolve. Add the golden syrup and bring to a boil, stirring from time to time. Reduce the heat and simmer, stirring occasionally, for 20 minutes. Add the cream, stir and heat until boiling. Remove from the heat and let cool.

To make the pudding, position a rack in the centre of an oven and preheat the oven to 180°C (350°F). Line the bottom of a 22-cm (9-in) springform pan with baking (parchment) paper. Butter the paper bottom and the pan sides.

In a bowl, beat together the butter and sugar until light and creamy. Beat in the eggs and then fold in the flour.

Place the dates in a bowl. Add the boiling water, bicarbonate of soda and coffee essence and mix well. Let stand for 5 minutes. Fold the date mixture into the butter mixture and then mix in the walnuts. Spoon into the prepared pan.

Bake in the centre of the oven until the pudding recedes from the pan sides and springs back when pressed lightly, about 1½ hours. Remove the pan sides and transfer the pudding to a wire rack to cool partially.

To serve, cut the warm pudding into wedges and transfer to individual plates. Spoon the toffee sauce and cream around and partly over the pudding.

SERVES 10

QUEENSLAND

GUAVA SORBET

On the Coral Coast in Far North Queensland, a tropical fruit industry is growing rapidly. The guava is one of the fruits cultivated there. It is a native of South America, from where the Spanish and Portuguese spread it throughout the world. There are two main species grown in Australia, the common guava, which has yellow, white or pink flesh, and the cherry guava, which has red flesh and is sweeter and more acidic. Guava is a scented fruit that must be perfectly ripe when used. The best guavas I have tasted were from Mossman, just north of Port Douglas.

200 g (6½ oz/¾ cup plus 1½ tablespoons) sugar
200 ml (6½ fl oz/¾ cup plus 1½ tablespoons) water
500 g (1 lb) strained, puréed guava (about 750 g/1½ lb unpeeled)

In a small pan over medium heat, stir together the sugar and water until the sugar dissolves. Let cool. Place the guava purée in a bowl and stir the cooled sugar syrup into it. Freeze in an ice cream maker according to the manufacturer's directions.

Serve at once, if possible, for the best flavour and texture. Or store in the freezer for up to several days.

MAKES ABOUT 400 ML (13 FL OZ/1⅔ CUPS); SERVES 4

MELBOURNE

WATTLESEED ICE CREAM

Wattleseeds are collected in the Australian bush. They have a flavour similar to that of coffee. This recipe comes from Melbourne chef Julie Robins, a specialist in indigenous bush foods.

500 ml (16 fl oz/2 cups) milk
180 g (6 oz/¾ cup) caster (superfine) sugar
4 egg yolks
2 tablespoons wattleseeds (see glossary)
250 ml (8 fl oz/1 cup) thickened (double/heavy) cream

In a saucepan, combine the milk and sugar. Bring slowly to a boil, stirring to dissolve the sugar.

Meanwhile, place the egg yolks in a bowl and beat until well blended. Slowly pour the hot milk mixture into the beaten egg yolk, whisking constantly. Stir in the wattleseeds and return the mixture to the saucepan. Whisk over low heat until the mixture thickens slightly, 7–10 minutes. Do not allow it to boil. Remove from the heat and place in a sink of iced water to cool completely, stirring from time to time to prevent a skin from forming.

Stir the cream into the cooled egg-milk mixture. Transfer to an ice cream maker and freeze according to the manufacturer's directions.

MAKES ABOUT 700 ML (20 FL OZ/1¾ CUPS); SERVES 6

ORANGE

STUFFED QUINCES IN THEIR OWN JELLY

A bowl of quinces on the kitchen table will fill the room with fragrance. The flesh browns quickly once cut, but it doesn't matter, since quinces should be cooked until they are at least the colour of salmon or as deep as burnished mahogany. Quince trees are easy to grow in the home garden; they bear fruit in the autumn, and the fruits should generally be picked when they are a golden yellow and thus fully ripe. If making jelly, however, pick them when pale green, before any yellow shows. The greyish down covering the skin must be rubbed off before cooking. You will need to make this dish one day before serving, to allow time for the flavours to mellow and the jelly to set.

1.5 l (48 fl oz/6 cups) apple juice, preferably made from
    Granny Smiths
250 g (8 oz/1 cup) sugar
6 quinces
60 g (2 oz/1 cup) crystallised ginger
75 g (2½ oz/½ cup) raisins

In a large, heavy pot in which the quinces will fit snugly, stir together the juice and sugar. Bring to a boil, reduce the heat and simmer while preparing the quinces.

Wash the quinces and rub off the fuzzy covering. Remove the cores with an apple corer and tie the cores and seeds in a piece of muslin (cheesecloth). Add the muslin bag to the syrup.

Cut the ginger into 1-cm (⅜-in) dice. Stuff into the cavities of the quinces alternately with the raisins. Add the quinces to the syrup, cover and simmer gently until just tender, 2–3 hours. The timing will depend on the size and age of the quinces; the older they are, the longer they will take to cook.

Using a slotted spoon, lift the quinces onto a serving dish. Turn up the heat and boil the syrup until it reaches 105°C (220°F), the jelly stage, on a sugar (candy) thermometer. Remove from the heat and let cool until just warm. Pour over the quinces.

Cover and refrigerate overnight. Bring to room temperature before serving.

SERVES 6   *Photograph page 10*

QUEENSLAND

ORANGE AND RAMBUTAN SALAD

The combination of these refreshing fruits in a simple salad is the perfect ending to a rich menu. For a description of rambutans, see the note for tropical fruit soup with Asian spice, page 235.

8 rambutans, peeled and seeded
4 oranges, peeled and segmented with all pith removed
2 nashi fruits, cored and cut into thin wedges
4 passionfruits, pulp removed
2 tablespoons Grand Marnier, cointreau or other high-
    quality orange-flavoured liqueur
8 kiwifruits, peeled and puréed
4 fresh mint sprigs

In a bowl, combine the rambutans, orange segments, nashis, passionfruit pulp and liqueur. Stir well and let stand for 1 hour. Spoon the kiwifruit purée onto 4 flat dessert plates. Top with the fruits, garnish with the mint and serve.

SERVES 4

Left to right: Orange and Rambutan Salad, Wattleseed Ice Cream, Guava Sorbet—photographed overlooking the Tallebudgera River, Queensland

YELLOW PEACH ICE CREAM WITH PRICKLY PEAR SAUCE

Australia grows beautiful peaches, but the season never seems to last as long as we want it to. The Riverland peaches from Renmark in South Australia are among the finest grown. Prickly pear, a member of the cactus family, is about the size of an elongated apple. This juicy fruit ripens to yellow and finally red. The flesh can be pink or white, with or without seeds.

FOR THE YELLOW PEACH ICE CREAM:

500 g (1 lb) ripe yellow freestone peaches
250 ml (8 fl oz/1 cup) light (single) cream
3 tablespoons caster (superfine) sugar, or to taste
few drops of almond essence (extract)

FOR THE PRICKLY PEAR SAUCE:

100 ml (3½ fl oz/7 tablespoons) water
3½ tablespoons caster (superfine) sugar
3–4 prickly pears, 400 g (13 oz) total weight, spines removed

2 tablespoons flaked (sliced) almonds, toasted

To make the ice cream, bring a saucepan three-quarters full of water to a boil. Plunge the peaches into the boiling water for 60 seconds. Using a slotted spoon, lift out the peaches. When cool enough to handle, peel, halve and pit the peaches. Place the peaches in a blender or a food processor fitted with the metal blade and purée until smooth. In a bowl, stir together the peach purée, cream, sugar and almond essence. Pour into an ice cream maker and freeze according to the manufacturer's directions. Transfer to a covered container and place in the freezer.

To make the sauce, in a small saucepan over medium heat, stir together the water and sugar until the sugar dissolves. Bring to a boil and boil for 2 minutes. Remove from the heat.

Halve the prickly pears and spoon out the pulp into a sieve. Push the pulp through the sieve into the sugar syrup. Return to the heat and bring to a boil. Reduce the heat and simmer gently for 10 minutes. Let cool and then chill. You will have about 375 ml (12 fl oz/1½ cups) sauce.

To serve, spoon the ice cream into chilled serving dishes. Ladle a little sauce over each and scatter with the almonds.

SERVES 4–6

LEMON MYRTLE AND MUNTHARI MOUSSE

Vic Cherikoff is the major supplier of Australian wild ingredients. This is his recipe. Agar-agar is a gelatinous product derived from seaweed that is sold in powder and thread forms and is used to set a variety of mixtures. It can be found in Asian shops.

6 tablespoons powdered agar-agar or 3 teaspoons
    unflavoured powdered gelatine
500 ml (16 fl oz/2 cups) apple juice or pear juice
2 tablespoons tahini (see glossary)
3 tablespoons golden syrup
¼ teaspoon lemon myrtle essence (extract)
200 g (7½ oz) munthari berries (see glossary)
1 egg white
6 fresh mint sprigs

In a small pan, mix the agar-agar or gelatine to a paste in a little of the apple or pear juice. Add the remaining juice and bring to a boil to dissolve the agar-agar or gelatine. Remove from the heat and let cool until the mixture is tepid.

Add the tahini, golden syrup, myrtle essence and munthari berries to the juice mixture and stir until well blended. In a small bowl, beat the egg white until stiff, shiny peaks form. Fold the egg white into the juice mixture and then pour into 6 individual serving glasses. Cover and refrigerate until set, about 2 hours, or refrigerate overnight. Garnish with mint sprigs and serve.

SERVES 6

CUSTARD APPLE ICE CREAM WITH POACHED PEARS AND PASSIONFRUIT SAUCE

The flesh of ripe custard apples has a sweet, aromatic flavour that makes an unusually delicious ice cream. The passionfruit sauce adds just the right tart counterpoint.

FOR THE ICE CREAM:

4 egg yolks
1 tablespoon sugar
300 ml (10 fl oz/1¼ cups) milk
350 ml (11 fl oz/1⅓ cups) custard apple purée (from 3 ripe
    custard apples)
1 tablespoon fresh lime juice, or to taste

FOR THE POACHED PEARS:

250 ml (8 fl oz/1 cup) water
250 ml (8 fl oz/1 cup) dry white wine
100 g (3½ oz/½ cup) caster (superfine) sugar
2 lime zest strips
3 Beurre Bosc pears, halved, cored and peeled, with stems
    intact

FOR THE PASSIONFRUIT SAUCE:

250 ml (8 fl oz/1 cup) fresh passionfruit juice, strained, with
    2 teaspoons seeds reserved
100 ml (3½ fl oz/6½ tablespoons) water
100 g (3½ oz/6½ tablespoons) granulated sugar

To make the ice cream, in a large bowl, beat together the yolks and sugar until the sugar dissolves. In a saucepan, heat the milk almost to a boil, then slowly pour it over the eggs, whisking constantly. Return the mixture to the saucepan and cook over medium heat, whisking constantly, until the mixture thickens enough to coat the back of a wooden spoon, 5–8 minutes. Do not allow it to boil. Remove from the heat and place the pan in a sink of iced water to cool, whisking from time to time to prevent a skin forming.

When the mixture is cold, stir in the custard apple purée and the lime juice. Pour into an ice cream maker and freeze according to the manufacturer's directions. Transfer to a covered container and place in the freezer until ready to serve.

To poach the pears, in a saucepan, combine the water, wine and sugar. Bring to a boil, stirring until the sugar dissolves. Add the lime zest and pears, reduce the heat to low and poach gently until the pears are just tender, 10–15 minutes. Let cool in the syrup.

To make the sauce, combine the passionfruit juice, water and sugar and bring to a boil in a saucepan, stirring to dissolve the sugar. Boil over high heat until the liquid is reduced by half, skimming off any scum that forms on the surface. The passionfruit syrup should be clear.

To serve, spoon the ice cream onto 6 large, flat plates. Place a pear half beside the ice cream. Spoon the sauce partially over the pears and onto the plates. Serve at once.

SERVES 6

Top to bottom: Lemon Myrtle and Munthari Mousse, Yellow Peach Ice Cream with Prickly Pear Sauce, Custard Apple Ice Cream with Poached Pears and Passionfruit Sauce

GLOSSARY

AKUDJURA
A native bush tomato collected by the Aborigines in arid areas, dried, ground into a powder and used as a seasoning. Available at health-food stores and selected delicatessens.

ARBORIO RICE
A plump, short-grain rice grown in the Po Valley of northern Italy and commonly used for the making of risotto. It has excellent absorption qualities, and its high starch content results in a particularly creamy dish. Arborio rice is carried in Italian specialty shops and well-stocked food stores.

BLACK WOOD FUNGUS
A type of fungus that grows on rotting wood and is highly prized by the Chinese. Commonly available dried, black wood fungus is easily reconstituted in hot water. It has a mild taste and pleasant crunch and is sold in Chinese markets.

CAPERS
The buds of a Mediterranean shrub, capers vary in size from quite small to the size of a shelled pea. They are preserved either in brine or in salt and have a sharp, tangy flavour. The former are easily found in most food stores; the latter are generally sold only in specialty-food shops.

CAPSICUM
How to roast: Place the capsicum on a griller (broiler) tray in a griller heated on high or on a rack over a charcoal fire. Grill, turning occasionally, until blackened and blistered on all sides. Transfer to a closed paper bag or plastic container until cool enough to handle, about 10 minutes. Then, using your fingertips or a small knife, peel off the blackened skin and remove and discard the stems, seeds and membranes. Cut as directed in individual recipes.

CHICKEN STOCK
Commercial chicken stock is a satisfactory convenience, but the flavour of homemade stock is superior and well worth the effort when time permits. To make chicken stock, in a large pot, combine 2 kg (4 lb) chicken parts (backs, wings, necks); 2 brown onions, cut in half; 2 carrots, cut in half; 2 celery stalks, cut in half; 1 bay leaf; 6 black peppercorns, lightly crushed; and 500 ml (16 fl oz/2 cups) cups dry white wine. Add water to cover by about 2.5 cm (1 in) and bring to a boil. Skim off any scum that forms on the surface and reduce the heat to medium-low. Simmer, uncovered, for about 1 hour, continuing to skim as necessary. Strain through a sieve lined with muslin (cheesecloth), cover and refrigerate for up to 3 days or freeze for up to 2 months. Makes 2–3 l (2–3 qt).

CHILLI-GARLIC SAUCE
A mixture of chillies, garlic, oil and salt sold in bottles in Asian stores. The sauce is used both in cooking and as a table condiment.

CHILLI OIL
This fiery oil can be purchased in Asian markets and well-stocked supermarkets. To make chilli oil at home, in a small saucepan, combine 250 ml (8 fl oz/1 cup) peanut oil and 2 tablespoons chilli flakes, or more as desired. Heat slowly until the oil just begins to smoke and the chilli flakes start to darken. Remove from the heat immediately. Strain through a fine-mesh sieve into a metal bowl to cool, then pour into a jar and cover tightly to store.

CHILLI SAMBAL
Also known as *sambal oelek,* this fiery chilli paste is a popular ingredient and condiment in Indonesia and Malaysia. It is available in Asian stores.

CHIPOLATA SAUSAGE
A type of small French sausage that is flavoured with onions and is sold in selected delicatessens.

COCONUT MILK
The liquid that results from soaking grated fresh coconut meat in hot water and then straining the meat thoroughly. Although it can be made at home from fresh coconuts, good-quality coconut milk is sold in cans in Asian shops and well-stocked food stores. The layer that forms on top of homemade or canned coconut milk is known as coconut cream and can be easily spooned off. Thick coconut milk is the first pressing from freshly grated coconut, or, in the case of a canned product, the cream stirred into the milk. Thin coconut milk is the second pressing from freshly grated coconut, or canned milk with the cream removed.

CORIANDER AND CORIANDER ROOT
Popular in cuisines around the world, fresh coriander is a pleasantly pungent, delicately leaved herb. Both the leaves and the roots, which are commonly sold still attached to the plant, are used in cooking. Also known as cilantro.

COUSCOUS
Tiny dried pellets of semolina made from durum wheat, this North African specialty is available in both regular and instant forms. The former is steamed over simmering liquid, while the latter is mixed with liquid. Couscous is sold in selected delicatessens and well-stocked supermarkets.

CURRY LEAVES
Small, aromatic leaves that are sold fresh and dried in Asian stores. An essential ingredient of many curries.

CURRY PASTE, GREEN
An incendiary mixture of green chillies, shallots, fresh coriander, lemongrass, gingerroot, oil and other ingredients used for flavouring Thai dishes. It can be made fresh or purchased in cans or plastic packets at Asian shops and well-stocked supermarkets.

CURRY PASTE, RED
A traditional Thai preparation made by grinding together red chillies, shallots, garlic, gingerroot, coriander roots, lemongrass, oil and other ingredients used for flavouring dishes. It can be made fresh or purchased in cans or plastic packets in well-stocked supermarkets and Asian shops.

DAIKON
A long, white radish that is typically used raw, cooked and pickled in Japanese, Korean and Chinese cooking. It can be 30–40 cm (12–20 inches) long and has a crisp texture and slightly tangy flavour.

DEMIGLACE
A classic French preparation that is made by reducing the brown sauce known as *sauce espagnole* to concentrate its flavour and colour. It is sold in jars in specialty-food shops.

DRIED SHRIMP
A staple throughout southern China and Southeast Asia, small, pink dried shrimp flavour a variety of dishes. They are usually soaked in water to soften before using. Dried shrimp are imported from Thailand, China and other Asia countries and are sold by weight in Asian shops.

FILO
Paper-thin pastry sheets sold by weight. A common ingredient in Greek and Middle Eastern cooking, the pastry is most readily available frozen; thaw in the refrigerator. The sheets dry out easily and must be kept well covered until just before using.

FISH SAUCE
A fundamental ingredient and condiment in Southeast Asia cooking, this thin, brown sauce is made from salted and fermented fish. It is sold in bottles in Asian shops.

FISH STOCK
Freshly made fish stock adds a naturally sweet flavour to soups and other dishes. To make fish stock, in a large pot, combine 2 kg (4 lb) heads (gills removed) and meaty skeletons of white fish; 2 brown onions, sliced; 2 celery stalks, sliced; 1 bay leaf; 8 black peppercorns, lightly crushed; 1 teaspoon salt; and 500 ml (16 fl oz/2 cups) dry white wine. Add water to cover by 2.5 cm (1 in) and bring to a boil. Reduce the heat to low and simmer, uncovered, skimming off any scum that forms on the surface during cooking, until the ingredients have imparted their flavours, about 30 minutes. Do not overcook or the stock will become bitter. Strain through a sieve lined with several layers of muslin (cheesecloth) and store in the refrigerator for up to 3 days or freeze for up to 1 month. Makes 2–3 l (2–3 qt).

GALANGAL
A relative of gingerroot, galangal is a pale yellow rhizome with a sharp taste. It is commonly used as a seasoning in Thai soups and curries, where it is known as *kha,* and in the dishes of Indonesia and Malaysia. It is sold in Asian stores.

GHEE
The Indian term for clarified butter, that is, butter from which the milk solids have been removed. It can be heated to much higher temperatures than regular butter without fear of it burning, and it imparts a distinctive flavour to foods. Sold in cans in supermarkets and Asian shops.

GINGER, PICKLED
An Asian condiment made by preserving gingerroot in vinegar and then thinly slicing or shredding it. Sold packed in its pickling solution, pickled ginger can be purchased in Asian shops and supermarkets and, once opened, keeps well in the refrigerator.

GREEN PEPPERCORNS
Soft, unripened pepper berries of the *Piper nigrum* vine. If left to ripen and then dried, these same peppercorns would become the familiar black peppercorns. Sold in brine or water or dry-packed in better food shops.

KAFFIR LIME LEAVES
These highly aromatic leaves, from a specific variety of lime tree, are used in the cooking of Thailand, where they are called *makrut,* and of other Southeast Asian countries. The rind of the limes is used as well. The leaves are sold fresh, frozen and dried in Asian shops. Other lime and lemon leaves may be substituted, although they will not be as fragrant.

KAKADU PLUM
Native to the tropical Top End and the world's highest fruit source of vitamin C, this small plum, which looks like an oversized green olive, has a mild apricot flavour. It is available fresh in the summer months and fresh-frozen year-round in health-food stores and selected delicatessens.

KUMARA
This delicately flavoured sweet potato has yellow flesh and red skin. Other vibrantly coloured sweet potatoes (or U.S. yams) can be substituted.

LEMONGRASS
Used in Southeast Asian curries and other dishes, this tall, fibrous, aromatic grass with a bulbous base and coarse leaves imparts a lemony perfume to dishes. Only the base is used in cooking. Lemongrass is also sold in dried pieces and powdered, but the fresh is preferred. Look for lemongrass in Asian stores.

LILLY PILLY
A small, crisp bush fruit that ranges in colour from red to white and has a sharp acid flavour. It is usually made into jams and chutneys. Look for lilly pillies in specialty-food shops.

MESCLUN
A tradition salad mixture of Provence, mesclun combines tender, young greens and herbs of various textures and flavours.

MUNTHARI
Berry that grows on bush creepers found primarily in South Australia and Victoria, where they trail along secondary sand dunes on the coast. These small berries, which have a flavour reminiscent of Granny Smith apples, are sold in specialty-food shops.

OYSTER SAUCE
Used both in cooking and as a condiment, oyster sauce is made primarily from oysters, salt and water. It is a standard ingredient in the Cantonese pantry, but is found in other Asian cuisines as well. It is sold in Asian shops and well-stocked supermarkets.

PALM SUGAR
Also known as jaggery, palm sugar is made by boiling the sap of various palm trees until it crystallises, thereby forming a compressed brown sugar. It is available in Asian markets. Dark brown (occasionally called black) unrefined sugar can be substituted.

PANCETTA
Italian unsmoked bacon cured with pepper, salt and spices. Look for *pancetta* in Italian shops and selected delicatessens.

PEPPERBERRY
A purple-black Tasmanian fruit about twice the size of a peppercorn. Fresh-frozen pepperberries are available year-round in health-food stores and selected delicatessens.

PEPPERLEAF
The leaf of a native plant commonly found in the southern highlands of southeast Australia. Often used ground as a seasoning. Pepperleaves can be found in health-food stores, specialty-food shops and supermarkets.

POLENTA
The Italian name for both the ground grain known as cornmeal and the dish made from it. It is sold in coarse, medium and fine grinds and is available in supermarkets and delicatessens.

PORCINI
Also known as cèpes, these fleshy, flavourful mushrooms are commonly sold dried and occasionally packed in oil. Most recipes call for reconstituting dried porcini in water before using. Add these prized mushrooms to dishes towards the end of cooking to preserve their excellent flavour. They are sold in better delicatessens and Italian food stores.

PUFF PASTRY
A delicate pastry made from flour, water and butter that 'puffs' when baked to form a particularly light, airy, delicate

texture. Puff pastry is painstaking to make, but it can be purchased frozen in sheets in selected food stores.

QUANDONG
A native peach found fresh in the summer months in New South Wales and South Australia. Quandongs are available fresh-frozen and dried in health-food stores and specialty shops year-round.

RED PEPPERCORNS
Available freeze-dried or in brine, red peppercorns (also known as pink peppercorns) have a sharp bite and pungent flavour. Look for them in specialty-food stores.

RICE FLOUR
Flour ground from white rice principally used for making noodles and sweets. Sold in well-stocked food stores and Asian shops.

RICE PAPER
Made from rice flour and water, rice paper is sold dried in fragile ultrathin rounds and sometimes triangles. It is used for making the popular Vietnamese spring roll, *cha gio,* and can be found in Asian markets.

RICE VERMICELLI
Also called rice sticks, these fine noodles made from rice flour are sold dried in cellophane packets in Asian shops and well-stocked food stores. They can be dropped dry into hot oil and will puff to several times their original size within seconds, or they can be soaked in hot water to soften and then added to soups or other dishes.

ROSELLA FLOWER
A tropical scarlet blossom that grows on a climbing vine and is related to the native hibiscus. It has a taste that recalls rhubarb and can be found in health-food stores and specialty-food markets.

SESAME OIL, ASIAN
Made from roasted sesame seeds, this oil has a strong flavour and aroma. It is generally used to season foods rather than as a cooking medium. It is available in Asian markets; the cold-pressed sesame oil sold in health-food stores is quite mild in comparison and is not an appropriate substitute.

SHRIMP PASTE, DRIED
Known as *blachan* in Indonesia and Malaysia, dried shrimp paste is made from dried fermented shrimp and is sold in firm, dense blocks. It is brownish, has a strong flavour and is pounded to form a seasoning for a variety of Asian dishes. It can be found in Asian stores.

SNAKE BEANS
Also known as yard beans or Chinese long beans, these thin, round green beans commonly run to 40 cm (16 in) in length. They are used throughout Asia and can be found in Asian stores and most vegetable markets.

SPECK
A type of smoked pork popular in Austria and northern Italy. Leaner versions are sliced and served as an appetiser or snack; fattier cuts are used for seasoning dishes.

SWEET CHILLI SAUCE
This fruity, full-bodied sauce is a delicious addition to seafood and other dishes. To make the sauce, in a nonreactive saucepan, combine 3 tablespoons chilli powder, 3 tablespoons crushed garlic, 2 tablespoons crushed, peeled gingerroot, 750 g (1½ lb/3 cups) sugar, 1 l (32 fl oz/4 cups) white vinegar, 300 g (10½ oz/ 1⅔ cups) sultanas (golden raisins) and 1 tablespoon salt. Bring slowly to a boil, stirring to prevent scorching. Reduce the heat to medium-low and simmer, stirring often, until the sultanas are plump and have risen to the surface, about 20 minutes. Using a slotted spoon, transfer the raisins to a blender. Purée until smooth, then return the puréed raisins to the saucepan. (Alternatively, working in batches, transfer the entire mixture to the blender and blend until smooth.) Return the pan to the heat and add 400 ml (13 fl oz/1⅔ cups) commercial tomato sauce (ketchup). Bring slowly back to a boil, stirring occasionally. Boil for a few minutes, then pour into jars. Let cool, cover and refrigerate for up to 1 week or freeze for up to 2 months. Makes about 1.5 l (48 fl oz/6 cups).

TAHINI
A paste made from ground sesame seeds used extensively in Middle Eastern cooking. Sold in jars in Middle Eastern shops, supermarkets and health-food stores.

TAMARIND
Tamarind pulp is extracted from the pod of the tropical tamarind tree. It has a strong acid flavour and is sold in a wet form in jars as well as dried in blocks. The latter requires soaking in hot water for 5 minutes and then pressing through a sieve or using your fingers to remove any fibrous material. Both forms are available in Asian stores.

TOMATO SAUCE
This easy-to-assemble Italian sauce complements all kinds of pastas. To make the sauce, in a heavy pan over medium heat, warm 1 tablespoon olive oil. Add ½ small brown onion, finely chopped, and sauté until it begins to caramelise, about 12 minutes. Add 1 small clove garlic, finely chopped, and sauté for 2 minutes longer. Stir in 1 can (400 g/ 13 oz) tomato purée; 1 can (400 g/13 oz) Roma (plum) tomatoes, drained; pinch of sugar; 3 tablespoons tomato paste and salt and freshly ground pepper to taste. Simmer, stirring occasionally to break up the whole tomatoes, until smooth and thick, about 1 hour. Transfer to a jar, cover and refrigerate for up to 1 week or freeze for up to 2 months. Makes about 500 ml (16 fl oz/2 cups).

VANILLA SUGAR
To make vanilla sugar, split a vanilla bean lengthwise and bury the halves in a 500-ml (16-fl oz/2-cup) canister of granulated or icing (confectioners') sugar. Let stand for about 2 weeks to infuse the sugar with the vanilla flavour, then use as directed. Replenish the canister with sugar; the vanilla bean will continue to impart flavour for months. If the seeds of the vanilla bean have broken free from the pod, pass the sugar through a sieve before using.

WASABI
A Japanese root that is used for making the pungent green paste that traditionally accompanies sushi. It is available in powdered form, for mixing with water to form a paste, and as paste in tubes. Mixing it fresh results in a sharper bite. It is sold in Japanese and other Asian shops.

WATTLESEED
A native seed that is sold finely ground. The brownish caramel powder has a coffee-chocolate flavour with a hint of hazelnut (filbert). It is used to flavour ice cream and other sweets and can be found in specialty-food stores.

WONTON WRAPPERS
Thin fresh dough wrappers used for encasing wonton fillings. They are most often small squares (about 9 cm/3½ in), but sometimes rounds, made from eggs and wheat flour. Look for wonton wrappers in Chinese markets and store in the refrigerator for up to 1 week.

ACKNOWLEDGMENTS

Elise Pascoe thanks the following for providing recipes: Glen Barber and Kim Walker, Maggie Beer, Lynette Bignill, Gay Bilson and Janni Kyritsis, Fabrice Boone, Megan Brown, Jean-Paul Bruneteau, Joan Campbell, Karen Carnie, Kit Chan, Vic Cherikoff, Michael Cook, Serge Dansereau, Narsai David, Penny Farrell, Liz Fines, Rea Francis, Consuelo Guinness, Genevieve Harris, Fem Hawke, Judith Henderson, Anthony Hendre, Diane Holuigue, Robin Howard, Belinda Jeffery, Lew Kathreptis, Kate Lamont, Hugh Longstaff, Sally Lowden, Susan Lowden, Jean Luc Lundy, Stefano Manfredi, Michael McMahon, Paul Merrony, Barry Mieklejohn, Anneka Mitchell, Cheryl Mohr, Ian and Jenny Morphy, Stephen Neale, David Novak Piper, Anders Ousback, Gordon Parkes, Neil Perry, Damien Pignolet, Cherry Ripe, Julie Robins, Rupert Rosenblum, Tony Sassi, Maureen Simpson, Gary Skelton, Charmaine Solomon, Leigh Stone-Herbert, Ros Sweetapple, Anne Taylor, Jane Tennant, and Liz Willis-Smith.

Elise Pascoe thanks the following individuals, companies and organisations for their advice and products: Andrew Black of Australian Farm Products Pty Ltd, Australian Meat & Livestock Corporation, Australian Pork Corporation, Matt Brown of Matt Brown's Greens Pty Ltd, Courtney Clark, Sue Dodd of Sydney Market Authority, Hayman Island Resort, Bill Hills of Hills of Darling, Simon Johnson and Toby Tyler of McDonald & Johnson, Gabrielle Kervella, Anna Phillips, Jan Power, Rob Robinson of The Market Cat, Nick Ruello of Ruello & Associates, Rosemary Stanton, John Susman and Martin Groen of The Flying Squid Brothers, Kaye Weatherall of Yandilla Mustard Seed Oil, and John Wilson of Mohr Foods.

Cherry Ripe thanks the following individuals, businesses and organisations for their assistance: Maggie Beer, Jean-Paul Bruneteau, Diane Cilento, Jim Darley, Cheryl Dix, Sarah Gough, Nick and Amelia Hannaford, Kate Lamont, Margaret Lehmann, John Maiorana, Chris Nathanael, Professor Patrick O'Farrell, Jan Power, Qantas Airways, Queensland Travel and Tourism, Professsor Henry Reynolds, Ricegrowers Cooperative, Nick Ruello, South Australian Tourism Commission, South West Development Authority of Western Australia, Kevin Strapp, Tasmanian Development and Resources, Tourism Victoria, Townsville Enterprise, Professor Robin Warner, Margie West, and Western Australian Department of Trade and Development.

The photographer and stylist thank the following for their assistance in the location photography: Victoria Alexander of The Bathers Pavilion, Karen Cotton, Rhonda and Stephen Doyle of Bloodwood Estate, Greg Fraser, Fem and Courtney Hawke, Peter Lewis of Porter's Paint, Trish Mullene and Dany Chouet of Cleopatra's Guesthouse, John Pegrum and Dayne Van Bree of Woodbyne Park, Penny Pillmar and Royce Lanham, Rob Robinson of The Market Cat, and Jerry Rogers of Bend of the River. The photographer and stylist thank the following for providing props for the studio photography in Sydney: Accoutrement, Mosman; Appley Hoare Antiques, Woollahra; Australian Heritage Linen, Neutral Bay; Bay Tree, Woollahra; Blast! Imports, The Rocks; Country Road Australia; David Jones, Sydney; De De Ce Design Centre, Redfern; Dinosaur Designs, Paddington; George Jenson, Sydney; Hale Imports for Pillivuyt, Brookvale; In Residence, Paddington; Jarass, Chipendale; Limoges Australia, Double Bay; No Chintz, Surry Hills; Orson and Blake, Woollahra; Ventura & Co, Lilyfield; and Villeroy & Boch, Frenches Forest.

PHOTOGRAPHY CREDITS

ILLUSTRATION GUIDE

Golden wattle *(Acacia pycnantha)*, page 15, the national floral emblem, is one of the 700 species of the genus *Acacia* that grow in Australia. The small tree, averaging 6 metres (20 feet) in height, occurs in the temperate regions of the country. Its fluffy, golden yellow blossoms, which appear in the spring, are each composed of nearly 80 tiny fragrant flowers.

Waratah *(Telopa speciosissima)*, page 27, the floral emblem of New South Wales, is a tall shrub that in the spring bears spectacular scarlet flower heads. It is widespread from the central coast to the lower elevations of the Blue Mountains.

Tasmanian blue gum *(Eucalyptus globulus)*, page 51, the floral emblem of Tasmania, is one of about 600 species of the genus *Eucalyptus* found in Australia. Growing 60 metres (230 feet) or taller, blue gums bear cream-coloured flowers that produce an intensely flavoured honey.

Common heath *(Epacris impressa)*, page 81, is a small evergreen shrub whose pink form is the floral emblem of Victoria. Appearing from late autumn to late spring, the graceful trumpet-shaped flowers are arranged in dense clusters along their erect stalk.

Sturt's desert pea *(Clianthus formosus)*, page 113, the floral emblem of South Australia, blooms prolifically after a heavy rain, bearing clusters of scarlet flowers whose petals are each accented by a black boss. It is named after Charles Sturt, who described it in the journals he wrote while exploring inland Australia in the mid-1800s.

Mangles' kangaroo paw *(Anigozanthos manglesii)*, page 151, the floral emblem of Western Australia, has a name that aptly describes the appearance of its woolly-textured red and green flowers. The blooms, borne on a striking red stalk, appear in late winter and early spring.

Sturt's desert rose *(Gossypium sturtianum)*, page 181, the floral emblem of the Northern Territory, is a small shrub that was collected by the explorer Charles Sturt. The large mauve flowers with crimson centres are at their peak from late winter into the spring.

Cooktown orchid *(Dendrobium bigibbum)*, page 215, the floral emblem of Queensland, grows from rocky outcrops or tree trunks in tropical, high-rainfall areas. The flowers bloom chiefly in autumn and winter in a range of colours, from white to deep crimson or lilac with darker centres.